Mixed Legal Systems at New Frontiers

JCL Studies in Comparative Law

A series dedicated to classic works in the field of comparative law, commonly with a modern introduction, contemporary monographs, and collected essays by leading and rising scholars:

No. 1: Constitutional Courts: A Comparative Study. Edited by Andrew Harding and Peter Leyland (2009). ISBN 978-0-854-900633

No. 2: Mixed Legal Systems at New Frontiers. Edited by Esin Örücü (2010)

No. 3: Building the Civilization of Arbitration. Edited by Thomas E. Carbonneau and Angelica M. Sinopole (2010)

No. 4: Foundations of Comparative Law: Methods and Typologies. Edited by W. E. Butler, O. V. Kresin, and Iu. S. Shemshuchenko (2010)

JCL Studies in Comparative Law

Mixed Legal Systems at New Frontiers

Edited by

Esin Örücü

Wildy, Simmonds & Hill Publishing

Mixed Legal Systems at New Frontiers

British Library Cataloguing-in-Publication Data:
A catalogue record for this book is available from The British Library

ISBN 9780854900701

First published in 2010 by
Wildy, Simmonds & Hill Publishing
58 Carey Street, London WC2A 2JB
England

Contents

Preface

The World Society of Mixed Jurisdictions Jurists (WSMJJ) held their First Congress entitled 'Salience and Unity in the Mixed Jurisdiction Experience: Traits, Patterns, Culture, Commonalities', in New Orleans in November 2002. The Congress considered mixed jurisdictions as belonging to a closed family, and concentrated on some shared traits, the most important being that all the members of this 'family' were crosses between the civil law and the common law traditions. The twenty-one papers presented were published in the *Tulane Law Review*. Colleagues from some of the member jurisdictions such as Scotland and South Africa, Louisiana and Quebec were already involved in joint projects. Closer ties followed the Congress with collaborative research.

The Second Congress of the WSMJJ on Mixed Jurisdictions was held in Edinburgh in June 2007. The title of the Congress was 'The Boundaries of Unity: Mixed Systems in Action'. As can be gleaned from the title of the Second Congress, the emphasis has started to shift from the closed family of 'mixed jurisdictions' towards a wider embrace, considering 'mixed systems' in addition to the classical 'mixed jurisdictions'. The plenary sessions corresponded to the first part of the title of the Congress, 'The Boundaries of Unity': Different views on what constitutes a mixed legal system; Mixed legal systems and European legal development; and Re-codification of civil law in mixed legal systems were aired. Parallel sessions corresponded to the 'Mixed Systems in Action' part of the title: Iniuria, Legal History, Contract and Commercial Law, Property, International Law and International Private Law, and finally, Procedure.

Most of the forty-three papers presented were first published in the (2008) 12:1 *Electronic Journal of Comparative Law* (www.ejcl.org/121) and subsequently, groups of papers appeared in a number of law journals.

Ten of these papers were selected to appear in a special issue of the (2008) 3 *Journal of Comparative Law*. The present volume assembles these ten essays, many in updated versions, with an additional one on the covert mixed legal system of Turkey.

The aim is to provide the reader with original views on and insight into mixed legal systems in general, and some mixed legal systems and ongoing mixes in particular. The hope is that the analyses in this volume will be helpful for scholars, students and practitioners who have an interest in comparative law and a special interest in mixed legal systems, and provide inspiration to pursue further inquiries.

This birth of this volume would not have been possible without the encouragement and help of William E. Butler, Nick Foster and Brian Hill, and the contributors. The editor would like to extend her thanks to them.

Esin Örücü
15 January 2010

List of Contributors

Anton Cooray, Professor of Law and Associate Dean of Law, School of Law, City University of Hong Kong, lwcooray@cityu.edu.hk

Seán Patrick Donlan , BA (Houston), JD (Louisiana), PhD (Trinity College, Dublin). Lecturer, School of Law, University of Limerick, Ireland, sean.donlan@ul.ie

Willemien du Plessis, North-West University, South Africa, Willemien.DuPlessis@nwu.ac.za

Dale Beck Furnish, Professor Emeritus, Sandra Day O'Connor College of Law, Arizona State University, Dale.Furnish@asu.edu

Jane Matthews Glenn, Professor, Faculty of Law, and Member, Institute of Comparative Law, McGill University, jane.glenn@mcgill.ca

Marissa Herbst, North-West University, Beyers & Day Ing, Pretoria, South Africa, marissa.beyers@vodamail.co.za

Esin Örücü, Professor Emerita of Comparative Law and Honorary Senior Research Fellow, University of Glasgow and Professor Emerita of Comparative Law, Erasmus University Rotterdam, e.orucu@law.gla.ac.uk

Vernon Valentine Palmer, Thomas Pickles Professor of Law, Director of European Legal Studies, Co-Director of the Eason Weinmann Center of Comparative Law, Tulane University; President of the World Society of Mixed Jurisdiction Jurists, vpalmer@law.tulane.edu

Colin Picker, The Daniel L. Brenner /UMKC Scholar and Professor of Law, University of Missouri, Kansas City, Law School. A.B. Bowdoin College, J.D. Yale Law School, pickerc@umkc.edu

Christa Rautenbach, Professor of Law, North-West University (Potchefstroom Campus), South Africa, PVRCR@puk.ac.za

Jan M. Smits, Professor of European Private Law and Comparative Law, Tilburg University and Research Professor of Comparative Legal Studies, University of Helsinki, jan.smits@uvt.nl

General Introduction Mixed Legal Systems at New Frontiers

ESİN ÖRÜCÜ

INTRODUCTION

Any attempt to undertake a comprehensive study of 'mixed legal systems' and to analyse what the concept entails and implies in general terms is a perilous and delicate task. The matters are initially complicated by the fact that a great variety of legal systems have developed from mixed sources and all modern systems of any sophistication or complexity are mixed to a certain extent.[1] Then there are additional issues and paradoxes to consider.

First, 'mixed legal systems' evoke the important area of study by comparative lawyers related to legal families. One can start by asking whether it is in fact possible, or even helpful, to divide and place all legal systems in family groups and to regard 'mixed legal systems' as 'exceptions'[2] in terms of the orthodox methods of classifying legal systems.[3] Indeed, the very existence of 'mixed legal systems' demonstrates that all legal systems cannot be classified on the basis of one single set of criteria and also, that existing classifications fail to account for a significant number of systems. There are, in fact, a few comparative lawyers who do use 'mixed legal systems' as a heading of a family.[4] Thus, engaging in the study of

[1] Patrick Glenn for instance, regards the mixing of different legal traditions as continuous and normal. See, Glenn, P (2007) *Legal Traditions of the World*, Oxford University Press, 3ed.

[2] See Baxter, LG (1983) 'Pure comparative law and legal science in a mixed legal system' XVI *CILSA*, 84 at 93.

[3] For instance Dainow calls Louisiana, a mixed jurisdiction, a 'systeme juridique sui generis'. See Dainow, J (1954) 'Le droit civil de la Louisiane' 6 *Rev.int.dr.comp*, 19 at 32.

[4] See Rheinstein, M (1968) 'Legal Systems: Comparative Law and Legal Systems' in *International Encyclopaedia of the Social Sciences* IX ed. Sils, 204. More recently, see Palmer VV (2001) *Mixed Jurisdictions Worldwide: The Third Legal Family*, Cambridge University Press. Du

mixed legal systems has the potential to contribute to a new approach to the theory of legal families.[5] It can be claimed that the existence of mixed legal systems in fact reflects, more than anything else, the shortcomings of classificatory schemes created and used by mainstream comparative lawyers. Yet, any new attempt to reclassify has its own inherent perils: the more complicated the classifications the more confusion is created. This is not particularly helpful, and also defeats the purpose, since classifications are made for the purpose of simplification. This dilemma has to be faced.

Second, it is nearly impossible to find a satisfactory definition of a 'mixed legal system'.[6] What kind of definition can cover all instances of mixing: historical or contemporary, overt or covert, structured or unstructured, complex or simple, blended or unblended?[7] Are mixed legal systems simply formations at the points of contact between different legal traditions? If we call mixed legal systems phenomena at points of contact, living on the outskirts or periphery of legal families, are we not also assuming definitions of legal families and accepted criteria for dividing and allocating legal systems to pre-determined groups? Do mixed legal systems come into being in areas of expansion of these families[8] or where

---

Plessis also supports the view that there must be an 'independent recognition of a separate family' du Plessis, J (2006) 'Comparative Law and the Study of Mixed Legal Systems' in Reimann, M and Zimmermann, R (eds) *Oxford Handbook of Comparative Law*, Oxford University Press, 477 at 510. Also note special attention being paid to mixed legal systems: Örücü, E (1996) 'Mixed and Mixing Systems: A Conceptual Search' in Örücü, E, Attwooll, E and Coyle, S (eds) *Studies in Legal Systems: Mixed and Mixing*, Kluwer Law International, 335; Palmer, VV (2006) 'Mixed Jurisdictions' in Smits, JM (ed) *Elgar Encyclopedia of Comparative Law*, Edward Elgar, 467; Örücü, E (2007)'A General View of Legal Families and of Mixed Systems' in Örücü, E and Nelken, D (eds) *Comparative Law: A Handbook* Hart Publishing, 169; and du Plessis id.

[5] See the contribution by Örücü, E, 'What is a Mixed Legal System: Exclusion or Expansion?' in this volume.

[6] For the originating and the historical development of the concept see, Reid, KCJ (2003) 'The Idea of Mixed Legal Systems' (78) *Tulane Law Review*, 5. As he points out, historically, the striking characteristic of mixed systems was their mutual isolation.

[7] See McKnight, J (1977) 'Some Historical Observations on Mixed Systems of Law' *Juridical Review* 177, at 177-186, who, in addition, uses such categories as 'mixed', 'mildly mixed', 'pervasive' and 'selective' mixes, 'mix superimposed upon mix', 'mixed by choice', and 'mixed by force'.

[8] A recent work by McPherson for instance, traces the history of the colonial expansion of Britain as far back as the twelfth century invasion of Ireland by England, and assesses the principal elements in the process of reception, and of how, why, where and to what extent reception took place, with what consequences. Similar to the English language, transposing English law overseas has 'produced different accents and usages involving adjustments and changes to many of its rules.' He looks at how English law was received (imposed) in early colonies: Canada, Australia, New Zealand and the Pacific, West Africa, East Africa and the Persian Gulf, India and South East Asia, at methods and formulae (standard and territorial) of reception: the 'natural birthright' (first used in 1655) or 'colonial birthright' (first suggested in 1693) or 'inheritance' doctrine as the theory behind the expansion, and its necessary

legal systems have drawn closer to each other at which point osmosis takes place?[9] What is to become of socio-cultural traditions? How can a 'mixed legal system' be differentiated from 'legal pluralism'?

It has been pointed out that in dealing with mixed systems, close attention should be paid not only to the way in which these mixes have come about - at the level of institutions, doctrine and individual rules themselves - but also a 'clear distinction must be drawn between legal dualism or pluralism (where laws of different origin operate side by side) and mixed laws (where the different laws have been blended together)'.[10] Is this distinction so clear-cut?

One definition on offer for 'mixed legal systems' is: 'those [systems] having substantive attributes (and those of method) derived from two or more systems generally recognised as independent of others'.[11] Another one, dealing with South Africa, states that a mixed system describes the co-existence of two regimes 'which, although both applicable to the same persons, did not necessarily create contradictions, since they were confined to specific subject areas, for example, common law was used for commercial transactions and procedure, and civil law for family law and property.'[12] Yet a much broader one states that:

> The term "mixed" was selected arbitrarily over "hybrid" or "composite". It should not be understood in the restricted sense employed by some authors. We will thus find in this category

supplement, legislation, adopting (local) or imposing (imperial) English law. McPherson also considers the impact of people and religion, geography, land use and socio-economic factors as differentiating factors. He discusses the role of 'tacit' reception through the use of the concepts of 'justice, equity and good conscience'. As McPherson says, 'to transplant a legal system from one country to another requires more than a bare legislative declaration that it is to be in force locally.' A compilation of the whole of the common law was not accessible and there was a scarcity of lawyers and law books in the colonies. Nevertheless, development of local skills, education in England, colonial legal training and the inter-relationship between the colonies helped to overcome these problems. This book presents a panorama of the historical beginnings of the reception of English law and derivative forms of it today in some of the legal systems of the hundred or more places that use it, and offers an insight and understanding of the reception process and also the coming into being of mixed systems. See McPherson, B H (2007) *The Reception of English Law Abroad,* Brisbane: Supreme Court of Queensland Library.

9 According to Ancel, when legal systems meet (or confront) each other, among the problems created, the most important one is the effect this meeting has on the definition and the classification of the systems; these problems are created as a result of the 'relativity', 'mobility', and the 'permeability' of the systems. See, Ancel, M (1981) 'Le comparatiste devant les systemes (ou "familles") de droit' in *Festschrift Zweigert,* at 358-359.

10 Baxter supra n 2, at 92 footnote 45.

11 McKnight, supra n 7.

12 Bennett. WT (2010) 'Legal Anthropology and Comparative Law: A Disciplinary Compromise' forthcoming in the April 2010 issue of *Stellenbosch Law Review.*

> countries in which two or more legal systems apply concurrently or interactively, as well as those in which systems are rather juxtaposed because they apply to more or less clearly distinct fields.[13]

Legal pluralism on the other hand, is said to be where laws of different origin exist side by side in a given society with different legal mechanisms applying to identical situations,[14] where a diverse collection of normative orders is generated by semi-autonomous social fields, at least two or more of which may be simultaneously applicable to the same person.[15] It entails 'the existence of more than one legal system in a country',[16] and appears either as 'deep legal pluralism'[17] or 'state law pluralism'.[18] Any of the above can be taken as working definitions, however, such attempted definitions are either too vague to be helpful or open to criticism for being over-simplistic.

Third, difficulty lies also in the fact that the so-called 'mixed jurisdictions', a sub-category of mixed legal systems, are so diverse. Though at a cursory glance, most mixed jurisdictions may appear to be simply combinations of Civilian law and Common law, which is particularly true when regarded from the viewpoint of European expansion and colonisation – two of the most common catalysts in the formation of mixed jurisdictions – this view is very narrow. The legal world cannot be seen as a binary world of civil law and common law. It is quite easy to detect other elements within these simple looking mixed jurisdictions, such as customary or religious laws,[19] as well as to spot covert mixed systems. TB Smith once said:

> I have been referring to the "mixed jurisdictions" in a special sense, namely one in which a basically civilian system has been under pressure from the Anglo-American common law and has in part been overlaid by that rival system of jurisprudence. There are,

[13] In the website produced by the Faculty of Law of the University of Ottowa, with the help of the Supreme Court of Canada Library on 'world's legal systems'. Available at <http://aix1.uottawa.ca/world-legal-systems/eng-systems.html>

[14] Reyntjens, F (1992) 'The Development of the Dual Legal System in the Former Belgian Central Africa', in Mommsen, WL and de Moor, JA (eds) *European Expansion and Law* (Oxford), 111.

[15] See Moore, SF (2000) *Law as Process: An Anthropological Approach*, 56. Also see Griffiths, J (1986) 'What is Legal Pluralism?' 24 *Journal of Legal Pluralism and Unofficial Law* 1 at 29-37.

[16] Prinsloo, MW (1990) 'Pluralism or unification of family law in South Africa' 23 *CILSA* at 324.

[17] Here different cultural or religious groups live within their own legal systems, or the law of a cultural or religious group not needing recognition by the state, is practiced by the group. This kind of legal pluralism can also be called the 'strong' version.

[18] This type, which can be regarded also as a 'weak' kind of legal pluralism, is where legal norms of various groups are recognised or adopted by the state.

[19] See in this volume the two contributions on South Africa.

of course, mixed jurisdictions even more complex, and we often overlook the fact that law as a world phenomenon is not partitioned between the heirs of Rome and of Westminster.[20]

Fourth, since the historical accidents leading to their coming into being are diverse, all legal systems designated as 'mixed' must be evaluated within their own set of factors rather than together in one theoretical framework. Nonetheless, a theoretical grid is necessary for an enhanced understanding and a meaningful analysis.[21]

Fifth, when analysing established mixtures, the comparative lawyer must try to offer an understanding of, and solutions to, the peculiar problems of systems that are at present shifting and in transition. For instance, a legal system in transition will be first poised on the verges of two legal traditions, hesitant for a while, and then move, leaving the first and moving into the second, often clinging to some well-established and settled peculiarities of the past. Thus it may never totally acquire the style of the second legal tradition, neither may it lose the style of the first altogether. Here a mixed legal system is born. The problems are both of the ongoing state of a 'mix' and conceptual, and the established categories must be reviewed in the light of peculiar developments.

Sixth, has the following question been answered? At what point can a system in transition be labelled as 'mixed' and placed in a subgroup according to its component elements? For instance, at what point does a legal system that borrows 20%, 30% or 40% etc; of its laws from outside sources, become a mixed legal system? Is there a percentage of borrowing that justifies using this label?

Seventh, when the coming into being of mixed legal systems is being analysed, the significance of 'transfrontier mobility of laws' becomes apparent. The fact that law is not static lies at the bottom of all mixed legal systems. Moving populations add yet another dimension to this phenomenon. The birth of a mixed legal system is one of the outcomes of mobility of law and mobility of peoples. Law moves across boundaries and crosses borders.[22]

[20] Smith, TB (1965) 'The Preservation of the Civilian Tradition in "Mixed Jurisdictions"' in Yiannopoulos, AN (ed) *Civil Law in the Modern World*, Baton Rouge, 5.

[21] See the contribution by Vernon Palmer in this volume.

[22] In historical terms, the simplest, most easily defined and understood forces behind these movements are expansion, occupation, colonisation and efforts of modernisation, and the ensuing impositions, imposed receptions, voluntary receptions, infiltrations, inspirations and imitations, and concerted or coordinated parallel developments. Along these paths, legal ideas, concepts, structures and rules have moved from legal order to legal order.

> Mobility of law takes various forms. The paths taken are diverse, the distances covered are long, the methods used are varied and the end results are, even when similar, never the same. The end-products vary depending on conditions such as the size of the movement, its characteristics, the elements of force or choice inherent in the movement and the socio culture surrounding the movement.[23]

Yet, we know that there is considerable discomfort among the comparative lawyers on terminology to be used to refer to such mobility. Concepts such as transplants,[24] contamination, reception and diffusion have all been put forward, defended and challenged. Further still, there are even those who refute the fact that such transfers are possible, and yet transfers, by any name, are in the essence of coming into being of all mixed legal systems.

Eighth, for those who adhere to the decisive role of the cultural context, the very existence of 'mixed legal systems' and the increasing number of new mixes is problematic. In fact it should prove to be a challenge. Which culture does a mixed legal system represent? If 'mixedness' is not a manifestation of a transition but the final outcome, which is the case in most 'mixed legal systems', then the answer must be: 'mixedness is itself the culture'.

As long as two legal systems remain separate, the potential relationship between them may remain speculative, yet in a mixed legal system 'two separate legal systems *are* related; their blending has already occurred. Thus [...] *how* the blend occurred, *why* it did so, and the *effect* it has had upon the legal system itself and those regulated by it', can be fruitfully examined; and 'the metamorphosis which the transplanted laws undergo during the blending process' can only be properly comprehended by a sound knowledge of the donor systems.[25]

Finally, a wide area of knowledge is required for the understanding of such mixtures: history of law, sociology of law, anthropology of law and comparative law must work together. Other subjects that have a bearing are political science, international law, development and law and cultural studies. Tom Bennett claims that one of the reasons why comparative lawyers have ignored African customary law in the South African mixture

23 Örücü (1996) supra n 4 at 342.

24 Especially this concept is quite controversial. See for instance, Cotterrell, R (2001) 'Is There a Logic of Legal Transplants?' in Nelken, D and Fest, J (eds) Adapting Legal Cultures, Ashgate, 71. However, de Plessis, in his conclusions, highlights the fact that 'aspects of the donor legal culture itself can be adopted, thereby facilitating the borrowing of the rules.' du Pleassis supra n 4 at 510.

25 Baxter, supra n 2 at 94-95.

is because customary law was regarded as being in the province of legal anthropology with the field of study being described as 'plural', while research into South Africa's Roman-Dutch/English legal heritage was seen to be in the province of comparative law and the field of study was described as a 'mixed legal system'.[26] He urges for a compromise between the two fields for a more meaningful understanding of such a system.

Today the emphasis on cultural studies, and the necessity of an appreciation of multiculturalism, socio-cultural pluralism, legal cultural pluralism and the concept of identity have added a new dimension to comparative law research and this is most poignant and useful in the study of 'mixed legal systems'. The task may seem daunting, but there is an increasing amount of scholarly research into individual mixed legal systems, both practical and theoretical. There are also most valuable recent projects comparing two mixed jurisdictions in action.[27]

The aim of any research into mixed legal systems today must be, first to assess the classical references to mixed jurisdictions and then to find a wider reference through both historical and contemporary approaches. The researchers must also offer an understanding of the relationship of mixed jurisdictions to the forces behind the movements of the law that are the main explanatory factors of mixtures. In addition, existing and new terminology used in analysing individual instances must be clarified in order to provide a workable grid for fitting legal phenomena into explanatory frameworks.[28] New mixes, ongoing mixes and legal systems in transition must then be approached with the understanding gained. Further than that, it is invaluable to consider legal systems, designated as legal pluralisms, in order to appreciate the relationship between official state law and religious and customary laws, not only as anthropologists but as comparative lawyers.

[26] Bennett supra n 12.

[27] See as illustrations: du Plessis, J (1998) 'The Promises and Pitfalls of Mixed Legal Systems: The South African and Scottish Experiences,' (9) *Stellenbosch Law Review*, 338; van der Merve, CG (2003) 'Interpenetration of Common Law and Civil Law as Experienced in the South African and Scottish Law of Property' (79) *Tulane Law Review*, 256; Zimmermann, R, Visser, D and Reid, K (eds) (2004) *Mixed Legal Systems in Comparative Perspective: Property and Obligations in Scotland and South Africa*, Edinburgh University Press; Reid, EC and Carey Miller, D (eds) (2005) *A Mixed Legal System in Transition* Edinburgh University Press (primarily Scots law but includes contributions from South Africa and Louisiana); MacQueen, H and Zimmermann, R (eds) (2006) *European Contract Law: Scots and South African Perspectives*, Edinburgh University Press; Reid, K, de Waal, M and Zimmermann, R (eds) (2007) *Exploring the Law of Succession:Studies National, Historical and Comparative*, Edinburgh University Press (includes South African, Scots and European essays); Palmer VV and Reid, EC (eds) (2009) Mixed Jurisdictions Compared: Private Law in Louisiana and Scotland, Edinburgh University Press.

[28] See Örücü (1996) supra n 23 at 337.

In fact, 'today, and it seems quite suddenly, mixed legal systems are back in fashion'.[29] Indeed, in the last decade such research efforts have culminated in significant developments, both in the form of joint research projects and the creation of a new Society, The World Society of Mixed Jurisdictions Jurists (WSMJJ).

THE WORLD SOCIETY OF MIXED JURISDICTION JURISTS AND ITS SECOND CONGRESS

The World Society of Mixed Jurisdiction Jurists (WSMJJ) was formed in November 2002 in New Orleans during the First Worldwide Congress on Mixed Jurisdictions. The driving force behind the movement was Professor Vernon Valentine Palmer and his edited volume, 'Mixed Jurisdictions Worldwide: The Third Legal Family'.[30] Professor Palmer regarded fifteen jurisdictions to be the ones that fall into this extended family and his volume covered seven members of it.

The main thrust of the Society was to enrich the understanding of mixed jurisdictions by international collaboration and to encourage comparative law research at an international level. The purpose was the study and advancement of mixed legal systems by scientific, literary and educational means. These objectives were to be pursued through congresses, meetings, publications and co-operation with similar institutions.

The First Congress entitled 'Salience and Unity in the Mixed Jurisdiction Experience: Traits, Patterns, Culture, Commonalities',[31] looked at mixed jurisdictions as belonging to a closed family and concentrated on some shared traits, the most significant being that all the members were crosses between the civil law and the common law traditions. Colleagues from some of the member jurisdictions such as Scotland and South Africa, Louisiana and Quebec were already involved in joint projects. Closer ties followed the Congress with collaborative research.

The Second Worldwide Congress on Mixed Jurisdictions was held in Edinburgh in June 2007. The Congress was hosted by the University of Edinburgh School of Law in association with the British Academy, Edinburgh University Press and Cambridge University Press. This time the title of the Congress was 'The Boundaries of Unity: Mixed Systems in Action'. As can be gleaned from this title, the emphasis has started to shift

[29] Reid (2003) supra n 6 at 16. Reid identifies three groups who have renewed interest in mixed legal systems today: Europeanists, comparatists and system-builders.

[30] Palmer (2001) supra n 4.

[31] For the twenty-one papers presented at that Congress see 2003 (78:1 & 2) *Tulane Law Review*.

from the closed family of 'mixed jurisdictions' towards a wider definition, considering 'mixed systems' in addition to the classical 'mixed jurisdictions'. The Congress began with plenary sessions corresponding to the first part of the title of the Congress, 'The Boundaries of Unity': Different views on what constitutes a mixed legal system; Mixed legal systems and European legal development; and Re-codification of civil law in mixed legal systems. Thereafter there were parallel sessions corresponding to the 'Mixed Systems in Action' part of the title: Iniuria, Legal History, Contract and Commercial Law, Property, International Law and International Private Law, and finally, Procedure.[32]

A LOOK AT THE CONTRIBUTIONS

The ten contributions that were included in the *Journal of Comparative Law* (JCL)[33] and now reproduced here in this volume, are a selection from the forty-three papers presented. It was our decision to publish most of the papers from the plenary session and others from the parallel sessions that appeared to us to be related to general issues of comparative law and mixed legal systems. In this volume there is also an additional contribution on Turkey's covert mixture.

This collection begins with two pieces that set the scene. The first is the opening address to the Congress, the WA Wilson Memorial Lecture by Vernon Valentine Palmer: 'Two Rival Theories of Mixed Legal Systems'. Accepting that there is no consensus as to the precise meaning to be given to 'mixed legal systems', or even to 'mixed jurisdictions', which are at times used interchangeably, Palmer now concedes that there are two approaches to the subject. While mainstream comparatists only consider the classical 'mixed jurisdictions' born out of interaction between the civil law and the common law traditions, scholars of the 'legal pluralism' camp talk of 'mixed legal systems', the ingredients of which could be indigenous, exogenous, religious or customary. However, Palmer is of the view that there is as yet no useful order in this latter approach for the purposes of comparative law. The first approach is restricted and narrow, limited to private law systems. Palmer defends this approach by pointing out its benefits. In an attempt to reconcile the two approaches, he comes to the conclusion that the classical mixed jurisdictions are a genus of the species 'mixed' and that 'plurality consciousness' and an appreciation of the 'non-western elements' in the legal orders in some of the mixed jurisdictions, such as South Africa and Sri

[32] All the papers were published first in the *Electronic J Comp. Law* (2008) www.ejcl.org. and subsequently groups of papers appeared in a number of law journals.

[33] 2008 (3:1) *The Journal of Comparative Law.*

Lanka, can enhance research. There are indeed articles in this volume on South Africa and Sri Lanka, which do exactly that.

Esin Örücü, though not a legal pluralist, is critical of the exclusivity of the legal family of 'mixed jurisdictions'. First, she is critical of grouping localisms under the broad headings of the 'civil law tradition' and the 'common law tradition' alone, and regarding other localisms as being derivatives of one of them. She is also critical of creating a third family of 'mixed jurisdictions' that only considers combinations between these two legal traditions. Instead she suggests a 'family trees' approach within which legal systems could be classified according to their constituent elements. The assumption is that all legal systems are mixed, whether covertly or overtly. Örücü thus advocates 'expansion'. If mixed systems are to be studied together, certain sub-groups would need to be formed: some would be combinations of common law and civil law, such as Louisiana, Quebec, Scotland and Seychelles; some of civil law, common law, religious law and, until quite recently, Ottoman law, such as Israel; some of civil law, religious law, socialist law and tribal law such as Algeria. In addition, there would be ongoing mixtures and systems in transition such as some legal systems in Europe, which have left the socialist sphere and veered towards the civilian tradition in the search for a new identity. Örücü claims that systems such as Malaysia, Singapore, Burma and Thailand, all meeting points between several legal traditions, and the whole of South East Asia would be better served by the 'family trees' approach, which could cater for off-shoots and sub-groups. The outcome would not be to suggest a new family but to pave the way for a theoretical and conceptual framework of analysis by expanding the notion of 'mixed legal systems'. This contribution points to examples of a number of overlaps of different types.

Again, helping in setting the scene, but this time with a more specific slant, we have Jane Matthews Glenn with her 'Mixed Jurisdictions in the Commonwealth Caribbean: Mixing, unmixing and remixing'. She demonstrates how history has created a microcosm of mixed jurisdictions in both traditional and non-traditional forms in the Commonwealth Caribbean. To illustrate this she deals with Guyana, Trinidad and St. Lucia, where the traditional mix is between British common law and Roman-Dutch, Spanish and French civil laws. The non-traditional mix is between European and aboriginal law in Guyana, secular and religious East Indian law in both Guyana and Trinidad, and European law and African custom in St. Lucia. Matthews Glenn assesses the process of reception as 'mixing', assimilation as 'unmixing' and the non-traditional forms of mixity as 'remixing'. This essay, by looking at the 'historical layering', portrays an intriguing attempt at the extension of the traditional 'mixed jurisdictions' picture, to encompass different mixities in the concept of mixed jurisdictions.

In the process, it gives us an insight into how 'mixidness' or 'mixity' can come about, first in its traditional forms and then in non-traditional forms.

Moving the conceptual framework on, Dale Beck Furnish deals with a three-ingredient mix hidden in the common law tradition of the United States, the Navajo law, where three sources have blended. Here, tribal, state and federal laws mix to form the Navajo legal system creating a special pool of sources of law for this developing system. The federal law, as one of the ingredients, has enjoyed peremptory authority over the Navajo nation and its members since the nineteenth century, because the federal government has a trust relationship with Indian tribes. The Navajo nation's written laws and court decisions, share common sources of law with the states; these are common 'American' law sources. The third ingredient, the traditional precepts of the 'fundamental principles', takes precedence and determines how a common provision or doctrine of 'American' law applies to a given case in Navajo courts. Furnish provides intriguing examples of how the system works.

Hidden by the monolithic civilian legal system of Turkey, we see the existence of a covert mixed legal system presented by Esin Örücü. In a two-part contribution, this synthetic legal system is first analysed as a 'hyphenated' one where the source laws of the early twentieth century are still referred to today with a hyphen such as the Swiss-Turkish law, the German-Turkish law and so on. The modern layers of law from a number of civilian European legal systems are melted together in the Turkish pot to form the overlay, the synthetically constructed official legal system. Then, in the second part we see how the judges blend this overlay with the underlay, the socio-cultures, which were ignored by the legislator at the time of the eclectic receptions, in order to forge a new identity for the people. Judges are presented as the navigators and their work analysed through cases when official law meets diverse indigenous cultures and traditional values of the people.

We then have two contributions on South Africa, both of which consider the hitherto neglected element of the South African legal system. The one by Marissa Herbst and Willemien Du Plessis looks at the hybrid approach to the law of marriage: customary law versus common law, and the other by Christa Rautenbach considers common (Roman-Dutch law) and customary law of intestate succession. Thus these two contributions probe the place of the third ingredient of South African law within a legal system ordinarily labelled as a classical 'mixed jurisdiction', a blend between the civil law (Roman-Dutch law) and the common law (English law). These are refreshing additions to the classical picture.

Herbst and Du Plessis show the conflict between customary law and common law, which they regard as the theme permeating the history of colonialism in Africa. The authors point out that what gave rise to conflict in the area under scrutiny, was the non-recognition of customary marriages. They then consider the Recognition of Customary Marriages Act 120 of 1998 and query whether this Act is a possible panacea or rather the suffusion of customary law by western legal thinking.

Rautenbach also considers such developments and asks whether Roman-Dutch common law and customary law are being codified and unified, or harmonised, or whether what is happening should be regarded only as interference into customary law by the common law. She discusses the issues of 'indirect intervention' by the judiciary and the 'direct intervention' by the legislature. Her preferred metaphor to visualise the mixture of the transplanted law and the customary indigenous law (first ignored, then tolerated and now eventually accepted though with reservations and conditions) is 'potjiekos', a uniquely South African food, which is a mixture of meats and vegetables packed in layers.

Both contributions illustrate that values, such as polygamy and distinctive patriarchal characteristics seen in the rule of male primogeniture, are vulnerable when facing codified laws and the Constitution. There is extensive analysis of Constitutional Court cases here.

Taking up another specific area, Anton Cooray considers the case of trusts in Sri Lanka, a legally pluralistic jurisdiction. We appreciate that, in Sri Lanka Kandyan law applies to Sinhalese inhabitants of the Kandyan provinces, Thesawalamai applies to the Tamil inhabitants of the Jaffna province, Muslim law applies to all Muslims in Sri Lanka and Hindu law applies to Tamils as a foreign law. The common law is an amalgam of Roman-Dutch law, English law and some elements of special laws. However, English law has replaced and modernised Roman-Dutch law: A principle of Roman-Dutch law would only be followed if it had been introduced into Sri Lanka and had not become obsolete, if the Roman-Dutch and English law principles were similar, unless the parties have agreed to be bound by English law. Sri Lankan courts have recognised that every person has the right to choose the law that governs him/her. This contribution compares *fidei commissum* and trusts in Sri Lankan law and Indian law, and looks at the place of customary laws; assessing whether oriental and occidental laws live in harmony.

We now turn to other intriguing questions.

The historian Seán Patrick Donlan presents eighteenth-century English and Irish laws as hybrid systems in transition, in his essay, 'All this together make up our common law', using the quotation, 'our laws are as mixed as our language'. Donlan uses 'grafting' as the process of this mix. We are shown here the selective incorporation into common law of laws as developed by the non-common law courts. Already complicated by the use of Law French, the hybrid Anglo-Norman law competed with jurisdictions of canon, local, feudal, urban and commercial laws. Over the centuries, voluntary reception and borrowing and considerable pluralism shaped a number of areas of English law, which in turn impacted the law in Wales, Ireland and in the English colonies. This work integrates developments in European and English legal history and studies the intellectual impact of both civilians and common lawyers on the English legal system, linking the 'internal' history of law and the 'external' history of European thought.

The following two pieces delve into the lessons to be learnt from the classical mixed jurisdictions for the European Union 'mix', and the assessment of public international law as a 'mixed jurisdiction', a cross between the civil law and the common law traditions.

Jan Smits investigates in the penultimate piece, the question: 'To what extent can classical 'mixed jurisdictions' serve as an example for the harmonisation of private law in the European Union?' He wants to discover what it is that these systems have to offer to the present European debate on harmonisation. According to Smits, if we want to learn lessons from their experiences, a detailed study must be carried out into both their successes and failures. The question of how to find the 'best' rules is one of the most problematic aspects of law making and mixed jurisdictions cannot serve as a successful model here. Another question the author considers is how to keep the law coherent. Smits does not consider substantive private law of mixed jurisdictions for future European developments, but looks at successful and unsuccessful mixes. He views comparative law as a means of providing inspiration and, for him, sharing ideas is the most important lesson offered by mixed jurisdictions.

Stressing the need to approach international law through comparative analysis, Colin Picker offers in the final piece, a novel approach for a new understanding of international law and specifically international trade law: 'Neither common law nor civilian – but perhaps like a mixed jurisdiction?' For Picker, international law has reached a turning point. Therefore looking for ideas from national legal systems, and specifically from the experiences of classical mixed jurisdictions, may be the way forward. He looks at international law in transition, as 'an emerging mixed system'. Picker set out to prove that there is congruence between international law and the classical 'mixed jurisdictions' in the way that international courts have emerged and codifications have increased, both reflecting the common and civil law constituencies. International law must find a suitable balance between the two traditions as to sources and evidence of law.

Four issues come to light in these eleven contributions. The first issue is related to the possible justification for the use of the term 'mixed' for only a specific number of jurisdictions, as was done in the past. The second is that even some of the systems so labelled have in fact a third element or layer, and are not just 'simple mixes' of the common law and the civil law traditions as hitherto portrayed. The contributions on South Africa and Sri Lanka demonstrate this fact. Third, covert mixtures abound as demonstrated by the example from Navajo in the United States and Turkey. The fourth issue is that all modern law, including international law and EU law have a 'mixed' character. All feature a combination of models stemming from different traditions. Nothing is simply 'home-grown'. The critical approach to mixed legal systems has definitely reached new frontiers.

There are examples here which indicate that even legal systems that aspire to being solely the creation of 'domestic legal genius' have been mixed (Donlan); that legal systems analysed until recently under the title of mixed jurisdictions, made up of a blend of the common law and the civil law components, contain other ingredients (Matthews Glenn, Du Plessis and Herbst, Rautenbach, Cooray); that there are hidden mixes in otherwise 'pure' legal systems (Furnish and Örücü); and that one does not have to be a legal pluralist to note these facts.

Though it did not appear as an article in the special issue of (2008) 3 *JCL*, or here in this volume, Nicholas Foster's oral contribution to the Congress presented another fascinating area of neglected study: the mixed systems of the Arab Middle East which are on the whole missing from the agenda of those studying mixed legal systems. Pointing to the recent increase in 'mixing', the unprecedented 'contaminations' in our present globalised environment and the new importance of the more 'exotic' mixed systems, Foster asserted that to regard the systems which combine Western and Islamic laws purely as Islamic, as is generally done, is erroneous, and that they should be viewed as 'mixed'. He specifically mentioned the Ottoman, Egyptian and North African basic models that would be worthwhile studying. In such contexts, in addition to selective receptions that lead to import and imitation, voluntary synthesis between Muslim inspiration and occidental law, and even a prolific exchange between civilisations come to mind.

The crucial lesson Foster brought to our attention sprang from his lamenting the fact that as a result of the mutual ignorance of scholars concerned with the Middle East and those dealing with mixed jurisdictions, there is total separation between these studies. He looked specifically at 'modernisation' in the legal systems of the Eastern Arab World and analysed them in terms of legal diffusion and re-diffusion, and legal pluralism, concentrating on the processes of mixing.

While readers consider what is on offer in these eleven pieces, they will note that our world of metaphors has been enriched by the terms 'sausage making' (Donlan) and 'potjeikos' (Rauterbach); that forms of mixing have been expressed in many ways with incorporation, extension, inoculation, grafting, interweaving, blending, hybridity, mutation, absorption, diffusion, infusion and suffusion, and that the dynamics of overlapping legal systems, interrelated legal systems, nestling systems, synthetic legal systems, hyphenated legal systems, layered law, reciprocal influence have been re-considered. Matthews Glenn, for instance, talks of innovative concepts such as 'formal versus informal mixity' and 'non traditional forms versus traditional forms of mixed jurisdictions'.

FURTHER DEVELOPMENTS

It is worth noting that three recent major Comparative Law Handbooks published by Edward Elgar, Hart Publishing and Oxford University Press have paid special attention to mixed legal systems, by allocating them a special place in their volumes.[34] Another remarkable recent development is to be found in the updating of the first and leading casebook on comparative law in the United States for the past sixty years, Schlesinger's Comparative Law.[35] Ugo Mattei, Teemu Ruskola and Antonia Gidi have thoroughly reconstructed this seventh edition. In their radical departure, the editors brought a much broader perspective, mostly reflected in Part I – though they warn that 'traditionally inclined colleagues may wish to skip' this part.[36] Here there is a chapter on 'Diffusion of Law',[37] where we see an effort to integrate the so-called 'radically different cultures' and Area Studies with the mainstream study of comparative law. To portray law in an interconnected world, this chapter provides, under the sub-title 'the Comparative Lawyer as a Geographer', awareness of, and information on, a large number of mixed legal systems, though be it in snippet form.[38]

[34] Palmer, VV (2006) 'Mixed Jurisdictions' in Smits, JM (ed) *Elgar Encyclopedia of Comparative Law* Edward Elgar 467; Örücü, E (2007)'A General View of Legal Families and of Mixed Systems' in Örücü, E and Nelken, D (eds) *Comparative Law: A Handbook* Hart Publishing 169; and du Plessis, J (2006) 'Comparative Law and the Study of Mixed Legal Systems' in Reimann, M and Zimmermann, R (eds) *Oxford Handbook of Comparative Law*, Oxford University Press, 477. Remember that earlier, already in 1996, Kluwer Law International also published a volume dedicated especially to mixed and mixing legal systems: Örücü, E, Attwooll, E and Coyle, S (eds) (1996) *Studies in Legal Systems: Mixed and Mixing*, Kluwer Law International.

[35] Mattei, U, Ruskola, T and Gidi, A (eds) (2009) *Schlesinger's Comparative Law: Cases - Text - Materials*, Foundation Press, 7th ed.

[36] id, at x.

[37] id between 190-213.

[38] Among the systems informed are Philippines, Puerto Rico, Louisiana, Quebec, Scotland, India, the Sudan, Hong Kong, Macau, South Korea, Liberia, South Africa, Guyana, Sri Lanka, Israel, Japan, China, Turkey, Thailand, Ethiopia, Egypt, Indonesia, Cuba, Bolivia and Ecuador. Compare to Palmer's list of mixed jurisdictions comprising 15 systems: Louisiana, Israel, Scotland, South Africa, The Philippines, Puerto Rico and Quebec, Botswana, Lesotho,

This is a highly commendable development and supplies a helpful starting point for understanding the legal world as largely constituted by numerous mixed legal systems.

Since the Second Congress of the WSMJJ in 2007, further developments have also taken place. In May 2009 a joint colloquium hosted by the International Academy of Legal Science and the WSMJJ took place in the University of Stellenbosch, South Africa over two days on 'Mixed Jurisdictions as Models?: Perspectives from Southern Africa and Beyond'. Speakers from Canada, Botswana, South Africa, England, Nigeria, the Netherlands, Scotland, Cameroon and the USA (Louisiana) considered mixed legal systems in Africa and especially in Southern Africa, the integration and interaction of traditional and modern law in Africa, mixed systems as models for European integration, and finally, harmonisation of African law.

In September 2009, a two day conference in Lausanne, Switzerland organised by the Swiss Institute of Comparative Law (SICL) considered 'Going Beyond Mixed Jurisdiction Theory: The Emergence of Hybrid Legal Systems and their Implications for the Comparative Lawyer', and specifically 'Negotiating Boundaries: Hybrid Legal Traditions and Comparative Lawyers'. Two sessions looked at 'living hybrids' and 'developing hybrids', and then comparative and methodological considerations were covered in the third session 'towards a new theory of legal families'. Papers on mixity as a constitutive element of the European legal order, the mixed jurisdiction elements within the WTO, legal hybridity and diffusion in European legal history, the role of African native law of informal commerce in the development of the new African law, and the co-existence of customary and state law, indicate that the subject of mixity has indeed reached new frontiers. In addition, some individual mixed systems were also considered, such as Cyprus as a mixed legal system, the Maltese mixing, Chinese law as a new hybrid, legal developments in Nepal, and Louisiana. At the end of the conference a round table discussion probed into the possibility of the creation of an international and interdisciplinary community focusing on legal hybridity and diffusion.

2010 saw the launch of an Interdisciplinary Centre for the Study of Legal and Normative Mixtures and Movements: 'Juris Diversitas'; and June 2011 will see the Third International Congress of the WSMJJ to be held in Jerusalem on the theme 'Methodology and Innovation in Mixed Legal Systems'.

Swaziland, Sri Lanka, Mauritius, the Seychelles, Saint Lucia and Zimbabwe. The number could be sixteen as Namibia is also mentioned in passing.

CONCLUDING REMARKS

In sum, a reading of the first two pieces (Palmer, Örücü) in this volume informs us of the multiplicity of approaches to mixed systems and widens the horizon, offering expansion though retaining the exclusivity. While those working on classical mixed jurisdictions will continue to produce valuable work with increasing cross-fertilisation among scholars, others will probe into other ingredients of the very same legal systems, and yet some others will analyse altogether different types of mixes between legal traditions other than the civil law and the common law, while some will revisit international law, international organisations and the European legal order from a new perspective, as seen in this volume. If comparative lawyers, regionalists, international lawyers and anthropologists can work more closely in the future, the outcome will prove to be extremely beneficial to all and to legal scholarship. The role of comparative law in the development of mixed legal systems is especially significant, since a 'continuous process of comparative re-evaluation' is needed in order to avoid the danger of stagnation brought about by a self-referential legal approach.[39]

> Mixed legal systems can be regarded as points of reconciliation and as models of the symbiosis of legal systems. They may even be depicted as the "ideal systems" of the future. Even if enrichment by cross-fertilisation is thought to be the only advantage of being a mixed jurisdiction, the consequent open mind can lead to successful law reform by reference to foreign models.[40]

What the future holds for legal systems and classificatory schemes, and for the comparative lawyers studying them, indicates a most significant turning point. The eleven contributions in this volume can cumulatively be considered as temerity's challenge to tradition. The aim is to provide the reader with original views on and insight into mixed legal systems in general, and some mixed legal systems and ongoing mixes in particular. The hope is that the analyses in this volume will be helpful for scholars and students with an interest in comparative law and a special interest in mixed legal systems, and provide inspiration to pursue further inquiries.

This Second Congress of the WSMJJ surely helped in putting paid to the belief that we can carry on our merry way of looking at classical, formal

[39] See du Plessis supra n 4 at 511.
[40] Örücü (1996) supra n 23 at 350.

and traditional mixed systems. Their 'simplicity' is in doubt and we are entering an era of studies involving all legal systems anew. The boundaries of unity will be further forced as mixed legal systems reach out to new frontiers, justifying the use of the term 'world' in the name 'World Society of Mixed Jurisdiction Jurists'.

Two Rival Theories of Mixed Legal Systems

VERNON VALENTINE PALMER

I am very much honoured to give the Wilson Memorial Address this evening. It seems especially fitting that we should meet in the oldest mixed jurisdiction in the world in order to explore the very subject of mixed legal systems. Over the next three days The World Society of Mixed Jurisdiction Jurists will hold its Congress in the very city and in the same distinguished University where so much was initiated, accomplished and written on behalf of the mixed jurisdictions. Here the spiritual founder of our organization, the late Sir Thomas Smith, after holding the chair of Scots law at Aberdeen, held successively the chairs of Civil Law and Scots Law. He is very much present tonight both in our thoughts and our affections.

This lecture is in memory of Professor W.A. Wilson, an illustrious member of this faculty whose teaching and writing made a significant contribution to Scots law. I was not privileged to know Professor Wilson personally, but what I have learned from his writings makes me regret that fact very much. There is one statement he made that I found striking and would like to quote. In an essay in the *Juridical Review* in 1982 he spoke of the distinctive contribution that the academic lawyer can make to his students and to the profession.[1]

'The first task of the academic lawyer, and the one which students, the legal profession and the public at large most strongly expect of him, is to know what the law is.' But to know the law was only the first task, for he then spoke of a higher contribution: 'It can be argued that a jurist's opinion as to what the law is, is of much less importance than his analysis of the setting in which the decision as to what the law is has to be made. Perhaps, indeed, analysis is the characteristic activity of the academic lawyer.' Wilson seemed to accept that analysis transcended territorial boundaries and

[1] 'Knowing the Law and Other Things' (1982) *Juridical Review* 259, at 269.

linked legal minds in different systems. Analysis could enlighten lawyer or judge wherever situated. He gave as an example a distinction drawn by the American academic Thayer between 'primary facts' and 'secondary facts'. He wondered why this distinction had not been accepted and used in Scotland. He stated that Thayer's insight could hardly be 'brushed off' with the dictum that 'it is no part of Scots law' since this sort of analysis is 'a matter of logic rather than law.' Professor Wilson's willingness to consider logic emanating from any legal source, from abroad, at home or over the border, reveals a critical intellect who had a faith in the role of reason, or as Peter Birks would say, a faith in the rational rather than the national.[2] It suggests that he was open to the use of comparative law ideas as a source of data and persuasive analysis. If he were among us now, I feel sure that he would be critically examining our papers and presentations. I can best honour his memory by trying, however modestly, to emulate his example.

INTRODUCTION

A Dispersed Unity

By way of introduction to my subject, let me set the stage by saying that the mixed jurisdictions, up until relatively recently, have lived their entire existence in a kind of physical and intellectual isolation, cut off from family members around the world. They have been great solitaries, separated by the oceans, the currents and the continents. Each seemed to be one of a kind, something unique and peculiar, a wayward child who was destined to develop introspectively, conscious of its 'otherness', unclear as to the nature of its laws, uncertain what to call itself, ambiguous as to its place among the world's legal systems. It is only recently, as mixed jurisdiction studies and scholarly exchanges have increased, that this feeling of isolation and estrangement has begun to change. The opening of this World Congress can be viewed as another step in a very necessary exchange of ideas and intercultural development.

Dispersed as they are around the globe, such places could be easily dismissed as a series of disconnected dots and dashes on the maps. All efforts at classification in standard works have resulted in their marginalisation and have not succeeded in giving closer analysis to their common traits and shared experiences. A few years ago, in a work devoted to the comparative treatment of these systems, I argued that the unity of

[2] 'The Foundation of Legal Rationality in Scotland' in Evans-Jones, R (1995) *The Civil Law Tradition in Scotland* OUP at 82.

the mixed jurisdiction 'experience' is palpable from the perspective of the jurists who live within them. I called them a third family:[3] 'The systems are mutually intelligible. Their jurists enjoy the possibility of great complicity and close understanding, stemming from their knowledge of civil law, common law and the English language. They speak similar bijural dialects [...].'

In the papers of the First World Congress published by the Tulane Law Review I wrote:[4]

> Mixed jurisdiction jurists are separated by oceans, by history, and by many cultural and linguistic differences, yet they tend to understand one another very easily and do not feel alien in each other's culture. They are brought together, it seems, by their knowledge of both common law and civil law and how these traditions interact within the same system, and the English language serves as their channel of international communications. Their desire for closer, more permanent relations led to the founding of a new organization, The World Society of Mixed Jurisdictions, and steps are already underway to convene a second World Congress in Scotland.

An Uncertain Identity

I begin with a problem that may be troubling to colleagues as we gather in the next three days. There i s no consensus among us as to the meaning we should give to the expressions 'mixed legal system' or 'mixed jurisdictions' (they are frequently used interchangeably, but with different meanings and applications). It apparently cannot be simply assumed that we agree upon *what* is a mixed legal system and *who* is a mixed jurisdiction jurist.

The subject of classification, though often regarded by lawyers as barren and boring, is actually vital and significant to jurists in the mixed jurisdictions. Obviously the way we classify legal orders affects attitudes, perceptions, self-esteem and cultural identities. Almost every mixed system has known its own *bellum juridicum*, its polemical literature on the nature of its system. Almost all of the skirmishes over the reception of controversial transplants like the floating charge, the trust, or free testation have been at the deeper level debates over the nature of these systems.

My Louisiana colleagues may remember well that a famous law review article published in 1937 by Gordon Ireland proclaimed that Louisiana had

[3] Palmer, VV (2001) *Mixed Jurisdictions Worldwide: The Third Legal Family* CUP at 3.
[4] Palmer, VV (2003) 'Salience and Unity in the Mixed Jurisdictions: The Papers of the World Congress' (78) *Tulane Law Review* 1 at 2.

ceased to be a civil-law state.[5] The article provoked an uproar of denial[6] and at the same time it launched an impressive programme of reform. Actually it touched the neuralgic nerve of the civilian identity so profoundly that this event and its aftermath are usually characterized as the beginning of the civilian renaissance in Louisiana.

What is often forgotten is that the art of classifying legal systems, as René David counselled, should be used purely for explanatory purposes. All classifications have their utility and none are completely wrong. 'It all depends on the point of view adopted by the writer in question and the aspects of the matter which interest him most.'[7] Individual objectives and perspectives thus play a significant role.[8] Indeed it is to be expected that the perspective of mixed jurisdiction jurists like ourselves may be quite different than that of European and American colleagues.

The chief benefit of a formal classification should be to provide 'the basis for a relatively uniform and internationally understood nomenclature, thereby simplifying cross-referencing and retrieval of information.'[9] It is supposed to cut through to the really essential distinctions. It should allow us to understand what is included and excluded and to know why. If a grouping is well-justified, a presumption of similarity may ensue. The comparatist may treat one or two countries within the group as representative and concentrate upon them.[10] Further, the criteria may lead us to comparable systems never previously considered as being similar to ones we already know, and thus we may discover a new field of comparative law.

[5] Ireland, G (1937) 'Louisiana's Legal System Reappraised' (11) *Tulane Law Review* at 585.

[6] Daggett, HL et al. (1937) 'A Reappraisal Reappraised: A Brief for the Civil Law of Louisiana' (12) *Tulane Law Review* 1 at 12.

[7] (1982) *Les Grands Systemes de Droit Comparé* Dalloz at 22.

[8] It can be assumed, for example, that a Martian visitor could well be disinterested in the classification of legal systems on Earth. From an extraterrestrial perspective it might be just enough to know they were all a single family –the family of 'human laws'. In the same way, but to a different degree, the perspective of Socialist jurists was markedly different than that of the Western comparatists. The Socialist jurists showed very little interest in distinctions between common law, civil law, religious law and so forth. They tended to make but one distinction — that between socialist and 'bourgeois law'. All others were regarded as secondary. See, for example, Eörsi, G (1979) *Comparative Civil (Private) Law* Budapest, who divided law types into (a) natural (pre-capitalist) civil law, (b) capitalist civil law, (c) socialist civil law.

[9] *Encyclopaedia Brittanica*, vol. 14, at 1089.

[10] Michael Bogdan observes that the greater the cohesiveness of a family, the more the comparatist will tend to bring out differences. On the other hand, when comparing systems from different families, the more s/he will tend to bring out similarities. (1994) *Comparative Law* Kluwer at 82-83.

A Classificatory Vacuum

It is however clear by now that the great writers on comparative law have to a large extent failed the mixed jurisdictions. They have found no way or no desire to classify these systems at all. The so-called mixed systems receive at best a kind of 'negative definition'. They are the odd-men-out who do not fit the scheme. As Jacques du Plessis has well put it, the mixed jurisdictions have been condemned to 'classificatory limbo'.[11] They have languished there without compass or map or means of exit for many years. As we presently celebrate the 300th anniversary of the birth of Carl Linnaeus and the founding of the Edinburgh faculty of law, this anomalous situation must be regarded as a serious disadvantage. Mainstream comparative law theoreticians have been unwilling to deal with complex mixtures and fractional identities. Every system must apparently be of a single type and there is no place for hybrids in their typology.

There is a historical parallel to this state of affairs in the physical world where biologists in the time of Linnaeus divided all organisms into two Kingdoms, plants and animals, but then later discovered that there were intermediate types of organisms (zoophytes) such as the sponge or coral that did not fit exactly into either of the two Kingdoms. And then later, with the discovery of the microscope, a host of new microscopic forms of life appeared. Many of these micro organisms also displayed both animal and plant characteristics and could not be classified in either Kingdom. This caused the two-Kingdom theory to break down and it was necessary to move to a more elastic and reticulated classificatory system in biology. So too in comparative law, closer study by anthropologists, sociologists, and comparative lawyers have brought the world's legal systems into microscopic focus and made evident the existence of legal phenomena that we can only describe at present as mixed systems. It is time to rethink what this means for comparative law.

Contemporary Taxonomy: Three Flaws

I shall pass quickly over the failure of existing classificatory schemes (for fear that the subject may be as boring as many say it is). Many of these attempts are already familiar to you.[12] It is paradoxical, however, that with globalisation advancing the horizons of comparative law seem to be contracting and looking more Eurocentric than ever. Twenty years

11 *EJCL* Vol 9.3, October 2005, Editorial.

12 From Esmein to Arminjon, Nolde & Wolffe, to René David, to Zweigert and Kötz.

ago in their 1987 edition Zweigert and Kötz recognised as many as eight legal families in the world (Romanistic, Germanic family, Nordic family, Common Law family, Socialist family, Far Eastern systems and Hindu Law), but ten years ago this was reduced to only four. These four are said to be the 'great legal systems of the world', yet all of them originate in Europe and within the European Union.[13] They are the Romanistic family, the Germanic family, the Nordic family and the Common Law family. Apparently nothing in Africa or Asia has a sufficiently distinctive style or content to warrant its own grouping. Even if we put aside the appearance of Eurocentrism, there are still three problems in this tableau. Firstly, hardly without recognizing it, we are forced to use private law terminology as a kind of proxy for judging the nature of entire legal systems. Terms like 'Common Law', 'Civil Law' and 'Muslim Law' are continually used even though they say little or nothing about the constitutional, administrative or criminal laws in such systems. The flaw lies in making it insufficiently clear that this is a classification of the world's private-law systems, not their entire legal systems. Secondly, these signifiers are not adequate even to describe the whole of a private law system. The words Common Law or Civil Law, for example, simply refer to one of the oldest or best-known taproots of the system. All other roots and branches — the mixtures — are put aside. It is a technique, as Patrick Glenn has underscored, of 'limited feature classification',[14] which leaves out all other important elements such as the law merchant, the canon law and so forth. The flaw here is that by dint of massive reductionism a private-law system is characterized as a single type rather than the mixture of many things. Finally the third defect is the most serious, even if it is only a sin of omission: Existing classification schemes make no space for hybrids or mixed systems. Yet according to a recent census by the Ottawa civil-law faculty, mixed systems outnumber all other kinds in the world.[15] This omission therefore seems to mean that a universal legal phenomenon is ignored and left untreated.

Incidentally the standard disclaimer for failing to classify the 'classical' mixed systems is that it is too soon to know what they are or what they

[13] Zweigert, K and Kötz, H (1998) *Introduction to Comparative Law* (3rd ed., trans T. Weir) Oxford University Press.

[14] Glenn, HP (2006) 'Legal Families and Legal Traditions' in Reimann, M and Zimmermann, R (eds) *Oxford Handbook of Comparative Law*, Oxford University Press, at 438.

[15] Mariani, N and Fuentes, G (2000) *World Legal Systems* W&L at 35. As indicated at 35, the study estimates that around 60% of the legal systems are mixed. The study's methodology, however, is perhaps flawed because it unwarrantedly assumes, as a point of departure, that 40% of the systems are 'pure' (civil law, common law, customary law and Muslim law). The assumption violates the study's stated criteria for identifying a mixed system and necessarily undercounts their number. See Appendix A for details of the mixtures recognized in the study.

will become. We should 'wait and see' whether they would eventually move in the direction of one of the established families. Yet since these systems have shown resiliency and stability for centuries and as there is actually no evidence of any movement to join another family, this approach seems to be the equivalent of waiting for Godot to arrive.[16] Another suggestion that has been made is to use the principle of 'predominance' and to ask to which family does the mixture *predominantly* belong?[17] To my mind here is a prescription for worse confusion. Under the principle of predominance, Scots private law may, depending on the evaluator, be deemed a common law system given the extent of English law influence, or it may be called a civil law system in light of its Romanist elements. But according to this approach it must be one or the other and not a mixture of both. South African private law, on the other hand, could be deemed to be a civil law system, or perhaps a common law system, or even a customary law system if the African laws followed by the majority of the population are considered the predominant factor. Again South Africa must be one of the three rather than the sum of its parts. Obviously the predominance principle results in the suppression of mixtures that otherwise embarrass a traditional ordering scheme.

This leads me at last to my theme tonight. In light of this classification vacuum, how do mixed jurisdiction jurists perceive themselves? How do they use and define the words 'mixed legal systems'?

TWO RIVAL THEORIES OF MIXED SYSTEMS

Introduction

There are two rival theories as to what these terms mean and how they should be applied. These give us different answers and different insights into the questions, 'What is a mixed jurisdiction and who is a mixed-jurisdiction jurist?' The first theory — which I believe is traditional and today more prevalent — produces a limited grouping which is sometimes denominated as the 'classical' mixed jurisdictions. The theory of selection has a prescriptive basis and has arisen, in part, for historical reasons. The second theory, on the other hand, yields an unlimited category because it

[16] This seems deficient as a scientific approach to comparative law. I would submit that if a biologist were to inform his readers that he had discovered a new and uncatalogued form of life, he would surely not claim that it is unnecessary to attempt to classify it, nor would he postpone such a task by arguing that the newly discovered life form may one day cease to be new or could draw closer to the previously classified forms of life.

[17] de Cruz, P (2007) *Comparative Law in a Changing World* (3rd ed) Cavendish at 38.

results from a factual rather than a prescriptive way of determining legal mixtures. This theory has arisen under the influence of legal pluralism. Before beginning this paper I assumed that the first theory was the better of the two and was essential to maintain because the second theory was defectively wide and imprecise. It will soon be apparent that my views have evolved. I hope to show that that these rival theories are not in conflict. They are complementary ideas. Once aware of their meaning and implication it becomes clear that our differences of opinion as to what constitutes a mixed jurisdiction are quite relative, more apparent than real. I believe we need both conceptions to make sense of the world we inhabit.

The Traditional View

The first theory, or if theory is too grand a word, then at least the first approach, may be regarded as traditional and somewhat restricted in scope. As early as around 1900 and thereafter, a few writers brought to the world's attention a group of systems whose private law was a western hybrid, characterized by a core of common law and civil law elements. These were geographically dispersed and societally different countries. Ranging over four continents, they included Scotland, South Africa, Quebec, Louisiana, Puerto Rico and about ten more countries.[18] It had not before been appreciated that such a group existed, it being counterintuitive that they might have much in common. These writers insisted however that a certain natural unity existed and the jurisdictions in this class were *numerus clausus.* They actually had a detailed knowledge of these systems and wrote from first-hand experience and study. The story is instructive, and I will briefly trace an outline. I believe that if ever the hundreds of varieties of mixed systems in the world were to be successfully classified on a rational basis, the process would have to start inductively, not in an armchair, but searching through one related cluster at a time, much in the manner of these earlier writers.

Historical Development

It is helpful to begin with Sir Thomas Smith and his intellectual predecessors. As previously indicated, in his writings Smith would use

18 These are listed in du Plessis, J (2006) *Oxford Handbook of Comparative Law* OUP, Reimann, M and Zimmermann, R (eds) and in Palmer supra n 3 at 4. It has been pointed out that there is no single style of being mixed. One may find an individual personality within each jurisdiction. See Palmer, VV (2009) 'Quebec and Her Sisters of the Third Legal Family' (54) *McGill L. J.* 321, 350.

the term 'mixed jurisdiction' in a restrictive and selective sense to signify a group of countries in which common law and civil law elements in the private law interacted and vied for supremacy. Obviously he regarded his native Scotland as a paradigm of a mixed jurisdiction. Interestingly, he always carefully placed the term in quotation marks. At times, for literary variation, he substituted the words 'mixed system' but this did not change the countries to which he was referring, and this phrase too was within quotation marks. In 1963 he introduced the expression 'mixed jurisdiction' into the title of one of his essays, the first author ever to do so,[19] and on that occasion he ventured a definition. He wrote that a mixed jurisdiction was 'basically a civilian system that had been under pressure from the Anglo-American common law and has in part been overlaid by that rival system of jurisprudence.'[20] This step occurred during an extensive international campaign in which Smith wrote a great deal on the subject and made extended visits to Louisiana, South Africa and Quebec.[21]

Within ten years writers from Quebec, Louisiana and Scotland such as Jean-Louis Baudouin, Joseph Dainow, Albert Tate and David Walker had adopted his terminology and his loose definition as well.[22] When Smith in 1973 contributed a chapter to Volume six (edited by F.H. Lawson) of the International Encyclopaedia of Comparative Law, he could now entitle the entry Mixed Jurisdictions with no quotation marks. The concept had come of age. The chapter begins with these words:

> The "mixed" or "hybrid" jurisdictions with which this subchapter is concerned are those in which CIVIL LAW and COMMON LAW doctrines have been received and indeed contend for supremacy.

[19] Smith, TB (1965)'The Preservation of the Civilian Tradition in 'Mixed Jurisdictions' in Yiannopoulos, AN (ed) *Civil Law in the Modern World* LSU Press 1. He had used the term 'mixed' in the title of an earlier essay published in South Africa, but provided no description or definition in the body of the article. See Smith, TB (1956) 'The Common Law Cuckoo: Problems of a 'Mixed' Legal System with Special Reference to Restrictive Interpretations in the Scots Law of Obligations' *Butterworth's SALR* 147.

[20] Smith (1965) id at 2-3.

[21] See Reid, K (2005)'While One Hundred Remain: TB Smith and the Progress of Scots Law' in Reid, K and Carey Miller, D (eds) *A Mixed Legal System in Transition* Edinburgh University Press 1.

[22] See Baudouin, J-L (1972) 'The Future of Civil Law in a Mixed Jurisdiction' (the Bailey Lecture at LSU in 1972). See generally Dainow, J (ed) (1974) *The Role of Judicial Decisions and Doctrine in Civil Law and in Mixed Jurisdictions* LSU Press, where the editor and contributors to the volume use the expression fluently: Walker, D at 202 ('Scotland is today one of the mixed systems.'); Baudouin, J-L at 2 *passim*; Tate, Judge Albert at 23 ('Louisiana is a mixed jurisdiction: our basically civilian tradition has been partly overlaid and replaced by Anglo-American common law.' (obviously paraphrasing Smith)); Chloros, AG (1977) *Codification in a Mixed Jurisdiction* Holland.

> Other hybrid systems where, for example, customary law or religious law coexists with western type law are not considered.[23]

Smith made clear that there were other kinds of mixed legal systems, which he was omitting and not considering. He was obviously aware that the narrow group of systems he described were but a genus of the mixed species. He acknowledged that other mixed systems might be more 'complex' than those in Scotland, Louisiana, South Africa or elsewhere.[24] It now seems clear why he had been so carefully placing quotation marks around the term. They were intended to place in relief his restrictive and selective meaning. There was also another reason. T.B. Smith was the inventor and populariser of the term 'mixed jurisdiction', and therefore he was apparently quoting himself.

Maps and Foyers: Oxford and McGill

Professor Kenneth Reid has rightly pointed out that the 'idea' of a mixed jurisdiction existed before Smith popularised the expression. It was incubating from the turn of the 20th century until mid-century, during the heady days of empire and colonialism. It seems clear the parentage is Anglo-Scottish and that Smith may have borrowed the idea from more than one source. At this time English jurists tended to conceive of the world's systems in bipolar terms. The map fell into two parts, on one side the empire of Common Law and on the other the empire of Civil Law. Their special vocation, however — novel at the time — was to point out, and indeed to champion, a small number of jurisdictions that straddled or combined the two laws and did not exactly adhere to either one. Thus the idea of mixed jurisdictions was born, in Professor Reid's words, 'the product of a failure of classification.'[25]

If there were any particular foyer of this thinking it appears to have been at Oxford and McGill universities during the first decades of the twentieth century. Oxford had attracted a coterie of intellectuals and comparatists who were in various ways (by birth, legal training, field experience and intellectual interest) intensely and intimately connected to these common law and civil law hybrids. Notable in this group were F.P. Walton, R.W. Lee and F.H. Lawson, all of whom wrote important articles stressing the value and desirability of studying the mixed jurisdictions from a comparative

23 *Encyclopaedia*, Vol. 6, Property and Trust, Lawson, FH (ed) (1974), at 115, no. 228.

24 See Smith (1965) supra n 19.

25 Reid, K (2003) 'The Idea of Mixed Legal Systems' (78) *Tulane Law Review* 5 at 8.

law point of view.[26] The first two authors had experienced these systems on an intimate basis, and McGill attracted both of them to Montreal to serve as dean of the law school. Walton and Lee had strong connections to Scotland, Quebec, Ceylon, South Africa and Egypt. After taking degrees in classics at Oxford, Walton studied law in Edinburgh and was called to the Scots bar. He lectured in Glasgow on Roman law for a number of years and wrote several treatises on Scots law. In 1897 he left for Montreal to become the dean of the McGill law school where he remained until 1914, writing penetrating studies on the dual traditions in Quebec. Afterwards he became director of the Khedivian School of Law in Cairo and wrote a treatise on the Egyptian law of obligations. In retirement he returned to Oxford to serve as secretary of the faculty club.[27]

Lee was another Oxford classics scholar who left for Ceylon in 1891 where he spent three years as a local magistrate. The experience awakened a life-long interest in Roman-Dutch law. He returned to England for reasons of health, practicing mainly before the Privy Council as a specialist in appeals from Ceylon. From 1906 on he held the chair of Roman-Dutch law at London University. In 1914 he replaced Walton as dean of the McGill faculty.[28] In 1915 he published his classic work *An Introduction to Roman-Dutch Law*, and in 1921 returned to Oxford to take up the chair of Roman-Dutch law, which he held for thirty-six years until retirement in 1956.

For chronological reasons, it may have been Lee and Lawson who made an impression upon TB Smith during his studies at Oxford. In a *festschrift* essay for Lawson, written in 1986, Smith acknowledged that Lawson was first among a mere handful of English jurists who had attained a deep knowledge of Scots law. Lawson once sought a chair of law at Edinburgh and had a Scottish wife. In his inaugural essay as holder of the chair of comparative law at Oxford in 1949, he referred to 'a most interesting group of laws, which, because they display the influence of English law

[26] Amos, S (1937) 'The Common Law and the Civil Law in the British Commonwealth of Nations' (50) *Harvard Law Review* 1249; Walton, FP (1899) 'The Civil Law and the Common Law of Canada' (11) *Juridical Review* 282; Lawson, FH (1949) 'The Field of Comparative Law' (61) *Juridical Review* 16 (esp. at 26-29 discussing 'hybrid' systems).

[27] Walton wrote major works on Scots law (e.g., (1893) *Scotch Marriages, Regular and Irregular* Edinburgh, on Quebec (1920) *The Scope and Interpretation of the Civil Code of Lower Canada* (reprinted ed. Toronto 1980), (1920) *Egyptian Law of Obligations* London, (1935) [1965] *Amos and Walton's Introduction to French Law* (with Sheldon Amos), on Roman Law (1903) *Historical Introduction to Roman Law* Edinburgh. It is said that 'He never wrote anything which was not first-rate.' He returned to Edinburgh in 1932 where he died in 1948. See entry by Hanbury HG *Dictionary of National Biography* 1941-1950. On his views about legal education at McGill, see Macdonald, R (1990) 'The National Law Programme at McGill: Origins, Establishment, Prospects' (13) *Dalhousie Law Journal* 211 at 243-48.

[28] For an assessment of Lee's deanship at McGill, see Macdonald supra n 27 at 249-56.

on a body of doctrine already profoundly Romanised, stand between the common and the civil law systems, and accordingly were regarded by the late Professor Lévy-Ullmann as the most likely focus around which a future uniform law of the world might group itself.'[29] Concluding a three page discussion of these systems, he ended by saying, 'I have spoken at length about these hybrid laws because I regard them as peculiarly favourable fields for comparative work in an English university. Most of the literature is in English and Quebec law leads one naturally into French law. Besides we have with us, and can always hope to have, one of the greatest masters of Roman-Dutch Law [referring to R.W. Lee].'[30]

In his first year as dean of the McGill Law School in Montreal, Lee published an unusual article in the *Michigan Law Review* entitled 'The Civil Law and the Common Law — A World Survey'.[31] Serving as a frontispiece to the article, was a most interesting full-page map that Kenneth Reid drew to our attention to at the First World Congress in 2002. A copy is found in Figure 1 below. The map filled in the common-law countries around the globe in black ink, and represented the civil law countries by dotted marks. As against these two monoliths the map showed a third category, the *demi-monde* of 'mixed jurisdictions', which were designated by the use of horizontal stripes. The striped areas were Louisiana, Quebec, Guyana, South Africa, Ceylon, Scotland, and Egypt/Sudan.[32] The words 'mixed jurisdiction' were printed on the legend of the map but did not actually appear anywhere in the text. They would not appear in anyone's text until T.B. Smith began to write on the subject four decades later. Yet obviously the idea of a mixed jurisdiction was clearly alive and well in Montreal and no doubt in other places long before.

[29] Lawson, supra n 26, at 26.

[30] Id at 29. Lawson made passing reference to a world beyond common law and civil law, pointing briefly to the existence of 'oriental and primitive law', but he had little interest in pluralism. His use of the word 'primitive' is one clue to his outlook, but even better is his statement that 'The range of primitive law in British colonial territories is truly terrifying and the tendency to find common traits in widely different regions must be kept in check much more consciously than when dealing with civil or common law.' Id at 34. In his best-known work he stated: 'common lawyers, and for that matter civilians too, are disposed to say that all western law belongs either to the Common Law or to the Civil Law systems' but he noted that this was only half correct: 'the Scandinavian laws [...] are really independent; and there are many systems, some of considerable importance, which are hybrids, as it were balanced between the two blocs and possessing many of the characteristics of both.' (1953) *A Common Lawyer Looks at the Civil Law* Greenwood at 2.

[31] 1915 (14) *Michigan Law Review* 89.

[32] For further analysis of the role of Egypt/Sudan in Lee's thought, see Palmer (2009) supra n 18, 328-329.

Figure 1

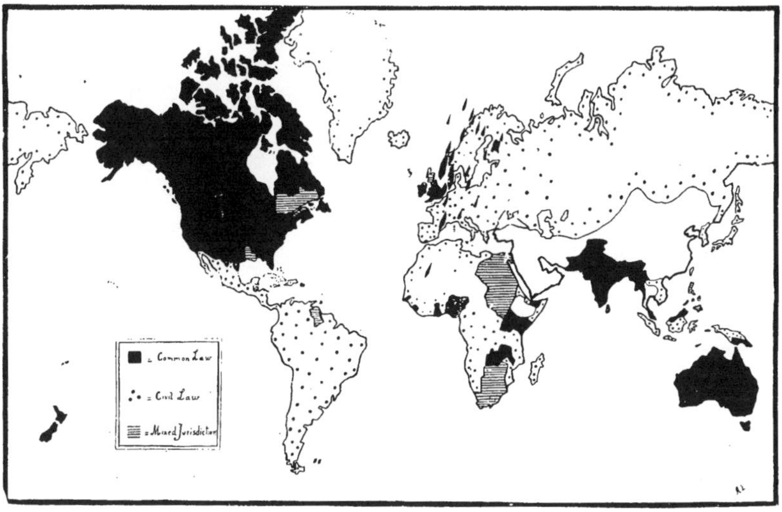

THE CIVIL LAW AND THE COMMON LAW --- A WORLD SURVEY

The Original Allure of the Mixed Systems

The early efforts seem rather innocent of any grand taxonomic purpose. Nor was there an evident interest in legal pluralism as such.[33] It appears they were simply building out from the conventional duality of their time and merely seeking to add a new in-between category. Why were they interested in this particular type of system? Aside from the novelty and the freshness of the subject, these systems were appealing for three general reasons. First, it seems that in the early part of the twentieth century there was far greater doubt than now as to the comparability of common law and civil law.[34] The study of the mixed jurisdictions was thought to be a means of helping common lawyers and civil lawyers reach across an epistemological gulf and gain better understanding of the tradition on the other side. But using a halfway house approach, an Englishman attempting to understand French law and culture might make a first approach

[33] As noted earlier, supra n 26, Lawson spoke of the 'terrifying diversity' of ethnic laws and chose to restrict himself to the European traditions.
[34] This was the same type of doubt, incidentally, that existed only twenty years ago about the comparability of western law and socialist law.

through Scots law, presumably because he/she would understand familiar common-law signposts and could assimilate civil law concepts more easily in the process. As Lawson pointed out, such systems could be excellent pedagogic devices in English-speaking law faculties.[35] Second, such study might eventually be of benefit to Europe by pointing the way for the future unification of private law, as Lévy-Ullmann had famously argued. Third, and this would be T.B. Smith's main focus, cross-comparative work within the group could help the beleaguered mixed jurisdictions like Scotland – where in his words the 'eleventh hour' had already struck – overcome their intellectual isolation and assist in efforts to preserve and maintain the civilian tradition.

The Boundless Neighbourhood

Smith was deeply impressed by the affinities between Scotland and South Africa. His 1959 essay 'Scots Law and Roman-Dutch Law: A Shared Tradition' emphasised the historical connections, shared civilian traditions and mutual challenges facing the two systems. Despite the geographical distance, he saw a certain intellectual proximity, which made them 'neighbours in law':

> Separated by two continents, Scots law and South African law during the 19th and first half of the 20th century were destined to work out, more or less independently, problems of remarkable similarity. Each system recognized essentially the same basic principles; the external factors correspond closely.[36]

He would later add that 'lawyers in these systems have hitherto tended to work in isolation, and to forget that "neighbours in law" are not necessarily those closest geographically.'[37] The notion of 'neighbours in law' meant for Smith a compatible legal order based on similar interests, methods and sources. Many of these similarities have been recently reviewed by Professor Reinhart Zimmermann, and in the following remarks, I am indebted to his outline.[38] Both systems were decisively moulded by the

[35] This utility still seems to be well appreciated, as evidenced by the prodigious use of mixed jurisdiction cases and examples in basic student texts on comparative law. *See, e.g.*, Schlesinger, R, Baade, H et al. (1998) *Comparative Law* (6th ed) Foundation Press (setting forth at length reported cases from the Philippines, South Africa, Guyana, Louisiana, and Puerto Rico).

[36] Smith supra n 20, at 46.

[37] 'Introduction' (1962) *Studies Critical and Comparative* Green at ix.

[38] Zimmermann, R (2004) ''Double Cross': Comparing Scots and South African Law' in

reception of Roman Law and Canon Law while retaining elements of indigenous customary law. Given these receptions, one could say there was already a mixture in place well before English influence was introduced.[39] The systems were far-flung provinces of the old *ius commune*, and since each remained uncodified, they were more open to accepting legal ideas and persuasive authority from one another. Secondly, both of their private-law systems came under the influence of English law, although this happened at an earlier time in Scotland. Thirdly, in both cases a reaction against the English influence occurred in the form of a neo-civilian renaissance in the second half of the twentieth century.

Beyond these broad parallels, however, there were also specific historical ties that linked the two systems. Each was intellectually indebted, though in different degrees, to old Dutch authorities. There was a famous intellectual connection between the two most respected institutional writers of the two countries. Lord Stair (sometimes called the 'Scottish Grotius') spent six years in exile in the Netherlands and was influenced by Hugo Grotius, who is considered the father of South African private law. Works by leading Dutch jurists were regularly cited in Scottish legal practice and exercised influence on the institutional writers.[40] Scottish students flocked to the law faculties of the Netherlands in great numbers during the 17th and 18th centuries.[41] They returned to Scotland with knowledge of the *ius commune* and, to some extent, the *ius proprium* of countries where they had studied. They returned with continental law books to place in Scottish libraries.

Zimmermann, R Visser, D & Reid, K (eds) *Mixed Legal Systems in Comparative Perspective* OUP.

[39] The phrase 'Roman-Dutch law', which Simon van Leeuwen invented in 1652 in his work *Paratitla Juris Novissimi*, acknowledges this fact. On the use of this phrase, see Lee, RW (1953) *An Introduction to Roman-Dutch Law* (5th ed) Oxford at 2. See also Carey Miller, D (1996) 'South Africa: A Mixed System Subject to Transcending Forces' in Örücü, E, Attwool, E and Coyle, S (eds) *Studies in Legal Systems: Mixed and Mixing* Kluwer at 166-69.

[40] Stair, for instance, relied on Vinnius and Grotius more than his direct cites to them would indicate. Bankton often echoes Johannes Voet without telling the reader. Zimmermann supra n 38, at 9-10.

[41] Zimmermann points out that in the period 1676-1725 Leyden University received 825 Scottish law students, 422 of them matriculating. In that same period the records of the Faculty of Advocates show that about 275 lawyers who were admitted to the bar (out of 637) had studied in the Netherlands. (2004) ''Double Cross': Comparing Scots and South African Law' in Zimmermann, Visser, Reid supra n 38 at 9. See also Cairns, JW (1996) 'Importing our Lawyers from Holland: Netherlands' Influences on Scots Law and Lawyers in the Eighteenth Century' in Simpson, GG (ed) (1996) *Scotland and the Low Countries 1124-1894* East Linton. This flow of students dried up by 1750 with the Napoleonic wars and the success of codification movements in France, Prussia, Austria and the Netherlands, together with a decline in the study of Roman law. Interestingly, students from the Cape were also sent for legal training to the Netherlands' universities in considerable numbers in the same century. Van der Merwe, CG, Du Plessis,J and De Waal, MJ 'South Africa Report' in Palmer supra n 3 at 146 n. 150.

The Bands of Unity

Today Scottish/South African legal studies may be described as flourishing. In the past ten years, in addition to many fine studies, we have been given three monumental works devoted to the connection between the two systems. Spearheaded by Reid, Visser and Zimmermann, this trilogy,[42] coming to more than 2000 pages and engaging more than 100 contributors, has not only greatly enriched the two systems doctrinally, but has produced an unprecedented intellectual exchange. It can no longer be seriously questioned whether the terrain for close comparative collaboration is as favourable as T.B. Smith imagined.[43] It is probably more fertile than he supposed. The papers from the First Worldwide Congress on Mixed Jurisdictions, totalling more than 500 pages, have been published[44] and will soon be augmented by the papers from this Congress. We also have impressive books and articles by Jan Smits, William Tetley, Jacques du Plessis, Hector MacQueen, Kenneth Reid, Lord Rodger, who have all made insightful contributions to this subject. I should also mention a new comparative study underway between Louisiana and Scotland involving 15 academics. As Jacques du Plessis has well said, the movement that was once a one-man band has become an entire orchestra.

The opportunities are clear and can be extended to the other mixed jurisdictions. The affinities and connections are neither fictitious nor exaggerated. The parallels that have been described in the case of South Africa and Scotland could be roughly repeated if we were to examine a different pair of jurisdictions, such as Louisiana and Puerto Rico, or Quebec and Scotland.[45] Here too we would find that initially a civil law was implanted that was shaped by the reception of Roman and Canon law, that a tide of common-law influence later ensued, and a neo-civilian reaction to that influence occurred in the 20th century.[46] But this by no means circumscribes the metes and bounds of their unity. There are other elements in common.[47] For example, in all these systems: (i) The civil law is brought to life through Anglo-American institutions, meaning that judges

[42] (1996) *Southern Cross*; (2000) *History of Private Law in Scotland*, vols I-II OUP; (2004) *Mixed Legal Systems in Comparative Perspective* OUP.

[43] A reviewer in the Edinburgh Review said that the 'resemblances and differences are presented, sometimes as if Scottish and South African law are the emanation of one and the same system of thought.' Review by van Erp, S (11) *Edinburgh Law Review* at 285-88.

[44] (2003) 'First Worldwide Congress on Mixed Jurisdictions' (78) *Tulane Law Review* 1-501.

[45] Walton FP pointed to the legal resemblances in his article (1901) 'Relationship of the Law of France to the Law of Scotland' (1) *Canadian Law Review* 442.

[46] That is by no means the end of history. The competitive dialectic will undoubtedly produce further stages.

[47] Palmer, supra n 3 at 76-80.

with creative mindsets and courts with inherent powers interpreted the civil law. The substance of the law was thus insensibly shaped by actors and institutions that were more than neutral conduits. (ii) Court decisions are accorded strong precedential value whether the civil law happens to be codified or not; indeed in these systems, court decisions are accepted as an official source of law second only to legislation. (iii) Civil procedure is adversarial and Anglo-American. The emphasis upon common law remedies has left a visible imprint on substantive civil law. (iv) Common-law influence follows a discernable pattern, penetrating the most porous points of entry, such as the law of delict, while leaving resistant institutions like property law relatively unaffected. (v) Anglo-American commercial law has everywhere replaced the law merchant originally in place, partly because of relatively weak cultural attachment to the latter, but more decisively because of pressure to conform to the norms of the dominant economy.

Shared characteristics such as these confer an identity or inner relationship to the cluster of 'common law/civil law' systems. It is true of course that several members in this 'classical' group have more than one private law system in place. South Africa and Sri Lanka, to go no further, concurrently combine religious, oriental and African personal laws, which further complexity the private law picture. Even if a comparative law researcher is primarily interested in the western law elements in those systems, s/he should know from her own legal history that the effects of these other personal laws can hardly be ignored, for they will be interacting with western law at some level in the society and will in time produce new internal combinations. These non-western personal laws are indeed the *fil conducteur* that may lead to the classification of other clusters of mixed systems. To explain this point more clearly, however, I now turn to the rival theory of mixed systems.

The Pluralist Conception of a Mixed Legal System

Introduction

More and more jurists and colleagues have been influenced by the insights of legal pluralism and have thereby been led to recognize a wider class of mixed legal systems. The principal criterion of the pluralist conception is simply the presence or interaction of two or more kinds of laws or legal traditions within the same system or 'social field'.[48] The existence

[48] Griffith's definition of pluralism, which is indebted to Sally Moore, is 'that state of affairs

of a mixed system in this sense sounds like a factual question. The mixed nature of a legal system can be discovered and confirmed in an objective manner by research and observation. The characterization does not depend upon an interpretation of 'legal styles' or a subjective judgment about the 'predominance' of one type of law over another. Nor does it necessarily depend upon what the subject of law perceives, though the subjective point of view is not entirely discarded.[49]

I need not try to define legal pluralism because it is clear that there is no widely accepted definition[50] nor do I wish to go into pluralism's battles with legal positivism, legal centralism, and Eurocentric biases about the meaning of law.[51] I merely want to draw attention to the general legal orientation and the fields of law (official and unofficial) that interest the legal pluralist.

Personal Laws and Private Laws

Pluralists tend to study post-colonial societies in Africa and Asia in which various personal laws coexist and interact with western law as continuing effects of legal history. A more liberal conception of the mixed legal system necessarily follows from their broader pursuit of legal phenomena, as when they study not only customary law, tribal law, and religious law recognised by the state, but also the unrecognised and unofficial laws which escape state control and constitute the living law.[52] The focus may be upon the Hindu, the Muslim, Jewish or African customary laws, which govern different communities within the same territory and which may necessitate the use of interpersonal conflict rules to determine which personal law applies to whom. There are of course differences between the notion of 'personal law' and 'private law'.[53] For purposes of this discussion personal

---

for any social field, in which behaviour pursuant to more than one legal order occurs.' Quoted from Menski, W (2006) *Comparative Law in a Global Context* (2d ed) CUP at 114. Michael Hooker's concept was similar.

49 Masija Chiba argues that the subjective perspective has significance when people living in pluralism may be formally allowed to choose among one or even competing legal rules. (2002) *Legal Cultures in Human Society* Shinzansha International, Tokyo at 182.

50 Id at 179.

51 *See* Griffith, J (1986) 'What Is Legal Pluralism?' (24) *Journal of Legal Pluralism and Unofficial Law* 1-56; Chiba supra n 49; Menski, supra n 48 at 115-16; Hooker, M (1975) *Legal Pluralism* OUP; Bennett, TW (2006) 'Comparative Law and African Customary Law' in Reimann, M and Zimmermann, R (eds) *Oxford Handbook of Comparative Law* OUP at 666-71; van Niekerk, GJ (2007) 'Legal Pluralism' in Bekker, JC, Rautenbach, C and Goolam, NMI (eds) *Introduction to Legal Pluralism in South Africa* (2nd ed) LexisNexis at 5-14.

52 The distinction for van Niekerk, id, lies in the difference between 'state' pluralism and 'deep' pluralism.

53 In some systems the term 'personal law' may not be recognised as such. For example, it

law may be regarded as a subset of private law, a restricted list of topics (perhaps the most culturally significant legal areas) within the larger area of private law.[54] In this sense personal law may signify an ethnic enclave or niche in the midst of official law.[55] Personal law and private law are therefore intertwined and overlapping ideas, and it is necessary to grasp their cultural connection in order to understand the characteristic structure of the mixed systems.

The creation of a mixed system, historically speaking, has often taken place when a people has lost its political sovereignty, yet somehow has preserved the right to keep living in accordance with its personal or private laws. Whether the personal law was the custom of an African people or the *Coutume de Paris* in Quebec, or the Roman-Dutch law of the Boers is only a difference in detail, for in each case there was a similar aspiration. The 'struggle for personal law' has been a hallmark of the classical mixed jurisdictions[56] as well as the *raison d'être* of complex pluralism in many parts of the world. No people that I am aware of has ever willingly given up its personal law or willingly accepted a different personal law than its own. In South Africa, when the Cape fell into British hands, the Roman-Dutch law was the personal/private law of the Dutch settlers, and retention was allowed. At the same time African custom was the personal law of various South African peoples, and that custom was retained as well. This has occurred throughout history and not, it seems, because of an international law norm (as has often been supposed),[57] but rather on account of cultural tenacity and political calculation. I would have to agree with Esmein's observation that the policy of allowing a subjugated people to retain their personal law is often not a matter of choice but a kind of necessity imposed upon the conqueror.

was unknown to classical Islamic jurists and did not gain currency until near the turn of the 20th century. Nasir, J (1990) *The Islamic Law of Personal Status* (2nd ed) London.

54 For example, the topics of Jewish personal law recognised in India only relate to successions and marriage/divorce, whereas though Hindu personal laws in India have a somewhat broader coverage (successions, marriage and divorce, guardianship, adoption; joint family and partition, and religious institutions) they by no means fill the field of private law. The topics of Muslim personal law in India have similar scope. *See* Rautenbach, Christa (2006) 'Phenomenon of Personal Laws in India: Some Lessons for South Africa' (xxxix) *CILSA*, at 244.

55 See Menski supra n 48, at 243.

56 See Palmer, supra n 3. The history of Quebec is one of the most transparent examples of the struggle. Thus Tancelin refers to Quebec private law as 'a law of survival' for the French-speaking community of Quebec. See his 'Introduction' (at 25) to Walton, FP (1980) *The Scope and Interpretation of the Civil Code of Lower Canada* Butterworths .

57 The usual reference to this norm is Lord Mansfield's statement in *Campbell v. Hall* (1774) 98 ER 1045, at 1047, that 'The laws of a conquered country continue in force, until they are altered by the conqueror.' For discussion and criticism, see Palmer, supra n 3, at 20-29.

> There is in effect a necessity which is imposed on the conqueror, *of allowing their laws to be conquered*, every time that a conquest brings together two races too different in the degree and form of the civilization. This is what is done in our time in great measure by the French in Algeria, by the English and the French in India and in Indo-China.[58]

It also explains British policy in southern Africa, which Bennett describes as 'no more than a frank acceptance of the fact that colonial administrations were in no position to force their subjects to comply with Roman-Dutch law.'[59]

Pluralism's Wide-Angle Lens

As stated previously, according to the pluralist viewpoint any interaction of laws of a different type or source — indigenous with exogenous, religious with customary, western with non-western — is sufficient to constitute a mixed legal system. This of course casts the net so widely that the quasi-totality of the legal systems of the world suddenly qualify as 'mixed legal systems'. Surprisingly, this extremely inclusive position has not been seen as a drawback or deterrent to its growing use. Professor Tetley, for example, treats Iran, Egypt, Syria, Iraq and Indonesia as 'mixed jurisdictions'. He describes Egypt as 'an intriguing mixed legal system blending civilian rules fashioned, in style, structure and content, on the model of the French civil code of 1804, with the law of Islam and, in family law areas, with a variety of religiously-founded personal laws.'[60] Esin Örücü, Elspeth Attwooll

[58] Esmein, A (1950) *Cours élémentaire d'histoire du droit francais* Paris at 50-51 (emphasis added). To Esmein, these considerations explained why Germanic tribes, after the collapse of Rome, allowed the Romans to keep their own law: 'It was an even more imperious necessity for the Barbarians' he writes 'as the Roman law was far superior to the Germanic custom.' Similarly Guterman points out that, 'Since the laws of the barbarians were tribal and, therefore, personal laws, it would have been difficult to apply them to the conquered people without transforming the latter into Germans. This plan was obviously not feasible.' In Guterman, S (1988) *The Principle of the Personality of Law in the Germanic Kingdoms of Western Europe from the Fifth to the Eleventh Century* P. Lang at 29-30. Kuhn adds, 'Il n'a pas de conquérant si impitoyable soit-il, qui puisse changer les habitudes et les coutumes d'un people par sa seule volonté. Il faut en exterminer les members; mais aussi longtemps que leur communauté de vie existera, il demeurera aussi un certain résidu d'identité juridique qui offrira autant de chances de modifier la loi du conquérant que d'être modifié par elle.' Kuhn, A (1938) 'La fonction de la méthode comparative dans l'histoire et la philosophie du droit' in (1938) vol I, *Introduction à l'Etude du Droit Comparé* (recueil d'études en l'honneur d'Edouard Lambert) Paris at 318-19.

[59] Bennett, TW (2007) 'The Conflict of Laws' in Bekker, Rautenbach and Goolam supra n 51 at 17.

[60] Tetley, W, 'Mixed Jurisdictions: Common Law vs Civil Law (Codified and Uncodified)',

and Sean Coyle have a particularly eclectic list of systems they regard as mixed, including Australia, Basque Country, Algeria, Hong Kong and the European Union.[61]

The reason behind this exponential expansion is clear. The world's legal systems may all be described as diversified blends with unlimited possible recombinations: chthonic laws, religious laws (Jewish, Hindu, Islamic or Canon Law), law merchant, natural law, Roman Civil Law, Common Law and so forth. It should not be at all surprising to discover five or six layers of exogenous elements in any single private law system one cares to examine. A visualization of this diversity is afforded by a colour-shaded map (Figure 2 below) and also by the chart of mixed systems found in Appendix A to this paper. Both documents were devised by the Ottawa Faculty of Law.[62]

Figure 2

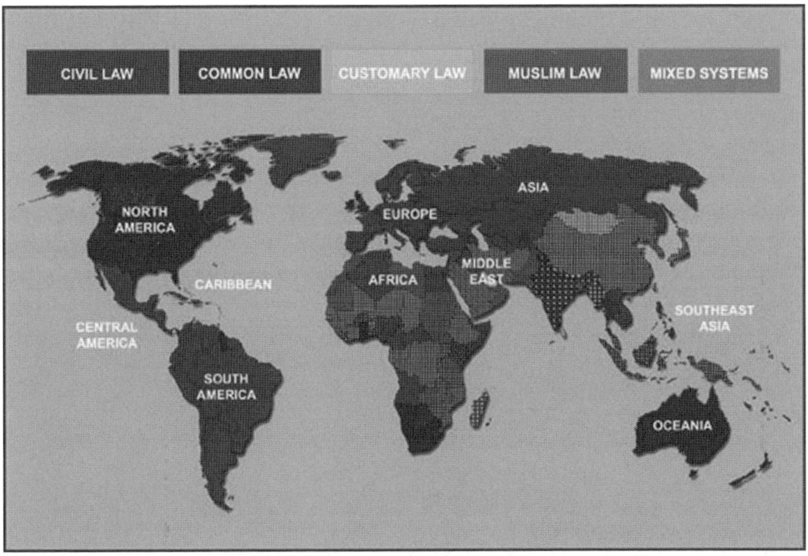

Implications for the 'Classical' Mixed Systems

Of course as this viewpoint gains acceptance, it goes without saying that the classical mixed jurisdictions like Scotland or Louisiana are entirely absorbed. Suddenly they are no longer odd and insular — and no longer

available at: www.cisgw3.pace.edu/cisg/biblio/tetley.html at 15.

61 Örücü, Attwooll and Coyle supra n 39.

62 *See* Mariani, N and Fuentes, G (2000) *World Legal Systems* W&L.

alone. Instead they become only another subgenus of the mixed species of laws. At this point the quality of being mixed must inevitably lose whatever pejorative cast it once had. Seeing hybridity as a universal fact is the first step in seeing our proper (though more banal) place in the world. It will necessarily alter the familiar attitudes and prejudices. For example, would it any longer seem useful or appropriate to speak of the classical systems as historical accidents[63] or to regard them as marginal cases in a binary civil law/common law world? How could mere 'accidents' happen so often and become so generalized? Furthermore, does it make sense to 'wait and see' whether they move in one direction or another? Obviously wherever they move (if in fact they do move) they can only move in a sea of mixed laws anyway. Further, if mixed systems have been all along at the centre rather than the periphery of legal evolution they cannot be regarded as unusual or strange. Logically, it is not easy to cast them both as paradigms and pariahs at one and the same time.[64] Perhaps then a useful classification scheme for the 21st century will have to begin with their centrality as a point of departure.[65] But we will have to abandon the conceit that 'pure' legal systems are somehow privileged or preferred, or that some mixtures are superior to others, or that the 'utility' of mixed systems lies in the incidental lessons or insights they may have for others rather than for themselves.[66] It has often been said that Scotland, Louisiana and others are 'laboratories of comparative law' and other systems may benefit from studying their experiences or their practices. In reality, however, all systems are laboratories of comparative law and any system's experience could be of some value for others.

Hector MacQueen has observed (in words which can be endorsed as an elevated approach to the study of plural systems generally) that,

[63] Glenn compares them to anomalies in the world of science where complex structures may represent 'frozen accidents' (1996) 'Quebec: Mixité and Monism' in Örücü, Attwooll, and Coyle supra n 39 at 2, 14.

[64] *Cf.* Maurice Tancelin's pained exclamation: 'But all that is established is that a mixed system is an atypical phenomenon; an embarrassment, indeed, to anyone attempting to make an ordered and systematic presentation of the national systems of law.' Tancelin, supra n 56, at 1.

[65] Esin Örücü argues that all legal systems are overlaps and mixes to varying degrees and thus their mixed nature should be the starting point of comparative classification. (2004) 'Family Trees for Legal Systems: Towards a Contemporary Approach' in van Hoecke, M (ed) *Epistemology and Methodology of Comparative Law* Hart at 363.

[66] For example, it has been asserted that Israel's continental drafting may reassure England of the feasibility of changing its drafting style; that Scots law or the McGregor code may serve as a template for the single European code; that Louisiana law may indicate to Europeans how common law/civil law ideas can be conciliated within a single civil code. *See* Kötz, H 'The Value of Mixed Legal Systems' (2003) 78 *Tulane Law Review* 435 at 438; Gandolfi, G (1993) 'Preface' in *Contract Code Drawn Up on Behalf of the English Law Commission* Giuffrè.

> [I]t is contrary to the spirit of mixed legal systems [to analyse them] on the basis that one part of the mix is good and the other bad. Instead, the mixed systems need to be evaluated on their own terms — that is as neither civil law nor common law — and analysts must accept that a mixed past means a mixed future.[67]

Thus if we wish to speak of their 'value' it is surely not in the form of their incidental or vicarious value to others, but rather in what they can reveal about the formation and evolution of legal systems everywhere. Their value to legal science can be better understood in terms of why they were originally formed, why they recurrently evolve, and what they have done for the profession and the peoples they have served.[68]

European Systems in the Pluralist Lens

The pluralist theory of mixed legal systems also tells us something valuable about those countries we customarily think of as being purely 'common law' or purely 'civil law'. This theory makes us re-examine the foundation of their identity. Perhaps the world is not ready to accept it, surely not just yet, but England, Canada, France, Germany and Switzerland, though hitherto thought of as common law or civil law systems are all mixed private law systems in a factual sense. Indeed, this view is increasingly accepted by legal scholars. It may of course suit their own projects and views about the future of Europe, but the disarming factual basis of the assertion seems unquestioned. Thus it is said that England is or soon will be a mixed legal system, that European transnational law is destined to be a mixed system, that the EU is becoming a mixed supranational system. Isolated legal subjects such as Admiralty or contracts are also discussed as mixed systems.[69] It may be simply a question of time before we hear

[67] MacQueen, H 'Looking Forward to a Mixed Future: A Response to Professor Yiannopoulos' (2003) 78 *Tulane Law Review* 411 at 412.

[68] The value-added in being mixed, I am suggesting, can be seen best from the internal rather than the external point of view. This is the light in which I interpret Lord Rodger's statements that 'If mixed systems do have a value, it is, surely, precisely in being mixed. For me one of the chief advantages of being a mixed system is that it has been expounded in the past by reference to some version of the [Roman law] template [...] at least we have these systematic expositions of the law [...] long before there was anything similar in English law.' Lord Rodger of Earlsferry, '"Say Not the Struggle Naught Availeth': The Costs and Benefits of Mixed Legal Systems' (2003) 78 *Tulane Law Review* 419, at 425-26 .

[69] Thus the title of a conference in Edinburgh in 2004 'Principles of European Contract Law: Another Mixed System?' which resulted in the book by MacQueen, H and Zimmermann, R (eds) (2006) *European Contract Law: Scots and South African Perspectives* Edinburgh University Press; as to the asserted mixed character of admiralty law, see Tetley, supra n 60.

that Roman law itself was a mixed legal system almost from the beginning. Reinhard Zimmermann, for example, seems to be in the forefront of a pluralist-historical view of European private law:

> All our national private laws in Europe today can be described as mixed legal systems. None of them has remained "pure" in its development since the Middle Ages. They all constitute a mixture of many different elements: Roman Law, indigenous customary law, canon law, mercantile custom and Natural Law theory, to name the most important ones in the history of the law of obligations.[70]

It will be noticed that the learned author is pointing to the imbedded, historical mixtures in European private law, and uses the word 'mixed' in a factual way to reveal what lies underneath the private law label. These elements, however, are not the product of a common law – civil law interaction and have nothing to do with that distinction. The mixture occurred before that distinction existed, that is, before there was a common law or civil law to differentiate.

I will return in a moment to the subject of mixed laws in contemporary Europe. I would like at this time to make a somewhat broader historical point about the antiquity of plural systems.

The Antiquity of Mixed Systems

Historically speaking, mixed systems have repeatedly incubated in conditions of increased contact, commerce and communication between peoples. Within ancient and modern empires mixing becomes unavoidable (and legal 'purity' unsustainable) once there is sufficient social and intellectual networking between foreign peoples. I would submit there is a recurrent historical pattern of mixed systems in the Roman, Ottoman and European colonial empires but for reasons of space I will confine my discussion to developments at Rome.

The Roman Empire in Construction and Collapse

The Roman Empire transformed the law of the Roman people into a mixed system and at the same time created a series of similar systems in Rome's provinces. One reason for this development appears to have been the sheer

[70] (2001) *Roman Law, Contemporary Law, European Law* OUP at 159.

number of foreign peoples brought together under Roman rule.[71] A second reason would be the value the Romans and others at that time attached to personal laws. Certainly prior to the 3rd century AD (but arguably even to the end of the Empire) the Romans followed the view that the law applicable to a person was determined not by the territory in which he lived but by the national group from which he came.[72] This was consistent with the view of many early peoples that law is a privilege of the race: the stranger is not admitted to participation.[73] The legal privileges of Roman citizenship were gradually extended to others (and in 212 AD citizenship became almost universal) but the personality principle still generally applied and ensured that Roman law was not imposed beyond the limits of citizenship. Indeed in reverse circumstances, it ensured that barbarian law would not be imposed upon conquered Romans.[74]

The makings of a mosaic were therefore inherent in the confrontation between Roman political rule and the personal laws of different peoples brought into proximity. In principle, the law applied to the *peregrini* inside Rome was their individual native or personal law. If disputes arose, however, between *peregrini* of different nations, then two or more personal laws could conflict and needed to be reconciled. Here the *peregrine praetor* needed to build up a composite legal system, the *ius gentium,* as an alternative system of justice. This *praetorian* creation exercised great influence upon the *ius civile.*[75] Eventually parts of the *ius gentium* applied not only to transactions involving *peregrines,* but to transactions between citizens. The *ius gentium* was thus partly 'received' by the urban praetor,

71 As to foreigners flowing in and out of Rome and the tribal networks, see Williamson, C (2005) *The Laws of the Roman People: Public Law in the Expansion and Decline of the Roman Republic* University of Michigan Press at 240-43, 262-67, 270-71.

72 Mousourakis, G (2003) *The Historical and Institutional Context of Roman Law* Ashgate at 418; Nicholas, B (1996) *An Introduction to Roman Law* Oxford at 59 ('Ancient law was in principle 'personal': [...] Roman law applied to Roman citizens, Athenian law to Athenian citizens.'); Lambris, M (1997) *The Historical Context of Roman Law* Sydney Law Book Co. at 44, 48. According to Mousourakis, the personality principle was no longer followed in Rome after the 3rd century, but Simeon Guterman sees no break in the continuity: 'In a very important sense the Roman law remained a personal law to the last days of the Roman Empire.' Guterman supra n 58 at 38. There may have been instances in which a people were admitted to the empire but did not retain their tribal custom, perhaps because they had already been sufficiently Romanised by living in close contact with the Romans society for several generations. *See* Barnwell, PS (2000) *Emperors, Jurists and Kings, available at*: www.JSTOR.org at 9-10.

73 Chénon, E (1926) vol I *Histoire Générale du droit francais public et privé des origenes à 1815* at 123.

74 Fleury, C (1724) *The History of the Origine of the French Laws* (English transl.) at 5.

75 Guterman supra n 58, at 39.

just as the *ius civile* was partly 'received' by the *peregrine praetor*.[76] The two legal orders constituted in effect a mixed system at Rome.

The collapse of the empire in the West (by 476 AD) reversed the political position of Rome but it did not arrest the interaction between Roman law and other personal laws. The ascendant German tribes now lived by their laws and customs, yet they permitted Romans and the clergy to be governed by Roman law.[77] Fleury notes that Charlemagne, after reuniting the Francs, Burgundians, Goths and Lombards into one empire, 'suffered' each nation to enjoy their own laws.[78] The Frankish capitulary of 768 AD stated: 'All shall follow their own law, both Romans and Salians; and those who come from other regions shall live according to the law of their own country.'[79] Saint Agobard, archbishop of Lyon from 816 AD, was a first-hand observer of the multiplicity of personal laws: 'It constantly happens that of five persons who are walking or sitting together, not one is subject to the same laws as another.'[80] Wessels notes that even fathers and sons or husbands and wives could live under different personal laws.[81] Some German kings tried to compartmentalize the laws to match the different peoples they governed. Hence codified rules for the Romans living in Gaul were contained in the *Lex Romana Visigothorum* issued by King Alaric II in 506 AD. At first this Lex was exclusively for the Romans and did not apply to the entire population, but by 654 AD it was extended to Romans and Visigoths alike.[82] In the course of time socialization between these peoples overcame the need to govern on the basis of personal laws.[83] Likewise, Romans in Burgundy were governed by the *Lex Romana Burgondionum*, and Burgundians and Romans were deemed equal but distinct under the law.[84]

[76] Thus it is believed that the actions *bonae fidei* were first introduced in the courts where foreigners were concerned and then borrowed from the *ius gentium* by the *ius civile*. Jolowicz, HF (1939) *Historical Introduction to Roman Law* CUP at 304-05. It is also clear that the contract of stipulation was made applicable to peregrines. Nicholas, supra n 72, at 58.

[77] Fleury, supra n 74 at 15-16; Wessels, JW (2005) 'Personal Laws' in *History of the Roman-Dutch Law* Lawbook Ex. Reprint at 45-49.

[78] Fleury id. at 38.

[79] Quoted in Lupoi, M (2000) *The Origins of the European Legal Order* Cambridge at 394-95.

[80] Mousourakis, supra n 72, at 419.

[81] Wessels, supra n 77, at 47.

[82] Lupoi, supra n 79, at 77-78.

[83] The Visigoths and Burgundians had settled among the Roman population as *foederati* and were among those Germans who most quickly and completely absorbed the old Roman traditions. Wieacker, F (1995) *A History of Private Law in Europe* Oxford (Weir transl) at 20-21. Lupoi states that the Burgundians adhered even more closely than the Visigoths to Roman institutions and established their own parity with the Romans, allowing mixed marriages, instituting courts with a Burgundian and Roman judge, and so forth. Lupoi, supra n 79, at 81.

[84] Lupoi, supra n 79, at 82. On the Italian peninsula the Lombards permitted Roman subjects to be governed by the law of Justinian. Mousourakis, supra n 72, at 419.

Lupoi notes that this split arrangement came about because the Romans raised resistance to being put under a single law with the Burgundians.[85] According to Mousourikas, respect for personal law was proved to be a major factor in the preservation of Roman law: 'As in Italy, so in Gaul and Spain, Roman law was preserved, even though in a vulgarised form, through the application of the principle of the personality of the laws, but also through the medium of the church whose law was imbued with the principles and detailed rules of Roman law.'[86]

Neither the laws nor the populations to which they applied stayed within watertight structures. Directly or indirectly Roman law exercised influence over the Germanic law and vice-versa.[87] As Roman and German elements in the population fused progressively, Germanic customs tended to become Romanised and Roman laws tended to be barbarised. The 'indigenous' custom of these peoples came to mean a transformed personal law that was partly exogenous.[88] The local customs had become 'a combination of elements of Roman law and Germanic customary law.'[89]

The point, then, is that the Roman Empire in the west, as much in its construction as in its disintegration, effectively generated mixed systems of private law from an early date. Of course the mixed elements in these systems would make it impossible to build any sort of 'pure' edifice of civil law out of their layered foundation. But these Romano-Germanic hybrid systems were a means of preserving and adapting personal laws, and at the same time they gave continuity to vulgarised Roman Law until the revival of Justinian's law.

Contemporary English Law and the European Union — Mixed Systems?

It is interesting to consider the implications of the pluralist analysis in

[85] Lupoi, supra n 79, at 82.

[86] Id at 420. Lupoi stresses however that this 'principle' was not spelled out in any source, id at 388, and he does not regard it as a principle, id at 393.

[87] Lupoi describes the interactive nature of this development: 'Visigothic legislation was invariably modelled on Roman legal sources and the various sources of vulgar Roman law, which were influenced by it in their turn.' Id at 75. King Euric was assisted in compiling his code by the Roman jurist, Leon of Narbonne. Kuhn, supra 58 ('Pendant la période oú la domination de l'Etat romain a été la plus complete, le système romain a été tres puissamment influencé par les peoples soumis.').

[88] Thus in de Ferriere's History, the French customs are seen as undergoing a process of Romanisation that lasted many centuries: 'our Customs have been partly taken from the Principles of the Roman Law; [...] they are nothing but a Mixture of different Laws which our Kings of the First Race suffer'd their Subjects to use, as they saw best. Now amongst these the Roman Law was followed in many Particulars and all the rest had a great deal borrow'd from it.' Ferrière, C (1724) *Histoire du droit Romain* London at 112.

[89] Mousourakis, supra n 72, at 421.

relation to English law. It is not uncommon to hear in recent years that English Common Law has become a 'mixed' system, but what is perhaps more remarkable to a foreign observer is that English lawyers are less inclined than in the past to deny that significant changes have indeed taken place.[90] Of course entry into the European Union has hastened harmonisation of English law with the Continent. In Lord Denning's famous allusion, 'the Treaty is like an incoming tide. It flows into the estuaries and up the rivers. It cannot be held back.'[91] English law has absorbed close to twenty EC Directives affecting the area of traditional private law and has been required to adopt continental reasoning, including the principles of proportionality and legitimate expectation, the distinction between private law and public law, the use of teleological and purposive reasoning, the concept of good faith and continental drafting style.[92] As a historical matter, however, England's openness to transnational had begun centuries earlier. Seán Patrick Donlan points to eighteenth-century English law as a system in transition in which England finally absorbed its civilian, ecclesiastical and equity jurisdictions.[93] Hector MacQueen maintains that over the past two centuries English law has been transformed. The field of obligations has been restructured as a system once based upon the forms of action into a continental taxonomy 'founded on the division of contract, tort and unjust enrichment.'[94]

[90] *See* Bingham, TH (1992) ''There is a World Elsewhere': The Changing Perspectives of English Law' (41) *ICLQ* 513; Levitsky, JE (1994) 'The Europeanisation of British Legal Style' (42) *American Journal of Comparative Law* 347; Lewis, X (1995) 'A Common Law Fortress under Attack: Is English Law Being Europeanized?' (2) *Columbia Journal of European Law* 1.

[91] *H.P. Bulmer Ltd v J. Bollinger SA* [1974] Ch 401 at p. 418. For an appraisal of the effects in the 1990s, see Markesinis, BS (1994) *The Gradual Convergence* OUP at 30-32.

[92] Bingham, supra n 90, at 522-24; Levitsky, supra n 90; Nestorovska, D (2005) 'Influences of Roman Law and Civil Law on the Common Law' (1) *Hanse Law Review* 79; Attew, M (1995) 'Teleological Interpretation and Land Law' (58) *Modern Law Review* 696. The incorporation in the year 2000 of the European Convention on Human Rights, thus effectively providing a written bill of rights for Britain, is another continental influence of major importance. See Simpson, AWB (2001) *Human Rights and the End of Empire: Britain and the Genesis of the European Convention* OUP.

[93] 'A System in Transition? Eighteenth-Century English Law', a paper delivered at the Second World Congress on Mixed Jurisdictions in Edinburgh (2007). See Donlan in this issue of the *JCL*

[94] MacQueen supra n 67 at 412. He cites a variety of evidence for this conclusion, including the decline of the doctrine of consideration, the continental pedigree of *Hadley v. Baxendale* and recent legislation which abolished the privity principle in order to bring English law into line with other jurisdictions of the European Union. Taking a longer historical perspective, David Ibbetson considers that the English law of obligations was fused with continental ideas from the time of Glanvil: 'The Common law of obligations grew out of the intermingling of native ideas and sophisticated Roman learning.' (1999) *An Historical Introduction to the Law of Obligations* OUP at 19.

As to the European Union, it too is being described as a mixed supranational system.[95] For instance European contract law has been considerably harmonised by measures such as the Vienna Convention on the International Sale of Goods, the Unidroit Principles of International Commercial Contracts, the Principles of European Contract Law, not to mention a host of Directives in the area of consumer law.[96] The much-discussed single Civil Code of private law, if this project someday materialises, will necessarily rely on these models and will produce a private law system based upon common law and civil law elements. Under the influence of the CISG, a comprehensive concept of 'breach of contract' has already been achieved across Europe.[97]

CONCLUSION

In conclusion, I have argued that there are two rival theories, which help us to see the mixed systems in a proper light. The theories are different but complementary. The first theory points us towards the sister jurisdictions where comparative work is the easiest to carry on and where the results thus far are impressive. We should not let go of this guiding concept — the idea of finding our neighbours in law. The reason is surely not the desire to found an exclusive club, but rather to frame our comparative work. Yesterday in Edinburgh I participated in a group of nine Scots and six Louisianians who sat down to a full day of conferences and the discussion of papers. There was not a moment in which I thought to myself, 'I don't understand this reasoning or this terminology.' We conversed, it seemed to me, nearly as easily as if we were all Louisianians or all Scots. It was another example of the irrelevance of distance to jurists on the same wavelength. This ease of communication and association extends throughout the classical group, as Smith predicted.

The justification for the classical grouping lies in the deeper measure of comparability that one encounters. This is not to say that comparisons between more divergent laws and societies are an impossible task, or an unrewarding one, but they may be more difficult and less fruitful than within the classical circle.

[95] Thus Kötz supra 66 at 439 ('It may sound a bit premature and starry-eyed, but I will say it nonetheless: let us hope that the gradual establishment of a European law as a mixed jurisdiction will allow us to combine the best of both worlds.').

[96] Loos, MBM 'The Influence of European Consumer Law on General Contract Law and the Need for Spontaneous Harmonization' (3-2007) *European Review of Private Law* 515.

[97] This required a break with a long tradition in certain civil law countries. *See* Basedow, J (2005) 'Towards a Universal Doctrine of Breach of Contract: The Impact of the CISG' (25) *International Review of Law and Economics* 487.

At the same time, I have tried to show that the pluralist conception of mixed systems opens a new vista in understanding the classical systems and their place in the world. It throws into relief the non-occidental personal laws within the systems and suggests the need to draw them into the comparative law work as best we can. The interaction of personal laws with Roman-Dutch law in South Africa and Sri Lanka should not be ignored, for their legal compartments are always leaking structures.

The pluralist insight has important consequences in studying contemporary Europe. It points to the imbedded mixtures within European private law and helps to explain the inevitable re-mixing now taking place at the national and supranational level. Most importantly, the pluralist theory demonstrates that the old catch words — common law, civil law, Islamic law, Hindu law — suppress more than they reveal and have lost their explanatory power. As we are ruled by predominantly mixed and plural laws, so it is perhaps time to recognise that *Mixitania rules the waves*. Someday the mixed systems should be the starting point — not the odd-men-out — of a new ordering of the world's legal systems.

Attempting to reclassify and reorder the mixed legal systems of the world in accordance with the information supplied by historical pluralism, ethnic pluralism, and transnational legal pluralism is the next daunting task of comparative law. If it can be accomplished, it would revolutionise the legal universe in a way comparable to the Copernican revolution on the old Ptolemaic system of astronomy. We are far from there at the present time. So far pluralism is an insight suggesting that the playing cards need to be reshuffled; it has yet to show how the cards can be re-dealt in a rational and coherent way. But I predict that if this task is one day accomplished, it will be done first by a mixed jurisdiction jurist, for he or she knows best that there is a need, and knows best the means to achieve the goal.

APPENDIX A

From: Mariani, N & Fuentes, G (2000) *World Legal Systems* 16-17 W&L.

Mixed Legal Systems
The term 'mixed', which we have arbitrarily chosen over other terms such as 'hybrid' or 'composite', should not be construed restrictively, as certain authors have done. Thus this category includes political entities where two or more systems apply cumulatively or interactively, but also entities where there is a juxtaposition of systems as a result of more or less clearly defined fields of application.

MIXED SYSTEMS OF CIVIL LAW AND COMMON LAW

BOTSWANA
CYPRUS
GUYANA
LOUISIANA (USA)
MALTA
MAURITIUS
NAMIBIA
PHILIPPINES
PUERTO RICO (ASSOCIATED TO USA)
QUEBEC (CD)
SAINT LUCIA
SCOTLAND (UK)
SEYCHELLES
SOUTH AFRICA
THAILAND

MIXED SYSTEMS OF CIVIL LAW AND CUSTOMARY LAW

BURUNDI
BURKINA FASO
CHAD
CHINA
CONGO, DEMOCRATIC
REPUBLIC OF THE CONGO,
REPUBLIC OF THE CÔTE D'IVOIRE
EQUATORIAL GUINEA
ETHIOPIA
GABON

GUINEA
GUINEA BISSAU
JAPAN
KOREA, NORTH
KOREA, SOUTH
MALI
MADAGASCAR
MONGOLIA
MOZAMBIQUE
NIGER
RWANDA
SAO TOME AND PRINCIPE
SENEGAL
SWAZILAND
TAIWAN
TOGO

MIXED SYSTEMS OF CIVIL LAW AND MUSLIM LAW

ALGERIA
COMOROS
EGYPT
IRAQ
KUWAIT
LEBANON
LIBYA
MOROCCO
MAURITANIA
SYRIA
TUNISIA

MIXED SYSTEMS OF CIVIL LAW, COMMON LAW AND CUSTOMARY LAW

DJIBOUTI
ERITREA
INDONESIA

MIXED SYSTEMS OF CIVIL LAW, COMMON LAW AND CUSTOMARY LAW

CAMEROUN

LESOTHO
SRI LANKA
VANUATU
ZIMBABWE

MIXED SYSTEMS OF COMMON LAW AND MUSLIM LAW

BAHRAIN
BANGLEDESH
OMAN
PAKISTAN
QATAR
SINGAPORE
SUDAN
UNITED ARAB EMIRATES

MIXED SYSTEMS OF COMMON LAW AND CUSTOMARY LAW

BHUTAN
HONG KONG (CN)
MALAWI
MICRONESIA, FEDERATED STATES
MYANMAR
NEPAL
SIERRA LEONE
SOLOMON ISLANDS
TANZANIA
UGANDA
WESTERN SAMOA
ZAMBIA

MIXED SYSTEMS OF COMMON LAW, MUSLIM LAW AND CUSTOMARY LAW

BRUNEI
GAMBIA
KENYA
INDIA
MALAYSIA
NIGERIA

MIXED SYSTEMS OF COMMON LAW, MUSLIM LAW AND CIVIL LAW

IRAN
JORDON
SAUDI ARABIA
SOMALIA
YEMEN

MIXED SYSTEMS OF TALMUDIC LAW, CIVIL LAW AND COMMON LAW

ISRAEL

What is a Mixed Legal System: Exclusion or Expansion?

ESİN ÖRÜCÜ

SUMMARY OVERVIEW

Can it be satisfactory in our so-called globalising age to group localisms under the broad headings of the 'civil law tradition' and the 'common law tradition' alone and regard other localisms as being only derivatives of one of them? As a better approach I suggested a 'family trees' approach[1] within which legal systems could be classified according to their constituent elements. This entailed deconstruction or 'productive disintegration' and reconstruction of the legal systems that seemed so well settled in their respective families.

I found it equally unsatisfactory to concentrate only on legal systems that display substantial civil law and common law influences co-existing or overlapping in their structure and substance, and further still to group these in a 'third family'.[2] First, not even all the legal systems that are mixtures of civil law and common law have been allocated a place in this family.[3] Second, there are other combinations that are not, and cannot be given a place within this 'third family' as it stands, and also, third, when the

[1] Örücü, E (2004)'Family Trees for Legal Systems: Towards a Contemporary Approach' Chapter 18 in van Hoecke, M (ed) *Epistemology and Methodology of Comparative Law* Hart Publishing 359. The present paper hails partly from this article as well as Örücü, E (2004) *Enigma of Comparative Law – Variations on a Theme for the Twenty-First Century* Martinus Nijhoff Chapter 10:3; and Örücü, E (2007)'A General View of Legal Families and of Mixed Systems' in Örücü, E and Nelken, D (eds) *Comparative Law: A Handbook* Hart Publishing 169.

[2] Palmer, VV (2001) *Mixed Jurisdictions Worldwide: The Third Legal Family*, Cambridge University Press.

[3] Palmer in id, states that there are fifteen such systems but only covers seven of them (Louisiana, Israel, Scotland, South Africa, The Philippines, Puerto Rico and Quebec) and leaves out Botswana, Lesotho, Swaziland, Sri Lanka, Mauritius, the Seychelles, Saint Lucia and Zimbabwe. The number could be sixteen as Namibia is also mentioned in passing.

theory of legal families itself is under challenge, it is not the time to create yet another monolithic one.

Thus 'exclusion' is a very narrow approach. 'Expansion' is to be advocated. Therefore, if mixed systems are to be studied together, certain sub-groups would need to be created: Some would be combinations of common law and civil law, such as Louisiana, Quebec, Scotland and Seychelles; some of civil law, common law, religious law and, until quite recently, Ottoman law, such as Israel; some of civil law, religious law, socialist law and tribal law such as Algeria; others, such as Hong Kong, that are combinations of traditional Chinese law, common law and socialist Chinese law, which itself embodies elements of the civilian tradition; some of common law, religious law and customary law such as India and Pakistan and so on. In addition, there would be ongoing mixtures, systems in transition, such as the legal systems looking for an identity, having left the socialist sphere in Europe and veered towards the civilian tradition. Poland, for instance, has a mixture of socialist law, Roman law, Polish law – itself a mix of German, French, Russian and Hungarian laws – traditional law and EU law. As some extreme examples one could also consider legally pluralist legal systems.

There is today an increasing interest in mixed systems in Europe. For instance, Jan Smits published a monograph 'The Making of European Private Law: Towards a *Ius Commune Europaeum* as a Mixed Legal System'.[4] Yet here too, though in a larger context, the exercise involves a common law-civil law marriage. However, as this is not a general but a specific enterprise, with its own political agenda, this approach may be regarded as appropriate.

My 'family trees' scheme starts with the given assumption that all legal systems are mixed, whether covertly or overtly, and groups them according to the proportionate mixture of the ingredients. Thus some continental systems are combinations of Roman, French and German laws and indigenous law such as the Dutch; and some such as the Greek, of customary, neo-canon, German, Greek and Roman laws. There are even more complicated crosses such as in Malta. All continental systems are better understood as overlaps. Nevertheless, when we talk of 'mixed systems', this obvious fact can be put to one side and serve merely as a reminder that there are no pure legal systems in the world.

[4] Smits, JM (2002) *The Making of European Private Law: Towards a Ius Commune Europaeum as a Mixed Legal System* Metro. Also see Smits, JM (1998) 'A European Private Law as a Mixed Legal System (5) *Maastricht Journal of European and Comparative Law* 328, and Smits, JM (ed) (2001) *The Contribution of Mixed Legal Systems to European Private Law* Intersentia.

The 'family trees' scheme makes it easier to classify systems such as Malaysia, Singapore, Burma and Thailand, all meeting points between several legal traditions. The whole of South East Asia would be better served by this approach. Off-shoots and sub-groups would be catered for, and the overlaps clearly seen, all being the outcome of transpositions.[5]

Influences other than the civil law-common law, and different types of mixes deserve as much attention by comparatists in our century. Exclusivity pleases those who are included but does not satisfy or do justice to the excluded.

This contribution seeks to make the case for considering such systems and looks at examples of a number of overlaps of different types. The outcome would not be to suggest a new family but to pave the way for a theoretical and conceptual framework for analysis by expanding the notion of 'mixed systems'.

INTRODUCTION

For taxonomic purposes and ease of organisation comparatists have placed legal systems in legal families, though it is universally admitted that 'the idea of a "legal family" does not correspond to a biological reality; it is no more than a didactic device.'[6] Biological and linguistic taxonomies have been used in classification as organising devices. A first point to make is that it has been the practice to study legal systems that best represent large groups and then make generalisations based on concepts such as originality, derivation and common elements.[7] The bases for classification have been similarities and relationships. Classifications rely on general characteristics, substance, sources and structure. The essence does not lie in diversity of rules in a given topic, nor in external criteria and context. Only the affinities are considered.

An entirely fresh approach is needed today, within which legal systems can be classified according to parentage, constituent elements and the resulting blend, and then be re-grouped on the principle of predominance. Obviously, parts of the new landscape will resemble the old, though the whole will look quite different.

[5] For an analysis of 'transposition', see Örücü, E (2002) 'Law as Transposition' (51) *International and Comparative Law Quarterly* 205.

[6] David, R and Brierley, JEC (1985) *Major Legal Systems in the World Today, An Introduction to the Comparative Study of Law* 3rd ed. Stevens and Sons at 21. Also see Husa, J (2004) 'Classification of the Legal Families Today' *Révue internationale de droit comparé* 12.

[7] For a summary of some past efforts at classification see Zweigert, K and Kötz, H (1998) *An Introduction to Comparative Law* (3rd edn trans. T Weir) Clarendon Press at 63-67. Also see Bogdan, M (1994) *Comparative Law* Kluwer Tano at 82-91.

A second point is that existing classifications rely on private law. They are Eurocentric and therefore heavily weighted towards the civil law and the common law families. Moreover, since legal systems may shift from one cluster towards another, classifications can have only a limited lifespan. Therefore, the placing of a legal system in the legal families framework would have to be re-thought from time to time.[8] New families may appear. It has been suggested, for example, that an 'African legal family' may be emerging;[9] and we know that interest in 'mixed jurisdictions' is increasing.[10]

Konrad Zweigert and Hein Kötz proposed using 'legal styles' to discover shared distinctive elements between legal systems.[11] However, they also pointed out that, 'as the example of "hybrid" systems shows, any division of the legal world into families, or groups is a rough and ready device.'[12] We are also warned: 'The suitability of any classification will depend upon whether the perspective is world-wide or regional, or whether attention is given to public, private or criminal law.'[13] Yet especially in Europe today it is commonplace not only to talk of civil law and common law families; but to treat them as if they are the only two monolithic entities. Such an approach is inadequate.

In addition, traditional classifications consider official law and the 'top-down' models exclusively. Groupings are all 'legally structured', and 'structure-specific'. An entirely culture-specific approach may not be conclusive, but the relationship between legal and social systems must be given due weight.

It is apparent that the 'legal families' division based solely on the 'law as rules' approach is collapsing. Other approaches are being put forward. One such suggestion, presented as being less biased, is the 'cultural families' division based on the 'law as culture' approach.[14]

Another such approach is the 'law and economics' approach, giving prominence to yet another context. Here we see how Ugo Mattei tries to

[8] Zweigert and Kötz, id at 66.

[9] Van Neikerk, G (2002) 'The convergence of legal systems in Southern Africa' (XXXV) *Comparative and International Law Journal of Southern Africa* 308-318.

[10] Note the launching of the World Society of Mixed Jurisdiction Jurists in New Orleans (November 2002). See, for instance, Zimmermann, R, Visser, D and Reid, K (eds) (2004) *Mixed Legal Systems in Comparative Perspective* Oxford University Press.

[11] Zweigert and Kötz, supra n 7 at 67-68.

[12] id at 72.

[13] David and Brierley supra n 6 at 21 and Bogdan supra n 7 at 85.

[14] On this basis van Hoecke and Warrington have distinguished four broad cultures: the African, the Asian, the Islamic and Western, that is, cultures with European roots: Europe, America and Oceania. See van Hoecke, M and Warrington, M (1998) 'Legal Cultures and Legal Paradigms: Towards a New Model for Comparative Law' (47) *International and Comparative Law Quarterly* 495.

draw the taxonomy away from the so-called Eurocentric axis to present a new map for the world's legal systems.[15]

Furthermore, Andrew Harding, whose main interest is in South East Asia, categorically tells us that all Eurocentric comparatists fall into the 'legal families trap'. He says that, 'Legal families tell us nothing about legal systems except as to their general style and method, and the idea makes no sense whatsoever amid the nomic din of South East Asia.'[16]

The above shows that scholars fail to agree on whether the notion of families is basic and scientific, or theoretically and descriptively useless. Those who do use the concept do not even agree on the criteria for classification and groupings.

Vernon Palmer, for example, places crosses between civil law and common law, in a 'third family' called 'mixed jurisdictions'.[17] To talk of a new family with the name 'mixed jurisdictions' however, is not satisfactory, as not all 'mixes' would have the same or similar ingredients. It would be difficult to place, for example, Quebec and Algeria, both mixed systems, into one family. Simple mixes, complex mixes, dual systems and systems adhering to legal pluralism cannot be pooled together.[18]

In the website produced at the Faculty of Law of the University of Ottawa with the help of the Supreme Court of Canada Library on 'world's legal systems', the categories of legal systems are cited as civil law, common law, customary law, Islamic law, Talmudic law, mixed law and dependent territories. The use of the term 'mixed law' is then explained:

> The term "mixed" was selected arbitrarily over "hybrid" or "composite". It should not be understood in the restricted sense employed by some authors. We will thus find in this category countries in which two or more legal systems apply concurrently or interactively, as well as those in which systems are rather juxtaposed because they apply to more or less clearly distinct fields.[19]

[15] This classification is based on the rule of professional law, the rule of political law and the rule of traditional law, these three forming a triangle on the apices of which all legal systems can be placed. See Mattei, U (1997) 'Three Patterns of Law: Taxonomy and Change in the World's Legal Systems' (XLV) *American Journal of Comparative Law* 1.

[16] Harding, A (2002) 'Global Doctrine and Local Knowledge: Law in South East Asia' (51) *International and Comparative Law Quarterly* 36 at 51.

[17] Palmer supra n 2.

[18] See Örücü, E (1996) 'Mixed and Mixing Systems: A Conceptual Search' in Örücü, E, Attwooll, E and Coyle, S (eds) *Studies in Legal Systems: Mixed and Mixing* Kluwer Law International 344.

[19] Available at: <http://aix1.uottawa.ca/world-legal-systems/eng-systems.html>

According to this source, 'mixed systems' appear in ten categories: mixes of civil law and common law (3.47% of the world population); civil law and customary law (28.54%); civil law and Muslim law (3.14%); common law and customary law (2.94); common law and Muslim law (5.25%), civil law, Muslim law and customary law (3.62%); common law, Muslim law and customary law (19.17%); civil law, common law and customary law (0.8%); common law, Muslim law and civil law (0.23%); and of civil law, common law and Talmudic law (0.09%). The number of jurisdictions that fall into the 'mixed systems with civil law' category are 65 (19.12% of the world's legal systems), 'mixed systems with common law' are 53 (15.59 %), 'mixed systems with customary law' are 54 (15.88%) and 'mixed systems with Muslim law' are 33 (9.70 %).

If a new family were to be created, 'mixed systems' would be a more appropriate name for it, with sub-categories. 'Mixed jurisdictions', as presented in the Palmer project, could be a sub-group within the sub-category of various crosses between common law and civil law.[20] This would be a most exclusive group indeed, if numbers and percentages above were to be taken as meaningful.

ENCOUNTER AND EXCHANGE

In any case it is a fact that 'the actual legal world is more to be seen as a world of "contaminations" than a world split up into different families', and 'practically every system, even in antiquity has grown through "contaminations"'[21] as the practice of borrowing has always been the normal path of development. A comparative lawyer can detect cross-pollination and 'horizontal transfers' between systems at all times.

What is necessary today is a re-assessment of individual legal systems according to the old and new overlaps, combinations and blends, and of how the existing constituent elements have mingled and are mingling with new elements entering them. As noted in the 'Summary Overview' above, I propose a scheme that regards all legal systems as mixed and overlapping, overtly or covertly, and groups them according to the proportionate mixture of the ingredients. To do this, it is essential to look at the constituent elements in each legal system and to regroup legal systems on a much larger scale according to the predominance of the ingredient sources from whence each system is formed.

[20] For some suggestions see my Maps in the Annex to this article.

[21] Monateri, PG (1998) 'The "Weak" Law: Contaminations and Legal Cultures' in *Italian National Reports to the XVth International Congress of Comparative Law*, Bristol, Giuffrè editore 83 at 107.

There are no purely 'home-grown' legal systems. All legal systems are combinations and overlaps. Some, such as the Dutch, are combinations of Roman, French, German and indigenous laws, and some, of Canon, Roman, French, Austrian and German laws and of *ius commune* such as the Italian. Then there are other combinations such as common law, religious law and indigenous customary laws as in countries such as India and Pakistan; and French, Socialist, Islamic and indigenous customary tribal laws as in Algeria. In fact, French, German and English common law are themselves all outcomes of overlaps of various ingredients. English law for instance, is becoming more and more an overlap of common law, various civilian systems and European law. Indeed, classical English common law itself was an overlap of Roman law, civilian ideas, canon law, equity and domestic common law.[22] Because layers may also shift their positions, the underlays and the overlays must be carefully distinguished. In Hong Kong, for example, English common law was the overlay until 1990, with Chinese customary law the underlay, but now, common law is becoming an underlay alongside Chinese customary law, both under a growing overlay of modern Chinese law. However, this re-thinking of legal systems may be seen as taking the expansion of the idea of 'mixed systems' a step too far.

The whole of South East Asia, with an abundance of off-shoots and sub-groups, profits mostly from such an approach. Two examples should suffice at this point. The first example is Thailand.[23] Never a colony, since the end of the nineteenth century it has had in its modern texture a real mixture of sources such as English, German, French, Swiss, Japanese and American laws. These sit alongside historic sources in existence since 1283: rules from indigenous culture and tradition, customary laws and Hindu jurisprudence are still to be found in some modern enactments. In addition, Thai Codes were originally drafted in English and French and subsequently translated into Thai. Thailand's modern texture has been formed from many sources and the legal system of today still grapples with problems of translation and connotation. How then are we to categorise Thailand? How should this legal system be labelled?

Similar questions can be posed for Malaysia. First there was the 'native' law of the aboriginal inhabitants, which is still today regarded as positive law by courts. Then came layers of transplanted law: *adat* law (a number of

[22] For contributions from Islamic and Talmudic laws into common law see the literature mentioned by Glenn, HP (2001) 'Are Legal Traditions Incommensurable?' (49) *American Journal of Comparative Law* 133 at 141-142. Also see Glenn, HP (2005) *On Common Laws* Oxford University Press.

[23] My thanks for kindling my interest in Thailand go to my PhD student Jutharat Compeerapap working on her thesis ' The Reception of Legal Language in Thai Contract Law: A Comparative Perspective' in Erasmus University Rotterdam in 2003-2005.

Malay customs), Hindu and Buddhist laws, Islamic, Chinese, Thai laws, the English common law tradition coloured by Anglo-Indian Codes and the USA model. There are further influences in South East Asia: French, Dutch, German, Swiss, Portuguese and Spanish Civilian traditions, American, Japanese and Soviet laws.[24] The region, says Harding,

> has an abundance of legal traditions, practically all of them having been "received" or "transplanted" in one sense or another, and encompassing all of the world's major legal world views and systems [...] except perhaps for African law and Eskimo law.[25]

What kind of a mixed system is this?

I have considered elsewhere four kinds of encounters between legal systems, legal cultures and socio-cultures:[26] those between systems of socio and legal cultural similarity, those between systems of socio-cultural similarity but legal cultural difference, those between systems of socio-cultural difference but legal cultural similarity, and those between systems of both socio and legal cultural difference. These encounters lead to overlaps, interrelationships, mixed and mixing systems and systems in transition. Law can always be approached as the product of a process of transposition.[27]

When legal systems are considered as overlaps, combinations, marriages and off-spring, terminology such as fertilisation, pollination, grafting, intertwining, osmosis and pruning can illuminate the processes of the birth of mixed systems.

The most significant theories explaining the birth of such systems however, come from linguistics: the 'family tree model' and the 'wave theory'.[28] The theory of the 'family tree model' of language development reflects an evolutionary approach and is the one generally used to explain ramification and divergence. The 'family tree' model (*stammbaum*) proposed

24 Harding, supra n 16 at 42-43.

25 Id at 47.

26 Örücü, E (1995) 'A Theoretical Framework For Transfrontier Mobility of Law' in Jagtenberg, R, Örücü, E and de Roo, A (eds) *Transfrontier Mobility of Law* Kluwer Law International 5.

27 The concept 'transposition', as in music, helps to highlight the crucial importance of the internal tuners who adjust the mix, adapting it to the new instrument, see Örücü supra n 5.

28 See for an exposition and analysis of these theories, Renfrew, C (1987) *Archeology and Language: The Puzzle of Indo-European Origins* Jonathan Cape especially at 105, 244-248. Also see Örücü, E (2007) 'Convergence and Divergence: Theoretical Issues' in Antokolskaia, M (ed) *Convergence and Divergence of Family Law in Europe*, (18) European Family Law Series, Intersentia, 27. Also consider my 'family trees for legal systems' in supra n 1 and note that it is not a derivative of these theories.

by Augustus Schleicher in 1862,[29] assumed that resemblances arose from common origin (understood in terms of parenthood), and languages closely similar and linked were thought to have separated or diverged from each other, with original divergence and further subsequent divergence. The underlying human reality was first thought to be migration of peoples.[30] Thus, when speakers are no longer in contact, they drift apart linguistically, becoming isolated (evolutionary theory). The 'family tree model' is coherent but only takes into account one of the ways in which change, difference and diversity occur. Exclusive reliance on the 'tree-model' of development can only explain ramification and divergence. The model overlooks 'the possibility that two languages may have passed through a period of common development, usually when their speakers occupied adjacent territories.'[31] In response, the 'wave theory' was developed.

The 'wave theory' or 'wave hypotheses', showing how changes spread like waves and disperse over a wide area, can also handle the equally important forces of convergence.[32] Introduced again in the 19th century by another German linguist, Johannes Schmidt in 1872, [33] the hypothesis was put forth that different linguistic changes spread like waves over a speech area thus leading to convergence. A subsequent wave may also move to areas not covered by the earlier wave. Schmidt drew lines (isoglosses) on a map to separate places where there were language differences, one isogloss enclosing one area with a particular linguistic form (divergence). Successive waves create a network of isoglosses. If however, 'one dialect gains a political or commercial predominance of some sort over adjacent dialects, those nearest to this central dialect may give up their own peculiarities and come in time to speak only that central dialect.'[34]

Following various local divergences (the tree model), the subsequent groupings would then have come about by the operation of the wave model. In this hypothesis, two or more closely related languages may each have features in common with their own neighbours that they do not share with each other. The relationships are far more complicated than any which could be conveyed simply by means of a 'family tree', as the 'wave model' caters both for convergence and divergence.

[29] Schleicher, A (1963) *Die Darwinsche Theorie und die Sprachwissenschaft*, Weimar. For the French edition see: (1968) *La Theorie de Darwin et la Science du Langage* in *Receuil de Travuax Originaux ou Traduit relatifs a L'Histoire Littérraire* 1 Franck.

[30] Renfrew supra n 28 at 101-102.

[31] Id at 104.

[32] Id at 105.

[33] Schmidt, J (1872) *Die Verwandtschaftsverhalnisse der indogermanischen Sprachen* Böhlau.

[34] Renfrew supra n 28 at 105.

However, similarities do not always arise from genetic relationships, neither does resemblance necessarily indicate common origin. There can be 'horizontal transfers' between adjacent systems. 'Horizontal transfer' can also explain why a borrowed concept or institution does not always exactly retain its original meaning. Areas nearest or adjacent to the initial change will change first and may even give up their own peculiarities. Subsequent re-groupings may come about on the 'wave model' mentioned above.

It follows from the foregoing that a wave need not start from a fixed centre either. Developments can take place in steps with no one locale as the prime mover. It is not necessary to depict one as the donor and the other the recipient, though there may be 'diffusion', 'infusion' and even 'suffusion'. There is no one localised homeland but 'cumulative mutuality' and interaction is in the essence. The 'tree model' and the 'wave model' can be used together to explain developments. As Renfrew says,

> [I]t is, in fact, the resemblances between languages most distant from each other spatially which can least easily arise from the wave-like diffusion of an innovation, and are thus most likely to be the result, rather, of a relationship explicable in family tree terms.[35]

Both on the 'tree model' and the 'wave model', a common ancestral origin is assumed. Yet, similarities can develop through time, by the process of convergence through contact. Therefore, common parentage is not in issue, since the ancestors could have been quite dissimilar, but through continuing contact, mutual influence and borrowing, the languages become significantly closer to each other, though never becoming identical. Thus waves cause diffusion and for dispersals to occur spontaneously through contact.[36]

Replace the term 'language' by 'law', and one can see that this combined approach could indicate a way forward for an understanding of how legal systems function, change and develop; converge or diverge. These combined theories can cater for our understanding of mixed systems.

For instance, civil law would appear near, but not necessarily as the prime innovating centre, as it would of course be possible to go right back to Greek laws, to the laws of Hammurabi, and earlier laws, even before

[35] Id at 111.

[36] A variant, 'wave of advance model', was also proposed to explain the random, unsystematic, slow, gradual and continuous convergence, as opposed to colonisation, which also creates convergence, but through intentional and deliberate settlement. See Ammerman, AJ and Cavalli-Sforza, LL (1979)'The wave of advance model for the spread of agriculture in Europe' in Renfrew, C and Cooke, KL (eds) *Transformations, Mathematical Approaches to Cultural Change* Academic Press 275.

considering Roman law, the ingredients of which possibly included elements of Hindu law through Egyptian and Greek channels. One sees that civil law and common law are but two of the ancestors, others being, according to one divide proposed by Patrick Glenn, Chthonic, Talmudic, Islamic, Hindu, and Asian.[37] Even then, Glenn says:

> In looking at (only) seven legal traditions of the world, it has been impossible to avoid the existence of other recognizable legal traditions. Some might say the other legal traditions are minor ones, which complement or oppose the traditions which have been examined. This may or may not be accurate, since there are no well established criteria for distinguishing major from minor traditions. [...] If the traditions in law which have been examined here [...] appear presently as the major ones of the world, it may be that this is only a conclusion of first impression, and that there are other legal traditions [...] which are still more profound and which await investigation, and recognition, as being of primary importance.[38]

More important, in a later work, Glenn considers the relations of common laws of the world with each other. His claim is that common laws, tolerant to particular laws, were also tolerant of each other. Not being aggressive, they shared information. Thus interrelationship and interaction were crucial, and we know that interrelationships breed mixedness.[39]

According to Glenn, although the English common law and the *ius commune* have been widely discussed within the context of Europe, the fact that there were many more common laws and that these common laws themselves were in dynamic relationship, has been neglected. Through this interaction and because individual legal systems appropriated notions, rules, institutions and principles from these common laws, another explanation of mixedness emerges. Until the nineteenth century the numerous common laws of Europe -- French, German, Spanish, Dutch and English -- lived in constant interaction with the local particular and with each other. As these common laws expanded both within and outside Europe, particular laws they met appropriated them. There was constant contact and intermingling. Common laws were the main instrument of 'conciliation' of laws. We see this best in mixed systems. Claims of universality were reconciled with claims of particularity at a time when law was not seen as an exclusive product of the State. Even later, at a time

37 Glenn, HP (2004) *Legal Traditions of the World* Oxford University Press, 2nd ed.
38 Id at 318-319.
39 Glenn(2005) supra n 22 at 119.

of legal nationalism this continued to be the case. This understanding only challenges 'exclusivity' and supports 'expansion'.

We see that combinations have taken place between systems and sub-systems of different origins. When there are many overlaps and much cross-fertilisation, reciprocal influence, fusion, infusion, grafting and the like, it may be difficult to determine with exactitude the degrees of hybridity. The simple conclusion must be that there are various degrees of hybridity in the legal world arising from different levels and layers of crossing and intertwining. This should be the starting point for mapping mixed systems.

The 'family trees' approach I proposed is initially deconstructive, disintegrative and critical. It rests on the assumption of fluidity. Following deconstruction, the aim is to re-construct a more reliable map of the legal systems of the world.[40] Distinctiveness cannot be ignored. Even when comparative law is used as an instrument of integration in Europe, one must be aware of the virtues in 'distinction' and 'diversity'. In the 'family trees' approach 'distinctiveness' matters as well as similarity, whereas in classical classifications only 'similarity' mattered. The relevant degrees of distinction and similarity decide on the place of a legal system.

In this attempt at re-aligning legal systems and placing them on their genealogical trees, we must consider transpositions, reciprocal influences and cross-fertilisation both horizontally and vertically.

Only some of the offspring show clear signs of their different legal cultural, racial, ethnic and religious origins overtly. Most of such systems have already been grouped as 'mixed jurisdictions', and treated as *numerus clausus*. However, there are many other overt and covert mixtures that are the offspring of the same or of other combinations.

One can see complicated crosses even within the continent of Europe, such as those in Malta.[41] Here legal history began with the Phoenician settlement and continued with the Roman conquest bringing the *Corpus Iuris*. Then the Normans invaded and brought feudal law as applied in Spain, Naples and Sicily. The invasion of the Moors had direct influence on the Maltese language. The sovereignty of the Knights of St. John recognised local usage and issued declarations of private law drawing on laws of other countries, mostly Italian. Then came the French with their Napoleonic laws. Finally the British brought the common law. So here in

[40] See, Örücü, E (2004) *Enigma* ... supra n 1, Chapter 10:3. Also (2004) 'Family Trees ..' supra n 1 at 359. The question still remains however, whether this approach could go far enough to embrace legal pluralism and all layers of law such as the global, international, regional, transnational, inter-communal, territorial state, sub-state and non-state, in the mapping. See Twining, W (2000) *Globalisation and Legal Theory* Butterworths at 136-141.

[41] Ganado, M (1996) 'Malta: A Microcosm of International Influences' in Örücü et al supra n 18 at 225.

Malta we see a good example of an eclectic Criminal Code drafted under a strong Italian influence but with pervasive English and Scottish impact, and a Commercial Code largely based on the French, with maritime law following English law. The 1873 Civil Code is predominantly based on the French and Italian Codes and also on the Municipal Code de Rohan, the Civil Code of Louisiana and the Austrian Civil Code. Canon law applies in family law where there is also the influence of English, German, Italian and French laws. Constitutional law is mainly British. The official languages are Maltese and English. The ingredients work cumulatively and interactively. Malta has now joined the European Union. What kind of new mixing can we expect? How is it possible to fit this mixture into any of the classical categories? Malta would not sit comfortably in existing 'legal families' but may be in a more refined 'mixed jurisdiction' category.

Sometimes, seeds are scattered even more widely leading to even more extreme and unexpected crosses. For example Turkey is a cross between Swiss, German, Italian, French and Roman laws, a covert Islamic law and local customary law, as well as more recently, European law and American law. This was brought about as a result of grafting, pruning, tuning and intertwining by an elite concerned with changing not only the law and legal culture but the people themselves and their way of life from the traditional to the modern by the introduction of radical social reform laws to accompany the forging of a new legal system by receptions from abroad.[42] Turkey aspires to European Union membership today. She is trying to assimilate many European Community directives and many of her laws are being re-aligned for a better fit with the EU *acquis communautaire*. One of the conditions is the 'improvement of the legal system' and further 'modernisation' of the law, 'modernisation' being understood to mean further elimination of 'traditional values'.[43] These should all be regarded as imposed receptions. What does the future hold for this mixture?

History tells us that when legal systems of diverse socio- and/or legal-cultures meet, the diverse elements co-exist side by side in the resultant legal system,[44] hence 'mixed systems' ensue.[45] Today, imposed

[42] Örücü, E (2006) 'A Synthetic and Hyphenated Legal System: The Turkish Experience' (1) *The Journal of Comparative Law* 27.

[43] And yet today, we also observe traditional values and religion gaining a new lease of life in Turkey.

[44] See Örücü (1995) supra n 26, and (2002) supra n 5.

[45] Any one of the following terms may be appropriate for the analysis of a specific move and for the explanation of a specific growth: 'seepage', 'contaminant', 'irritant', 'underlay', 'overlay', 'cross-fertilisation', 'incremental reception', 'competing systems', 'hyphenated' legal systems, 'layered law', 'chance', 'choice', 'prestige', 'efficiency', 'elite' and 'historical accident'.

receptions are frequently seen in the Central and East European States, and within the context of European integration. While the Continental civilian systems are trying to impose civilian type Codes on the English common law, the English common law is introducing the system of judge-made law to them. Whatever the means, the end result will be more transposition, more intertwining and mixing, and more new shoots.

Past receptions from civil law and Roman law into English law for instance, have been called 'sporadic receptions' or 'injections', with 'civil law based reasoning filtering into common law'[46] ensuring that English law was constantly enriched. However, any rules based on Roman law or the later *ius commune* 'were immediately cut off from their roots', and 'assimilated into the specifically English framework, and given life outside their original context'. The resultant new law 'did not remain in dialogue with the old law from which it derived'; and 'once the borrowings are cut off from their roots they cease to be part of the same culture' as they grow in the new soil. Therefore, the influences were not systematic and the solutions did not remain the same. Nevertheless, these affected the growth of the 'English oak'.[47]

Our main work as comparative lawyers is now to deconstruct the conventionally labelled pattern of legal systems and reconstruct them with regard to origins, relationships, overlaps and interrelationships, and diverse fertilisers such as the social and cultural context, and the grafting and pruning used in their development. In this way the comparative lawyer can re-analyse legal systems, leaving ample space for newly forming growths, and new mixes.

MIXING SYSTEMS

It has already been indicated that all legal systems are mixed. Only the ways of mixing and the character of the ensuing mixtures are different and the levels of combination and therefore the extent of the mix vary. The term 'mixed' is now much more frequently used and has acquired many different meanings: a 'combination of various legal sources', a 'combination of more than one body of law within one nation, restricted to an area or to a culture', 'the existence of different bodies of law applicable within the whole territory of a country', 'countries in which two or more legal systems

[46] Ibbetson, DJ (1998) 'A Reply to Professor Zimmermann' in Watkin, TG (ed) *The Europeanisation of Law* (18) United Kingdom Comparative Law Series London, UKNCCL 224 at 228. Also see the contribution of Donlan, SP in this volume.

[47] So regarded by Denning LJ (as he then was) in *Nyali Ltd. V Attorney General* [1955] 1 All ER, 646 (CA) at 653.

apply concurrently or interactively', and 'legal systems that have never had a single dominant culture'.

Normally 'mixed' implies a historic fact, a reality and a 'local jurisdiction', especially as used in the concept 'mixed jurisdictions', whereas, as has been convincingly suggested, the emphasis should be on 'experiences in encounters' and therefore, the 'encounter' and the ensuing dynamic exchange should be highlighted.[48]

Patrick Glenn specifically referred to 'mixed jurisdictions' when he analysed the encounters between the various 'common laws' of the world, which he calls 'relational laws'. 'Appropriation of common laws' can form the basis of an explanation of mixedness. He sees 'mixed jurisdictions' as places of confluence of common laws, as 'ongoing interdependence'; places where we see an unsuccessful 'process of exclusive appropriation of one of the common laws'. However, Glenn also points out that 'with the increase in importance in the world of overlapping laws', [49] their significance may decline, possibly because more and more legal systems become mixed. Hence, another reason for no exclusion but expansion.

Indeed, instances of mixing are complicated. They may be overt or covert, structured or unstructured, complex or simple, blended or unblended; and often difficult to define. When talking of 'mixed legal systems', the importance of the 'ongoing mixing' of legal systems must also be considered. In ongoing states of 'mix', a wide knowledge is required to fully analyse this phenomenon, since many systems are shifting and in transition, and new types of mixes are constantly coming into being. However, their future is uncertain.[50] How the legal elite reacts to the mix, handle it and tune the incoming legal elements and mould them into a legal system is crucial. In addition, systems differ as to how the mix is sustained, nurtured or killed.[51] In all these senses each system is unique. However, as well as having features that are unique, each has features shared with others and features common to all. This enables us to study mixed systems both separately and together.

A study of a legal system fifty years ago and again today may reveal considerable changes in its structure, context and conceptual infill and

[48] Kasirer, N (2003) 'Legal Education as *Métissage*' (78) *Tulane Law Review* 481 at 488.

[49] Glenn (2005) supra n 22 at 119.

[50] In these new legal mixes the degree of success cannot be measured easily. Neither can 'success' be defined from a single standpoint. Pre-determined economic, social, cultural, religious or ideological ends are all factors by which success can be measured. Efficiency, internalisation, cultural shift, and the actual use of the new legal structures can all be criteria for measurement.

[51] du Plessis, J (1998) 'The promises and pitfalls of mixed legal systems: The South African and Scottish Experiences' (3) *Stellenbosch Law Review* 338.

also in the attitude of lawyers, academics and people to it and its 'mix'. Sometimes 'mixedness' can be the manifestation of a transition, sometimes it can be the final outcome of the process. 'Mixedness' is usually a result of historical accident and accidents can lead to unexpected outcomes along unexpected paths.

Here we need a caveat. The existence of 'mixed legal systems', the creation of new mixes, and the present process of mixing may prove to be problematic for those who adhere to the definitive role of the cultural context. Unless one starts from the premise that 'mixedness is itself the culture', there is no easy way forward. Even if one does start from that premise, one has to probe into the generation of the 'mixedness'. This is related to 'horizontal transfer', the possibility of which in turn is refuted by those who state that 'legal transplants are impossible'.[52] So we can end at an impasse.

Since through cross-fertilisation and horizontal transfers all legal systems within the European Union will eventually mix to some degree, a study of legal systems already mixed can provide valuable lessons for these mixing systems, and the study of how they work is fruitful. In fact, mixed legal systems have always been the 'laboratories' of comparative lawyers, their 'vantage point'.[53] As already alluded to, today such systems have gained a special place in the process of European integration. Jan Smits says that mixed legal systems will provide 'inspiration' and that the experiences of South Africa, Scotland, Quebec and Louisiana are consequently of great importance for the future developments of European private law.[54]

Mixed systems can be viewed along a spectrum. As a general observation, one can start with simple mixes[55] where the blend is mainly between two Western traditions - the civilian and the common law. It is here we see the so-called 'mixed jurisdictions'. This blend is as to content and substance, and not necessarily as to structure, although some of these systems have codified their civil laws, such as that of Louisiana, and some have not, such as that of Scotland. Scotland for instance, is designated as a classical 'mixed jurisdiction', and has one of these simple mixed systems, a system 'mixed' only at the substantive level. Its history is unusual. The path of the migration of law from different sources into Scots Law was seepage,

52 Legrand, P (1997) 'The Impossibility of "Legal Transplants"' (4) *Maastricht Journal of European and Comparative Law* 111, and (2001) 'What "Legal Transplant"?' in Nelken, D and Feest, J (eds), *Adapting Legal Cultures* Hart Publishing 55.

53 Kasirer supra n 48 at 481.

54 Smits (1998) supra 4 at 33, and (2001) supra n 4 at 9. Also see his contribution in this volume.

55 See for an analysis of mixed systems, Örücü (1995) supra n 26 and Örücü (1996) supra n 18.

imitation, inspiration, voluntary reception and imposed reception. The starting point was Scots customary law, which was then overlaid by Anglo-Norman, canon, Roman and European civil laws and later in modern times by English law. Further, the system now has to absorb European Community law and European human rights law.

The Scottish mix resulted from the close cultural and political ties with the jurisdictions of both traditions 'at different stages of its history', rather than from the 'imposition of the common law upon a civilian system by a colonial power, as in Louisiana or South Africa'.[56] The Scottish legal system has been regarded as being a system 'mixed from the very beginning',[57] with Scottish jurists creating the 'mix' by selecting 'the best' of the ingredients from various sources. Yet, the exact balance between the elements of this 'mix' in modern Scots law has long been, and still is, the subject of constant controversy.

The mixed legal systems that attract most attention in the European integration process are such simple ones, the 'mixing bowl' type,[58] with only a limited number of ingredients. For seekers of a new *ius commune*, one of the obstacles is that the ingredients to be blended or interlocked come from two different legal cultures - the common law and the civil law – and this, notwithstanding the variety that exists among the systems that belong to the so-called civil law tradition.

Nevertheless, we must not limit our view of the world of 'mixing' to the confines of the European Union or the Western world. When looked through the lens of history, we see that many of the mixes of the past were formed by strong movements of transmigration of legal institutions and ideas, mostly in the form of impositions, and of divergent linguistic, communal or religious traditions. Legal systems, like cake mixes, are constantly mixing, blending, melting, and then solidifying into new shapes as they cool down, while transposition and tuning take their effect. Special attention must be paid to legal-cultural convergence and non-convergence that may come about as a result of legal import, and to any ensuing socio-cultural non-convergence. In this context, cultural pluralism, clash of diverse cultures, and the consequences for the importing legal system are of particular

[56] Reid, E (2001) 'Comparative Law: Perspective from a Mixed Jurisdiction', in *HLS Cahier Nr.2 Methodology and its application* Facilitair Bedrijf 49.

[57] Sellar, WDH (2004) 'Scots law – mixed from the very beginning? A tale of two receptions' (4) *Edinburgh Law Review* 3. Also see Zimmermann, R (2004) ''Double Cross': Comparing Scots and South African Law' in Zimmermann, R, Visser, D and Reid, K (eds) *Mixed Legal Systems in Comparative Perspective* Oxford University Press.

[58] See for coining and explanation of such terminology, Örücü (1995) supra n 26; and Örücü (1996) supra n 18.

contemporary interest and legal pluralism is another significant concern. All can be examined within the context of 'mixed systems'.

Thus, visualised along a spectrum, at one extreme end is the position where the transmigration works smoothly, because of extensive similarities in structure, substance and culture and fine 'tuning' such as in Scotland (a simple mix).[59]At the other extreme is the position where transposition has not worked and the official legal system has 'curdled' and is dysfunctional, as is the case in Burkina Faso and Micronesia.[60] Between the two extremes lies a range of places on the spectrum.

When elements from socio-culturally similar and legal-culturally different legal systems come together forming mixed systems of the already mentioned 'simple' kind - the 'mixing bowls'- the ingredients are still in the process of blending but in need of further processing if a 'purée' is to be produced. Next to 'simple' mixes come the 'complex' mixed systems, where the elements are both socio-culturally and legal-culturally different. I have called this type elsewhere the 'Italian salad bowl' where, although the salad dressing covers the salad, it is easy to detect the individual ingredients clearly through the side of the glass bowl.[61] A good example of this is Algeria. Then, there is what I called the 'English salad plate', the ingredients sitting separately far apart on a flat plate with a blob of mayonnaise at the side into which the different ingredients can be dipped before consumption. Examples of this are the Sudan and Zimbabwe (legal pluralisms), which lie towards the far end of the spectrum. The examples become more extreme along the path, ending in 'curdling', with a dysfunctional legal system, as already mentioned.[62]

The composition of each mix depends on conditions such as the size of the transmigration, the characteristics of the legal movement, shared language, proximity to the model, the degree of success of transpositions and 'tuning', the element of 'force' or 'choice' inherent in the move and the social culture of the new environment.

More complex mixes might appear in places where the legal system or the law is based on, or heavily determined by, religion or belief. However, they could also be in places where unexpected events are taking place. An example of this is Hong Kong, where in its relationship with China there is talk of 'one country two systems'. Transmigration of laws might occur

[59] This could also occur under the pressure of a ruling elite and the legal profession, as is the case of Turkey, a seemingly civilian but covert mix, as seen in this volume.

[60] See Tamanaha, B (2001) *General Jurisprudence of Law and Society* Oxford University Press at xi-xii.

[61] See Örücü supra n 18 and 26.

[62] For a picture of this spectrum, see id.

between legal systems of both legal and socio-cultural diversity creating legal pluralism, a mixed or a hybrid system, or unexpected results under pressure from an '*élite dominante*'. Sometimes there are overlaps between these meanings and a place could have a 'complex' system in any or in all these senses. Such systems obviously defy the traditional theory of 'legal families', classical paradigms being totally inadequate.

Once she removes her Eurocentric spectacles, the comparative lawyer immediately sees that indigenous laws rarely consist of single homogenous systems. A number of indigenous legal orders and social orders can live side by side. To find, understand and re-present such indigenous law can be difficult though, especially when some of it is unwritten and, some written but imperfectly translated. For example, in many Asian systems Western law was added to the religious laws of Hinduism, Buddhism, Confucianism and Islam, which themselves co-existed prior to colonisation. The mixture was also complicated by the fact that not all laws were applicable to all peoples, different parts of the population being classified as 'foreign Orientals', 'assimilated Asians', 'Europeans', 'non-natives' or 'natives'. In countries such as Indonesia, Taiwan and Malaysia, the resultant mixture continues to give rise to problems even today.

Thus, we see that transmigration of law has followed the paths of colonisation, re-settlement, occupation, expansion, and inter-relationship. The methods of these migrations were imposition, reception, imposed reception, co-ordinated parallel development, infiltration, imitation and variations and combinations of these. The consequences have been the birth of systems in transition and mixing, mixed jurisdictions, inter-related systems, evolving systems, layered-law, hyphenated legal systems, harmonisation, unification and standardisation. In all this there are different conceptual implications.

The clearest 'reciprocal influence' today is within the European Union, but transpositions from the Western legal traditions to the Central and East European legal systems, where a number of mixing systems are coming into being, are more significant. Outside Europe, there are other cross-fertilisations. So we see the birth of more 'complex' mixes, the blurring of the demarcation lines between the generally accepted classifications of legal families, and the emergence of new clashes between legal cultures themselves, and legal cultures and socio-cultures. This is mostly due to voluntary reception rather than colonisation and imposition as in the past, but there are some cases of imposed reception.

Systems are in transition and are experiencing fundamental upheaval. Some systems are re-shaping themselves in social, economic and legal terms with the help of outside models from competing systems. Others, in certain regions or groupings, are necessarily affected by reciprocal influences. Some others are affected by globalisation. Comparative lawyers need a fresh approach.

It has already been noted that Vernon Palmer suggested that we should be talking of a new 'third legal family' with the name 'mixed jurisdictions' to include a number of historically determined mixes, which he regards as sharing certain characteristics. This means that these systems 'are built upon dual foundations of common-law and civil-law materials', that is, there is a 'specificity of the mixture'; the mix is obvious to both insiders and outsiders, that is, 'obvious to an ordinary observer'; and the private-law sphere has 'the outward appearance of a "pure" civil-law system', whereas the public law sphere 'will appear to be typically Anglo-American', that is, there is a 'structural allocation of content'. Palmer regards these as 'the lowest common denominators of a mixed jurisdiction'[63] and talks of a 'closed family' of fifteen members, with seven of them studied in his work.[64]

According to my analysis, the concept of 'mixed jurisdictions' is used by Vernon Palmer in a narrow and conventional sense, considering only co-existing and commingling between the civil law and the common law, that is 'simple' mixes - very few in number.[65] It also disregards the impact of the 'indigenous' laws present in some of these very same systems.[66] His is only a partial answer. As noted above, clearly not all 'mixes' can be pooled together and not all the existing members of such a family would have the same or similar ingredients. Though not all regarded as 'mixed jurisdictions', it would be difficult for example, to place Scotland, Quebec, Hong Kong, Thailand, Sierra Leone, Pakistan, Indonesia and Algeria, all mixed systems, into one family. Even if we were to accept Palmer's claim that fifteen individual legal systems share certain characteristics to justify placing them together in a group as a 'third family of mixed jurisdictions', what of contemporary mixing systems and systems in transition? Palmer's 'third family' may serve his purposes, but does not address the problems of understanding and analysing the world we live in today.

[63] Palmer supra n 2 at 7-9. Also see Palmer, VV (2006) 'Mixed Jurisdictions' in Smits, JM (ed) *Elgar Encyclopedia of Comparative Law* Edward Elgar 467, where he refers to mixed jurisdictions as 'Mixed jurisdictions as they are classically called, make up roughly 15 political entities, of which 11 are independent countries. Most (excluding Scotland and Israel) of these are the former colonial possessions of France, the Netherlands or Spain, which were subsequently transferred to Great Britain or the United States'. For a more extensive treatment see du Plessis, J (2006) 'Comparative Law and the Study of Mixed Legal Systems' in Reimann, M and Zimmermann, R, *Oxford Handbook of Comparative Law*, OUP, 477.

[64] For the list of systems covered see supra n 3.

[65] Zimmermann also regards Palmer's use of the term in a technical sense, restricted. See Zimmermann supra n 57 at 3. However, see the contribution of Palmer VV in this volume.

[66] See for example the contributions on South Africa (Herbst, M and Du Plessis, W, and Rauterbach, C) and Sri Lanka (Cooray, A) in this volume.

Another approach is offered by Anthony Ogus. He looks at mixed or 'hybrid' systems through the lens of a 'law and economics' scholar and places them into three categories.[67] His first group includes those systems 'where a culture was imposed by a colonialist power, but where a native culture persisted to some degree'. Here, the native culture 'competes' with the imposed culture. Ogus gives a number of African countries as examples. 'Countries which have experienced successive colonialist or other occupation' fall into his second category. In this category, each successive foreign culture has had a major impact on the legal culture and competes with the others. He chooses as examples of this category Quebec, Louisiana and South Africa. Countries 'which experienced industrial and commercial development relatively late and where rulers recognised the need to look elsewhere for more sophisticated legal input than the domestic legal system could provide' form his third category, the examples being Japan, Turkey and Greece.[68] He says that in this category 'there were effectively "tenders" from several major legal cultures to supply the necessary set of specifications'. East European States using Western models for law reform are also regarded as falling into this category, though 'in somewhat different circumstances'.[69]

Some predictions for the future are also offered. Ogus is of the opinion that the three categories share characteristics that separate them from legal systems with one dominant culture. The expected outcome is that mixed systems will be 'more efficient, and adapt more readily to changing external variables, than those with a single dominant culture', though much depends on how the competition works. Of course, there is always the possibility that optimal selections may not be made from between the different 'tenders'; the 'rents' to be enjoyed by a particular foreign legal system may be too attractive for domestic lawyers trained in that system to resist. Despite such problems however, from the 'law and economics' point of view, the future is quite bright for mixed systems; they should, 'unless obstructed by private interest groups allied to a particular culture, adapt more readily to efficient legal reform'.[70] Comparative lawyers need to consider what contribution does a 'law and economics' approach have in assessing 'mixed systems' over and above other approaches.

[67] Ogus, A (2001) 'The Contribution of Economic Analysis of Law to Legal Transplants' in Smits, JM (ed) *The Contribution of Mixed Systems to European Private Law* Intersentia 27.

[68] Zweigert and Kötz also regard Greece as a mixed system. See supra n 7 at 72.

[69] Ogus supra n 67 at 37.

[70] Id at 36-37.

CONCLUDING REMARKS

Although not 'mixed jurisdictions' in Vernon Palmer's sense, the examples referred to in this study are all certainly 'mixed' and 'mixing' systems, the various elements from different sources being woven into 'the tapestry' of their laws, in various degrees. We know that all legal systems are born of different parentage, from marriages between different systems and sub-systems.

It is difficult to determine the exact level of hybridity in each legal system. However, what is clear is that combinations of disparate legal and social cultures do give birth to mixed systems. Overlap, cross-fertilisation, reciprocal influence, horizontal transfer, fusion, infusion, grafting and the like all contribute to the coming into being of mixed and mixing systems. All are forever in flux, as are all legal systems. The various degrees of hybridity arise from various degrees, levels and layers of encounters, crossing and intertwining.

When there are clear signs of their different legal cultural, racial, ethnic and religious origins, it is naturally easier to handle such legal systems. As noted, some of these systems have already been grouped as 'mixed jurisdictions' and are treated as *numerus clausus*. Yet, as also pointed out, there are many other overt mixes with different origins. Furthermore, there are also covert mixtures, the results of the same or of other combinations. It is the covert and the ongoing mixes that really tease the comparative lawyer and it is the study of 'mixedness' that can illuminate the path towards the comprehension of the interaction of law and culture everywhere.

Let us end this study with a number of rough maps, thus expanding the concept of 'mixidness':[71]

[71] In each category only samples are given. Apart from the 'mixed jurisdictions category' none are numerous clauses. Compare with the Ottawa mapping at supra n 19.

ANNEX

Map I

Mixed Systems
1. Simple mixes (hybrids with civil law and common law as their ingredient – mixed at substantive level – mixing bowl)

'Mixed jurisdictions': (numerous clauses -15 - as a concession to Vernon Palmer): Botswana, Lesotho, Louisiana, Mauritius, Namibia, the Philippines, Puerto Rico, Quebec, Saint Lucia, Scotland, the Seychelles, pre-1996 South Africa, Sri Lanka, Swaziland, Zimbabwe.

Other simple mixes: Jersey, Malta, Cyprus.

2. Complex mixes (hybrids with civil law, common law, (socialist law), religious law and customary law in different combinations)

Complex mixes 1 (hybrids with civil law, common law and customary law: Cameroon, pre-1997 Hong Kong, Lesotho, Sri Lanka, post-1996 South Africa, Thailand, Vanuatu)

Complex mixes 2 (hybrids with civil law, common law and religious law: Israel, Jordan, Saudi Arabia, Somalia, Yemen)

Complex mixes 3 (hybrids with civil law and customary law: Burundi, Burkina Faso (dysfunctional), Chad, China, Ethiopia, Gabon, Korea, Japan, Mali, Niger, Rwanda, Taiwan, Togo)

Complex mixes 4 (hybrids with civil law and Islamic law: Algeria, Egypt, Iraq, Kuwait, Lebanon, Morocco, Mauritania, Syria, Tunisia)

Complex mixes 5 (hybrids civil law, Islamic law and customary law: Djibouti, Indonesia, Senegal)

Complex mixes 6 (hybrids with common law, religious law and customary law: Pakistan, India, Kenya, Nigeria, Uganda)

Complex mixes 7 (hybrids with socialist law, civil law, common law, customary law: post-1997 Hong Kong, China, Cuba, North Vietnam, North Korea)

3. Legal Pluralisms (Dualist systems with layers of law co-existing and applicable to different members of the population such as: The Sudan, Zimbabwe)

Map II

Mixed Systems
Systems in Map I could also be re-arranged according to the primary parentage such as:

The **French** Group: (e.g. Algeria, Andorra, Benin, Burkina, Burundi, Louisiana, Quebec, Mauritius, Mauritania, Morocco, Senegal, Seychelles, Sainte Lucia, Togo, Tunisia)
The **Dutch** Group (e.g. South Africa, Sri Lanka, Indonesia, Botswana, Lesotho, Swaziland)
The **Spanish** Group (e.g. Andorra, Belize, Bolivia, Louisiana, Puerto Rico, the Philippines)
The **Portuguese** Group (e.g. Angola, Goa + Diu + Daman (Goa Union Territory of India), Guinea Bissau, Macau, Sri Lanka)
The **British** Group (e.g. Burma, Belize, Bhutan, Hong Kong, Malawi, Scotland, South Africa, Seychelles, Tobago, Pakistan, India)
The **US** Group (e.g. Louisiana, Micronesia, Puerto Rico, the Philippines)

This Map however would be quite unwieldy when indigenous laws are considered and legal systems start appearing under more than one Group.

Map III

Mixed Systems
1. Overt mixes (all the mixed systems – unblended - cited under **Map I**)
2. Covert mixes (systems that do not appear as mixed - blended)

Covert mixes 1 (Compounds – purée – blended - where the ingredients are from similar legal and social cultures: all civil law and common law systems considered as pure which are combinations of Roman law, Canon law, various common laws and each other: France, England, Italy, The Netherlands, New Zealand, Spain, the USA (minus Louisiana))

Covert mixes 2 (Compounds – purée – blended - where elite or the political pressure is the prominent mixer, therefore unexpected outcome: Albania, Argentina, Belgium, Bulgaria, Cyprus, Croatia, Estonia, Hungary, Kazakstan, Martinique, The Former Yugoslav Republic of Macedonia, Russia, Turkey, Uzbekistan, Vietnam)

Map IV

Mixed systems
1. Unstructured mixes – (understood in a different way to Glenn, where civil law is not codified): Scotland, South Africa, Israel
2. Structured mixes (where civil law is codified): Quebec, Louisiana, Sainte Lucia

Map V

Mixing systems
1. Ongoing mixes (European systems covered by the regional organisations such as the EU and the ECHR mixing with each other and under the pressure of these organisations; African systems modernising and democratising)
2. Systems in transition (moving from one orientation to another: East and Central European systems, Russia, Ukraine)

Mixed Jurisdictions in the Commonwealth Caribbean: Mixing, Unmixing, Remixing

JANE MATTHEWS GLENN *

INTRODUCTION

The vagaries of history have made the Commonwealth Caribbean a microcosm of mixed jurisdictions in both their traditional and non traditional forms. The traditional form is one of mixity of different European legal systems – of common law and civil law – and most examples result from the ebb and flow of military success in the imperial clashes of the 17th to early 19th century, coupled with the colonial doctrine of reception. Three examples in the Commonwealth Caribbean are Guyana, Trinidad and Saint Lucia, where the mix is between British common law and Roman-Dutch, Spanish and French civil laws, respectively. Of the three, Saint Lucia is the clearest example of ongoing mixity, as Spanish law in Trinidad gave way almost entirely to the common law in the mid 19th century and only vestiges of Roman-Dutch law in Guyana survived an early 20th century reform.

The three jurisdictions also provide examples of possible non traditional forms of mixed jurisdictions.[1] Guyana raises the issue of mixity between European and aboriginal law; Trinidad poses the question of formal mixity

* This paper draws on research undertaken in the context of a project on access to housing in Caribbean countries, which is supported by the Social Sciences and Humanities Research Council of Canada.

1 Levasseur, A and McCreary, JM (2002-03) 'Book Review –Mixed Jurisdictions Worldwide: The Third Legal Family' (63) *Louisiana Law Review* 69 at 70 (suggesting that a country could be regarded as a mixed jurisdiction if its legal system 'were a mixture of written law and customary law, or religious law and secular law').

between secular and religious (Hindu and Muslim) law; and Saint Lucia provides an example of informal mixity between European law and African custom.

This paper looks at the process of reception (*mixing*) and assimilation (*unmixing*) which is at the heart of the traditional analysis of mixed jurisdictions, before considering possible non traditional forms of mixity (*remixing*). But first, a few words of introduction to the three Commonwealth Caribbean examples are in order.

Guyana, the only one of the three countries located on mainland South America, is the largest of the three, at 83,000 square miles.[2] It consists of a narrow but fertile coastal plain (much of which lies below sea level and is protected by a Dutch-introduced system of dikes) where about 80% of the population live, and an extensive but sparsely inhabited upland interior where most of the Amerindian population live. It is drained by numerous rivers, and the name 'Guyana' (formerly Guiana) comes from an Amerindian word meaning 'land of waters'.[3] Guyana is the second most populous country of the three, at around 750,000 people, almost half (43%) of whom are of East Indian descent, almost half of African (30%) or mixed (17%) descent, and the rest made up of Amerindians (9%) and a catch-all 'others' (1%). The economy is based mainly on agriculture (notably sugar and rice), with mining (especially gold and bauxite) playing an increasingly important role. It is the poorest country of the three, with a GDP per capita of US $ 4,439, and ranks lowest (103rd) on the United Nation's Human Development Index.

Trinidad, an island of about 1,900 square miles, is located just off the South American mainland and is a geographical extension of it. Trinidad consists mainly of rolling fertile plains, with some low mountains along the northern coast. It is the most populous of the three countries, at just over a million people (about 1,050,000) who, like Guyana, are divided mainly between descendants of African slaves and East Indian indentured labourers, in almost equal proportions (38% African, 40% East Indian), with the remaining being mixed (20%) or others (2%). Agriculture (notably sugar) continues to play an important economic role, but it is being replaced by petroleum ('black gold'). It is the richest country of the three, with a GDP per capita of US $12,182 (although the wealth is unevenly divided and 21%

2 The factual information in this paragraph is drawn mainly from Central Intelligence Agency, *The World Factbook*, available at <https://www.cia.gov/library/publications/the-world-factbook/index.html> and from the Guyana Bureau of Statistics *2002 Population and Housing Census*, available at <http://www.statisticsguyana.gov.gy/>.

3 Hawkins, J (ed) (1986) *The Oxford Reference Dictionary* Clarendon Press at 363.

live below the poverty line). Its Human Development Index ranking (57th) is the highest of the three.

Saint Lucia is the smallest of the three countries, at 238 square miles. It is located in the middle of the Windward chain of islands in the south-eastern Caribbean; it is a volcanic island and thus mountainous, but with some broad fertile valleys. Its population of some 168,000 people is largely African (83%) or mixed (12%), with East Indians making up only 2% and other, 3%. As in the other two countries, agriculture dominated until recently (originally sugar, then bananas – 'green gold'), but tourism ('white gold') now drives the economy.[4] Saint Lucia ranks about midway between the other two countries in its economic indicators (GDP per capita of US $6,324) and social development (76th on the Human Development Index).

MIXING

Mixing of civil and common law in Guyana, Trinidad and Saint Lucia was triggered by Britain's success in the global struggle between the colonial superpowers of the late 18th and early 19th centuries. But the stage was set several centuries earlier, with Columbus' voyages of discovery.[5] All three countries were sighted by Columbus (Guyana and Trinidad in 1498, Saint Lucia in 1503), and Guyana and Trinidad were then claimed by Spain.

Spanish presence in Guyana was limited at best,[6] and Dutch traders met with little opposition when they established up-river trading posts in the late 1500s and a first precarious coastal settlement in 1613. A Dutch presence was formalised in 1621 with the creation of the Dutch West India Company (*West-Indische Compagnie*) along the lines of the East India Company, and was formally recognised by Spain in 1648.[7] Dutch Guiana

[4] Payne, A (2006) 'The End of Green Gold: Comparative Development Options and Strategies in the Eastern Caribbean Banana-producing Islands' (41:3) *Studies in Comparative International Development* 25.

[5] 'Columbus did not, of course, discover [the New World] [...]. What Columbus did was to establish contact between two worlds, both already very old; between the restless, expansionist, technologically advanced states of Western Europe and the Amerinidian communities of Central and South America': Brereton, B (1981) *A History of Modern Trinidad 1783-1962* Heinemann Educational Books at 1.

[6] The limited Spanish presence was mainly in the most westerly area (Essequibo), and this forms the background to an on-going boundary dispute between Venezuela and Guyana today: see Donovan, TA (2004) 'Challenges to the Territorial Integrity of Guyana: A Legal Analysis' (32) *Georgia Journal of International and Comparative Law* 661. However, the Spanish 'largely avoided' the remaining areas, 'long known as the Wild Coast': 'Guyana', *Encyclopaedia Britannica*, available at <http://www.search.eb.com>.

[7] Bisschop, WR (1908) 'Modern Roman Dutch Law' (24) *Law Quarterly Review* 157 at 167; Besson, J (2003) 'History, Land and Culture in the English-speaking Caribbean' in Williams, AN (ed) *Land in the Caribbean: Issues of Policy, Administration and Management in the English-*

consisted initially of three colonies: Essequibo in the west bordering Venezuela (site of the first Dutch settlement), Berbice in the east bordering Surinam (established by the Dutch in 1626), and Demerara in the middle (founded in 1770).[8] Essequibo and Demerara were subsequently united into a single colony (Essequibo-Demerara) but Berbice remained separate, although both colonies remained under Company control. The two colonies were captured by the British in 1796, restored to the Dutch by the Treaty of Amiens 1802, and recaptured by the British in 1803. British sovereignty was confirmed by the Treaty of London 1814. The colonies were ultimately united as British Guiana in 1831.

Spanish settlement in Trinidad was more extensive and long-lasting than in Guyana. Interest in the colony was initially spurred (1530s) by its strategic importance at the mouth of the Orinoco watershed in neighbouring Venezuela, reputed site of the fabled El Dorado, and was later fuelled by the production of tobacco (late 1500s and early 1600s) and cocoa (a century later).[9] The first permanent settlement dates from 1592[10] although for most of the Spanish period, Trinidad remained 'neglected and undeveloped; a "colonial slum" of the Spanish empire'.[11] In fact, the island's population did not increase significantly until Spain issued a *Cédula de población* [Population Decree] in 1783 to encourage immigration from the nearby, mainly French, islands.[12] The result was that the population of Trinidad

speaking Caribbean Terra Institute at 3; Donovan supra n 6 at 670.

8 The three colonies were named after three of the major rivers draining the interior of Guyana.

9 Eg Leiter, J and Harding, S (2004) 'Trinidad, Brazil and Ghana: Three Melting Moments in the History of Cocoa' (20) *Journal of Rural Studies* 113. Cocoa was also responsible for an increased Spanish population in the late 1800s, as a second cocoa boom drew workers from Venezuela (the so-called 'cocoa panyols' [espanols]). Hulme, P (2006) 'Book Review of Forte, Maximilian C *Ruins of Absence, Presence of Caribs: (Post)colonial Representations of Aboriginality in Trinidad and Tobago*' (12) *Journal of the Royal Anthropological Institute* 957. See also Moodie-Kublalsingh, S (1993) *The Cocoa Panyols of Trinidad: An Oral Record* British Academic Press.

10 Forte, MC (2004-05) 'Writing the Caribs Out: The Construction and Demystification of the "Deserted Island" Thesis for Trinidad' (VI:3) *Issues in Caribbean Amerindian Studies* at 3, available at <http://www.centrelink.org/Papers.html>.

11 Brereton supra n 5 at 8. Trinidad, like the Spanish colonies in Guyana, was under the Captaincy-General of Venezuela during this period: Dupont, J (2001) *The Common Law Abroad: Constitutional and Legal Legacy of the British Empire* Rothman Publications at 295.

12 Under the *Cédula*, immigrants had to be Catholics and subjects of nations friendly to Spain (ie France); white immigrants were granted an area equivalent to 30 acres for themselves and for each family member, and 15 acres for each slave; free coloured were granted half that amount. The *Cédula* extended a practice started in the mid 1770s, which was aimed initially at French planters from islands ceded to Britain in 1763 after the Seven Years War, and later at those loyal to the French crown in the revolutionary period; its slave-based land grant formula transformed the island into a slave society: Brereton supra n 5 at 11-14.

was largely French when the British captured the island in 1797.[13] British control was confirmed by the Treaty of Amiens 1802.

As for Saint Lucia,[14] it was – like many of the island colonies – 'visited, settled, abandoned, and resettled, handed about from one owner to another in the competition of nations, thrown first into one scale and then into the other, in order to adjust for the time being the claims of rival governments.'[15] Like Guyana, Saint Lucia was under proprietary rule for most of its early history, although the picture is complicated by the fact that both the English and French crowns, as well as the Carib Amerindians, claimed the right to grant the island. Several conflicting conveyances and unsuccessful attempts at settlement followed, until a French grant of the island to the French West Indies Company (*Compagnie des Indes occidentales*) in 1642 resulted in the first successful settlement the same year. Saint Lucia continued to be tossed between the two countries over the next 150 years[16] until it, like Guyana, fell into British hands for the last time in 1803. British sovereignty was confirmed in the Treaty of Paris 1814.

Reception

When the three colonies were taken by the British, they became 'colonies of conquest' in which, under the doctrine of reception and British colonial practice, the laws and customs in force at the time of conquest remained in force, generally speaking, until subsequently changed. The usual practice

13 After the *Cédula*, the old Spanish elite, 'impoverished and isolated, lost all influence over the affairs of their native island. Some of them joined the Spanish armed forces, others emigrated to the continent; a number relapsed into poverty and obscurity, and disappeared from the historical record': Brereton supra n 5 at 20. The first British governor, Picton, is reported to have observed in 1802 that 'there were only six or seven Spaniards "of any respectability" in Trinidad': Forte supra n 10 at 16, citing Newson, *Aboriginals and Spanish Colonial Trinidad* at 194.

14 The discussion of Saint Lucia draws largely on Matthews Glenn, J (1997) 'Civilian Survival: Upper and Lower Canada and the Saint Lucia Civil Code' in Brierley, JEC et al (eds) *Mélanges Paul-André Crépeau* Éditions Yvon Blais 327.

15 Lucas, CP (1888) *A Historical Geography of the British Colonies* Clarendon Press vol ii at 14, as quoted in Reis, CE (1914) 'Spanish Law in the British Empire' (14) *Journal of the Society of Comparative Legislation* (New Series) 24 at 28.

16 Including a brief exchange during the Seven Years War, when the British captured Saint Lucia in 1762 but returned it to France under the Treaty of Paris 1763 in exchange for Quebec. Contemporary opinion was that France got the better of the bargain: Voltaire's dismissive '*quelques arpents de neige*' ['several acres of snow'] still rankles Canadians, but some British opinion was equally dismissive, comparing adversely the 'frozen wastes of Canada' to the valuable sugar islands of the Caribbean: Belleau, C (1984) 'The Law of Civil Procedure in the Province of Quebec with Special Reference to the Field of the Execution of Judgments as Compared to the St. Lucia Experience' in Landry, RA and Caparros, E (eds) *Essays on the Civil Codes of Québec and St. Lucia* University of Ottawa Press 265 at 267

might be reaffirmed, supplemented or varied by articles of capitulation, proclamations, instructions, treaties, and the like.[17]

In Guyana, the principle of continuity was affirmed in the Articles of Capitulation of Essequibo and Demerara dated 18 September 1803, which provided not only that the Dutch 'Laws and Usages of the Colony' were to remain in force and be respected[18] but also that the existing institutions of governance were to be continued.[19] These provisions were not repeated in the Treaty of London 1814.

In Trinidad, the Articles of Capitulation were silent on the retention of Spanish law, but the British military commander issued a proclamation several days after capitulation guaranteeing the continuation of Spanish civil and criminal law and the maintenance in office of all judicial and administrative officers until the permanent nature of the island's government could be decided.[20] This position was reiterated some sixteen years later in a Royal Proclamation issued on 19 June 1813:

> that all such public acts and judicial proceedings which before the surrender of the said island to us were in the name of his Catholic Majesty shall henceforth be done, issued, and performed in our name; and that the same Courts of Judicature which subsisted in the said island previous to its surrender thereof to us shall be continued in the exercise of all the judicial powers belonging to them, in all criminal and civil cases, and that they shall proceed according to the laws by which the said island was then governed .[21]

17 See generally Côté, JE (1977) 'The Reception of English Law' (15) *Alberta Law Review* 29; see also Reis supra n 15 at 28-30; Lennard, FB (1933) 'Some Aspects of Colonial Law' (19) *Transactions of the Grotius Society* 41 at 56. The leading English case on reception and continuation of law, *Campbell v Hall* (1774), Cowp 204, 98 English Reports 1045, arose in relation to the nearby island of Grenada.

18 Janki, M (nd) 'Customary Water Laws and Practices: Guyana' at 1, available at <http://www.iucn.org/themes/law/pdfdocuments/LN190805_Guyana.pdf>; see also Lee, RW (1914) 'Roman-Dutch Law in British Guiana' (14) *Journal of the Society of Comparative Legislation* (New Series) 11 at 12. This protection was, in a sense, continued in the letters patent of 1831 unifying British Guiana, which provided that 'nothing herein contained shall extend, revoke or abrogate any law or lawful usage now in force in the said United Colony of Demerara and Essequibo or in the said Colony of Berbice respectively': Lee at 12.

19 Ramkarran, HN (2004) 'Seeking a Democratic Path: Constitutional Reform in Guyana' (32) *Georgia Journal of International and Comparative Law* 585 at 586.

20 Brereton supra n 5 at 33; Reis, supra n 15 at 29-30; John, AM (1988) 'The Smuggled Slaves of Trinidad 1813' (31) *The Historical Journal* 365 at 365.

21 *Report of His Majesty's Commissioners of Legal Inquiry on the Colony of Trinidad* (1827) (*Trinidad Report* 1827) as quoted in Reis supra n 15 at 30.

In Saint Lucia, retention of existing law was provided for in a Proclamation of the military authorities issued shortly after conquest, on 23 June 1803, which stipulated:

> Although the said Island was taken by storm and without a surrender or stipulation of any sort, nevertheless, to reassure the inhabitants and property owners about their present status pending a declaration of His Majesty, their Excellencies guarantee them full and complete enjoyment of all their property, under the laws existing in the Colony in the period immediately preceding the last cession.
> All duly constituted authorities are charged to conform to this proclamation.[22]

The Treaty of Paris 1814 similarly guaranteed the continuation of existing French laws,[23] but concerns remained and in 1817 the Governor of the colony issued a further reassurance: 'The laws, customs and regulations in force in the Colony at the moment of publication of the present ordinance will continue to be followed and enforced.'[24]

In the result, some or all of the old laws continued in force in Guyana, Trinidad and Saint Lucia. What laws were these?

Old law

The applicable laws in force in the three colonies at the time of British conquest were the Roman-Dutch, Spanish and French laws as they themselves had been received into the former colonies at the time of their earlier settlement or subsequently introduced. The content of law might therefore vary from country to country of the same Imperial power; however, the sources of law in civilian Guyana, Trinidad or Saint Lucia have a familiar ring to someone familiar with the legal history of, say, South Africa, California or Quebec.

[22] Reproduced (in French) as No 4, Appendix II, Saint Lucia Revised Ordinances, 1957 [author's translation]. Although the reference to 'the period immediately preceding the last cession' is said to refer to the period prior to an earlier capture by the British on 26 May 1796 (it was subsequently returned to the French by the Treaty of Amiens 1802), the generally accepted cut-off date for retention of French law is 23 June 1803: Liverpool, NJO (1984) 'The History and Development of the Saint Lucia Civil Code' in Landry and Caparros (eds) supra n 16, 303 at 307. See also Wood Renton, J (1909) 'French Law within the British Empire' (10) *Journal of the Society of Comparative Legislation* (New Series) 93 and 250 at 103-104.

[23] The Treaty provision is not reproduced in the historical appendix to the Saint Lucia Revised Ordinances.

[24] As quoted (in French) in Liverpool supra n 22 at 308 [author's translation].

The Dutch West India Company colonies in Guyana thus received Roman-Dutch law generally similar to their sister colonies under the East India Company. It was set out in a Company order (*Ordre van Regieringe*, or Order of Government) of 13 October 1629, sanctioned by the States-General, as including:

> Art. 59. In matters of marriage, rights between husband and wife, in intestate succession and the drafting of wills, and all that is connected therewith, there shall have force of law over all countries, towns and peoples belonging to the dominions of the States-General and the West India Company, and everywhere be observed as law, the political ordinance issued by the States of Holland in the year 1582, as its provisions are best known, can be easily used as the common custom of South Holland and Zeelandt, and will introduce the least obscurity and change.
> Art. 60. All conveyances, as well as bonds or mortgage deeds [...] to grant proprietary rights or real rights, shall be passed before the said three members of the committee of civil justice, and the letters to be made thereof shall have to be sealed by them, and thereupon be registered in a register to be kept by the assessor, also in conformity with what is customary in the United Provinces.
> Art. 61. In other matters of diverse contracts and transactions the ordinary *beschreven Rechten* [written law] shall be followed.[25]

A further statement was provided some 150 years later, in a resolution of the States-General dated 4 October 1774 and relating to the colony of Demerara-Essequibo. It identified the applicable law as being,

> all the laws of Holland in general and more particularly all Laws, Statutes, Resolutions, and Ordinances of Their High Mightinesses [ie the States-General] or of the Committee of Ten with the approbation of Their High Mightinesses, heretofore transmitted, or hereafter to be transmitted, to the Director General and the Court of Essequibo, or to the Commander and Court of Demerara.[26]

Matrimonial matters were to be governed by the Political Ordinance of Holland and West Vriesland of 1580; intestate succession, by the law

[25] As quoted in Bisschop supra n 7 at 167. For a detailed discussion of Guyanese legal development generally, see Ramsahoye, FHW (1966) *The Development of Land Law in British Guiana* Oceana Publications.
[26] As quoted in Ramsahoye supra n 25 at 307; see also Lee supra n 18 at 12.

of North Holland; civil matters, by the enactments of the Council of Ten; and all other matters, by written law (i.e. the statute law of Holland and, failing that, Roman law).[27] In applying the law, the courts were to look first to the laws and customs of the colony, followed by those of the United Provinces and ultimately Roman law if necessary. But in practice, Bisschop argued, application of the laws and customs of the United Provinces in the colonies would have been difficult, as the inhabitants came from different provinces and printed material was scarce; local courts thus most probably looked immediately to Roman law (as expounded by such leading authors as Grotius, van Leeuwen, Voet, Groenewebern, van der Linder and van der Keessel) if local laws and customs did not provide a solution to the issue at hand.[28] This was echoed by Lee:

> In these circumstances the exported law lost sharpness of outline. It furnished a somewhat blurred background to a picture, the details of which were supplied by the legislative authorities competent in the colony in question. The administration of the criminal law left much to the discretion of the judges. In civil matters, when a judge or advocate had occasion to go behind the local ordinances to inform himself as to the fundamental principles of the law, he would have recourse for the most part to the well-known textbooks, the *Inleiding* of Grotius, Van Leeuwen's *Roomsch-Hollandsch Recht*, Voet's *Commentary on the Pandects*.[29]

The law applicable in Trinidad, as elsewhere in Spanish America, was found in a variety of specific and general sources, including instructions to governors, royal orders (*Ordenamientos*) adopted from time to time for the colonies, and statutes (*Fueros*) setting out the ancient customs of the realm. The *Ordenamientos* and *Fueros* included:[30] the *Fuera Real de España* (1255) governing such matters as public officials (including judges, lawyers and notaries), procedure, and matrimonial and inheritance rules;

[27] Lee supra n 18 at 12. Similar provisions applied in the colony of Bebice, with the exception of intestate succession which was to be governed by the law of South Holland: id citing Charter of Berbice, 6 December 1732, art 30.

[28] Bisschop supra n 7 at 167-169. He also mentioned the importance of a compilation of ordinances adopted by the East India Company in 1642 and approved by the States-General in 1650 (the Statutes of Batavia) which were followed generally (id at 164-167); but their use appears to have been limited to East India Company colonies, and not followed in West India Company ones.

[29] Lee, RW (1930) 'What has Become of Roman-Dutch Law?' (12) *Journal of Comparative Legislation and International Law* (Third Series) 33 at 35.

[30] List drawn from Reis supra n 15 at 27, who referred to the *Trinidad Report* 1827, supra n 21. See also Glenn, HP (2005) *On Common Laws* Oxford University Press at 40-41 and 75-78

the fundamental *Siete Partidas* [Seven Parts, or Books] (1260) setting out canon law, the decrees of the great councils of Spain, the rules concerning judgments, contracts and testaments, and criminal law provisions;[31] the *Leyes de Estilo* (1525) dealing with the functions of notary publics; the important *Recopilación de las Leyes de las Indias* (1681) compiling all laws, *cédulas* and orders enacted for the colonies; and finally the *Leyes de Bilbáo* (1732) governing commercial relations. The applicability of these laws in Trinidad was confirmed in an 1807 trial by a number of expert witnesses who, in response to a question about 'the law of Old Spain and the island of Trinidad, or either of them' at the time of surrender in 1797, responded in substantially the same terms:

> The laws that existed in Old Spain and this colony at the time of the capture of the island in 1797 are the same as those in force now. They are the Recopilacion des Indies, the Recopilacion de Castilla, the Laws of the Seven Partidas, and warranted by [such authors as] Elizondo, Colom, Febrero, Martinez, Bobadilla, Curia Phillipica and Herrera.[32]

As for Saint Lucia, the applicable law at the time of surrender consisted of the *Coutume de Paris*, the *Ordonnances*, Edicts and Declarations of the French monarchy relating to matters of a general nature, other laws relating to colonial matters emanating from the Governor or the Intendant in the name of the King and published in the *Code de Martinique*,[33] and Roman law and the works of French writers, particularly Pothier. The *Coutume de Paris* was said to apply 'because the 33rd Article of the *arrêt* [decree] of the "*Conseil d'État du Roi*," of May, 1664, establishing the *West India Company*, expressly declares its obligatory effect in the *West India Colonies*, as it had been established in the French Colonies in the East'.[34] The best-known

[31] The importance of the *Siete Partidas* has been described as follows: 'At the time of its compilation it was not only superior to anything of the kind that had ever been attempted at the time of Justinian; it stood alone and unrivalled in the medieval world; and for over six hundred years it remained not only the greatest textbook of Spanish jurisprudence but the greatest exclusively national code of laws of Europe': Burke, UK *A History of Spain*, vol i at 282, as quoted in Reis supra n 15 at 27. See also Lobingier, CS (1913) 'Las Siete Partidas and Its Predecessors' (1) *California Law Review* 487; and Lobingier, CS (1929) 'Las Siete Partidas in Full English Dress' (9) *Hispanic American Historical Review* 529.

[32] Howell, TB and Howell, TJ (eds) (1822) *A Complete Collection of State Trials and Proceedings for High Treason and Other Crimes and Misdemeanors* (Vol XXX 1806-1808) Longman & TC Hansard at 594-596.

[33] A five-volume work containing the local laws of Saint Lucia, then administratively part of Martinique.

[34] Per Woodcock, Chief Justice of Tobago, speaking for the majority of the Court of Appeal for the Windward Islands, in the leading case of *DuBoulay v DuBoulay* (1867-69) LR 2 PC 430

statement of the ancient French law in Saint Lucia is that of Mr Justice Porter Atthill, Chief Justice of Saint Lucia:

It is, however, necessary here to state, that the Civil Law of the Island, besides the local *Ordonnances*, the Maritime and Commercial law, are nearly the whole of the French Laws anterior to 1789, which are scattered over a great number of authorities, such as the *Coutume de Paris*, which is part of the ancient '*lex non scripta*' of *France*, the *Ordonnances*, Edicts and declarations of the French Monarchy, the *Code de la Martinique, Pothier, Merlin, Ferrière, Denisart, Domat, Pigeau, Jousse*, and many others unnecessary to mention.[35]

In sum, at the time of their conquest, all three colonies were subject to laws of some antiquity, but with substantially similar sources in that they included a wide range of specific instructions or general rules applicable in the colony or a group of colonies (eg decrees and regulations issued by the King or his representative, company by-laws, etc) as well as a large body of law applicable in the mother country and found in a disparate range of statutes, regulations, compilations, general principles and doctrine. The extent to which the latter was available for consultation, or even known, in a given colony is a matter of conjecture.

Received law

How much of this old law continued to be applicable in the British colonies following conquest? Did a colony become a mixed jurisdiction at the time of conquest, automatically by the very fact of conquest? Or did it become a self-enclosed, but unmixed, enclave of old law, with mixity coming later with incremental changes to the law? Part of the answer is provided for a given colony by a close analysis of the terms of the articles of capitulation, proclamations, instructions, treaties, etc. issued at the time of conquest. But part of the answer might be found by looking at the general principles of the doctrine of reception.

It is well accepted that, under the doctrine of reception's presumption of continuity, the private law applicable in colonies of conquest continues in force following conquest absent specific provisions to the contrary. However, the position as to public law is not as clear-cut. Walton, writing

(JCPC) at 434. This *arrêt* became effective on its subsequent registration, on 5 November 1681, with the *Conseil supérieur de l'Île Martinique*.It has been carried forward and reprinted, in the original French, in the various compilations of the laws of Saint Lucia (see presently Saint Lucia Revised Ordinances, 1957, No. 1, Appendix II (on 'Ancient French Law (*Ancien Droit Français*)'). See also Wood Renton supra n 22 at 103-104 and 117-118.

35 Speaking in dissent at the Court of Appeal, in *DuBoulay* supra n 34 at 438 [italics in original].

about Quebec in 1907, suggested an approach of discontinuity of public law: 'The conquest of Canada in 1763 had the effect of substituting the public law of England for that of France.'[36] This would mean that all colonies of conquest became fully mixed jurisdictions by the very fact of conquest coupled with the interplay of the two presumptions, continuity of private law and discontinuity of public law. But approaches elsewhere are more nuanced. As one author put it, 'Great obscurity attaches to the result of the change of sovereignty in its effect on a system of law which is not English. How much of the public law of England is thus introduced *by the mere fact of the change*?'[37] There is general agreement about the immediate application of Imperial legislation in force *proprio vigore* and of some or all principles of constitutional law touching the Royal prerogative. And it is also generally accepted that laws contrary to public order (such as torture) would not survive the conquest, although this principle is not uniformly applied.[38] The terms of the articles of capitulation can also affect reception of public law.

A more nuanced approach, according a larger place to continuity of public law, is suggested by the practice in the three colonies. Continuity is clearest in Guyana, where the Dutch government structure remained in place until it was substantially modified in 1891 and ultimately abolished and replaced by a more familiar British structure in 1928. According to HN Ramkarran,

> The British inherited Dutch institutions of governance which were the Court of Policy, the College of Electors, the College of Financial

[36] Walton, FP (1907) *The Scope and Interpretation of the Civil Code of Lower Canada* Wilson & Lafleur at 26-27, as quoted in Côté supra n 17 at 42. See also Walton, FP (1913) 'The Legal System of Quebec' (33) *Canadian Law Times* 280 at 281 ('it is generally agreed that there are certain rules of law and especially certain rights and privileges of the subject which belong to public and not to private law. As part of the constitutional law of the British Empire they are the same in all portions of it, and, therefore, the same in the province of Quebec as in the rest of Canada. It can hardly be disputed for example that such charters of liberty as Magna Carta or the Bill of Rights formed part of the law of Quebec as soon as English sovereignty was introduced. [However] [...] the line of demarcation between public and private law is in some cases by no means easy to draw') and Côté at 42 ('One need only look at the Quebec cases to note that the discussion of constitutional principles and the prerogative, or indeed of public law generally, is always in terms of English law and never that of France or any province of old France'). However, even Quebec followed the practice of maintaining the existing court structure in place until changed, but that could be regarded as coming with a guarantee of on-going private law (ie treating court structures as part of private law, rather than public law).

[37] Keith, AB (1916) 'Book review of C Reis, *The Government of Trinidad* (London: Sweet & Maxwell, 1915)' (16) *Journal of the Society of Comparative Legislation* (New Series) 87 at 87 [emphasis added].

[38] See below, the text at note 40.

> Representatives, and the Combined Court, and were obliged to continue them by Article 1 of the Capitulation Treaty. These continued until 1891 when the Constitution was amended to enlarge the Court of Policy, abolish the College of Electors, directly elect a section of the Court of Policy, and create the right of the Governor to dissolve the Court of Policy.
> The [British] Crown Colony Constitution was enacted in 1928. The Court of Policy and the Combined Court were abolished and replaced by the Legislative Council and the Executive Council. This constitutional formula of a legislature and a cabinet, with a majority of members nominated by the British-appointed governor, constituted the type of Crown Colony favoured by Great Britain.[39]

However, this might have occurred because continuation of the existing institutions was expressly provided for under the Articles of Capitulation, as Ramkarran points out.

There is some evidence of continuity in Trinidad as well. For example, the 1807 court case mentioned above was in fact the trial of the first Governor, Thomas Picton, for the misdemeanor of causing torture to be inflicted on a free coloured woman,[40] and the issue in the case was whether or not torture was acceptable under the Spanish law applicable in Trinidad immediately prior to conquest. This supports the principle of continuity of public law, and casts doubt on the existence of a 'public order' exception to it. As well, the *cabildo* (a multi-faceted body fulfilling legislative, administrative and judicial functions at both the central and municipal levels in Spanish colonies) continued to play a role after conquest.[41] But as in Guyana, the

[39] Ramkarran 'Seeking' supra note 19 at 586. See also Dupont *Common Law Abroad* supra note 11 at 208-210; Osgood, HL (1891) 'Book review of C.P. Lucas, *An Historical Geography of the British Colonies*, 2 vol. (Oxford: Clarendon Press, 1888 & 1890)' (6) *Political Science Quarterly* 369 at 371. For a detailed description of the change from Dutch to British institutions, see Penson, LM (1926) 'The Making of a Crown Colony: British Guiana, 1803-33' (9) *Transactions of the Royal Historical Society* (4th Series) 107.

[40] 'Proceedings before the Court of King's Bench, Westminster, in the Case of Thomas Picton, Esq., sometime Governor and Commander in Chief over and in the Island of Trinidad in the West Indies, on an Indictment for a Misdemeaner, in causing the Torture to be inflicted upon Luisa Calderon, a free Mulatta, in the Island of Trinidad aforesaid, A.D. 1804-1812' in Howell and Howell supra n 32.

[41] The 'illustrious *cabildo*' has been described as 'a "body corporate, that partook of the mixed nature of an ecclesiastical council, a parish vestry, a municipal corporation, a council of government, and a legislative and executive council, over which the Spanish governor presided". This corporation was a self-elected body, exercising jurisdiction partly general, partly municipal and judiciary. It had power to levy duties and taxes, and to appoint alcaldes (judges)': Reis supra n 15 at 26, quoting Joseph (1933) *History of Trinidad* at 146. As late as 1832, for example, the *cabildo* tried to delay the imposition of imperial rules to better the conditions of slaves by invoking a Spanish public law rule that Ordinances restricting property rights

proclamation issued in Trinidad immediately following capitulation guaranteed the maintenance of judicial and administrative offices[42] until the nature of the new government was decided, and this did not happen until 1832 (as decision about the form of government was caught up in concerns about the slave trade and abolition of slavery).[43] The *cabildo* was not formally abolished until 1840.

In Saint Lucia, finally, the *Conseil superieur* continued to exercise legislative as well as judicial powers, as it had done under the French regime, until it was stripped of its legislative powers in 1817. In the case of Saint Lucia, the continuity of public law was not provided for under the terms of surrender, as the proclamation issued immediately following capitulation was in private law terms only.[44]

The effect in principle of conquest on the public law of a colony is thus an open question. However, it seems likely that the public law rules of the conqueror, if not introduced automatically on conquest, would be rapidly introduced subsequently (which makes the longevity of Dutch institutions in Guyana particularly interesting). What of private law?

UNMIXING

Following conquest, Guyana, Trinidad and Saint Lucia were three enclaves of civil private law in a British empire in which the common law obviously dominated. They thus came under pressure to assimilate, which each colony resisted with varying degrees of success. Generally speaking, assimilation seems to have taken place in three stages. The first stage was one of informal assimilation, with local officials and judges ignoring or changing laws with which they disagreed or did not understand. For example, Brereton wrote that by the early 1810s, 'the legal system in Trinidad [...] was a confusing and uneasy mixture of Spanish law and British procedures. Spanish law had been greatly modified, partly through ignorance, and partly through the hostility of British judges and officials to laws that they tended to regard as unnecessarily complex and often obsolete.'[45] The second stage

had to be suspended until the King's pleasure was known: Brereton supra n 5 at 62.

42 See above, the text at note 20.

43 Eg John supra n 20. Putting off a change in form of government meant that Imperial policies to improve the lot of slaves and free coloured adopted in response to humanitarian pressures in England could be tried out in Trinidad before being applied more generally, as 'the island had no elected assembly that could resist legislation unpopular with the slave-owners': Brereton supra n 5 at 52. Trinidad was preferred over Guyana and Saint Lucia for this purpose as the colony's Spanish legal heritage was thought to make slavery there 'milder than in those territories where the legal tradition was French or Dutch': id at 58.

44 See above, the text at note 22.

45 Brereton supra n 5 at 71-2.

was the piecemeal introduction of English law and procedure in a number of discrete areas. During this stage, the on-going civil law continued as the general norm, with common law exceptions engrafted on it. The third phase was a generalised, wholesale introduction of the common law which reversed the hierarchy between the two systems, with the common law now being the general norm and civil law enclaves remaining as exceptions to it. RW Lee captured the flavour of the difference between the last two stages as follows:

> What we call a system is in many respects a conglomeration. It is not so entirely one that great sections of it cannot be modified, or even replaced, without fatal results to the whole. Constitutional law depends on political allegiance, commercial law is peculiarly responsive to external influences, great changes in procedure may leave the substantive law unchanged. As compared with these, what we call specifically the civil law of a country is stubbornly unwilling to change. If this, the kernel of the legal system, retains its character substantially unaltered through successive ages, we shall say that the 'system' continues to exist.[46]

All three stages of assimilation were substantially completed in Trinidad and Guyana, and but Saint Lucia continues to resist the last stage.

Piecemeal introduction

A detailed consideration of the piecemeal legislative changes in each colony would be overly fastidious, and various authors have identified different patterns of introduction.[47] At the risk of over-generalisation, one might suggest that piecemeal introduction of English law reflected the concerns of the English elite (planters and merchants): the more influential the elite, the more rapid the pace of assimilation. One set of concerns would be to be able to acquire, keep and dispose of their wealth and possessions in

[46] Lee supra n 29 at 34.

[47] See eg Lee, RW (1915) 'The Civil Law and the Common Law: A World Survey' (14) *Michigan Law Review* 89 at 94-100; Anthony, KD (1994) 'The Reception of the Common Law Systems by the Civil Law Systems in the Commonwealth Caribbean' in Doucet, M and Vanderlinden, J (eds) *La réception des systèmes juridiques: Implantation et destin* Bruylant 15 at 31-36; and Lennard supra n 17. See also, for Guyana, Lee supra n 18, and Ledlie, JC (1917) 'Roman-Dutch Law in British Guiana and a West Indian Court of Appeal' (17) *Journal of the Society of Comparative Legislation* (New Series) 210; for Trinidad, (1897) 'Modes of Legislation in the British Colonies' (2) *Journal of the Society of Comparative Legislation* 258 at 291-98, and Reis supra n 15 (Trinidad); and for Saint Lucia, Wood Renton supra n 22.

the manner with which they were familiar, so that English mercantile law (company law, sale of goods, bills of exchange, insurance, bankruptcy law, etc)[48] and English family property law (separation of matrimonial property, freedom of testamentary disposition,[49] English form of wills, etc) would be among the first to be introduced. Another set of concerns would be to be governed and protected in a way they could trust, and this would mean the introduction of English forms of government, English criminal law and English judicial institutions and procedure. This pattern is borne out in the three colonies, with a key step leading to assimilation being the naming of a Commission in 1823 to enquire into the administration of criminal and civil justice in the West Indian and South American colonies.[50] The Commission reported in 1827 for Trinidad, 1828 for Guyana and 1830 for Saint Lucia,[51] and in each case the result was an increased pace of piecemeal assimilation.

Generalised introduction

The pressures to assimilate were strongest in Trinidad, and Spanish law gave place almost entirely to English once the colony was granted a local (albeit nominated) Legislative Council[52] in 1831, as the 1827 Commission report had recommended, and the Governor was given permission in 1842 to proceed with law reform. The ensuing flood of piecemeal legislation was

48 Macdonell, J (1916) 'The Codification of the Commercial Law of the Empire' (16) *Journal of the Society of Comparative Legislation* (New Series) 265 at 266 ('Of a Civil Code for the Empire there can be no question; there exist within it profound differences in the legal systems in force. No doubt these are being effaced. [...] But even if the assimilation were complete as to contracts and torts, the differences in the law as to status are likely to remain for a considerable time. No similar obstacles bar the way to an assimilation of mercantile law; it would be only the completing of a work already far advanced'); Lee 'Civil Law' supra n 47 at 97 ('As regards commercial and maritime law there has scarcely been a struggle. The principles and rules of English Law have prevailed in all the British Colonies, whether in consequence of statutory enactment or by tacit acceptance and judicial decision').

49 Lee 'Civil Law' supra n 47 at 98 ('No legal proposition seems so ingrained in the Common Law as that a man may leave his property to whom he will, and that no one, not even a child, has any claim upon a testator's bounty').

50 See especially Anthony supra n 47.

51 *Trinidad Report* 1827 supra n 21; *Second Report of the Commissioners of Enquiry into the Administration of Criminal and Civil Justice in the West Indies and South American Colonies, United Colony of Demerara and Essequibo and Colony of Berbice* (1828) (*Guiana Report* 1828); *Third Report of the Commissioners of Enquiry, Saint Lucia* (1830) (*Saint Lucia Report* 1830).

52 The council consisted of the leading local government officials (the 'official members') and private citizens selected by the governor from amongst the major landholders (the 'unofficial members'). Trinidad was thus an example of a 'pure' Crown Colony, and this remained the case until 1924: Brereton *History* supra note 5 at 136. On Crown Colonies generally, see Bryce, J (1907) 'Some Difficulties in Colonial Government Encountered by Great Britain and How They Have Been Met' (30) *Annals of the American Academy of Political and Social Sciences* 16.

such that it brought in its wake, implicitly, the generalised introduction of English law. This is illustrated in an 1897 article by Clarence Bourne, the then Examiner of Titles for Trinidad and Tobago, about legislative changes in the field of property which, in essence, imported a series of 19th century English statutes up-dating some of the more antiquated provisions of its feudal-based property law.[53] The Trinidad copies thus contained an array of detailed provisions expressed in the technical language of common law property with no reference to Spanish law. Bourne described it as English legislation being 'dumped down on a Spanish foundation', and asked whether the legislature, 'while replacing Spanish bricks by English, [had thereby] substituted the foundations on which alone the latter could rest'.[54] The issue was not put to rest until 1914, when the *Judicature (Amendment) Ordinance* set 1 March 1848 as the general date of reception of English law in Trinidad.[55] However, Spanish law continues to apply, through transitional provisions in the piecemeal legislation, to the construction of deeds made before 10 June 1844, the disposition of property made by wills made before the same date, the form of wills made before 13 January 1845, the institution of the heir in cases of birth before 12 March 1846, intestacy and succession before the same date, and the succession rights between mother and illegitimate child born before 12 March 1846.[56] These transitional provisions are basically spent, but they provide a theoretical after-life for some elements of Spanish law in Trinidad today.

Guyana resisted assimilation more successfully than Trinidad, and it was not until the early 20th century that English law was generally received into the colony. The 1828 Commission report for British Guiana recommended adoption of English criminal procedure and court structure, but was more supportive of retaining Roman-Dutch civil law than was its Trinidad counterpart of Spanish law, writing that 'the examinants in both Colonies [Essequibo-Demerara and Berbice] concurred in stating that the Civil Law

[53] Bourne, HC (1897) 'Real Property Law in Trinidad and Tobago' (2) *Journal of the Society of Comparative Legislation* 318.

[54] Id at 319 and 321-2.

[55] No 23 of 1914, s. 2 ('Subject to the provisions of any written law in operation on 1st March 1848, and to any written law passed after that date, the Common Law, Doctrines of Equity, and Statutes of general application of the Parliament of the United Kingdom that were in force in England on that date shall be deemed to have been enacted and to have been in force in Trinidad as from that date': see now Laws of Trinidad and Tobago, chapter 4:01, s.12. The 1st March 1848 is the date on which Ordinance No 4 of 1848 was adopted, which repealed Spanish law 'so far as the same relates to actions and rights of action and the forms of actions, and the form and mode of procedure in the same, and as to costs' (Reis supra n 15 at 31) and provided every person with 'the like relief in equity, or the like remedy by action at law, as he would be entitled to and have in the like cases in England' (Bourne supra n 53 at 321).

[56] Reis supra n 15 at 32; Lee 'Modes' supra n 47 at 294-295.

in force there, as contra-distinguished from the Criminal Law, is simple and well adapted to the wants and usages of the people.'[57] Although piecemeal changes were made to the civil law during the ensuing years, these did not seriously affect the underlying principles of Roman-Dutch law[58] until the pace of change rapidly accelerated following the move towards a more English form of government in 1891.[59] By the 1910s, 'The result of all this comprehensive legislation was to leave the Roman-Dutch law [...] a mere "husk", a "skeleton", a "shattered remnant"'.[60] A commission was therefore appointed in 1912 to consider the advisability of making changes to the common law of the colony 'and whether such changes, if any, should be made by the substitution of English law or otherwise'.[61] The Common Law Commission, as it came to be called, reported in 1914 and recommended a sweeping introduction of the English common law

> in regard to all mercantile matters, to all domestic relations (including marriage, judicial separation and divorce, the law of husband and wife, parent and child, guardian or curator and minors, and master and servant), to the law of delict or torts, agency, suretyship, liens, intestate succession, and in fact *to all the law of persons, things, obligations, inheritance, and every other description of matters whatsoever not dealt with by legislation, or otherwise expressly exempted.*[62]

[57] Lee supra n 18 at 13, quoting *Guiana Report* 1828 supra n 51 at 3. Although the author of the Report, Jabez Henry, was common-law trained, he was equally at home in Roman-Dutch law, having served as President (ie Chief Justice) of Essequibo-Demerara from 1813-1816 and authored a ten-volume translation (published in 1828) of van der Linden's *Institutes of the Laws of Holland* during the period he served on the Commission. See Graham, D (2001) 'Discovering Jabez Henry: Cross-border Insolvency Law in the 19th Century' (10) *International Insolvency Review* 153.

[58] The most extensive change was the wholesale introduction of English mercantile law in 1864: Ledlie supra n 47 at 214. See also eg the entries on 'British Guiana' in the annual 'Review of Legislation': for 1913, Crossley Rayner, T and 1914, Nunan, JJ (1916) 16 *Journal of the Society of Comparative Legislation* (New Series) 183; for 1915, Nunan (1917) 17 *Journal of the Society of Comparative Legislation* (New Series) 169; for 1916, Nunan (1918) 18 *Journal of Comparative Legislation and International Law* (New Series) 227; for 1917, Nunan (1919) 1 *Journal of Comparative Legislation and International Law* (Third Series) 159.

[59] See above the text following note 38.

[60] Ledlie supra n 47 at 215, quoting the 1914 *Report of the British Guiana Common Law Commission (Common Law Commission)*. Ledlie observes, echoing Bourne's analysis of the Trinidad situation (supra the text at note 54), that because the earlier changes were adopted 'not on any definite system, but rather piecemeal, as the exigencies of the time seemed to call for them, and without reference to the provisions of Roman-Dutch law which they superseded, the relation between the new (English) law thus imported and the existing (Roman-Dutch) law was often a matter of great difficulty to determine, and the resulting confusion and uncertainty was considerable': id.

[61] Id at 215, quoting instructions to the Common Law Commission.

[62] Id at 216, quoting *Common Law Commission* [emphasis added].

Only the law of immovables was spared, as the commissioners expressed 'no desire to introduce the complicated incidents of (English) real property law'.[63] A second commission, the Statute Law Commission, was then struck to consider how to give effect to the recommendations of the Common Law Commission.[64] Its 1916 report formed the basis of the *Civil Law of British Guiana Ordinance, 1916*,[65] which came into effect on 1 January 1917. The heart of the legislation is section 3, which provides in large and general terms for the abrogation of Roman-Dutch law[66] and the introduction of English common law,[67] although some aspects of Roman-Dutch property law are specifically preserved, notably the principle of absolute ownership of land[68] and the rules relating to conveyancing by judicial transport, mortgages and real servitudes.[69] In the result, therefore, the old law in Guyana gave way almost completely to the English common law in 1916. Only vestiges of Roman-Dutch law, notably relating to land,[70] remain.

Saint Lucia has been the most successful of the three countries in resisting the assimilation of its French civil law heritage, although it faced similar pressures to do so. Piecemeal substantive reform and anglicisation of the judicial system (replacement of the existing court structure by an English model, with English-trained judges and English rules of procedure in 1831; adoption of English as the language of the courts in 1842) took their toll there, as in the other two colonies. However, the adoption in 1876 of

[63] Id at 217, quoting *Common Law Commission*.

[64] Both of these Commissions were chaired by JJ Nunan, then Solicitor-General and later Attorney-General of the colony, who thus played a key role in the process. Ledlie describes the Common Law Commission report, in particular, as 'a document of considerable legal and historical interest': id at 216.

[65] No 15 of 1916. See now *Civil Law of Guyana Act*, Laws of Guyana, chapter 6:01.

[66] S 3(a): 'the law of the Colony relating to [a long list of general areas of law, including 'tacit and legal hypothecs or mortgages', 'movable or personal property', and 'immovable or real property and chattels real'] and the law of the Colony relating to all other matters whatsoever, whether *eiusdem generis* with the foregoing or not, shall cease to be Roman Dutch law, and as regards all matters arising and all rights acquired or accruing after the date hereof [ie 1 January 1917], the Roman-Dutch law shall cease to apply to the Colony'.

[67] S 3(b): 'the common law of the Colony shall be the common law of England as at the date aforesaid including therewith the doctrines of equity as then administered or at anytime hereafter administered by the courts of justice of England'.

[68] S 3(d)(i). This is also implicit in the introductory provision to s 3(d) assimilating real property to personal property.

[69] S 3(d)(ii): 'the law and practices relating to conventional mortgages or hypothecs of movable or immovable property, and to easements, profits *a prendre*, or real servitudes, and the right of opposition in the case of both transports and mortgages, shall be the law and practice in those matters now administered by the Supreme Court'.

[70] Some traces may still remain in matrimonial law. See Patchett, KW (1959) 'Some Aspects of Marriage and Divorce in the West Indies' (8) *International and Comparative Law Quarterly* 632 at 643-647, 351-352.

the Saint Lucia Civil Code, modelled on the Civil Code of Lower Canada (ie Quebec),[71] did much to curb the erosion of the civil law in the colony, although this was not its principle purpose at the time. Like its Quebec precursor, the Saint Lucia Civil Code was adopted as 'a technical reordering of a complex body of norms that was intended to make this private law more accessible in both its language and substance to legal professionals'.[72] But in Saint Lucia, unlike Quebec, the Civil Code has not taken on the larger role of defining its society, so that the country has been less vigilant in carving out a special place for itself and protecting its distinct civilian heritage in subsequent regional structures.[73] This helps explain why it agreed to revise its Civil Code in the 1950s so as to 'assimilate the Code to the Law of England where they differ, in the light of the present needs of the Colony'.[74] A main reason for this was the drive towards federation:

> It has long been recognized that it is necessary to bring up to date the whole body of the Civil law and align it with current thought and practice in the West Indies. In this connection the value of the French civil law as the basic law of the colony requires reassessing and it is probable that a larger infusion of English law is necessary if the law of St. Lucia is to be put on a more satisfactory footing. This is of particular importance having regard to the possibility of West Indian Federation.[75]

[71] Saint Lucia's Code is sometimes said to be based on the Napoleonic Code. However, this Code never applied in Saint Lucia as the island came under British control in 1803, a year prior to the adoption of the Napoleonic Code. The 1866 Civil Code of Lower Canada was itself a codification of French customary law. On the history of Code, see Liverpool supra n 22; see also Cenac, WF (nd) *Coutume de Paris to 1988: The Evolution of Land Law in St. Lucia* Voice Publishing. For additional information on the Canadian connection, see Matthews Glenn supra n 14.

[72] Brierley, JEC and McDonald, RA (eds) (1993) *Quebec Civil Law: An Introduction to Quebec Private Law* Emond-Montgomery at 25. As Sir Robert Torrens, then Governor of Barbados and the Windward Islands, put it in an address to the Saint Lucia Legislative Council in 1845: 'The Head of the Local Government, the Judge on the Bench, the Law Officer, the Barrister, the Special Magistrate and Justice of the Peace are each unprovided with [ie lack] an entire manual of the laws, which, in their various spheres, they are to administer and enforce, and which it is their duty to know: and her Majesty's subjects in St. Lucia have no means of general acquaintance with the laws under which they live save by hearsay, custom and such uncertain means': as quoted in Liverpool supra n 22 at 326-327, citing Colonial Office Document 321/22.

[73] Anthony, KD (1988) *The Mixed Legal System of Saint Lucia: Its Establishment and Decline* PhD thesis, University of Birmingham at 574.

[74] Laws of Saint Lucia (Reform and Revision) Ordinance, No 21 of 1954, s 4 (3).

[75] Saint Lucia, Legislative Council Meeting [undated], as quoted in Anthony, KD (1984) 'The Viability of the Civilist Tradition in St. Lucia: A Tentative Appraisal' in Landry and Caparros (eds) supra n 16, 33 at 58.

Reform of the Code thus began in 1954; the revised Code was adopted as the *Civil Code (Amendment) Ordinance* in 1956;[76] and it came into force on 30 June 1957. The main technique of reform was to retain the existing provisions of the Code but to engraft upon them, by open receptions clauses, large areas of the common law, particularly in regard to torts, contract, agency, trusts, guardianship and matrimonial offences.[77] This technique, which might be described as 'incorporation by interpretation' rather than 'repeal and replace', is illustrated by the provision relating to delict, which provides that

> the law of England for the time being relating to contracts, quasi-contracts and torts shall *mutatis mutandis* extend to this Colony, and provisions of [the relevant articles of the Code] shall be construed accordingly; and the said Articles shall cease to be construed in accordance with the law of Lower Canada or the 'Coutume de Paris'.[78]

The result is an intense intermingling of the common and civil law, and the Saint Lucian legal system is sometimes described as 'hybrid':[79] the phrase 'the delict of trespass'[80] does not ring too strangely to Saint Lucian ears. The 1956 revision reinforced the tendency, already strong in the common law-trained Bench and Bar, to have 'uninhibited recourse'[81] to English authorities in deciding cases; at the same time, however, Saint Lucian jurists continue to cite Quebec decisions of the Privy Council, and

[76] Ordinance No. 34 of 1956.

[77] Anthony, KD (1995) 'The Courts and the Interpretation of a Civil Code in a Mixed Legal System: Saint Lucia Revisited' (5) *Caribbean Law Review* 144 at 195. Other than the introduction of the trust, which would obviously have an effect, property law went largely untouched. As a leading Saint Lucia civilian observed, 'It would be lamentable if the complicated English law of real property were ever substituted for the simple system which we inherited from France through Quebec. The fundamental right called ownership and the owner's liberty to burden his radical title with emphyteuses, leases, servitudes, usufructs, hypothecs and other encumbrances are concepts intelligible to the simplest layman': Floissac, VF (1985) 'The Interpretation of the Civil Code of Saint Lucia' in Landry and Caparros (eds) supra n 16, 339 at 353.

[78] Art. 917A (1). However, subsection (3) provides, somewhat contradictorily, that 'Where a conflict exists between the law of England and an express provision of this Code or of any other statute, then the provisions of the Code or of such statute shall prevail'.

[79] White, D (1981) 'Some Problems of a Hybrid Legal System: A Case Study of St. Lucia' (30) *International and Comparative Law Quarterly* 862; Huxley, A (1984) 'How Hybrid is Saint Lucian Law?' in Landry and Caparros (eds) supra n 16, 371.

[80] *Ferry v Gifford and LeJeune* (unreported, 1968) as cited in Anthony supra n 77 at 208.

[81] Id at 146. See also Anthony, KD (1992) 'Which Estoppel in the Law of Saint Lucia?' (2) *Caribbean Law Review* 149 (discussing the courts' preference for the English law of estoppel, rather than the Quebec notion of *fin de non recevoir* and the relevant articles of the Code).

the Privy Council continues to apply the civil law in deciding cases from Saint Lucia.[82]

Saint Lucia now appears to be at a crossroads in protecting its civilian heritage. In 2000, the then government of Saint Lucia announced plans to revise the Code to have it reflect the 'values and beliefs underpinning the society', which have changed dramatically since 1879, particularly in the area of family law;[83] this societal emphasis was echoed in a statement by the then Minister for Justice in 2003: 'That is what the law and important laws like the Civil Code really are, they define our culture, define our social relations, defining who we are and how we relate to each other';[84] the project had the support of the then government of Canada, and is to draw upon Quebec's experience in reforming its Civil Code in 1994. On the other hand, the 2000 announcement identified as a key goal of the project 'to assist in developing a more positive legal framework for private sector development', a statement also echoed in 2003: 'We also want to reflect the interests and values of our business community, which is why the business sector is so well represented by way of committee membership in this project'. Foreign direct investment is important in Saint Lucia's tourist-driven economy, and most of the investors come from common law jurisdictions. And governments change, so the extent to which Civil Code revision remains a priority for the present governments of either Saint Lucia or Canada is no longer clear.

The three jurisdictions thus provide examples of traditional mixed jurisdictions, where the mixity is between different European legal systems, and their story of mixing and unmixing is a familiar one. What of non traditional mixity?

[82] See eg *Polinere et al v Felicien* [2000] 1 WLR 890 (JCPC) at 893 ('Their Lordships consider that anyone attempting to interpret the Civil Code must bear in mind that it is derived, in most cases word for word, from the Quebec Civil Code of 1865 [...]. In adopting the St. Lucia Civil Code, the legislature must in their Lordships' view have intended that its terms should be construed with due regard to what they had been understood to mean in Quebec and France. The jurisprudence which has been attached to the provisions of the Code by the courts and legal writers of those countries must at the very least have considerable persuasive authority. Their Lordships therefore consider that it was unwise for the judge and the Court of Appeal to have attempted to construe them without any reference to their civilian background').

[83] Government of Saint Lucia (2000) 'Throne Speech, 4th Session, 7th Parliament' at 15, available at <http://www.stlucia.gov.lc/addresses_and_speeches/governor_general/throne_speeches/ThroneSpeech2000.pdf>

[84] Government of Saint Lucia (2003) 'Civil Code Reform Project Committee Members Appointed', available at <http://www.stlucia.bov.lc/pr2003/civil_code_reform_project_committee_members_appointed.htm>.

REMIXING

Some have argued that the concept of mixed jurisdictions should not be restricted to its traditional form, but should be extended to encompass other forms of mixity. Three possibilities are mixity between European and aboriginal law, between secular and religious law and between formal and informal law, and these possibilities are illustrated by Guyana, Trinidad and Saint Lucia, respectively.

European and Aboriginal Law

The clearest example among the three colonies of possible mixity between European and aboriginal law is Guyana,[85] where Amerindians make up some 9% of the overall population and constitute the majority of people living in the country's vast interior. Amerindian rights were recognised in some measure by the Dutch prior to conquest, when their relationship reflected partnership more than power – a relationship captured in the notion of the 'middle ground':

> In this "Middle Ground", settlers and indigenous peoples met and "constructed a common, mutually comprehensible world", in which the institutions of the two groups accommodated each other, found new meaning and established a shared basis for interaction. The Middle Ground depended on the inability of both sides to gain their ends through force. The Middle Ground was created because both parties wanted to trade, neither had a monopoly on power, and they had to find mutually intelligible and acceptable means of dealing with each other.[86]

[85] There is no aboriginal population remaining in Saint Lucia and few, if any, in Trinidad. See Forte 'Writing' supra note 10 (suggesting that descendants of the original inhabitants remain in Trinidad). The information about Guyanese Amerindians is drawn from Colchester, M (1997) 'Guyana: Fragile Frontier' (38:4) *Race & Class* 33; Colchester, M; LaRose, J and James, K (2002) *Mining and Amerindians in Guyana* North-South Institute, available at <http://www.nsi-ins.ca/english/pdf/guyana/guyana_final_report.pdf>; James, T (2003) 'Indigenous Land Rights in Guyana: Past, Present and Future', available at <http://www.cpsu.org.uk/downloads/Land_Rights_Guyana.pdf>; Colchester, M and MacKay, F (2004) *In Search of Middle Ground: Indigenous Peoples, Collective Representation and the Right to Free, Prior and Informed Consent* Forest Peoples Programme, available at <http://www.forestpeoples.org/documents/law_hr/fpic_ips_text_only_aug04_eng.pdf>; Bartlett, T (2005) 'Amerindian Development in Guyana: Legal Documents as Background to Discourse Practice' (16) *Discourse & Society* 341; and Janki supra n 18.

[86] Colchester and MacKay supra n 85 at 3, quoting White, R (1991) *The Middle Ground: Indians, Empires and Republics in the Great Lakes Region, 1650-1815* Cambridge University Press at ix-x.

The British continued this recognition after conquest, although Amerindian rights were continually eroded by demands for their lands to support ranching, forestry and mining activities. The Amerindians are governed by the paternalistic *Amerindian Act*, first adopted in 1951 as a compilation of a number of laws adopted in the early 20th century and revised in 1976.[87] A new Act was adopted in 2006, but it is not supported by the Amerindians, who challenge its constitutionality.[88] The British had made recognition of Amerindian land rights a condition of independence in 1966; an Amerindian Lands Commission set up at that time recommended granting indigenous communities title to about a quarter of Guyana (half of what the communities had claimed). The on-going process of titling is slow, however, and its very existence casts doubt on the nature of their title: is it a recognition of pre-existing rights, or a grant of new rights?

In a leading Canadian article on the doctrine of reception, JE Côté describes how the doctrine as applied in the early colonies of the New World (ie the Americas and Australia) largely ignored aboriginal law: either the presence of indigenous peoples was disregarded and the colony classified as terra nullius and hence a colony of settlement where British law applied, or they were regarded as having no laws or perhaps laws and customs that were 'too unfamiliar, or too primitive, to justify compelling British subjects to obey them'.[89] However, these attitudes began to change with the spread of British colonisation in the more settled east and southeast Asia, and resulted in a recognition of personal laws, with Europeans being governed by English law and local inhabitants being governed (except for some areas of commercial practice) by their own religious and customary practices. 'This was an eminently practical solution, but it owes nothing to the old theory of settled and conquered colonies, and if anything is quite subversive of that theory'.[90]

Our attitudes to aboriginal law have changed considerably since the 1970s, and aboriginal rights are presently understood in terms that parallel the doctrine of reception. A Canadian authority on the doctrine of aboriginal rights, Brian Slattery, describes it as having two main sources, ancient custom and basic principles of justice, which operate in tandem. The 'principal source' is 'an ancient body of inter-societal custom that emerged from relations between British colonies and neighbouring Indian nations in eastern North America' as informed by 'the actual circumstances

87 Ordinance No 22 of 1951; Act No 6 of 1976; see now Laws of Guyana, chapter 29.01.

88 Act No 6 of 2006. See Rainforest Foundation (2006) *Annual Report* at 10, available at <http://www.rainforestfoundation.org/files/RF2006annualreport.pdf>.

89 Côté supra n 17 at 38.

90 Id at 39.

of life in America, the laws and practices of indigenous societies, imperial law and policy, and broad considerations of comity and justice'.[91] These customs eventually coalesced into a distinct branch of unwritten British colonial, or imperial, law.

> The doctrine of aboriginal rights developed at the same time as other basic doctrines of British imperial law and shared essentially the same juridical character. Just as imperial law governed such matters as the status of colonies and their lands, *the application of English law,* and the relative power of local assemblies and the Imperial Parliament, it also harboured rules concerning the status of indigenous peoples and their lands, the operation of their laws, and the relationship between aboriginal and colonial institutions.[92]

Slattery stresses that the doctrine of aboriginal rights, like other doctrines of imperial law, is a part of fundamental constitutional law and thus applied automatically to all new colonies, whether acquired by settlement or conquest. He continues:

> When the Crown gained suzerainty over a North American territory, the doctrine of aboriginal rights provided that the local customs of the indigenous peoples would presumptively continue in force, except insofar as they were unconscionable or incompatible with the Crown's suzerainty. *This provision resembles the imperial rule governing conquered or ceded colonies,* which holds that the local law of the colony remains in force, subject to similar exceptions. However, the doctrine of aboriginal rights has a broader application than the imperial rule regarding conquests and takes effect regardless [of] whether the territory was acquired by conquest, cession, settlement, annexation, tacit acquiescence, or some other method.[93]

[91] Slattery, B (2000) 'Making Sense of Aboriginal and Treaty Rights' (79) *Canadian Bar Review* 196 at 200. See also Slattery, B (1987) 'Understanding Aboriginal Rights' (66) *Canadian Bar Review* 727 (identifying a key issue as follows (at 735): 'Assuming that the Crown did, in some way, gain sovereignty over native Canadian peoples, how did this affect their legal position? What happened to their laws, property rights, and political institutions? Did these disappear overnight, to be replaced by a new set of rights and rules? Or did they survive the transition basically intact, or in some modified but recognizable form?').

[92] Slattery supra n 91 at 200 [emphasis added].

[93] Id at 201 [emphasis added].

As part of colonial or imperial law, the doctrine of aboriginal rights, and its principle of continuity would apply in Guyana in the same way that it applies in Canada.

Secular and Religious Law

A second example of possible non traditional mixity is between secular and religious law or, more precisely, between laws of general application and formal changes to them or in their application to accommodate the beliefs and customs of newcomers. This is illustrated by legislative changes in Trinidad[94] to accommodate indentured East Indian labourers and their descendents.

East Indians owe their presence in Trinidad, and elsewhere in the Caribbean, to the planters' need of a stable supply of manageable labour following the full emancipation of slaves in 1838.[95] This need was particularly acute in the larger, more sparsely settled colonies such as Trinidad, where the former slaves left the sugar estates in great number, mainly to squat on the available vacant land.[96] Attempts to encourage black immigration from elsewhere (nearby islands, the United States, Africa) were unsuccessful, and India became the solution of choice to the labour problem.[97] The British government authorised Indian immigration to Trinidad and other Caribbean colonies in 1844, and a steady stream of immigrants arrived in the colony from the first boatload in 1845 until the end of the programme in 1917.[98] Because the immigrants received free passage to Trinidad and, at the insistence of the Indian government, were entitled to free passage

[94] Similar changes occurred in colonial Guiana, as well as Jamaica: see generally Patchett supra n 70 at 653-665.

[95] Slavery was abolished throughout the British empire in 1834, but it was followed by a transitional four-year 'apprenticeship' period during which the former slaves had to continue working on the plantation.

[96] 'When, by an Act of the British Parliament, slavery was abolished in all British territories, the emancipated slaves left the sugar plantations in thousands, preferring to acquire their own plots and work the land for themselves. West Indian sugar planters were faced with severe labour shortage': Colonial Office of Information (1958) *The West Indies – A Nation in the Making* Reference Pamphlet No 30 at 49 as quoted in Patchett supra n 70 at 654. See also Matthews Glenn, J; Labossiere, RP and Wolfe, JM (1993) 'Squatter Regularisation: Problems and Prospects – A Case Study from Trinidad' (15) *Third World Planning Review* 249 at 251.

[97] See Ballinger, R (2006) 'Empire in the Present: Exploring the Indies through the Cultural Geography of the Commonwealth' (16) *Anthropological Forum* 277 (stressing the importance of 'colony-to-colony' relations).

[98] Brereton supra n 5 at 96-102; Brereton, B (1979) *Race Relations in Colonial Trinidad 1870 -1900* Cambridge University Press at 176. Application of the programme was suspended, for financial reasons, from 1848 to 1851. It ended in 1917 under pressure from the Indian government: Eldering, L (2005) 'The Bhojpuri Diaspora: A Rich Field for Comparative Acculturation Research' (17) *Psychology & Developing Societies* 237 at 243.

back to India, the programme was highly regulated to ensure that the Indians fulfilled their agricultural obligations. It was based on a system of indentures, backed by criminal sanctions, under which the immigrants contracted to work on the plantations for a period of tied labour (five years, later extended to ten) before being entitled to passage home.[99] In fact, a large majority of the immigrants did not return to India at the end of their period under indenture, and remained in Trinidad largely as agricultural labourers. In 1869 the Trinidad government opened up Crown land to small purchasers, and also began to grant labourers who had accomplished their indentureship 10 acres of land in lieu of return passage;[100] the commutation programme lasted until 1879, but it symbolised the extent to which the East Indian immigrants were not simply transient labourers. Many left the estates and became smallholding farmers either under the commutation programme or by purchasing land on their own.[101] They lived in their own villages which echoed the religious, social and governance structure of rural villages in India.

The Indian community has grown in size and social and political importance since 1917. They have not been assimilated but rather have 'retained their identity as an Indian community in which the Hindu and Muslim religions are paramount considerations'.[102] This explains why Trinidad, like Guyana and Jamaica, adopted legislation permitting marriage and divorce according to these religious rites. This was first provided for in the Immigration Ordinance, which permitted Indians brought in as indentured labour and their descendents to marry according to their religious law.[103] More general Trinidad legislation, encompassing East Indians who did not come within the scope of the immigration provisions, was adopted in 1936 for the smaller Muslim population and in 1946 for the Hindu majority.[104] The issue of marriage validity is important not only in

[99] For details of the system, see Brereton supra n 5 at 101-102.

[100] Id at 107.

[101] Over 90% of indentured labourers remained in Trinidad: Singh, S-A (2005) 'Hinduism and the State in Trinidad' (6) *Inter-Asia Cultural Studies* 353 at 353.

[102] Patchett supra n 70 at 654.

[103] The secondary sources do not indicated the original date of this ordinance, but it could have been in 1851 when immigration of indentured labour resumed after a brief hiatus and the office of Superintendent (later Protector) of Immigrants was created: Brereton supra n 5 at 102.

[104] *Muslim Marriage and Divorce Ordinance*, see now Laws of Trinidad and Tobago, chapter 45:02; *Hindu Marriage Ordinance*, see now chapter 45:03. Hindis made up some 88% of the Indian population brought in under the indenture system: Singh 'Hinduism' supra note 101 at 353. For details of the legislation see Patchett supra n 70 at 660-665. See also Brereton supra n 98 at 182; and Singh supra n 101 at 356-357 (also discussing recognition of Hindu cremation traditions). In 1999, the *Orisa Marriage Act*, No 22 of 1999 (see now chapter 45:04) was adopted to accommodate the increasing number of persons adhering to this traditional

regard to the status of husband and wife but also the legitimacy of their children and their maintenance and inheritance rights.

Mixity of secular and religious law is increasingly an issue, as states struggle to accommodate an increasingly multi-ethnic population in a globalising world. Canadian examples of formal mixity include legislative accommodation of religious courts[105] and judicial accommodation of religious practices.[106]

Formal and Informal Law

A third possible example of non traditional mixity is between formal law and informal law. One example is the concept of 'family land', which is present in many Caribbean jurisdictions, most notably Saint Lucia.[107]

Family land is land that is regarded by the family as belonging to successive generations of the family and not just to its present members. The concept developed after emancipation of the slaves and some explain it as an on-going echo of customary land tenure in West Africa, the ancestral homeland of most of the former slaves.[108] Under formal private law, the owners for the time being hold the land in indivision (a form of co-ownership roughly equivalent to the common law's tenancy in common),[109] and the law recognises extensive property rights to the present owners of the land acting together (a right to sell the property in its entirety) and to individual family members acting alone (a right to use the land in conjunction with other family members,[110] a right to sell one's own share in

---

African religion.

105 See eg Saris, A (2006) 'Les tribunaux religieux dans les contextes canadien et québécois' (40) *Revue Juridique Themis* 353.

106 See eg Landheer-Cieslak, C (2006) *La religion devant les juges français et québécois de droit civil* Bruylant/Yvon Blais; *Syndicat Northcrest v Amselem* [2004] 2 S.C.R. 551

107 Other Commonwealth examples include Guyana and Belize (in Central America). Family land is sometimes called 'heirs' land', 'children's land' or 'generation land'.

108 Yelvington, KA (2001) 'The Anthropology of Afro-Latin America and the Caribbean: Diasphoric Dimensions' (30) *Annual Review of Anthropology* 227. Others attribute it to restrictive land acquisition policies adopted by planter-controlled island governments after emancipation in an effort to tie the former slaves to the plantations; in response, extended families pooled their resources to be able to afford the land, and the land thus acquired was regarded as belonging to the family, both present and future: Barrow, C (1962) *Family Land and Development in St Lucia* University of the West Indies at 14-16. Still others explain it, at least in part, by the difference in inheritance patterns under French (shared succession) and English (single succession) law: id at 14-16; Vargas, A and Stanfield, D (2003) 'St Lucia Country Study of Land Administration and Management Issues' in Williams (ed) supra n 7, 281 at 283-284.

109 Cenac supra n 71 at 13-18.

110 In practice in Saint Lucia, some co-owners live on and farm the land; but those who do not do so nevertheless have a right to come back and farm if they wish, and this is readily

the land, a right to chose one's own heir by will, and a right to apply to end the co-ownership by partition). Informal law, on the other hand, frowns upon individual recourse to formal law for reasons that are contrary to the spirit and purpose of family land, and informally limits the formally recognised private law rights. Formal law thus applies one set of rules, which informal law overrides in order to keep the land in the family. The inalienability of family land became a concern in the neo-liberal 1980s, and a 1984 reform package provided that one or more family members could be registered on title as trustees having the authority to sell or mortgage the property on behalf of all family members.[111] However, little use has been made of this possibility, illustrating the strength of the informal law.[112]

The Saint Lucia example of family land is somewhat similar to the Trinidad example of indentured labour, in the sense that it accommodates other customs and beliefs; it differs, however, in that the accommodation occurs informally rather than through changes to the formal law.

Other examples of informal law are less historically conditioned, and can range from the informal property laws applying in squatter settlements[113] through, perhaps, even to rules governing everyday comportment.[114]

CONCLUSIONS

The three Commonwealth Caribbean jurisdictions of Guyana, Trinidad and Saint Lucia are thus examples of mixed jurisdictions in both their traditional and non traditional forms. In the three, traditional mixity between civil and common law resulted from British military successes in the imperial clashes of the 17th to 19th centuries. The Roman-Dutch, Spanish and French civilian heritages survived with mixed success in the three jurisdictions. All three were subjected to similar legal pressures to assimilate: substantive changes to large areas of the law; largely inaccessible civil law sources,

accepted in time of need. In this way, family land is a social and economic safety net. See eg Besson, J (1987) 'A Paradox in Caribbean Attitudes to Land' in Besson, J and Momsen, J (eds) *Land and Development in the Caribbean* Macmillan at 27-30.

111 Cenac n 71 at 88-93; see also Dujon, V (1997) 'Communal Property and Land Markets: Agricultural Development Policy in St Lucia' (25) *World Development* 1529.

112 Eg Barnes, G and Griffith-Charles, C (2007) 'Assessing the Informal Market and Deformalization of Property in St Lucia' (24) *Land Use Policy* 494.

113 See eg de Sousa Santos, B (1977) 'The Law of the Oppressed: The Construction and Reproduction of Legality in Pasargarda' (12) *Law and Society* 5; Edésio, F and Varley, A (eds) (1998) *Illegal Cities: Law and Urban Change in Developing Countries* Zed Books; and Matthews Glenn, J and Bélanger, V (2003) 'Informal Law in Informal Settlements' in Holder, J and Harrison, C (eds) *Law and Geography* (Current Legal Issues Volume 5) Oxford University Press 281.

114 Eg Reisman, M (1985-1986) 'Lining Up: The Microlegal System of Queues' (54) *University of Cincinnati Law Review* 417.

written in languages which few were able to read; adoption of English as the language of the laws, the government, and the courts; administration of justice following common law procedures by common-law trained lawyers and judges who were by-and-large unfamiliar with and unsympathetic to the civil law traditions they were administering; and so on. But the extent to which each of the three colonies succumbed to assimilation pressures is probably due more to extra-legal factors than to legal ones.

The chances of survival of a minority legal tradition are much stronger where there is a degree of affinity between the population and its legal system, where the majority of the population regards it as part of their heritage and a reflection of their own identity. It is admittedly difficult, even artificial, to look for widespread affinity in the population of the three colonies to any legal system, as the vast majority were slaves, indentured labourers or otherwise disenfranchised.[115] The choice of legal system was largely a matter for the elite. That said, the concordance was strongest in Saint Lucia, which was an established, settled colony at the time of the conquest. The colony had been French for some 150 years prior to conquest; the population remained relatively stable after conquest, without a sudden influx of new English planters and merchants, new slaves or indentured labourers. The population remains largely Roman Catholic, and the French language (creole) has not only survived but is increasingly treated with pride.[116] This bodes well for a continued survival of the French legal system on the island. The concordance between population and legal system was weakest in Trinidad, where Spanish settlement never really caught hold and the population was largely French even prior conquest. Moreover, both Trinidad and Guyana were the 'wild west' of the Caribbean, with much vacant land available for newcomers.[117] The composition of the elite of two colonies thus changed rapidly, becoming more English, and this happened more quickly in Trinidad than in Guyana. By the end of the 19th century,

[115] Early statistics show that around the time of the emancipation of the slaves in the 1830s, inhabitants of European origin constituted around 3% of the population in Guyana, 8% in Trinidad and 12% in Saint Lucia: Dupont supra n 11 at 208 and 295; 'Saint Lucia' *Encyclopaedia Britannica*, available at <http://www.search.eb.com/>.

[116] See eg Lieberman, D (1975) 'Language Attitudes in St Lucia' (6) *Journal of Cross-Cultural Psychology* 471; and Frank, DB (1993) 'Political, Religious and Economic Factors Affecting Languages Choice in St Lucia' (102) *International Journal of the Sociology of Language* 39; Nwenmely, H (1999) 'Language Policy and Planning in St Lucia: Stagnation or Change?' (13) *Language and Education* 269. The 2000 Throne Speech, by the Governor General at the opening of the legislative session of the Saint Lucia Parliament, was delivered partly in Creole: see supra n 83.

[117] Abolition of the slave trade in 1809 thus created difficulties for the two colonies, Trinidad in particular; and in 1812 a registration system for slaves was put in place – not without difficulty – to control the smuggling of slaves: see John supra n 20.

there were few or no descendents of the original continental Spanish settlers in Trinidad, and only about 1% of the population of Guyana was Dutch.[118] It is not surprising, therefore, that assimilation in Trinidad was virtually complete by the mid 19th century, and took about 60 years more in Guyana to be almost complete.

As for possible forms of non traditional mixed jurisdictions suggested by the three jurisdictions, mixity between European and aboriginal law, as with the Guyana example, seems closest to traditional mixity. Both ask the same questions about on-going application of pre-existing law, and both invoke similar principles of continuity in response. The two principles differ, however, in that the aboriginal principle of continuity envisages aboriginal rights applying only to the original inhabitants, with the newcomers being subject to their own laws,[119] whereas in traditional mixed jurisdictions, continuity results in an on-going generalised application of the old law, until changed, to newcomers and old residents alike. However, both principles were developed at about the same time and form part of the same imperial constitutional law. Extending the notion of mixed jurisdictions to include aboriginal law would share the logic of historical layering that is inherent in most traditional examples of mixed jurisdictions.

The other two examples – formal mixity between secular and religious law, as in Trinidad, and informal mixity between formal and informal law, as in Saint Lucia – are both possible extensions of the notion of mixed jurisdictions, although these are less compelling than the previous example. Formal mixity between secular and religious law does not always have the same historical dimension as traditional mixity, not does it result in a generalised layering of laws but rather in the creation of pockets, or enclaves, of personal law; nevertheless, the formality of the mixing helps ensure a certain 'crispness' in the analysis of the relationship between the two sets of laws, similar to that applying to traditional mixity. Mixity between formal and informal law is the furthest removed from traditional mixed jurisdictions. It raises interesting questions, and there is mixing. But to include it within the notion of 'mixed jurisdictions' runs the risk of extending the notion beyond recognition.

118 Dupont supra n 11 at 210.

119 The extent to which aboriginal law can have a territorial as well as a personal dimension is still being worked out in Canada. See eg Matthews Glenn, J (1999) 'Aboriginal Rights and Sustainable Development in Canada' (48) *International and Comparative Law Quarterly* 176.

The Law of the Navajo Nation: A Three-Ingredient Mix of Consensual (Indigenous) and Adversary (Common Law) Systems

DALE BECK FURNISH

INTRODUCTION

> *The Navajo Nation has a mixed judicial system. That is, the Navajo Nation courts follow general American models of practice, procedure and substantive rules while retaining traditional Navajo substantive law and procedure.*~ Reservation Business Services v. Albert, 7 Navajo Rptr. 123, 126 (Navajo 1995)(Yazzie, C.J)

The Navajo Nation, or *Diné*,[1] has contrived to combine in a single legal

[1] No one should be fooled into thinking that I am an Indian Law scholar, nor that I have pretensions in that direction. Nonetheless, there is a certain fascination. As a boy, I read everything that I could get my hands on by James Willard Schultz and, later, by Ross Santee. Today, I read everything that Tony Hillerman writes. I live in a state where Indians and Indian Law constantly make their presence felt, and for parts of four decades, have taught at the law school with one of the most active Indian Law programmes in the United States, where Indian law students are a significant part of the student body. I long ago incorporated a section in my Creditor-Debtor teaching materials on the impact of Indian Country on that area of the law. See Furnish, DB (2003) *Creditor/Debtor Relations: Cases & Materials* Sandra Day O'Connor College of Law, 14th ed. 354-416.

For the current effort, I have relied on true Indian scholars, specifically on the published scholarship of, among others, colleagues like Judge William C. Canby, Jr., Robert N. Clinton, Rebecca Tsosie and Kevin Gover, to a degree that will be obvious to anyone who knows their work. What may be less obvious is the debt that I owe to two research assistants, Deborah Ann Begay and Cherie Espinosa, both members of the Navajo Nation and 2007 graduates of

system a working mixture of indigenous consensual, or horizontal, and Common Law adversary, or vertical, legal systems. The Navajo Nation's mixed jurisdiction – ultimately answerable to traditional, pre-Columbian Navajo law – incorporates two other legal systems that define its limits and affect its tribal members: federal Indian Law and American Law.

Federal Indian Law consists of case decisions by the Supreme Court of the United States, legislation by the Congress and administrative actions by the Executive Branch. The federal Indian Law of the United States creates a top-down regime, a framework on which tribal law depends. It enables and defines tribal systems, while reserving plenary authority to supplant them. If Congress had so chosen, it might have completed the framework with a full structure, imposing on Indians an entire normative system and courts to apply it. In purest doctrine, it still has the power to do so. In practice and in fact, Congress has left much of tribal government and laws to tribal self-determination. At the beginning of the 21st century, that approach seems permanently stitched into the fabric of the United States federal system.

Federal Indian Law has not, however, gone out of its way to support the Navajo Nation's – or any other tribe's – emergence as an independent legal system. The Navajo Nation has achieved success in forging an autocthonous legal system not because it always was encouraged to do so by the federal government, but because it has remained committed to its tribal identity and has been astute in exploiting the opportunities presented by federal Indian Law.

The second extraneous legal system that forms a part of the Navajo Nation's mixed jurisdiction is American Law, the general legal structure of procedural rules and substantive laws that have developed within the United States. The federal system divides the nation into 50 states, the District of Columbia, and various territories, all (with the exceptions of Louisiana and Puerto Rico, an island whose exact legal status remains

---

the Sandra Day O'Connor College of Law at Arizona State University. Their sure sense of their traditions and their Navajo inheritance, combined with their increasing knowledge of the law, have guided me to many revelations and insights.

My purpose here is to organise existing scholarship from a new perspective, perhaps most accurately characterised as viewing Navajo Law through a comparative lawyer's eyes, after long contacts in Latin America and a commitment to the possibilities of working economic and social change through the reform of commercial laws and free trade agreements. Commercial law reform often creates mixed jurisdictions, and free trade agreements raise intriguing questions of sovereignty.

The Navajo people's term for itself, *Diné*, means simply 'the people'. *Diné* does not mean the Navajo government, any more than 'the public' means 'the government'. Further, while the Navajo people constitute a tribe, they officially call themselves the 'Navajo Nation,' a term used in the Treaty of Fort Sumner in 1868.

an enigma) of which share a common legal heritage. The hallmark of the system — the basis for the term 'American Law'— is its homogeneity, consummated in the first half of the 20th century[2] by such events as the advent of the American Law Institute and its Restatements of American Law;[3] the decision in *Erie v. Tompkins*, abolishing 'federal general common law' in favour of that of the states;[4] and the adoption of uniform rules of procedure and evidence in federal and state courts.[5] Today, United States jurists routinely approach a legal topic by analysing case law and statutes from all states as if they were one body of law, and a series of authoritative Restatements drafted by the American Law Institute which sets out the 'American Law' of Contracts, Property, Torts, Trusts, Conflicts and most other major fields of the law.

The Navajo Nation has assimilated American Law into its court procedures and into its substantive laws. An American lawyer attending a hearing in a Navajo trial or appellate court will feel at home, gratified to observe the application of familiar rules of procedure and evidence in pursuit of familiar substantive issues defined by familiar statutes and doctrines, giving rise to a system of reported case law, all in English. The Navajo judicial style resembles the American standard; indeed, most of the Navajo judiciary and bar graduated from American law schools. American Law provides the Navajo Nation a structural paradigm for its mixed jurisdiction, then.

Just as an 'American' lawyer begins to feel comfortable in the Navajo legal system, however, s/he runs into a series of distinguishing characteristics that make it seem quite foreign. The Navajo Nation does not have a constitution,[6] and it is not subject to the United States Constitution.

[2] See Friedman, L (2005) *History of American Law* (3rd ed.); (2002) *American Law in the 20th Century*

[3] See Reese, WLM (1970) 'Unification of Common Law Rules: the Role of the American Law Institute' in Hazard, J & Wagner, W (eds) *Legal Thought in the United States of America Under Contemporary Pressures* Emile Bruyland 171.

[4] 304 U.S. 64, 78 (1938).

[5] Originally under authority of an Act of Congress of June 19, 1934, Pub. L. No. 73-651, 48 Stat. 1064 (1934), today codified after extensive amendments at 28 U.S.C. §§ 2072-2075. See Clark, CE & Moore, JW (1935) 'A New Federal Civil Procedure' (44) *Yale L J.* 387.

[6] On three different occasions, the Navajo Nation rejected proposed constitutions, in 1937, in 1953 and in 1968. See Wilkins, DE (1987), *Diné Bibeehaz'aanii: A Handbook of Navajo Government* Navajo Community College Press at 51-52, 58-59. Despite the past efforts to create a constitution, it appears that the *Diné* have grown comfortable with a form of government in which 'since [its] powers are *not defined*, they are also *not limited*.' Id. at 57.
The Navajo Nation Code [hereinafter NNC] does include, as Chapter 1 of its first Title, a Navajo Nation Bill of Rights which tracks — but does not duplicate exactly — that of the first ten amendments to the U.S. Constitution. See NNC tit. 1, §§1-9 (2005). These provisions complied with the Indian Civil Rights Act (ICRA), Pub. L. No. 90-284, §§ 201-202, 82 Stat. 73, 77-78 (1968), which provided 'constitutional rights' (consisting of most of the U.S.

Most notably, however, pre-Columbian principles provide the system with its Fundamental Law, the source of its most basic, overriding rules and attitudes.[7] This special characteristic of Navajo justice means that the resolution of a given case or controversy may be different in a Navajo court than in a state court, or at least turn on the application of uniquely Navajo concepts and doctrines. The Navajo system — however much it may resemble the state systems around it — is distinctly its own system.

Navajo law sits on a deeper source than American Law. The Navajo Nation adds to that paradigm its own component of Navajo traditional sources, or Navajo Common Law, ultimately affecting both procedural and substantive law in ways quite surprising to any lawyer steeped in American Law method. Pre-Columbian principles of Navajo Law have not disappeared. They form the vital, preemptive foundation of Navajo law today; the bottom-up source of its legal system.

The combination of all three elements — federal Indian Law, American Law and Navajo traditional law — in a single system under the aegis of the Navajo Nation makes a fascinating success story. Navajo law functions as an effective, vital interface between cultures that manifest quite different attitudes, activities and organisations at the most fundamental level of their legal culture. The U.S. legal system today is characterised by its concern for the rights of the individual and its vindication of diversity at the expense of collective rights and responsibility to the community. Under American Law's constitutional form, the individual makes a social contract with society: to exist within it, in exchange for society's guaranty that s/he shall enjoy a high degree of autonomy from the state and any societal consensus regarding one's own beliefs, attitudes and life style.[8]

In fact, the American approach — which Europe, or at least parts of it, may join — stands as iconoclastic when viewed against the broader humanity and the sweep of history. In most of the world, an individual's personal

---

Constitution's Bill of Rights guaranties) that no Indian tribe might abrogate in its exercise of self government.. See ICRA, 25 U.S.C. § 1302(1)-(6), (8)-(10) (2001).

[7] See Austin, RD (2009) Navajo Courts and Navajo Common Law: A Tradition of Tribal Self-Governance University of Minnesota Press. While this recent book, by a sixteen-year former Justice of the Navajo Supreme Court (1985-2001), offers the most comprehensive and thoughtful treatment of Navajo Fundamental Law, other helpful sources include Navajo Nation Council (2002) Navajo Common Law Project available at http://www.navajocourts.org/NCLP/commlawproj.pdf; and Heeter, C (2009) Navajo Common Law, a collection of all references to Navajo Common Law by the Navajo Supreme Court, available from the author at curtisheeter@navajo.org.

[8] This insight is not new. See, e.g. Glendon, MA (1991) *Rights Talk: The Impoverishment of Political Discourse* Free Press at 11-17; Tsosie, R (1994) 'Separate Sovereigns, Civil Rights and the Sacred Text: The Legacy of Justice Thurgood Marshall's Indian Law Jurisprudence' (26) *Ariz. St. L.J.* 495 at 531-32.

identity depends on clan, kinship, family and religion. That individual's rights and responsibilities derive from, are defined by and exist only within that communal or social framework, not separate from it or counter to it. Ironically, the American legal culture, dedicated to tolerance and diversity, often has trouble finding points of reference within its system by which to apply societal and/or communal approaches to issues. The Navajo Nation and its laws have far less difficulty dealing with the group, or consensus, views. Within the Navajo context, any treatment of individual claims includes tribal concerns from the outset, with deference to the latter.[9]

The Navajo Nation and its legal system tend to perceive individual interests where the American legal culture perceives individual rights. The individual's interests then exist within and as defined by group interests.[10] Navajo law assumes as part of its fundamental task the necessity to mediate between the individual and the tribe in ways that maintain harmony within the group, vindicating valid individual interests by resolving them within group consensus. One set of interests (individual) cannot exist without the other (communal). Thus communal interests provide the well-spring for those of the individual, who cannot stray too far from his or her obligations to the community in conduct and attitude. Tension exists between the individual and the community, but it is the law's task to reconcile the individual's interests and concerns to those of the community, and vice versa, so as to maintain harmony between them.

Summary

The Navajo Nation and its mixed jurisdiction provide a well-developed legal system, serving a vibrant community with a significant land base[11]

[9] This is not to say that there is no friction between generations or that the blandishments of the modern world have made no inroads in the Navajo Nation. As in most societies today, the Navajo Nation has experienced a generational shift toward more overt assertion of individual rights and movement away from traditional life styles. In 1968, the Indian Civil Rights Act (ICRA), Pub. L. No. 90-284, §§ 201-202, 82 Stat. 73, 77-78 (1968), imposed most of the constitutional Bill of Rights guaranties, with concomitant emphasis on individual rights, into Navajo law. See ICRA, 25 U.S.C. § 1302(1)-(6), (8)-(10) (2001). The advent of ICRA and the rights discussions that it engenders, among other factors, have influenced this shift. The shift may manifest itself in younger Navajo members who prefer not to use tribal courts, with their Navajo language, traditional attitudes and law sources, nor to live on the Reservation.

[10] See supra n 6.

[11] The *Diné* number about 300,000 in tribal membership, the better part of which occupies a reservation roughly the size of Ireland, comprising about 70,000 square kilometres of land upon which they have lived since before Columbus. The Navajo Nation's reservation sits on its traditional lands in northeastern Arizona, northwestern New Mexico and southeastern Utah, within the area bounded by the *Diné*'s original Four Sacred Mountains. For a time — from 1863 to 1868 — the Navajos were forcefully removed, on the 'Long Walk', east to lands

and a sophisticated system of tradition and belief. The Navajo Nation has never lost its sense of itself. It can and does assert a world view different from that held by the larger society with which it shares geography and the United States' federal system, and it affirms that world view at the most fundamental level of its legal culture.[12]

The *Diné*'s legal system is not a prototype, although other tribes might well consider it worthy of imitation. There is no archetypical tribal system. There may well be other tribes possessing similar elements in their legal systems. There may well be other tribes whose legal systems deserve analysis. We focus on the Navajo Nation, because it lends itself especially well to setting out the essential elements of an unlikely mixed jurisdiction that blends indigenous, consensual traditions with Common Law, adversary traditions in a successful, functioning, developing legal system.

THE FIRST INGREDIENT: FEDERAL LAW

> *[Tribes] may, more correctly, perhaps, be denominated domestic dependent nations. They occupy a territory to which [the United States] assert[s] a title independent of their will, which must take effect in point of possession, when their right of possession ceases. Meanwhile, they are in a state of pupilage; their relationship to the United States resembles that of a ward to his guardian. ~ Cherokee Nation v. Georgia,* 30 U.S. (5 Pet) 1, 17 (1831) (Marshall, C.J.).

> *Congress (rather than some other part of the government) can regulate virtually every aspect of the tribes without rendering tribal sovereignty a nullity. ~ United States v. Lara,* 541 U.S. 193, 214 (2003)(Thomas, J., concurring).

Once upon a time, during and after its successful revolution against England, the new American nation considered Indian tribes to be sovereign nations. Tribal laws and legal systems were their own devices, setting internal policies and external relationships with other nations, including

---

near the Pecos River in Texas, at Bosque Redondo. They suffered greatly during that time. They were restored to their traditional lands by the Treaty they negotiated with General William T. Sherman at Fort Sumner on June 1, 1868, and have remained there since.

12 See Yazzie, Hon. R (1994) '"Life Comes From It": Navajo Justice Concepts' (24) *N.M.L.Rev.* 75 at 187 (Judge Yazzie's article is also found in Nielsen, MO and Zion JW (eds.) (2005) *Navajo Nation Peacemaking* University of Arizona Press, 2 at 50); Tso, Hon. T (1992) 'Moral Principles, Traditions and Fairness in the Navajo Nation Code of Judicial Conduct' (76) *Judicature* 15; Tso, Hon. T (1986) 'The Tribal Court Survives in America' (Spring) *Judges' J* 22.

the United States.[13] That policy broke down rapidly in the face of demand for Indian lands by European immigrants, and the attendant military domination of the Indian tribes by the United States. It fell to the new nation's Supreme Court to articulate the status of the tribes in the federal system.

The Court has fulfilled its charge. Despite shortcomings in common sense, logic and orderly development, and resulting tensions, the Indian Law[14] of the United States at the beginning of the 21st century seems reasonably settled. Early on, the Supreme Court defined the Indian tribes as 'domestic dependent sovereigns' to whom the federal government owed fiduciary duties.[15] While it decisively insulated the tribes from action by states,[16] the Court invested Congress with plenary power to legislate regarding Indians.[17] The threat of such untrammelled legislative power may not prove comforting to Indian tribes, but in fact and in practice – after two centuries of misadventure and tragic consequences – federal Indian policy has stabilised in a way that allows a tribe like the Navajo Nation a large degree of self-determination.

The federal powers of oversight and the trust responsibility did not spring up as settled doctrine with the advent of the new Constitution of the United States in 1787. No plain-meaning legal source exists for their exercise. They have developed over time, by accretive process. The riparian analogy is especially apt, for both the judicial development of Indian Law doctrine and Congress' Indian policies ebb and flow, and have been highly fluid concepts. Federal Indian policy has fluctuated over the last two centuries,

[13] See U.S. Const. art. I, § 8, granting Congress the power to regulate commerce 'with foreign Nations, and among the several States, and with the Indian tribes'; Id art. 2, § 2, cl. 2., granting the President the power to make treaties with the advice and consent of the Senate, a power exercised to make treaties with Indian tribes.

[14] See Hon. William C. Canby, Jr. (2004) *American Indian Law* (4th edn) Thomson-West. Judge Canby notes that,

> The term 'Indian Law' is a catchall with various meanings, but it refers primarily to that body of law dealing with the status of the Indian tribes and their special relationship to the federal government, with all the attendant consequences for the tribes and their members, the states and their citizens, and the federal government. In this application, 'Indian Law' might better be termed 'Federal Law About Indians.' [...] Although [the term] legitimately might be thought to include the internal law that each tribe applies to its own affairs and members, that is not the common definition. [...] Instead, that body of law is separately referred to as 'tribal law.' Id at 1, 3.

[15] *Cherokee Nation v. Georgia*, 30 U. S. (5 Pet.) 1, 17 (1831).

[16] *Worcester v. Georgia*, 31 U.S. (6 Pet.) 515, 561 (1832).

[17] *United States v. Kagama*, 118 U.S. 375 (1886). See also, *Lone Wolf v. Hitchcock*, 187 U.S. 553 (1903), which held that Congress had the power to overturn existing treaties with Indian tribes, in pursuit of its legislative will.

carving one course and then shifting — sometimes wildly — to another, until it seems to have settled into a more stable streambed. Nonetheless, the proper federal attitude and practice toward Indians still seek a clearly-articulated doctrinal base.

Criminal law is a special case. Congress has never been shy about expanding the jurisdiction of federal courts over criminal matters involving Indians, in or out of Indian Country. An 1817 law,[18] since become the General Crimes Act and much expanded in its effects,[19] and the 1885 Major Crimes Act, expanded from its original seven to include thirteen felonies,[20] still apply. In 1825, Congress passed a forerunner of what today is known as the Assimilative Crimes Act, making any act within United States territory (clearly including Indian Country[21]) 'a like offense and subject to a like punishment' in federal court whenever the act is defined as a crime by the laws of the State within which the territory is located.[22] Finally, Indian Law drastically limits tribal courts in the criminal sentences they may impose,[23] effectively restricting them to no more than misdemeanor jurisdiction. Although these limitations still leave a substantial number of criminal misdemeanor cases on the Navajo Nation courts' calendar, running into tens of thousands of cases a year,[24] the United States Supreme Court curtailed even the tribes' misdemeanor jurisdiction in 1978, when

[18] Pub. L. No. 14-92, 3 Stat. 383 9 (1846). See 18 U.S.C. §§ 1151-1170 (2000), for the current codification, in particular § 1152. If this seems quite natural today, consider how incongruent it would be for the United States Congress to attempt to vest criminal jurisdiction in the federal courts over Mexicans or Canadians who committed any crime *in Mexico or Canada* against U.S. citizens. The Congress may have tried to do so more recently, in contemplation of terrorist activity against U.S. citizens abroad. See, e.g., 18 U.S.C. §§ 7(7), 32(b), 111, 115, 1114, 1117, 1201, 1203, 2331(2000). The major difference between the modern legislation and the 1817 legislation is the immediate ability of the federal government to assert the jurisdiction, and the will and ability of the foreign jurisdiction to resist.

The 1817 law further permitted prosecution in federal court of all crimes committed by non-Indians in Indian territory.

[19] See 18 U.S.C. § 1152 (2000).

[20] See 18 U.S.C. § 1153(a) (2000).

[21] Because under 18 U.S.C. § 1152 (2000), 'the general laws of the United States as to the punishment of offences committed in any place within the sole and exclusive jurisdiction of the United States [...] shall extend to Indian Country.' The provisions of 18 U.S.C. § 13 (2000) are just such a general law of the United States.

[22] 18 U.S.C. § 13 (2000).

[23] 25 U.S.C. § 1302(7) (2000) (limiting the maximum sentences that a tribal court may impose to a $5,000 fine and one year in prison).

[24] For example, in fiscal 1998 the Navajo courts handled well over 27,000 criminal misdemeanor cases. *Means v. District Court of Chinle*, 7 Navajo Rptr. 382, 386 (1999). The Navajo Nation publishes its Supreme Court and select other opinions in the Navajo Reporter. This Reporter appears sporadically, most recently in 2009 with Volume 8, including opinions for the years 2000 to 2005. Navajo tribal court opinions — including more recent opinions — also appear online at www.versuslaw.com (by year and Navajo courts, e.g., at 2006. NANN.0000002) and also at www.navajocourts.org/suctopinions

it decided that no tribal court may exercise criminal jurisdiction over a nonmember.[25] Thus, perhaps the only sort of criminal act that might totally escape federal jurisdiction is a misdemeanor found only in a tribal code committed by an Indian against an Indian. When one adds up the cumulative effect of the federal statutes and case law, they provide absolute federal criminal jurisdiction over felonies in Indian Country, and the tribal courts' limited criminal misdemeanor jurisdiction shall never extend to any non-Indian.[26] Perhaps the only sort of criminal act that might totally escape federal jurisdiction is a misdemeanor found only in a tribal code committed by an Indian against an Indian, subject to limited sanctions.

Apart from criminal law, much of the federal law component does not intrude so much on the substance of tribal laws as it creates rules of oversight by the federal government, most of it in areas where the federal government exercises similar oversight of the states as well. It is classic federal public law, dealing with the general categories of land and other resource use;[27] health, education and welfare;[28] and some special concerns.[29] Congress, then, has generally focused its legislative energies on implementing federal Indian policy, protecting Indian resources, defining relations between Indians and non-Indians, and addressing special Indian interests that have arisen over the course of United States history.

In still one other area of federal legislation, Indian Law also adds a singular dimension: those rules that set out the terms and practices for relations between the federal and Indian governments,[30] and the rules that

[25] *Oliphant v. Suquamish Indian Tribe,* 435 U.S. 191 (1978).

[26] 18 U.S.C. § 1152, ¶ 2 (2000). See Canby supra n 14 at 153-170.

[27] See 25 U.S.C. §§ 311 to 416j (2001), comprising Chapters 8 (Rights-of-Way Through Indian Land), 9 (Allotment of Indian Lands), 10 (Descent and Distribution; Heirs of Allottee), 11 (Irrigation of Allotted Lands), 12 (Lease, Sale or Surrender of Allotted or Unallotted Lands); 25 U.S.C. §§461 to 494 (2001) (Subchapter V — Protection of Indians and Conservation of Resources); 25 U.S.C. §§ 2101 to 2221 (2001), comprising Chapters 23 (Development of Tribal Mineral Resources) and 24 (Indian Land Consolidation); 25 U.S.C. §§ 3101 to 3120 (2001) (Chapter 33 — National Indian Forest Resources Management); and U.S.C. §§ 3701 to 3746 (2001) Chapter 39 (American Indian Agricultural Resource Management).

[28] See 25 U.S.C. §§174 to 202 (2001), Chapter 5 (Protection of Indians); 25 U.S.C. §§ 305 to 310 (2001), Chapter 7A (Promotion of Social and Economic Welfare); 25 U.S.C. §§ 450 to 458bbb-2 (2001), Subchapter II on Indian Self-Determination and Education Assistance (contract and grants funding and administration); 25 U.S.C. §§ 501 to 510 (2001), Subchapter VIII (Indians in Oklahoma; Promotion of Welfare); 25 U.S.C. §§ 1641 to 1683 (2001), Chapter 18 (Indian Health Care); 25 U.S.C. §§ 1901 to 1963 (2001), Chapter 21 (Indian Child Welfare).

[29] For example, Congress has passed special laws to protect Native American grave sites, 25 U.S.C. §§ 3001 to 3013 (2001); to control the custody and adoption of Indian children, reserving that jurisdiction to the child's tribe, 25 U.S.C. §§ 1911 to 1923 (2001); to regulate Indian gaming, as casinos have proliferated in Indian Country, 25 U.S.C. §§ 2701 to 2721 (2001); and to guaranty the operation of the Bill of Rights in Indian Country, 25 U.S.C. §§ 1301-1303 (2001).

[30] See 25 U.S.C. §§ 1 to 88 (2001), Chapters 1 (Bureau of Indian Affairs) and 3 (Agreements

may limit Indians' exercise of self-determination.[31] One should note that Indian tribes operate free of the constraints of the United States Constitution and its enumerated powers for governmental exercise, so that to the extent that Congress provides some restraints, it may fill in the constitutional void.

With exceptions created by the vestiges of unfortunate past,[32] since about 1970 Congress has chosen to fulfil its fiduciary relationship[33] to the tribes by providing for their greater autonomy and self-determination. While the exceptions may chafe sorely on the Navajo Nation and other tribes, federal Indian Law does provide a stable, top-down framework for tribal government, and the Navajo Nation has prospered within that framework.

In 1968, Congress passed the Indian Civil Rights Act (ICRA),[34] applying to the tribes most of the United States Constitution's fundamental guarantees,[35]known as the Bill of Rights.[36] In this respect, the ICRA was a back-handed prop to tribal sovereignty, since it assumed the continued existence of the tribes and their laws.[37] The real benchmark occurred on

---

with Indians); 25 U.S.C. §§ 211 to 264 (2001), Chapter 6 (Government of Indian Country and Reservations); 25 U.S.C. §§ 450 to 458bbb-2 (2001), Subchapter II (Indian Self-Determination and Education Assistance); 25 U.S.C. §§ 4001 to 4046 (2001), Chapter 42 (American Indian Trust Fund Manageme nt Reform).

[31] These provisions come from parts of Title 25 on Indians of the United States Code already cited for other effects, but are interspersed therein. See 25 U.S.C. §§ 211 to 264 (2001), Chapter 6 (Government of Indian Country and Reservations); 25 U.S.C. §§ 1301 to 1341 (2001), Chapter 15 (Constitutional Rights of Indians);

[32] Principally, in the area of criminal law for Indians, which seems irretrievably federal. There are other major areas, however.

[33] One aspect of the trust relationship is the principle that interpretations of treaties and statutes (after they wholly replaced treaties for all transactions after 1871) begin from the premise that ambiguities should be resolved in favour of Indians. See, e.g., *County of Oneida v. Oneida Indian Nation of New York*, 470 U.S. 226, 247 (1985); *Choctaw Nation v. Oklahoma*, 379 U.S. 620, 631 (1970); *Winters v. United States*, 207 U.S. 564, 576-7 (1908); *United States v. Winans*, 98 U.S. 371, 380 (1905).

An important application of this approach states that with regard to disposition of lands, treaties do not constitute 'a grant of rights to the Indians, but a grant of rights from them — a reservation of those not granted.' *Washington v. Washington State Commercial Passenger Fishing Vessel Association*, 443 U.S. 658, 680 (1979); accord *United States v. Winans*, 198 U.S. 371, 381 (1905); *Worcester v. Georgia*, 31 U.S. (6 Pet.) 515, 582 (Justice McLean concurring)

[34] Supra n 6.

[35] See 25 U.S.C. § 1302 (2001). In overall effect, then, ICRA utilised federal statutory powers to require that Indian tribes' judicial regimes provide a good part of the constitutional Bill of Rights. The ICRA did not include the establishment clause, rights to appointed counsel, the necessity of grand jury indictments, nor the guaranty of civil jury trial. See Canby supra n 14 at 354-363.

[36] Contained in its first ten amendments.

[37] Indian tribes historically have no obligation to provide constitutional guaranties, since they are neither the federal government (limited by the Constitution proper) nor a state (to which its provisions and guaranties apply under the 14th Amendment). See *Talton v. Mayes*, 163 U.S. 376 (1896).

The effects of ICRA as a remedy in a federal court against the actions of tribal courts

July 8, 1970, however, when President Richard Nixon appeared before Congress with a President's Message on Indian Affairs. The 37th President of the United States delivered a statement on federal Indian policy, decrying 'the historic and legal relationship between the Federal government and Indian communities [that] has oscillated between two equally harsh and unacceptable extremes',[38] and calling on Congress for a set of new laws that would 'strengthen the Indian's sense of autonomy without threatening his sense of community'.[39] President Nixon promised to propose a series of laws that would implement 'a new and coherent strategy [...] turn[ing] from the question of *whether* the Federal government has a responsibility to Indians to the question of *how* that responsibility can best be fulfilled.'[40] The Watergate scandal and related events forced Nixon to resign in 1974, leaving his presidency sullied in the American mind, but some of the promised new legislation followed his 1970 statement and it largely set the course of federal Indian policy since.

Since that time, Congress has responded with a steady flow of enabling legislation through subsequent presidential administrations.[41] Among the

---

have been notably curtailed by the Supreme Court decision in *Santa Clara Pueblo v. Martinez*, 436 U.S. 49 (1978). *Santa Clara* held that the writ of habeas corpus under § 1303 of ICRA, 25 U.S.C. §1303 (2001), available 'to any person, in a court of the United States, to test the legality of his detention by order of an Indian tribe', provided the only possible federal remedy under ICRA, overturning broadly-established lower court precedent. The *Santa Clara* decision reduced the ICRA remedy to one against actions by tribal courts in criminal cases, exclusively. Even further, the party aggrieved must first exhaust remedies in tribal courts before turning to ICRA remedies before a federal court. See, e.g., *Selam v. Warm Springs Tribal Correctional Facility*, 134 F.3d 948 (9th Cir. 1998); *McCurdy v. Steele*, 506 F.2d 653 (10th Cir. 1974); *O'Neal v. Cheyenne River Sioux Tribe*, 482 F.2d 1140 (8rh Cir. 1973).

38 'President's Message to Congress on Indian Affairs' (6) *Weekly Comp. Pres. Doc.* 894, 895 (July 8, 1970), also in 116 Cong. Rec. 22355 (1970). Nixon identified the two extremes as (1) termination of the 'trusteeship relationship between the Federal government and the Indian people', id, and (2) 'excessive dependence on the Federal government [...] so great that the Indian community is almost entirely run by outsiders who are responsible and responsive to Federal officials in Washington, D.C.' id at 896.

39 Id.

40 Id. at 905.

41 See Canby supra n 14 at 29-33. Early in the process, in 1975, Congress promulgated a 'statement of findings' and a 'Congressional declaration policy'. 25 U.S.C. §§ 450-450a (2001). Congress specifically found and enacted into law the statement that,

> the prolonged Federal domination of Indian service programs has served to retard rather than enhance the progress of Indian people and their communities by depriving Indians of the full opportunity to develop leadership skills crucial to the realization of self-government, and [...] the planning and implementation of programs [...] which are responsive to the true needs of Indian communities, [and that] The Indian people will never surrender their desire to control their relationships both among themselves and with non-Indian governments, organizations and persons. 25 U.S.C. § 450(a)(1)-(2) (2001).

early initiatives, in 1975 Congress passed the Indian Self-Determination Act [42] after it had established an American Indian Policy Review Commission, including Indian representation.[43] The Commission reported in 1977, calling for 'a firm rejection of assimilationist (sic) policies, reaffirmation of the status of tribes as permanent, self-governing institutions, and increased financial aide to the tribes.'[44] The federal government has generally maintained that approach since.[45] Nonetheless, Judge Canby, perhaps the Indian Law scholar with the longest tenure, maintains scepticism. In 2004, he commented, 'It is perhaps possible that the contending forces in Indian affairs have reached some sort of final balance, and that no further major changes of direction will occur. Nothing in the history of federal Indian policy, however, justifies confidence in such a conclusion.'[46]

[42] Pub. L. No. 93-638, 88 Stat. 2203 (1976). Notably, that statute was amended in 1988 to add to 25 U.S.C. § 450a(b) (2001) a provision for the 'development of strong and stable tribal governments capable of administering quality programs and developing the economies of their respective communities'. Pub. L. No. 100-472, § 102, 102 Stat. 2285 (1990). Prior to the amendment, the language of the statute did not recognise tribal governments as an objective for federal support.

[43] Pub. L. No. 93-580, 88 Stat. 1910 (1976).

[44] Canby supra n 14 at 31.

[45] In 1994, President William Clinton issued a Memorandum for the heads of Executive Departments and Agencies 'to ensure that the Federal Government operates within a government-to-government relationship with federally recognized Native American tribal governments [...] reflecting respect for the rights of self-government due the sovereign tribal governments.' Government-to-Government Relations with Native American Tribal Governments, 59 Fed. Reg. 22951 (May 4, 1994). For a similar statement by President Clinton's successor, President George W. Bush, see Proclamation of American Indian Heritage Month, 67 Fed. Reg. 67773 (Nov. 6, 2002).

President Clinton issued several Executive Orders on Indian matters establishing guidelines still valid, including an especially important one toward the end of his time in the White House. Exec. Order No. 13,175, Consultation and Coordination with Indian Tribal Governments, 65 Fed. Reg. 67,249 (Nov. 9, 2000).

Executive Order No. 13,175 included three 'Fundamental Principles' that federal agencies should follow in 'formulating or implementing policies that have tribal implications', including

> (1) 'a unique legal relationship with Indian tribal governments' based on an extensive body of federal laws 'that establish and define a trust relationship with Indian tribes';
>
> (2) recognition that, 'As domestic dependent nations, Indian tribes exercise inherent sovereign powers over their members and territory', and that the United States should respect that sovereignty by working with the tribes 'on a government-to-government basis to address issues concerning Indian tribal self-government, tribal trust resources, and Indian tribal treaty and other rights'; and
>
> (3) 'The United States recognizes the right of Indian tribes to self-government and supports tribal sovereignty and self-determination'.

[46] Canby supra n 14 at 33.

Summary of the Federal Indian Law Component

Federal Indian Law provides a significant component of Navajo Nation law, or the law that applies to Navajos and non-Indians within the Navajo Nation. It deals principally with the tension between three sources of governmental power within the United States — tribal, state and federal — created by federal controls over Indian tribes. Federal Indian Law exerts oversight of the Navajo and other tribal systems. The nature of that oversight — as developed by case law, laws of Congress and Executive Orders over more than two centuries — must be seen as a trust responsibility, with a fiduciary duty to preserve Indians' domestic dependent sovereignty.[47] That oversight must also be seen as a source of great tension, attempting to reconcile plenary legislative power with fiduciary duty, and to mediate between competing jurisdictions in the tribes and states, while neither dominating them nor dictating to them.

Within that framework, imposed from the top down, most American Indian tribes retain a broad opportunity to pass their own laws and apply them through their own courts. As we shall see with the *Diné*, the effectiveness of a given tribe in taking advantage of that opportunity will vary with its degree of self-sufficiency, which in turn depends on its economic resources and viability, and the constituent will of its people to take control of their own destiny. Today, the Navajo Nation enjoys a unique form of government of its own invention and a highly developed legal system notable for its vigor and self-definition.[48]

Viewed dispassionately, federal Indian Law affects the Navajo Nation and other American tribes in much the same way that federal law affects the states and their citizens. Beyond its stark assertion of criminal jurisdiction, federal Indian Law has become a relatively benign and innocuous element in Navajo law in particular and in the laws of Indian tribes in general. Generally, except for criminal law, the federal law component of the Navajo Nation and other Indian legal systems empowers and enables rather than limits. As with the states of the federal union, it functions as a

[47] See Clinton, RN, Goldberg, C E and Tsosie, R (2003)*American Indian Law: Native Nations and the Federal System, Cases and Materials* (4th edn) Lexis-Nexis at 497-525; Newton, NJ (ed.) (2005 ed.) *Cohen's Handbook of Federal Indian Law* Lexis-Nexis at 418-42

[48] I have had the good fortune to teach at a law faculty with one of the largest contingents of Native American law students in the United States. The special aspects of the Navajo system have come home to me in the light of remarks by law students from other tribes, and the respect (in some cases approaching awe) in which they hold the Navajo Nation. For example, once when I was advising a law student clerking for a tribal court and urging him that the court should exercise jurisdiction regarding a commercial matter that had contacts both on and off the reservation, noting that the Navajo Nation courts had done so in similar situations, he responded, 'Sure, the Navajos would, but nobody else can be like the Navajos.'

framework of preemptive laws and regulations upon which the states and tribes may construct their own systems, usually enjoying the broadest sort of latitude to do so as long as they respect federal limitations.[49] That said, Indians probably feel less able to take a dispassionate view of the federal law component in their laws and more vulnerable because of it than do common citizens of the United States.

Indians feel special tensions based on a long history of unhappy circumstances and events visited on Indians through federal Indian Law.[50] Indians are not simply citizens of a given state, which in fluid United States society is likely to be more an accident of opportunities to study, work or marry than of identification with a given region or society. Even when s/he identifies strongly with where s/he was born and/or grew up, a non-Indian may think of him or herself as 'an American citizen who happens to live for the moment in Colorado', or, perhaps, 'Maryland', or any other of the 50 states, until something better comes along. A Navajo more likely thinks of him or herself as a tribal member with primary ties to a specific land and tribe, and a desire — even an imperative — to live on those particular lands among those particular tribal members, though events may place them temporarily in some other venue.

THE SECOND INGREDIENT: AMERICAN LAW/STATE LAW

> *[T]he question has always been whether the state action infringed on the right of reservation Indians to make their own laws and be ruled by them. [...] Today the Navajo [tribal courts] exercise broad criminal and civil jurisdiction which covers suits by outsiders against Indian defendants. No Federal Act has given state courts jurisdiction over such controversies. ~ Williams v. Lee, 358 U.S. 217, 219-20, 222 (1959).*

> *The inherent sovereign powers of an Indian tribe do not extend to the activities of nonmembers, [except where:] 1) nonmembers enter into consensual relationships with the tribe or its members, or 2) the conduct of non-Indians on fee lands within the reservation . . . threatens or has some direct effect on the political integrity, the economic security, or the health or welfare of the tribe. ~ Montana v. United States, 450 U.S. 544, 565-66 (1981).*

[49] Federal Indian Law provides the frame of reference for an eternal debate regarding when and how the federal government may encroach too far on tribes'/states' rights; i.e., the relative virtues of big central government versus local control.

[50] 'The strong and distinct Navajo identity is a result of enduring the swings in federal policy toward Indians.' Tso (1986) supra n 12 at 22, 53.

[T]he existence and extent of a tribal court's jurisdiction will require a careful examination of tribal sovereignty, the extent to which that sovereignty has been altered, divested, or diminished, as well as a detailed study of relevant statutes, Executive Branch policy as embodied in treaties and elsewhere, and administrative or judicial decisions. ~ National Farmers Union Insurance Co. v. Crow Tribe, 471 U.S. 845, 855-56 (1985).

Absent congressional direction enlarging tribal-court jurisdiction . . . the civil authority of Indian tribes and their courts with respect to non-Indian fee lands [within a reservation] generally "do[es] not extend to the activities of nonmembers." ~ Strate v. A-1 Contractors, 520 U.S. 438, 453 (1997), quoting Montana v. United States, 450 U.S. 544, 565 (1981).

[T]he ultimate question is whether the exercise of state court jurisdiction in a given case will "frustrate federal policy or violate traditional notions of tribal sovereignty. ~ Begay v. Roberts, 167 Ariz. 375, 379, 807 P.2d 1111 (Ariz. Ct. App. 1990), citing Smith Plumbing Co. v. Aetna Cas. & Sur. Co., 149 Ariz. 524, 529, 720 P.2d 499 (Ariz. 1986).

[Where an Indian files suit in state court against a non-Indian] the Indian interests which the infringement test seeks to protect are not present. ~ State v. Zaman (Zaman I), 190 Ariz. 208, 210, 946 P.2d 459 (Ariz. 1997).

[T]he status of the defendant as an Indian or a non-Indian is the sine qua non of federal Indian law. ~ State v. Zaman (Zaman II), 194 Ariz. 442, 984 P.2d 528 (Ariz. 1999).

There are many non-Indian actors who impact the Navajo Nation in various and significant ways that may escape the authority of the Navajo Nation if our courts are required to apply the Montana[-Strate] exceptions to every civil case involving non-Indians. [...] Further, application of Montana[-Strate] to every civil case with a non-Indian defendant undermines the federal policy encouraging the development of tribal courts. [...] Finally, our responsibility to protect the sovereignty of the Navajo Nation counsels that we do not surrender authority unnecessarily. ~ *Nelson v. Pfizer, Inc.*, 8 Navajo Rptr. 373, 376-77 (2003).

The above introductory sampling of snippets from United States Supreme Court, Arizona State Supreme Court and Court of Appeals, and Navajo Supreme Court opinions probably tried the reader's patience and elicited the thought that it served no discernible purpose. Nonetheless, begging the reader's indulgence, it is meant to provide sound bites that reveal the development of coherent – if fractious – judicial doctrine, beginning from about the time tribal courts began to function as viable tribunals and exercise significant civil jurisdiction. As the excerpts demonstrate, the geographical proximity of tribal and state courts, as policed by the United States Supreme Court, does not make for easy relations between jurisdictional neighbours. This section shows, because of Navajo's mixed legal system, how Navajo and state legal systems share a common recent ancestor, American Law, but the *Diné* system's insistence on mixing American Law with its own Common, or Fundamental, Law creates tension with state systems and courts true only to the former. In the end, Navajo tribal courts have found ways to assert their civil jurisdiction and the sovereignty of their mixed legal system.

In those areas in which federal Indian Law permits the tribe to draft its own laws, the bulk of Navajo law is drawn from the body of 'American Law'. At first exposure, an 'American' lawyer may feel reassured that Navajo law is cut from the same legislative and judicial cloth as the 'American Law' found in the 50 states.[51] Judicial proceedings before Navajo tribunals look and feel like those before state and federal courts. The greatest portion of the substantive and procedural rules that constitute the Navajo Nation's legal system consists of the 'American' law found in uniform laws and procedural rules, state statutes, and the case law of state and federal courts. The Uniform Commercial Code is part of the Navajo Nation's statutes.[52] The Federal Rules of Civil and Criminal Procedure and of Evidence may be found virtually intact in the Navajo Courts,[53] as they are in each of the state systems.

The Supreme Court of the Navajo Nation publishes its written opinions,[54] which bind lower tribal courts as precedent, thereby creating common law. Its opinions cite the decisions of the Supreme Court of the United States and lower federal courts, and state court appellate decisions, as well as its own prior decisions. The opinions are written in English, in a style familiar to any American lawyer.

Once inside the Navajo system proper, however, the feeling of familiarity begins to wane. As the third section of this study will set out

[51] Indeed, the Navajo Supreme Court will admit to practice before the Navajo judiciary any lawyer who has graduated from a law school in the United States and passes the Navajo bar examination.

[52] NNC tit. 5A (2005).

[53] Adopted by the courts under authority of NNC tit. 5, § 601 (2005).

[54] Bound volumes of the Navajo Reporter exist for cases through 2005. Online sources for Navajo Nation opinions include www.versuslaw.com or at www.navajocourts.org/suctopinions. See supra n 24.

in greater detail, the Navajo legal system rests on a bedrock of indigenous Common Law which predates the American legal system. That original source justifies the Navajo system. It explains why in its version of the Uniform Commercial Code, for example, the Navajo legislature introduced various deviations and modifications,[55] and included 'Special Plain Language Comments' following the Official Comments for many articles.[56]

Navajo Common Law, or Fundamental Law, provides a potential overriding rule for any case.[57] It may negate an apparently applicable rule of American law at the same time that it recognises it, so that a lawsuit in a Navajo court — applying the 'same' law as a state court — might reach a different result.[58]

Perhaps most important to differentiate, the Navajo judicial system resolves its cases by consensual, rather than adversary, approach. The system has provision for an extensive system of Peacemaker Courts at the local, or chapter, level — reliant on wise mediators who are not lawyers — as an alternate venue.[59] Even when the case is before a *Diné* judge sitting in a 'typical' American courtroom and applying American rules of procedure and evidence, proceedings may involve some surprising turns and results. Perhaps most disconcerting to state law practitioners, parties to a case in Navajo court may return to the controversy several times until they have had sufficient opportunity to satisfy themselves that the court has considered all conceivable avenues to resolution.

The special prism through which the Navajo courts view and apply the generic American Law source within their own system contrasts with a second source of American Law that affects the Navajo Nation, from outside that tribal system proper. Federal Indian Law fixes jurisdiction of the tribal courts, defining those circumstances in which state courts must give way to

[55] For example, the NNC adds NNC tit. 5A, §1-110 (2005) that renders the Navajo UCC inapplicable to 'any exclusively barter transaction in which the aggregate market value of all the goods and services involved in the transaction does not exceed ten thousand dollars.' This exempts, e.g., any such barter transaction from the statute of frauds. NNC tit. 5A, § 2-201(D) (2005). Another exemplar deviation 'does not permit a secured creditor to repossess personal property of Navajo Indians without judicial process.' NNC tit. 5A, § 9-503 (2005).

[56] For example, the Special Plain Language Comment for NNC 5A, § 1-201 (2005) (General Definitions) states, 'When reading any sections in this Code, it is very important to check to see if any of the terms are defined and to read the definitions of those terms. Unless one reads the definitions, the full meaning of a statute may not be understood.' See also, e.g., the Special Plain Language Comments for NNC tit. 5A, § 1-102, §§ 2-204 to 2-206, § 2-305, §§ 2-312 to 2-316, § 2-403, § 9-103, §§ 9-107 to 9-110, § 9-203, § 9-208, § 9-307, § 9-312, § 9-315, etc. (2005).

[57] See the discussion in Austin supra n 7 at 37-51; infra ns 118, 120-121, 132-133, 140-150, 159, 162-171 and accompanying text.

[58] See infra ns 169-172 and accompanying text.

[59] See NNC tit. 7, §§ 409-412 (2005).

or share jurisdiction with tribal courts, and also those in which tribal courts have no adjudicatory powers and the matter falls exclusively to state courts. State courts, innocent of any allegiance to the Navajo system, apply their specific versions of American Law to Navajo tribal members and to events occurring on or affecting Navajo Indian Country when federal Indian Law grants them exclusive or concurrent jurisdiction to do so. In such cases, the American Law applied will be that found in the statutes, rules and case law of a given state.

Federal Indian Law prohibits state courts from taking jurisdiction over tribal members and events whenever they are preempted from doing so by congressional legislation or a treaty, or whenever to do so would infringe on Indian sovereignty. The Supreme Court of the United States' development of the preemption and infringement doctrines is a work in progress, and continues to generate a steady stream of decided cases. To date, it has achieved no rule that would curtail parties' race to the state or tribal courthouse[60] whose law most likely favours their side.

The Infringement Doctrine

The infringement doctrine provides the original standard for determining when tribal courts should have exclusive jurisdiction. *Williams v. Lee*,[61] handed down in 1959, articulates the doctrine. The case involved a merchant operating a general store on the Navajo Indian Reservation, who filed suit in Arizona state court to collect a debt for goods that he had sold to a Navajo tribal member and his wife, who lived on the Reservation. The state court entered judgment for the merchant, and the Arizona Supreme Court affirmed. The Supreme Court of the United States reversed, casting the question as 'one of state power over Indian affairs', and stating that,

> [A]bsent governing acts of Congress, the *question has always been whether the state action infringed on the right of reservation Indians to make their own laws and be ruled by them*.[…] Congress recognized this

[60] As *Erie v. Tompkins*, 304 U.S. 34 (1938), did for the disparity between state and federal courts. Before the decision in *Erie* courthouses on opposite sides of the street might predictably reach different resolutions, applying different law (federal common law often was different from state common law) and giving rise to races to file in one court or the other, since the place of filing determined the outcome. This sort of jurisdictional determinism exists today between state and tribal courts, and parties know it.

[61] 358 U.S. 217 (1959). The relatively late date for *Williams* may be explained by the fact that only in the mid-20th century, after the Indian Reorganization Act of 1934 and more especially with the advent of Indian self-determination in the 1960's, did tribal courts applying tribal laws become a viable factor. There were jurisdictional decisions before *Williams*, but the 1959 case sets the benchmark for modern analysis of the issue.

authority in the Navajos in the Treaty of 1868, and has done so ever since.[62]

Note that *Williams'* infringement test cannot determine concurrent jurisdiction; it functions only to determine exclusive subject matter jurisdiction. If infringement occurs, the state must stand aside. Therefore, *Williams* may not apply to a case in which an Indian plaintiff sues a non-Indian defendant, even if it arose in Indian Country.[63] That set of facts might give rise to concurrent jurisdiction in both the state court and the tribal court.[64] On the other hand, the Supreme Court has held that a state court could not entertain a lawsuit between two tribal members.[65]

A more recent case whittled away at tribal courts' subject matter jurisdiction, without changing the essential infringement doctrine. *Strate v. A-1 Contractors*[66] involved an automobile accident between non-Indians[67] on a state highway through the reservation. When the tribal court retained jurisdiction despite the defendants' objection, defendants took the question to federal district court. Ultimately, the United States Supreme Court granted certiorari, and held that tribal courts had no jurisdiction over a dispute between nonmembers growing out of events on a right-of-way (lands ceded to the state for the highway) through the reservation.[68]

Strate walks an interesting line. The high court applied analysis of tribal *legislative* jurisdiction it had set out sixteen years earlier in *Montana v. United States,*[69] finding a common issue in the 'forms of [tribes'] civil jurisdiction' that also defined their judicial power over civil matters, and held that a tribe's 'adjudicative jurisdiction' could not surpass its legislative

[62] Id. at 219-20, 222, 223 (citations omitted)(emphasis added).

[63] See *Three Affiliated Tribes of the Fort Berthold Reservation v. Wold Engineering, P.C.*, 467 U.S. 138, 148 (1984).

[64] Some tribal courts would hesitate to exercise such jurisdiction by their own tribal laws. Judge Canby notes that 'a number of tribal codes provide for civil jurisdiction over non-Indian defendants only when they stipulate to it.' Canby supra n 14 at 189. But the fact that they could exercise such jurisdiction upon defendant's consent indicates that the subject matter is appropriate to the tribal court.

[65] *Fisher v. District Court,* 424 U.S. 382, 386 (1976). There may be a question regarding nonmember Indians from another tribe or reservation, however. See *Duro v. Reina,* 495 U.S. 676 (1990). The *Duro* case held that a tribal court did not have criminal jurisdiction over a nonmember Indian, but Congress reversed that result by a statute that did not pertain to civil jurisdiction. 25 U.S.C. §1301(2).

[66] 520 U.S. 438 (1997).

[67] Although the court characterised the parties as 'nonmembers', apparently making the decision valid as to cases including Indians of a tribe different than the tribal court.

[68] In other words, the accident occurred in Indian Country, as defined at 18 U.S.C. § 1151. In *Strate,* the Supreme Court created a special category of Indian Country, less subject to Indian jurisdiction.

[69] 450 U.S. 544 (1981) (6-3 vote).

jurisdiction. To create its neo-infringement test the *Strate* case addressed the concept of 'inherent sovereignty' and stated:

> *Montana* delineated — in a main rule and exceptions — the bounds of the power tribes retain to exercise 'forms of civil jurisdiction over non-Indians.' [...] Absent congressional direction enlarging tribal-court jurisdiction, we adhere to that understanding [that] the civil authority of Indian tribes and their courts with respect to non-Indian fee lands generally 'do[es] not extend to the activities of nonmembers of the tribe.'[70]

Montana had limited legislative jurisdiction by stating a general rule that activities of nonmembers are not subject to tribal regulation.[71] Then *Montana* set out two exceptions to its rule: 1) where the nonmembers had entered into 'consensual relationships with the tribe or its members', or 2) 'the conduct of non-Indians on fee lands within [a] reservation [...] threatens or has some direct effect on the political integrity, the economic security, or the health or welfare of the tribe.'[72] The exceptions borrow the criteria from *Williams,* expressed as a particular circumstance in the first exception and as a general concept in the second. *Strate* showed the Supreme Court less inclined to find infringement, but any test so subjective as *Montana-Strate* leaves great discretion in the court applying it. As we shall see, the Navajo

[70] 520 U.S. at 453 (citations omitted).

[71] The *Montana* rule might be seen, in its own right, as an exception to the broader traditional rule that tribes have authority to regulate activity within their territory, i.e., within Indian Country. By 1997, however, the Supreme Court stated in *Strate v. A-1 Contractors,* 520 U.S. 538, 446 (1997), '*Montana* thus described a general rule that, absent different congressional direction, Indian tribes lack civil authority over the conduct of non-members on non-Indian land within a reservation', and expressed a concern that the exceptions to the '*Montana* rule' should not be applied in a way that 'would severely shrink' it. Id. at 458. With that formulation, *Montana* should best be seen as a new rule, replacing the old rule in favour of general tribal authority over their territory. But see *Iowa Mutual Insurance Co. v. LaPlante,* 480 U.S. 9, 18 (1987), which stated, 'Tribal authority over the activities of non-Indians on reservation lands is an important part of tribal sovereignty. [...] Civil jurisdiction over such activities presumptively lies in the tribal courts unless affirmatively limited by specific treaty provisions or federal statute.'

Judge Canby notes,

> Although *Montana* announced an exception to the general rule that a tribe has governmental power over its territory unless some statute or treaty takes it away, subsequent Supreme Court opinions have tended to refer to the '*Montana* rule,' not the '*Montana* exception.' As a 'rule' limiting inherent tribal sovereignty, it continues to gain strength; indeed, it appears to have become the foundation case for contemporary Indian law in the Supreme Court. Canby supra n 14 at 78.

[72] 450 U.S. at 565-66.

Nation's Supreme Court has used that test aggressively to countervail any limitations on infringement of its tribal court jurisdiction.

In 2008, the Supreme Court revisited the question of infringement in the case of *Plains Commerce Bank v. Long Family Land & Cattle Co.*[73] Chief Justice John Roberts' opinion for a 5-4 majority—Justice Ruth Bader Ginsburg, the author of the unanimous decision in *Strate*, wrote the dissent—did nothing to change the neo-infringement test established in *Strate*, but may demonstrate the subjectivity of that test. The justices divided by the narrowest of votes over whether the first *Montana* exception applied when a non-Indian bank foreclosed on fee land within the reservation, given nine years before by tribal members in guaranty for a loan, and then sold the land to non-Indian individuals. Was the sale a simple transaction between non-Indians involving fee lands? Five justices thought so, and prevailed.[74] Was it a clear case for application of the consensual-relationships exception? Four justices thought that a more accurate characterization of the facts in issue, and lost.[75]

The Preemption Doctrine

Throughout the development of the infringement and neo-infringement doctrines, looms another, more powerful doctrine: preemption. Infringement begins from the proposition that, 'The inherent sovereign powers of an Indian tribe do not extend to the activities of nonmembers,'[76] but Congress may countermand that principle at any time. Federal treaties and statutes may preempt state courts from exercising jurisdiction by consigning matters to tribal sovereignty. That proposition springs from the well-established premise — dating from the early 19th century and the *Worcester* decision[77] —that relations with Indian tribes exclusively belong to the federal government and that states can exercise no unilateral authority over Indians or Indian Country. In other words, Congress may intervene whenever, and to whatever extent it finds warranted, mindful of the trust relationship it serves through its legislation, to set tribal courts' jurisdiction, but state courts and legislatures have no independent authority to affect that jurisdiction.

[73] 554 U.S. __, 128 S. Ct. 2709 (2008). See Furnish, DB (2009) 'Sorting Out Civil Jurisdiction in Indian Country After *Plains Commerce Bank*: State Courts and the Judicial Sovereignty of the Navajo Nation' (33) *Am. Ind. L.Rev.* 385.

[74] 554 U.S. at __, 128 S.Ct. at 2714.

[75] Id. at 2727.

[76] *Montana v. United States*, 450 U.S. at 565.

[77] See supra n 16 and accompanying text.

In *McClanahan v. Arizona State Tax Comm'n*,[78] decided fourteen years after *Williams*, the Supreme Court of the United States read the applicable treaties and statutes with the 'tradition of sovereignty in mind'[79] to decide that the State of Arizona was preempted from taxing the income earned by a Navajo Indian on the Navajo Reservation. In reaching its decision, the Supreme Court turned away from the possibility that the tribe might possess any inherent sovereignty,[80] since all of the tribes' inherent sovereignty had been delivered up in trust to the federal government, implicitly, by the events of the 19th century.

McClanahan shifted the focus to the concept of federal preemption, turning to treaties and statutes to see what areas might be foreclosed to state exercise.[81] In Judge Canby's phrase:

> By reducing sovereignty to a backdrop and relying on the preemptive effect of federal law to exclude state power, *McClanahan*'s analysis appears to alter the presumption that the tribe has governmental power over all matters affecting the tribe on the reservation, and that the state does not. It seems instead to assume that the state has power unless federal law (including federal Indian policy) has preempted it.[82]

Searching written sources for preemption usually takes on a historical cast. Congress cut off the possibility of treaties with tribes in 1871, but not before many had been executed. The Navajo Treaty of Fort Sumner of 1868 contains an Article that states that the reservation shall be set apart for the 'use and occupation of the Navajo tribe of Indians',[83] retaining criminal and civil jurisdiction by inherent sovereignty.[84] The acts by which states were admitted to the union typically contained provisions by which the new states disclaimed all right and title to jurisdiction over land and property held by Indians.[85]

78 411 U.S. 164 (1973).
79 Id. at 173.
80 The Navajo Supreme Court seems less prepared to define its tribal sovereignty by federal preemption doctrine, however. See *Means v. District Court of Chinle*, 7 Navajo Rptr. 382, 386 (1999) The *Means* opinion states, 'A treaty is not a grant of rights to Indian nations but a grant of rights from them, with reservations of all rights which are not granted.' Id. at p. 6.
81 411 U.S. at 172.
82 Canby supra n 14 at 89.
83 Treaty of Fort Sumner, Article II.
84 *Williams v. Lee*, 358 U.S. 217, 221-223 (1959).
85 See, Act to Enable the People of New Mexico to Form a Constitution and State Government and Be Admitted into Union on an Equal Footing with the Original States; and to Enable the People of Arizona to Form a Constitution and State Government and Be Admitted into Union

At the end of the day, then, laws and treaties provide a rich trove of Indian sovereignty — be it residual inherent sovereignty or sovereignty created by federal grant — that persists under the preemption doctrine.[86] The infringement doctrine preserves that sovereignty from incursion by state courts or legislatures. Preemption defines sovereignty; freedom from infringement preserves it. There may be deeper, more venerable sources of Indian sovereignty, inherent in the history and status of the tribes, but at the end of the day it does not matter. Federal Indian policy today supports tribal autonomy, having laid a sturdy preemptive basis for such autonomy in 19th century treaties and a series of 20th century laws. Preemptive sovereignty provides a sufficient base, even if there were no other, for tribal courts' civil jurisdiction. Paired with the infringement doctrine as developed to date, preemption establishes that there is ample —if not unlimited — opportunity to vindicate tribal court jurisdiction in the face of a state court's claim.

Case Law from Arizona, New Mexico and Utah State Courts on Civil Jurisdiction of Tribal Courts

While the United States Supreme Court may delineate the doctrines of infringement and preemption at the intervals marked by its ponderous deliberations, lower courts must work through their calendars without the luxury of deciding when to unleash their decisional powers.[87] In the ensuing wash of decisional law, state courts exercise workaday discretion in applying the federal doctrines. The case decisions from the courts of the three states which encompass the Navajo Nation thus far show no consensus on a coherent application of the United States Supreme Court doctrine.[88]

The nature of the overlapping civil jurisdiction created by the advent of tribal courts creates a special predicament within the federal system of the United States. State courts exercise general jurisdiction, with authority over any civil claim sufficiently connected to their respective territories to meet due process requirements. Federal courts exercise limited jurisdiction, as specifically authorized to them by Congress. While state-

on an Equal Footing with the Original States, Pub. L. No. 61-219, § 2, ¶2 (N.M.); § 20, ¶ 2 (Ariz..), 36 U.S. Stat. 557 (1910); ARIZ. CONST. art. 20 ¶4; N.M. CONST. art. XXI, § 2.

[86] E.g., *Oliphant v. Suquamish Indian Tribe*, 435 U.S. 191, 195-97 (1978); *Duro v. Reina*, 495 U.S.676, 684 (1990).

[87] State supreme courts also enjoy the right to decide which of many appeals they will hear. For example, Arizona's five-judge Supreme Court writes about 50 cases a year, out of about 3,000 appeals.

[88] See Furnish, DB supra n 73 at 419-37.

federal coincidence in civil jurisdiction may arise, such potential conflicts are usually resolved in favor of the federal courts, whenever the parties can and wish to take advantage of the limited federal jurisdiction. Tribal courts do not submit to the same judicial hierarchy. Tribal courts, like state courts, pretend to general jurisdiction of all civil matters properly before them through sufficient contacts with their territorial sovereignty.

Tribal courts' jurisdictional ambitions run head-on into the state courts' jurisdictional purchase, and bid to occupy the same space. Whereas between two state courts concurrent jurisdiction may often exist, between state and tribal court concurrent jurisdiction might always exist — contact with the territory of one must create contact with the territory of the other — if federal Indian law did not sift the circumstances to assign some to the exclusive jurisdiction of the state court and others to the exclusive jurisdiction of the tribal court. This does not exclude the possibility of concurrent jurisdiction in state and tribal court, but it certainly complicates the mix. The complication springs from the hard fact that two sovereigns — both disposed generally to do so — must decide when to exercise jurisdiction and when to cede it to the other. They find their common guidelines for making that decision in the Supreme Court precedents on infringement and preemption discussed above.

The process of sorting out civil jurisdiction between tribal courts and state courts is beset with inherent uncertainties today. The three state courts touched by the issue of Navajo judicial sovereignty have all wrestled with the problem on repeated occasions. I have elsewhere analyzed the resulting case law and tend to classify their respective positions — at least as articulated in their most recent Supreme Court opinions on the subject — as protectionist (Arizona),[89] inclined to mutual recognition and respectful coexistence (New Mexico)[90] and flexible within a common sense framework (Utah).[91] Certainly the state courts will continue to develop their views of when they must step aside for tribal courts, and when they should exclude tribal courts. One hopes that they will do so while keeping in mind that tribal courts — in this case the Navajo Nation tribal courts — will simultaneously engage in the same process. If state and tribal courts diverge too drastically in their application of the Supreme Court precedents, judicial antagonism may develop between sovereign authorities occupying the same space. The state courts have work to do, but let us assess the progress of their common partner in the process.

[89] Id. at 420-29.
[90] Id. at 429-35.
[91] Id. at 435-37.

The Navajo Nation's Case Law on Civil Jurisdiction of Tribal Courts

While state courts apply preemption-infringement doctrine to decide when they may take subject matter or personal jurisdiction of events and persons implicating Indian Country,[92] the Supreme Court of the Navajo Nation also applies the same doctrines to the same ends. The major difference may be that a non-Indian defendant who finds himself in a tribal court typically objects to its jurisdiction as a first defence, so that there are a great many Navajo court decisions discussing the issue and the tribal judges have become adept at resolving it, to a greater degree than most state courts. Stoking this process, the United States Supreme Court has imposed an exhaustion requirement by which no federal court shall consider the question of tribal court jurisdiction until after the tribal forum has had 'the first opportunity to evaluate the factual and legal bases for the challenge.'[93]

The Navajo Tribal Council has set down a solid statutory base from which to derive jurisdiction. The NNC provides for the broadest possible civil jurisdiction, modelling its law on state long-arm statutes.[94] In 2001, the legislature added an article that includes a provision specifically titled, 'Long-Arm Civil Jurisdiction and Service of Process Act'.[95] Finally, the territorial reach of the tribal courts also is defined as broadly as possible.[96] The legislative purpose of the Navajo Nation, in common with most states, is to take its civil jurisdiction to the furthest extension permissible, aware

[92] See, e.g., *State v. Zaman (Zaman II)*, 194 Ariz. 442, 984 P.2d 528 (Ariz. 1999); *State v. Zaman (Zaman I)*, 190 Ariz. 208, 946 P.2d 459 (Ariz. 1997); *Astorga v. Wing*, 211 Ariz. 139, 118 P.3d 1103 (Ariz. Ct. App. 2005); *Begay v. Roberts*, 167 Ariz. 375, 807 P.2d 1111 (Ariz. Ct. App. 1990); *Tempest Recovery Services, Inc. v. Belone*, 134 N.M. 133, 74 P.3d 67 (N.M. 2003); *Maryboy v. Utah State Tax Comm'n*, 904 P.2d 662 (Utah, 1995).

[93] *Nat'l Farmers Union Ins. Co. v. Crow Tribe*, 471 U.S. 845, 856 (1985). See *Iowa Mutual Ins. Co. v. LaPlante*, 480 U.S. 9 (1987).

[94] 7 NNC § 253(A)(2), which states,

> A. The District Courts of the Navajo Nation shall have original jurisdiction over: [...]
> 2. Civil Causes of Action. All civil actions in which the defendant: (1) is a resident of Navajo Indian Country; or (2) has caused an action or injury to occur within the territorial jurisdiction of the Navajo Nation.

[95] 7 NNC §253a(C) adds a provision detailing the circumstances that may create personal jurisdiction based on conduct, § 253a(E) provides for *forum non conveniens* practice by Navajo courts, and §253a(F) provides that, 'A Court of the Navajo Nation may exercise jurisdiction on any other basis authorized by law, including the inherent and treaty jurisdiction of the Navajo Nation.'

[96] 7 NNC §254 extends territorial jurisdiction to 'Navajo Indian Country', which the same provision defines in the broadest possible terms, making no exception for non-Indian fee lands or rights of way so long as they fall within the exterior boundaries of the reservation or the Eastern Navajo Agency, largely composed of allotment and fee lands.

that its expansive language will be checked by the federal Indian Law pertaining to its jurisdiction to adjudicate civil claims.

One must also bear in mind the difference in judicial perspective when a tribal court looks at jurisdiction. The Plaintiff has already filed the case in a tribal court when the defendant objects to tribal jurisdiction.[97] The question is not whether the connections to the tribe are so powerful as to create exclusive jurisdiction in its court, but rather whether there are enough contacts to sustain jurisdiction in that court, regardless of concurrent jurisdiction in a state court. There is at play no concept of infringement on sovereignty, nor of preemptive sovereignty in favor of the state; the only sovereignty in the balance is that of the tribe. Not surprisingly, the Navajo Nation courts show a tendency to find proper subject matter jurisdiction and retain cases, rather than to surrender them to exclusive state court jurisdiction by finding that the tribal court has no connection that would allow it to keep the case.

A definitive body of Navajo case law dealing with the jurisdiction question began to emerge in 2003.[98] Five cases decided by the Supreme Court of the Navajo Nation in the five years thereafter seem quite complete in their discussion of the issue. They form a full doctrine of civil jurisdiction from the Navajo Nation perspective, taking full account of the United States Supreme Court doctrine to date.

[97] The NNC allows no special appearance to contest jurisdiction; any appearance is a general appearance and submission to the tribal court's jurisdiction. In any case, the effect is the same. The party that makes a special appearance to contest jurisdiction and loses is thereafter bound by the substantive proceedings in the case. The party that wins an objection to jurisdiction before a court that does not permit special appearances achieves the goal: the case terminates at that point.

[98] My selection of the cases discussed here may be somewhat arbitrary. There are certainly other Navajo Supreme Court cases that discuss the jurisdictional question. Perhaps the first effort by the Navajo Supreme Court to deal with the issue of tribal sovereignty in a systematic opinion occurred with the case of *Means v. District Court of Chinle* supra n 80. *Means* was a criminal case and that opinion's connection to the cases analyzed here seems less direct than the bond shared by cases beginning with *Nelson v. Pfizer*, infra ns 99-102 and accompanying text. Nonetheless, *Means* and other earlier cases include concepts and analysis which have coalesced since 2003.

The Benchmark: Nelson v. Pfizer, Inc., and the Responsibility to Protect Inherent Tribal Sovereignty

The Supreme Court of the Navajo Nation decided its benchmark case on jurisdiction, *Nelson v. Pfizer, Inc.*,[99] in 2003, after the relevant decisions of the United Supreme Court, and was able to assimilate them to the Navajo Nation reservation. *Pfizer* was a products liability case brought by a group of Navajo reservation residents[100] against the manufacturer of Rezulin, a medication for diabetes.[101] The Navajo trial court applied the *Montana-Strate* test, found neither of the exceptions present, and dismissed for lack of jurisdiction. On appeal, the Navajo Supreme Court reversed, in an opinion that seems calculated to establish guidelines.

The *Pfizer* opinion rejects the proposition that *Montana* might create a rule applicable to non-Indian activities that occurred on tribal land.[102] The opinion sets out a checklist of 'several sources' for tribal court jurisdiction over non-Indians: 1) 'its broad inherent sovereignty over non-Indian conduct anywhere within its territory;' 2) 'federal and state statutes, regulations and intergovernmental agreements' delegating such authority; 3) treaties that recognize such authority; and 4) 'a tribe's authority as landowner.'[103]

Pfizer held that the tribal court had jurisdiction because of inherent sovereignty, thereby finding it unnecessary to consider the alternative

[99] *Nelson v. Pfizer, Inc.*, 8 Navajo Rptr. 369 (2003).

[100] Including only one person who was not an enrolled member of the Navajo Nation.

[101] *Pfizer* supra n 99 at 373.

[102] *Pfizer* barely cites *Strate*, and does not discuss it, presumably because that case applied *Montana* to events which did not occur on tribal lands. Instead, the opinion provides a Navajo view of federal Indian Law dealing with jurisdiction:

> The implications of *Montana* for the Navajo Nation's power over its territory are clear. . . . There are many non-Indian actors who impact the Navajo Nation in various and significant ways that may escape the authority of the Navajo Nation if our courts are required to apply the *Montana* exceptions to every civil case involving non-Indians. . . . Further, application of *Montana* to every civil case with a non-Indian defendant undermines the federal policy encouraging the development of tribal courts. See *Iowa Mutual Ins. Co. v. LaPlante*, 480 U.S. 9, 15 (1987) ('Tribal courts play a vital role in tribal self-government . . . and the federal government has consistently encouraged their development.') . . . Finally, our responsibility to protect the sovereignty of the Navajo Nation [found in Canon One of the Navajo Nation Code of Judicial Conduct, adopted November 1, 1991, by the Navajo Nation Courts] counsels that we not surrender authority unnecessarily. . . .
>
> Based on these considerations, and the explicit restrictions in *Montana* and later cases . . . we decline to extend *Montana* to activity on tribal land . . . Id. at 376.

[103] Id. at 374 (citations omitted).

proposition argued by the plaintiff, delegation by treaty.[104] The opinion lists any number of aspects of the case that have significance for the Navajo Nation, but never identifies precisely what specific factors triggered inherent sovereignty.[105] Instead, oracle like, the court states, 'our subject matter jurisdiction over matters occurring on tribal land is broad.'[106] It is not a finding of exclusive jurisdiction, excluding all possibility that a state might have heard the case, but of sufficient jurisdiction.[107]

Further Refinement: Dale Nicholson Trust v. Chavez, and Treaty-Based Jurisdiction

Within a year, the Navajo Supreme Court refined its jurisdictional analysis further in *Dale Nicholson Trust v. Chavez*.[108] The case raised the issue of whether the tribal court could 'restrain state officials from seizing property located within the Navajo Nation.'[109] Noting that the *Pfizer* opinion had not considered the treaty basis for tribal jurisdiction, since it based that decision on inherent sovereignty, the court held that the 1868 Treaty of Fort Sumner, interpreted 'as our ancestors understood it,' specifically recognized the Navajo Nation's 'authority to regulate all non-members, including non-Indians, other than certain federal employees on its lands.'[110] The treaty preempted the *Montana-Strate* test for jurisdiction. Therefore, so long as a civil claim arises on Navajo tribal land, the 1868 Treaty of Fort Sumner preempts state court jurisdiction under the *Montana-Strate* test.[111]

104 Id.

105 Id..

106 Id. at 377.

107 *Pfizer* takes pains to instruct tribal trial courts in the use of the *Montana* exceptions. It states that it 'does not want to discourage' lower courts from evaluating for the *Montana* exceptions, since 'fulfillment of either one will satisfy the lower threshold we hold applies today.' Id. at 377. In other words, if one of the *Montana* exceptions were present in a given case, that would clearly justify tribal civil jurisdiction, but the jurisdictional threshold is lower than that. Failing the exceptions, the analysis must continue against the lower threshold and the various sorts of factors indicated in *Pfizer*, or, one surmises, any other aspects of the case that might bear on the Navajo Nation's interest.

108 8 Navajo Rptr. 417 (2004).

109 Id. at 423. There is special concern for actions by state officials in light of *Nevada v. Hicks*, 533 U.S. 353 (2001), where the Supreme Court approved a search on Indian Land of an Indian's home by state officials looking for evidence of illegal hunting.

110 Id. at 428. The court noted that *Montana* itself recognized such language in the 1868 Treaty of Fort Laramie with the Crow Tribe, 450 U.S. at 558, and the case of *Atkinson Trading Co., Inc. v. Shirley*, 532 U.S. at 650, reiterated that power from the same treaty. Also in 1868 the Cheyenne River Sioux Tribe signed a treaty with the federal government, containing a similar power, recognized in *South Dakota v. Bourland*, 508 U.S. 679, 687-88 (1993). The Navajo Treaty of Fort Sumner of the same year 'contains almost identical language.' Id. at 429.

111 The court did note that inherent sovereignty would have failed as a jurisdictional base in *Nicholson Trust*, because of the presence of state agents as parties. *Montana-Strate* exceptions

When *Nicholson Trust* is read with *Pfizer*, one sees that the Supreme Court for the Navajo Nation has established that its courts will exercise civil jurisdiction over events and parties on tribal land, without any need to demonstrate infringement or a *Montana-Strate* exception. Inherent sovereignty, or, more potently, the Treaty of 1868 that preemptively grants sovereignty over its lands to the Navajo Nation, provides the basis for such territorial jurisdiction.[112]

Final Touches: Montana-Strate Exceptions Applied

By the *Pfizer-Nicholson Trust* doctrine, the only time that *Montana-Strate* exceptions become relevant to Navajo tribal court jurisdiction is when events involving nonmember parties occur on non-Indian land. The Supreme Court of the Navajo Nation took up that question in 2005, in *Allstate Indemnity Co. v. Blackgoat*,[113] dealing with a traffic accident on U.S. Highway 160 within the Reservation, in which two Navajo children died. The children's guardians, Larrison and Suzy Holly Blackgoat, a Navajo couple, claimed compensation from the insurer of the Navajo driver. After fruitless negotiation among several claimants to limited insurance funds, the insurer (Allstate Insurance) filed an interpleader with the tribal court, tendering the maximum liability under the policy, $30,000. The Blackgoats requested pre-judgment interest beyond the cap amount, and Allstate objected that the court had no jurisdiction to award it.

Allstate argued that *Montana-Strate* applied. Perhaps the *Blackgoat* court could have ruled that the place of the accident had nothing to do with jurisdiction to distribute insurance proceeds paid into tribal court under interpleader instigated by the insurer, or it might have based jurisdiction on the fact that all involved in the accident were tribal members. Instead, it accommodated Allstate's argument by assuming that 'U.S. Highway 160 is the type of right-of-way that requires a *Montana* analysis.'[114] That

might have been required, but the preemption in the Treaty of 1868 overrode them; it would not do so if the cause of action arises on non-Indian owned fee land within the Navajo Nation. Id. at 429.

[112] Both Arizona and New Mexico were required to respect that sovereignty as a condition to their admission as states of the Union. See supra n 85 and accompanying text.

While such preemption makes jurisdiction clear, it does not mandate its exercise. A Navajo court may abstain in favor of proceedings in another court with concurrent jurisdiction. PacifiCorp v. Mobil Oil Corp., 8 Navajo Rptr. 378 (2003)(two off-Reservation corporations operating on Reservation were parties to pending suit in federal district court).

[113] 8 Navajo Rptr. 660 (2005).

[114] It complains in a footnote that, under questions from the bench,

> both sides demonstrated a lack of understanding of [*Nicholson Trust*] and its identification of the exclusion provision of the Treaty of 1868

assumption allowed the court to confront *Montana-Strate* directly and to find the first exception, a consensual relationship by Allstate in its contract with a Navajo tribal member.

The *Blackgoat* opinion then went further, and held that the tribal court's jurisdiction went beyond the simple distribution of the interpleaded funds, which Allstate urged should be the limit of its consensual relationship and the court's jurisdiction.[115] The court reasoned that 'the actual U.S. Supreme Court test allows jurisdiction if the asserted jurisdiction has a "nexus" to a consensual relationship,'[116] and held that 'the question whether the cap provision precludes an award of pre-judgment interest clearly has a nexus to the contract itself.'[117] The Navajo court then applied the 'Navajo public policy' of *nályééh*, under which 'injured parties should be compensated fully so that there are no hard feelings,'[118] to support an award of pre-judgment interest against the insurer.

In 2006, the Supreme Court of the Navajo Nation decided a preliminary procedural matter in *Green Tree Servicing, L.L.C. v. Duncan*.[119] The Plaintiff, a national lender specialising in mobile homes, asked for enforcement of an arbitration clause in its financing contract with defendant. State courts generally defer to arbitration clauses, but the tribal court required the parties to submit supplemental briefs to address the issue of whether the arbitration clause violated Navajo public policy, specifically in light of the 'test for the validity of contract provisions announced' in the *Blackgoat*

> as the source of absolute jurisdiction over non-Indians on tribal lands within the Navajo Nation. . . . We state again that the *Montana*[-*Strate*] test is only relevant within the Navajo Nation on non-Indian owned fee land or on certain types of rights-of-way. It is only the fact that the accident occurred on a federal right-of-way that makes the *Montana*[-*Strate*] test relevant to our jurisdiction over this case. Id. at 666, n. 2.

115 Id. at 667. Allstate supported its argument by citing *Ford Motor Co. v. Todecheene*, 394 F.3d 1170 (9th Cir., 2005) and *Wilson v. Marchington*, 127 F.3d 805 (9th Cir. 1997), which had rejected tribal jurisdiction over a products liability claim against a vehicle manufacturer based on a finance agreement by the manufacturer's subsidiary and a simple car accident between a tribal member and a non-Indian driving through the Reservation. The court distinguished the two cases on their 'unique circumstances . . . under the fact-intensive *Montana* test.' Id. at 667.

116 Id. at 666. citing *Atkinson* supra n 110 for that proposition.

117 Id.

118 Id. at 668. The court noted that 'some [state] jurisdictions have awarded pre-judgment interest beyond contractual liability caps by ruling such contractual caps may be overridden by public policy considerations.' (citations to three state court decisions omitted.) Austin supra n 7 defines *nályééh* and discusses the *Blackgoat* case at 79-80

119 No. SC-CV-46-05 (Navajo 2006) at 2006.NANN.0000011 in www.versuslaw.com or at http://www.navajocourts.org/suctopinions2007.htm (follow 'SC-CV-46-05' hyperlink)

decision[120] and 'the Court's emphasis on the importance of homes in Navajo thinking.'[121]

In a short period of time the *Nicholson Trust* case seems to have become a solid precedent. As frequently happens, when a court has occasion to address an issue repeatedly it soon identifies the analysis best suited to the task, sharpens its articulation of that analysis and creates standing, formidable doctrine. Every year since 2003 the Navajo Supreme Court has honed its articulation of doctrine by deciding new civil jurisdiction cases, turning ever more confidently to *Nicholson Trust* and its finding of preemption based on the 1868 Treaty of Fort Sumner, which appears to have become the Navajo Supreme Court's touchstone of choice for its assertion of civil jurisdiction free from *Montana-Strate* and other inhibiting rules.[122]

At the end of 2008, the Navajo Supreme Court wrote an opinion that provides a benchmark articulation of its doctrine to date, deciding a matter that took a complicated procedural path to reach the court,[123] *Ford Motor Co. v. Kayenta District Court*.[124] The case holds that the Navajo tribal court has proper long-arm jurisdiction over the automobile company, whose vehicle had an allegedly defective seat belt, allegedly causing the death of a tribal policewoman when the vehicle overturned on the reservation.

Although Ford Motor Co.'s connection to the reservation was tenuous, based on the presence of the vehicle it had manufactured, the Court began its substantive analysis by stating that 'The Navajo Nation retains jurisdiction over claims arising within the Nation by inherent sovereignty under Article II' of the1868 Treaty of Fort Sumner. Further, the Court stated, 'To the Navajo, the Treaty is organic law. . . . a sacred document,' and that it relied on the Treaty 'as the primary source of the Nation's authority over non-Indians within the Nation.'[125] It cited *Nicholson Trust* for the proposition

120 Id. at 2. Apparently, the reference is to that part of the *Blackgoat* opinion that invoked Navajo public policy — specifically, the concept of *nályééh* — to test the validity of a contract provision to cap recovery by the claimants against the insurer, and applied it to override such a contractual limitation.

121 Id.

122 See notably Thinn v. Navajo Generating Station, SC-CV-25-06 (Navajo Oct. 19, 2007) available at http://www.navajocourts.org/suctopinions2007.htm (follow 'SC-CV-25-06' hyperlink); *Cedar Unified School District v. Navajo Nation Labor Comm'n*, SC-CV-53-06 and SC-CV-54-06 (Navajo Nov. 21, 2007), available at http://www.navajocourts.org/suctopinions.htm (follow 'SC-CV-53-06 SC-CV-54-06' hyperlink).

123 See the federal courts' handling of the case in *Ford Motor Co.v. Todecheene*, 488 F.3d 1215 (9th Cir. 2007); *Ford Motor Co. v. Todecheene*, 394 F.3d 1170 (9th Cir. 2005); *Ford Motor Co. v. Todecheene*, 221 F. Supp. 1070 (D. Ariz. 2002).

124 No. SC-CV-33-07 (Navajo Dec. 18, 2008) available at http://www.navajocourts.org/suctopinions2008.htm (follow SC-CV-33-07 hyperlink).

125 Id. at 4.

that Article II of that Treaty 'specifically recognizes the Navajo Nation's authority to regulate all nonmembers other than certain federal employees on its lands,'[126] and found that Ford Motor Co. had sufficient contacts with Navajo lands to create a reasonable expectation that it could be sued in Navajo tribal court.[127]

For good measure, the court found that, '*Montana[-Strate]* does not apply in this case,'[128] but nonetheless devoted several pages to demonstrating why it believed that the facts in *Ford Motor* satisfied 'both *Montana[-Strate]* exceptions.'[129] The Navajo Supreme Court dismissed the 2008 United States Supreme Court opinion, *Plains Commerce Bank*, on its own terms as a 'simple sale of non-tribal land between nonmembers;'[130] *i.e.*, a fact situation completely distinct from that in *Ford Motor*, where in the view of the court the company had ample contacts with tribal members on tribal land.

Summary of the Navajo Nation's Case Law on Civil Jurisdiction of Its Tribal Courts

The Supreme Court of the Navajo Nation has demonstrated a sure grasp of United States Supreme Court case law and has no inhibitions about applying it in ways that take Navajo civil jurisdiction out to permissible limits, consistent with declared tribal policy. When one traces the doctrine from *Pfizer* to *Nicholson Trust* to *Blackgoat* to *Greentree* to *Ford Motor*, it becomes clear that the *Montana-Strate* test cannot — at least in the vision of the Supreme Court of the Navajo Nation — control the civil jurisdiction of Navajo tribal courts save in the limited circumstance of a non-Indian defendant for activities arising on non-Indian lands. Even then, when one of the two *Montana-Strate* exceptions must be present to create jurisdiction, the Navajo court reads those exceptions expansively.

In *Greentree* and *Blackgoat* and *Ford Motor*, the Navajo Supreme Court could find consensual relationships with tribal members, the particular circumstance that creates the first exception in *Montana-Strate.*[131] It is certainly possible, however, that the same reasoning that led the tribal court to apply Navajo traditional law as overriding public policy might support finding the second jurisdictional exception from *Montana-Strate*, because 'the conduct of non-Indians on fee lands within [a] reservation [...]

[126] Id. at 6.
[127] Id at 2, 9.
[128] Id. at 10.
[129] Id. at 10-13.
[130] Id. at 7.
[131] See supra note 72 and accompanying text.

threatens or has some direct effect on the political integrity, the economic security, or the health or welfare of the tribe.'[132]

At the further extension of developing Navajo doctrine, the *Greentree* and *Blackgoat* cases demonstrate the possible special aspects and different law that may control when Navajo civil jurisdiction does apply. Both cases utilise concepts and doctrines drawn from Navajo common law (Fundamental Law) as their preeminent source, dictating that Navajo tribal courts may well resolve a case involving the same parties and circumstances differently than might be expected in a state court. Even so, the Navajo legal system acknowledges the sources from American Law — along with and subordinate to Navajo sources — as part of the mix that resolves the controversy.

THE THIRD INGREDIENT: NAVAJO COMMON (FUNDAMENTAL) LAW

From here growth began and the journey proceeds.
Different thinking, planning, life ways, languages, beliefs, and laws appear among us,
But the fundamental laws placed by the Holy People remain unchanged.
Hence, as we were created and with living soul, we remain Diné forever.
~ Fundamental Law, Navajo Nation Code tit. 1, §201.

The Structure of our courts is based on Anglo court systems, but the law we apply is our own. Our law is a combination of federal, Navajo and some state law. ~ Hon. Thomas Tso, C.J., Navajo Supreme Court, (Spring, 1986) 'The Tribal Court Survives in America' *Judges J.* at 22, 54.

The Navajo courts apply Navajo customs and traditions, or Navajo common law, before they apply any other form of law. ~ *Ben v. Burbank,* 7 Navajo Rptr. 222, 224 (Navajo D. Ct. 1996).

On 27 March 2007, in the Great Hall at the Sandra Day O'Connor College of Law at Arizona State University in Tempe, Arizona, the Navajo Supreme Court heard oral argument in *Tso v. Navajo Housing Authority.*[133] Lawyers for the two sides sat at counsel tables on either side of a podium, dressed in suits and ties and shuffling through their briefs and notes. They looked

[132] Id.

[133] The author attended the oral argument and took notes, which form the basis for the description and analysis included here [hereinafter *Author's Notes*]. To my knowledge, no court reporter or other source of trial transcript is available.

up at an elevated bench. Behind them rose an amphitheatre seating 350, with perhaps 150-200 people in attendance. The bailiff called, 'The Navajo Supreme Court is now in session. All rise.' The lawyers and the audience rose, as Chief Justice Herb Yazzie, Associate Justice Lorene Ferguson, and District Judge T.J. Holgate, sitting by designation, entered from a door behind the bench. When the court sat down, so did opposing counsel and the audience. The Chief Justice called the case, and asked counsel if they were prepared to proceed.

Oral argument began in a fashion familiar to appellate courts throughout the United States. The Appellant's counsel started his argument by identifying two central issues: Navajo Law and Federal Law, which he said left his client 'between a rock and a hard place.' The bench soon interrupted with questions, and dialogue between bench and counsel continued during the Appellant's allotted time. The Appellee Tso had a $36,000 judgment from tribal court against the Navajo Housing Authority (NHA) for his wrongful termination in violation of the Navajo Employment Preference Act (NEPA),[134] but the NHA pleaded federal law[135] to block Tso's enforcement of his judgment.

Alternatively, the NHA alleged that Navajo law[136] blocked execution of Tso's judgment against the NHA. The Navajo Supreme Court earlier had rejected that argument in a written opinion, holding that the NHA's assets enjoyed a statutory exemption from execution, overridden by the subsequent language of the NEPA.[137] The immediate appeal argued that subsequent amendments to the statute, creating not mere exemption but sovereign immunity for the NHA, should have retroactive effect and change that result.[138] The possibility of returning to the Supreme Court with new arguments after the case had been decided and legislative amendments had ensued, unavailable in American Law systems, presents an important aspect of Navajo law's consensual nature. The court will continue to entertain arguments until the parties are satisfied that they have exhausted all possibilities, so that repeat opinions on the same appeal are common.[139]

134 NNC, tit. 15, §§ 601-619.

135 The Appellant argued that the Secretary of Housing and Urban Development would revoke the NHA's funding if it paid the judgment from federal funds, based on OMB Circular A-87, Cost Principles for State, Local and Tribal Governments, 2 C.F.R. pt. 225, Appendix B, § 16, stating that 'damages and other settlements resulting from violations [of] Indian tribal laws and regulations are unallowable.' 62 Fed. Reg. 45934 (Aug. 29, 1997).

136 NNC tit. 6, § 623.

137 See *Tso v. Navajo Housing Authority*, 8 Navajo Rptr. 548 (2004).

138 See *Author's Notes.* The Navajo Council amended the NNC in 2005 with the clear intent of investing the NHA with sovereign immunity, a direct response to the decision in the first *Tso* appeal. See NNC tit. 6, §§ 602(A), 616(B)(1), 623.

139 For example, there also are two opinions in the *Blackgoat* case, one of which is referred to

The laws treating NHA's alleged immunity from execution are complicated, and the statutory landscape is cluttered.[140] While it might be fascinating to sort out all of the nuances, more germane to our discussion here, the oral argument went well beyond the applicable statutory sources in its inquiry as to the controlling law.

Accepting for purposes of argument that tribal and/or federal law might bar execution against the NHA, the justices immediately raised the issue of *nályééh*, the Navajo common law concept invoked in the *Blackgoat* case.[141] *Nályééh* compels compensation in forms and amounts sufficient to salve feelings on all sides of any controversy, leaving no hard feelings and 'returning people to good relations with each other in a community', thereby working 'restorative justice' in which 'the community must arrive at a consensus about the problem' and 'helping a victim is more important than determining fault'.[142] Stated another way, *nályééh* serves as a gift and an apology, as well as compensation, to make people whole, restore harmony to the community and end all dispute.[143] But does *nályééh* — Navajo Common Law — override the federal and tribal law barring execution of a judgment against the NHA?

The oral argument of the *Tso* appeal made an excellent forum for discussion of precisely that issue, and the larger issue of how Navajo common law relates to federal law and tribal statutes. Chief Justice Yazzie asked the Appellant's counsel at one point, 'Can the NHA exist in a bubble on Navajo land free of the application of Navajo Law?' The counsel replied, not meeting the question head on, that it was the tribal Council's policy to limit NHA funds exclusively to residential uses.[144] Perhaps the larger question contained in the Chief Justice's question is, 'Does the employee who complains about the NHA do so under federal law or Navajo Law?' Presuming the answer to that question is, 'Navajo Law', then, 'What is Navajo Law as defined by its proper sources?' The NNC provides that the courts of the Navajo Nation 'shall apply any laws of the United States

---

in supra ns 113-118. See www.navajocourts.org/suctopinions for a second *Blackgoat* opinion issued in 2006.

140 See supra ns 134-136 and accompanying text, and *Author's Notes.*

141 See supra n 118 and accompanying text.

142 Yazzie supra n 12 at 184-85.

143 As defined in the oral argument of counsel for the Appellee in *Tso*. See *Author's Notes.* Justice Austin supra n 7 at 79 defines *nályééh* as 'the end product of a process that uses apology, forgiveness and "talking things out" to correct a wrong. During the discussions, an agreement is reached on the amount of restitution that will restore an injured party to *hózhó*,' or to 'balance, harmony and peace.' Id. at 204.

144 Id.

that may be applicable and any laws or customs of the Navajo Nation not prohibited by applicable federal laws.'[145]

Concentrating on the issue of *nályééh* focuses the debate. The Appellee, who wished to enforce his judgment, argued that the NHA had at its disposition many funds not directly traceable to the federal government, which might properly be tapped consistent with the Navajo Common Law concept of paying debts by the debtor's clan through a collective effort recognising joint liability.[146] The Appellant countered that while that perception of *nályééh* might work well where an individual owed a debt, the ancient principle must be filtered through modern business practices and modern business structures.[147] Where a corporate structure – specifically, a public entity funded by the federal government, which has a policy that the entity should not pay judgments on peril of losing its federal funding – owes the debt the ancient Navajo Common Law may have to give way to modern concerns.

The Navajo Supreme Court handed down its decision in the *Tso* case in December 2007, holding that the legislative amendments to the NNC could not retroactively provide the NHA with sovereign immunity from NEPA judgments,[148] but that the NHA could not use federal monies to satisfy the judgment.[149] The Court then held that the NHA should pay Mr. Tso's judgment with monies not traceable to federal sources, invoking the

> [...] central principles of *Diné bi`ó'ool'jjl* (the Navajo Life Way) that affirmatively require the NHA to satisfy the judgment. The NHA has been found responsible for injuring or causing damage to Mr. Tso, and the amount of damages has been determined. Whether that amount is considered 'damages,' 'restitution' or 'nályééh' is unimportant here; the important thing is that the NHA have respect for others and for decision made by the Labor Commission, the lower court, and this Court. *Diné bi`ó'ool'jjl* recognizes our relationships to

[145] NNC tit. 7, § 204(a). The provision became part of the NNC recently, by Tribal Council Resolution CO-72-03 of October 24, 2003, implementing Tribal Council Resolution CO-69-02 of November 13, 2002, which had added the Fundamental Law provisions now found in NNC tit. 1, §§ 201-206.

Interestingly, NNC tit. 7, § 204(c) recognises the 'laws of the state in which the matter in dispute may lie' as a residual source of Navajo Law, applicable for 'Any matters not covered by the traditional customs and uses or laws or regulations of the Navajo Nation or by applicable Federal law and regulations.'

[146] See *Author's Notes.*

[147] Id.

[148] See *Tso v. Navajo Housing Authority*, SC-CV-20-06 (Navajo 2007) at www.navajocourts.org/suctopinions (follow 'SC-CV-20-06' hyperlink).

[149] Id. at 5-6.

> each other and the responsibilities that those relationships create. There was an employer-employee relationship between the NHA and Mr. Tso. That relationship created duties and responsibilities between the NHA and Mr. Tso. It has been determined that the NHA wrongfully damaged that relationship. [...] The NHA now has the responsibility to compensate Mr. Tso as directed by the courts. To disregard the responsibilities of a relationship, or to refuse to make amends as required, is shameful and without rationale. [...] We hold that the NHA must satisfy Mr. Tso's judgment against it with non-federally granted money.[150]

In any event, the ultimate decision in *Tso* is not necessary to discern the nature of the mixed jurisdiction in which it arises and is resolved. In a public session following the oral argument in that case, the question of the accommodation of Navajo Common Law within the sources of law applied by Navajo courts came up again, and Chief Justice Yazzie answered as follows:

> Our laws derive from two systems, and there will be conflicts. Our traditional customs, acknowledged by our Common Law, define who we are. Those customs exist and must be used in everything that we do. Our courts are obligated to interpret all law, not just legislative provisions and case law. Those sources must be applied in the light of traditional law, consisting of those concepts and principles that must exist absolutely if we are to remain Navajo. It is our job to conform the new law to traditional law. Traditional law comes from time immemorial. Traditional law meets new laws as mere laws enacted by human beings, and therefore inferior to laws established by our ancestors and holy people. We must always consider the source of the law.[151]

In fact, as we have seen herein, the federal Indian Law has left a good deal of leeway to the Navajo courts to apply their own law from their own indigenous sources. The Supreme Court of the United States recognised some time ago that '[t]ribal laws and procedures are often influenced by tribal custom and can differ greatly from our own. Thus, tribal courts are important mechanisms for protecting significant tribal interests.'[152]

[150] Id. at 6-7.

[151] Reconstructed from *Author's Notes*.

[152] *United States v. Wheeler*, 435 U.S. 313, 332 n. 34 (1978). Chief Justice Thomas Tso, after he had retired from the Navajo Supreme Court, noted that

Do those tribal interests include application of the concept of *nályééh* to overcome a federal prohibition against execution? The Navajo Supreme Court seems to have answered affirmatively; but even asking the question makes a statement about the mixed nature of the Navajo legal system.

The Navajo Nation has developed its current legal system, indeed its whole government structure, within the last half century, beginning from the creation of a Tribal Council in 1923 to approve oil and gas leases on the Reservation. Thereafter, when the Indian Reorganization Act of 1934 presented the Navajo Nation with an opportunity to organise tribal government under a constitution,[153] the Nation referendum vote rejected that possibility, but the incident gave impetus to the development of modern Navajo Nation government from that date forward. The Navajo Tribal Council became a de facto governing body (with a Chairman, and recognising a Chapter System of local government), slowly wresting control of Navajo internal affairs from the federal government and steadily adding sophistication to its own structure and rules.

The creation of a tribal court system played a significant part in that process. Into the 1950's, the only 'Navajo Courts' were the Courts of Indian Offenses established in 1883 by the Bureau of Indian Affairs to apply criminal law on Indian reservations, known as 'CFR Courts' because they operate under the Code of Federal Regulations.[154] Staffed by tribal elders appointed by federal authorities, three Navajo CFR courts began operating in 1903.[155] In 1958, however, the Tribal Council created a Judicial Branch of the Navajo Nation, with seven professional trial court judges and a three-judge Court of Appeals, consisting of one full time judge and two trial judges sitting by assignment.[156] In 1985, the Court of Appeals became the Navajo Supreme Court, with three permanent justices.[157] Since 1982,

---

> the 'fundamental moral principles, traditions and feelings of the Navajo people' give rise to Navajo Common Law in the same way that Justice Felix Frankfurter memorably invoked the concept of due process as embodying 'a system of rights based on moral principles so deeply embedded in the traditions and feelings of our people as to be deemed fundamental to a civilized society as conceived by our whole history.' *Solesbee v. Balkcom,* 339 U.S. 9, 16 (1950) (dissent). ~ Tso (1992) supra n 12 *at* 16.

153 Among a welter of other changes in rights and obligations.

154 25 C.F.R. §§ 11.100-11.104.

155 Tso (1986) supra n 12 at 25. For the most complete discussion of the development of the Navajo court system to date, see Austin supra n 7 at 1-36.

156 Id. at 53. The original act of the Tribal Council issued on October 16, 1958, and its provisions now appear in NNC tit. 7, §§ 201 et seq., much amended since.

157 Tso (1986) supra n 12 at 53. That act issued on December 4, 1985, and its provisions now appear in NNC tit. 7, §§ 301 *et seq.*, also much amended since.

Navajo Peacemaker Courts have offered an alternative form of dispute resolution under a headman in each local Chapter.[158]

Perhaps most significant of all, in their short existence the Navajo Nation Courts have assimilated forms, procedures and substance from the American legal system into the tribal system. The American legal system may appear to predominate at first encounter, but it serves much older Navajo values and traditions, and must give way in case of conflict. 'Navajo common law is not about rules that are enforced by authority; it deals with correcting self to restore life to solidarity. Navajo justice is a product of the Navajo way of thinking.'[159]

The United States Supreme Court has referred to tribal courts as courts of limited jurisdiction,[160] and we have seen that they may lack jurisdiction even when the circumstances of a given case or controversy arise on the reservation or otherwise have significant contacts with it. Nonetheless, from their viewpoint, the Navajo Nation's tribal courts start from the same general jurisdictional base as state courts.[161]

The special Navajo character of Navajo justice and courts shows up in many places. One of the most visible is in the Navajo Nation Code of Judicial Conduct, adopted by the tribal courts on November 1, 1991. An earlier version, in 1978, had adopted word-for-word the American Bar Association's 1972 Code of Judicial Conduct. The second effort by the Navajo courts again worked from the ABA's 1990 Model Code of Judicial Conduct, and adopted most of its language and principles. This time, however, the Navajo Code added a uniquely Navajo principle in its Canon One: The Obligation to Promote Navajo Justice.[162] The opening Canon takes as its Principle that,

> A Navajo judge should decide and rule between the Four Sacred Mountains. That means that judges, as Navajos, should apply

[158] See supra n 59.

[159] Yazzie supra n 12.

[160] See *Nevada v. Hicks*, 533 U.S. 353, 367 (2001).

[161] See *Pfizer* supra n 99. As the *Pfizer* case states, 'Our district courts are courts of general jurisdiction under the Navajo Nation Code, 7 N.N.C. §253, but their jurisdiction is limited by federal statutes and by United States Supreme Court case law.' Id. at 373-374. We must distinguish tribal courts whose jurisdiction springs from the inherent sovereignty of their constituent tribe and lands. These courts have appeared in the latter half of the 20th century. The Navajo Nation courts are general jurisdiction courts, limited by outside preemption, much as state courts must give way to certain federal peremptory exercise. Federal courts are courts of limited jurisdiction, exercising only those adjudicatory powers allocated to them by Congress, but have the power to override state and tribal courts' 'general' jurisdiction whenever Congress gives it to them.

[162] Alluded to in *Pfizer*, id at 376. Note that Canon One predated the amendments that added Fundamental Law to NNC tit. 1, § 201 and specified Fundamental Law as the first source of applicable law, in NNC tit. 7, § 204. See supra ns 145-147 and accompanying text.

Navajo concepts and procedures of justice, including the principles of maintaining harmony, respecting freedom, and talking things out in free discussion.

More specifically, Canon One of the Code of Judicial Conduct obligates a Navajo judge to understand and apply four primary values that would be foreign to any Anglo judge: 'clan relationships, harmony, traditional leadership and taking care of victims.'[163] If those terms appear foreign, however, they invoke Navajo concepts weighted with history, tradition and sense of place and identity, at the very heart of everything Navajo: *k'é*, *dooneeike'*, *hózhó*, the personal qualities that make a leader a *naat'áanii*, and *nályééh*.[164] No simple definition can suffice for any of the terms, and they are all essential to Navajo identity. Let us finish by working through the implications of *k'é*, apparently preeminent among the traditional concepts,[165] as it was applied in a case that should be startling to Anglo legal sensitivities.

K'é has been described as a 'wide range of deeply felt emotions that create solidarity of the individual with his or her clan.'[166] These emotions dictate how Navajos greet each other (by clan reference back to grandparents), give rise to folk sayings or maxims that impose duties and define relationships, set the ways of resolving conflict, and generate group empathy extending even to 'mountains, plants, animals, Mother Earth and all of creation.'[167] The same emotions explain how Navajos might adopt at the same time a non-judgmental attitude ('It's up to him.') regarding most personal behaviour and yet condemn wrongdoing by the ultimate expression of disapproval, 'He acts as if he had no relatives.'[168]

How does the concept of *k'é* affect the law and decision of individual cases? Rather dramatically, it can turn out. In *Ben v. Burbank*[169] Lucy Ben

[163] Tso (1992) supra n 12 at 17.

[164] These spellings seem to be phonetic renderings, and alternate spellings may be encountered. Both Austin supra n 7 at 203-206 and 8 Navajo Rptr. at xxiii-xxiv include excellent glossaries of Navajo terms.

[165] See NNC tit. 7, § 354(A)(5), entitled 'Knowledge of Navajo Language, Culture and Tradition', which requires all judicial applicants to speak Navajo and English, 'and have some practical knowledge of the fundamental laws of the Diné.' In addition, however, the statute specifies that the applicant must be able to demonstrate (a), 'an understanding of K'é, including the *Diné* clan system.' No other traditional concept is specified.

[166] Yazzie supra n 12 at 182. Even as he tries to define it, however, Chief Justice Yazzie cautions, 'it is difficult to translate into English because of its strong connotations.' Id., at fn. 40. Undaunted, an English-speaking student of the Navajo translated it as 'solidarity'. Witherpsoon, G (1975) *Navajo Kinship and Marriage* University of Chicago Press 37.

[167] Tso (1992) supra n 12 at 17.

[168] Id.

[169] 7 Navajo Rptr. 222 (Navajo D. Ct. 1996). Austin supra n 7 discusses *Ben* at 46, 134-35, within the context of a whole chapter devoted to the concept of *k'é*, id at 83-135.

orally instructed Tom Burbank, her cousin, to make additions on a house he was building for her. Burbank agreed and completed the work, but Ben did not pay him. After four and a half years had passed, Burbank sued Ben in tribal court and secured a judgment for $403.50. Ben appealed, alleging that the statute of limitations had run and barred the claim. In fact, the time for bringing suit on the contract had run.[170] In the state court, the case would have terminated there, the Plaintiff out of luck and out of court, with no further remedy. The Navajo Supreme Court, however, dismissed the appeal without even waiting for a reply brief from the Appellee, stating:

> The Navajo courts apply Navajo customs and traditions, or Navajo common law, before they apply any other form of law. [,,,] the Navajo way of *k'é* is the prevailing law to be applied. *K'é* recognizes 'your relations to everything in the universe,' in the sense that Navajos have respect for others and for a decision made by the group. It is a deep feeling for responsibilities to others and the duty to live in harmony with them. It has to do with the importance of relationships to foster consensus and healing. It is a deeply–felt emotion which is learned from childhood.[…] Appellant admits there was an oral agreement [and] when people make promises between one another, oral or written, they should honor those promises. […] These parties are related by clan and Appellee trusted Appellant to pay for the work because of this relationship[;] one must respect his or her relatives in order to maintain social order. […] It appeared that Appellant was hiding behind her statute of limitations claim in order to avoid paying for the work. This is not the Navajo way.[171]

FINAL WORD: A DYNAMIC MIXED JURISDICTION

The Navajo Nation's mixed jurisdiction manifests vitality and a balance, combining older ingredients in a new mix, to build an autonomous legal system in about half a century. The Navajo legal system appears to serve and preserve the traditional values of the *Diné* while it moves with that people into a larger society. It strives to maintain *Diné*'s identity as a special community unto itself, not hostile to the larger community in which it lives, but insistently assertive of its own distinctive character at the same time embracing elements of the society all around it.

170 NNC tit. 7, § 602(B) (1)(three years).

171 7 Navajo Rptr. at 224.

Turkey's Synthetic Legal System and Her Indigenous Socio-Culture(s) in a 'Covert' Mix

ESİN ÖRÜCÜ

INTRODUCTION

Turkey is not a mixed jurisdiction in the classical sense. Neither does she have an overt mixed legal system. Yet, the Turkish legal system is mixed in two other and different senses. In the first sense, it is a synthetic legal system, legislatively constructed by receiving, adapting and mixing laws from various foreign western sources and melting them down in the Turkish pot, to form the overlay. In the second sense, it is a mix of these diverse laws with a people the majority of whose values reflect a different socio-culture related to one past element of the legal system, that of the Ottoman Empire - erased by the Turkish Republic - significantly different to the socio-cultures represented by the incoming laws. It is this unique composite that makes it worthwhile to consider the Turkish legal system in the context of this volume, as a covert mixed legal system.[1]

First, in Part I, the synthetically constructed legal system, the modern overlay, will be assessed with its diverse sources still alive and used as source-laws. Here, my intention will not be to make a case for or against 'legal-change-as-legal transplant', or as I call such movements, 'law as transposition'.[2] Neither will I discuss in this part how law deals with culture in Turkey. My concern will be to demonstrate the 'synthetic'

[1] This piece is an aggregate of two of my previously published articles: (2006) 'A Synthetic and Hyphenated Legal System: The Turkish Experience' 1:2 *The Journal of Comparative Law*, 27, and (2008) 'Judicial navigation as official law meets culture in Turkey' 4.1 *International Journal of Law in Context*, 35.

[2] See Örücü (2002) 'Law as Transposition' (51*) International and Comparative Law Quarterly* 205, and also Part II of this contribution.

and 'hyphenated' nature of Turkish law. Second, in Part II, the efforts of Turkish judges will be considered as they navigate, always keeping within the synthetic framework, and yet catering for the needs of the people with clashing values – the underlay - for whom the laws were made with a view to changing their traditions and culture(s). The purpose here will be to assess the work of the courts when law meets culture in Turkey, since the culture of the official legal system and the culture of the people do not always accord and the courts must navigate and steer within the framework of the 'synthetic' and 'hyphenated' legal system as best they can.

Gessner says: 'Empirical evidence in history and from contemporary reception processes [shows] that a legal culture is rooted very deeply in society and cannot easily and quickly be changed by top-down measures.'[3] Does the Turkish experience successfully challenge this observation in a country where we can speak not only of a 'hyphenated legal system',[4] but also of a 'hyphenated socio-culture'?

PART I. THE SYNTHETIC AND HYPHENATED LEGAL SYSTEM

THE CONCEPTUAL FRAMEWORK

The legal system of Turkey is an 'eclectic', 'synthetic' and 'hyphenated' one, being directly borrowed from, and significantly influenced by, foreign models. These models are all Continental European.[5] None of the models represent an Eastern or religious viewpoint. The present legal framework of Turkey is the product of law being moved across frontiers from societies and laws socio- and legal-culturally diverse from her own. This framework has been synthetically constructed through 'imposed receptions', voluntary 'receptions', 'imitations', 'adaptations' and 'adjustments'.[6] Thus, rather

[3] Gessner, V (1994)'Global Legal Interaction and Legal Cultures' (7) *Ratio Juris* 132 at 136.

[4] The term 'hyphenated', which I use as part of my vocabulary of analysis, has been borrowed from Çağlar. See, Çağlar, A.S (1997) 'Hyphenated Identities and the Limits of Culture' in Madood, T and Werbner, P (eds) (1997) *The Politics of Multiculturalism in the New Europe,* Zed Books Postcolonial Encounters Series 169. The term is an apt one to use not only for the legal system and the laws and but also for the peoples of this country. In the form used by Çağlar, the term 'hyphenated' corresponds to my 'hyphenated socio-culture'. In the manner I analyse it however, it fits well with the character of the Turkish legal system. In Çağlar's discourse the terms 'hybrid', 'creolised' or 'hyphenated' are used interchangeably, for my purpose the only appropriate one at this stage is 'hyphenated'. The 'hyphenated' character of the law in modern Turkey, and the 'hyphenated' nature of the existence and identity of her people apply today as well as in the past.

[5] With the exception of some recent American influence. See Örücü, E (1999) 'Turkey: A Survey of the Public Law Framework' (5) *European Public Law* 30.

[6] Örücü, E (1996) 'Turkey: Change Under Pressure' in Örücü, E, Attwooll, E, and Coyle,

than being homegrown, legal evolution has been through a succession of imports and has relied on major translation work. Legal evolution was instigated through a strong desire to become western and contemporary, and still today rapid law reforms are being made in order to fulfil the requirements of the European Union *acquis communautaire* in the hope of joining the European Union.[7] The roles of 'historical accident', 'chance', 'choice', 'prestige' and 'competing legal systems' can all find a place in the experience of Turkey.

Turkey, heir to the Ottoman Empire, has been through a number of phases of development: between 1299 and 1839 an Islamic state, from 1839 to the fall of the Empire in 1920 a mixed legal system with considerable French influence, and since 1923 a modern, western, laic and civilian democracy. Now as in the past, legal and social evolution is through voluntary receptions and at times also through 'imposed receptions', law being principally regarded in instrumental terms: no 'mirror thesis' here.[8] When the ideological and technological decision was made in 1924 to move outside the framework of the indigenous system of laws rather than to integrate and modernise the existing systems, and to receive foreign codes, and use the tool of reception as the sole method of law reform, a commission of twenty-six members was set the task of translating first the Swiss Civil Code from its French version. Subsequently, a number of special committees translated most of the important commentaries on various branches of law into Turkish. Within the year 1926 Turkish legal experts produced four entirely new codes, and there were more to follow, the main aim of this 'purposive use of law' being to demolish the foundations of the old legal system by creating completely new laws, and 'to regulate and legislate the [...] relationships of the people according to what was thought these relationships ought to be, and not according to existing customs, usages, and religious mores. This [...] was revolutionary and radically reformist, [...] -- a prime example of "social engineering through law".'[9]

S (eds) *Studies in Legal Systems: Mixed and Mixing* Kluwer Law International 89; Örücü, E (1992)'The Impact of European Law on the Ottoman Empire and Turkey' in Mommsen, WJ and de Moor, JA (eds) *European Expansion and Law* Berg Publishers 39; Örücü, E (2003) 'Comparatists and extraordinary places' in Legrand P and Munday, R (eds) *Comparative Legal Studies: Traditions and Transitions* Cambridge University Press 467; Örücü, E (1999) *Critical Comparative Law: Considering Paradoxes for Legal Systems in Transition* Nederlanse Vereniging voor Rechtsvergelijking No: 59 Kluwer Law International 80.

[7] See Örücü,E (2004) 'Seven Packages Towards Harmonisation with the European Union' (10:4) *European Public Law* 603

[8] The received legal culture is a synthesis of predominantly Swiss, German, Italian and French legal cultures, and the legal system is based totally on large-scale eclectic receptions from Western models.

[9] Örücü (1992) supra note 6 at 53. It is worth noting here that Iraq, which was part of the

The Turkish Republic had an aspiration and her political, legal and social systems were constructed and geared towards the achievement of this. Developments over the years must all be assessed in the light of this vision. When discussing 'legal transplants', the Turkish experience was referred to by Watson and other scholars, as the most extreme example.[10]

The theory of 'competing legal systems', used in our day mainly in the rhetoric of 'law and economics' analysis, was, in a different sense, the basis of the reception of laws that formed the Turkish legal system in the years 1924-1930. The various Codes were selected from what were seen to be 'the best' in their field for various reasons. No single legal system served as the model. The choice was driven at times by the perceived 'prestige' of the model, and at other times by 'efficiency', sometimes by 'chance', or 'historical accident'. Modernisation[11] and westernisation were not based on any one dominant culture, and the fact that a number of different models were chosen may have given the borrowings 'cultural legitimacy'.[12] The civil law, the law of obligations and civil procedure were borrowed from Switzerland, commercial law, maritime law and criminal procedure from Germany, criminal law from Italy and administrative law from France; all translated, adapted and adjusted to solve the social and legal problems of Turkey and to interlock.[13]

Ottoman Empire from 1534 until the First World War, produced a Civil Code in 1953, one of the first modern civil codifications in the Arab World. Unlike other codes such as of Lebanon, Egypt and Syria, this Code received the French Civil Code as a model whilst, in contrast to the Turkish experience, reserving a considerable place for legal rules borrowed from Islamic law, which was at the root of Iraqi law, forming a voluntary synthesis between Muslim inspiration and occidental law. This Code then became a model for Jordan. See Al Dabbagh, H (2005) 'La réception du modèle juridique français par le code civil irakien' (2) *Révue Internationale de Droit Comparé* 263, who calls this a 'supple reception', a 'brassage' and a 'métissage'.

[10] See for example, Zweigert, K and Kötz, H (1998) *An Introduction to Comparative Law* (3rd ed), trans. Weir, T Clarendon Press. As recently as 2000, Alan Watson cited the Turkish example to support his views. See Watson, A (2000) *Legal Transplants and European Private Law* Ius Commune Lectures on European Private Law: 2. So does William Twining consider this example in Twining, W (2005) 'Social Science and Diffusion of Law' (32) *Journal of Law and Society* 203 at 223-228.

[11] We know that there is no settled definition of 'modernisation' and 'development', both being concepts influenced by subjective values as to the desired direction of a society. We also know that 'success' has never been satisfactorily defined.

[12] See Ajani, G (1998)'The Role of Comparative Law in the Adoption of New Codifications' in *Italian National Reports to the XVth International Congress of Comparative Law* Giuffrè editore 65 at 68-69 and at 80.

[13] The existence of choice differentiates a reception from an imposition where the recipient has no say. If 'competing systems' were not comparative alternatives, then, there could be no justification, or no reasonable ground for choice of the most efficient system or solution or rule. See, Chang, R (1998) 'Comparison and the Justification of Choice' (146) *University of Pennsylvania Law Review* 1569 at 1573. On this criterion alone, the Turkish legal experience is a substantial case in 'reception' and translation. See also Glenn who opposes the term

Although Hoffman claims that distortions occur in translation of even a single word in 'transporting human meaning from one culture to another' unless 'the entire language' around the word or its audience are transported,[14] and that 'legislation cannot make mores',[15] the entire Turkish legal system is built on such institutional transfers and translations.

In an attempt to marry social science research on diffusion and legal research on transplantation and reception, Twining has looked at 'diffusion of law' research carried out by Everett Rogers[16] and tested it in the Turkish experience.[17] I do not however agree that the testing of Rogers' key elements or conceptual scheme in Turkey, furthers our understanding of the Turkish experience. Though the questions posed are valid ones used by many analysts studying reception processes, be they legal or social science researchers, regardless of whether these questions are initially posed in the domain of social science research or not, I do not believe that the diffusion theory has a monopoly on these straightforward questions. As a plethora of metaphors and vocabulary is suggested and used both in social science discourse on diffusion and legal discourse on transplants and receptions, Twining rightly asks: Which of the metaphors of this vast heritage are relevant to a particular project?

The assertion; 'The occasion, the condition, the timing, what is received, formal channel of initial reception, change agents and heterophily' put forward by Rogers and tested by Twining in Turkey breaks up the account of the process into convenient sections: a neat arrangement which however does not add much that is analytically useful to the hitherto presented exposé.[18] Are we better placed in any way if we recount the story under these headings, or use the term 'diffusion'? Does one have to be a sociologist or anthropologist to ask questions about 'occasions, motives, agents, recipients, pathways, obstacles, trialability, observability, impact and so on'?[19]

It is also important to note that in the Turkish experience the exporter's perspective does not exist and the whole process must be assessed from the importer's perspective.[20] Though Twining claims that, used as a generic

---

imposition and talks of 'reception as alliance' and 'reception as construction': Glenn, P (1987) 'Persuasive authority' (32) *McGill Law Journal* 261at 265.

14 Hoffman, E (1991) *Lost in Transplantation* Minerva, at 272, 275.

15 Used by Legrand, P (1997) 'The Impossibility of Legal Transplants' (4) *Maastricht Journal of Comparative and European Law* 111 at 119.

16 Rogers, EM (1995) [1963] *Diffusion of Innovations* Free Press.

17 Twining (2005) supra n 10, 203 at 210-221 and at 223-228.

18 See works by Örücü, supra n 6.

19 Twining (2005) supra n 10 at 228.

20 Contrast with Greenhalgh, T et al (2004) in Twining (2005) supra n 10 at 223.

term, 'diffusion' includes imitation, spread, transposition, adoption and reception, to me 'diffusion' implies emanation and spread from a single source or centre and therefore, has 'an export bias'[21] and therefore cannot accurately be applied to the Turkish experience. The standpoint of any analysis of this experience must be 'an import bias'. In fact, one could rather talk of 'appropriation'.

As observed above, the theory of 'competing legal systems' prevails in the evolution of the Turkish legal system. When problems arise, models are sought according to the 'prestige' and/or the 'efficiency' of the model, always within the framework of a democratic, liberal market economy, human rights and the overall requirements of the 'immutable articles' of the Constitution. For example, the area of administrative law, born from the French model, has been influenced recently by Anglo-American institutions.[22]

In addition to the selective approach to Continental Codes, the *Yargıtay*[23] (The Court of Last Instance) was enabled to make adjustments to the law by the flexible rules present in the 1926 Civil Code sections 1, 2 and 4, which correspond *verbatim* to sections 1, 2 and 4 of the Swiss Civil Code. These are rules on justice and equity, objective good faith and the principles of the rule of law. For the development of the Turkish law and legal system, the importance of section 1 cannot be overstated:

> The law must be applied in all cases that come within the letter and the spirit of its provisions. If no relevant provision can be found in the statute, the judge must decide in accordance with the customary law and, in its absence, in accordance with the rule which he would lay down, were he the legislator. In so doing, he must be guided by accepted legal doctrine and case law.

[21] Twining (2005) supra n 10 at 232. Also see Twining, W (2004)'Diffusion of Law: A Global Perspective' (49) *Journal of Legal Pluralism and Unofficial Law* 1 at 5.

[22] The 'independent regulatory agency model' is becoming increasingly important as a model for Turkish administrative institutions, such as in the case of the Supreme Board of Radio and Television and the Board for the Protection of Competition, two public corporate bodies, both established in 1994. In the last few decades, there has been a 'growing tendency to create an independent Turkish administrative law based on a balanced merger of universal, modern institutions - including the French model - with local realities, needs and concepts.' And, this development is not confined to administrative law alone. Güran, S (1996) 'Administrative Law' in Ansay, T and Wallace D (eds) (1996) *Introduction to Turkish Law* (4th edn) Kluwer Law International 50 at 50.

[23] For readers unfamiliar with the Turkish alphabet: it contains the letters ç, ş, ğ, ö, ü and ı (undotted i) both in the lower case and the upper case.

It is also worth remembering that in a legal system such as the Turkish, 'in which the source of law is determined by the formal legal framework, custom and tradition become a source of law only when recognised by courts,'[24] as will also be seen in Part II

When Turkish courts look for new ways of dealing with emerging problems and difficult cases where matters of principle are to be settled, Turkish legal scholars and the higher courts scrutinise the reception models, the so-called 'source laws' (*kaynak kanunlar*), thus the term 'hyphenated legal system' becomes appropriate in depicting this legal system: at times reference is made to *İsviçre-Türk Hukuku* (Swiss-Turkish Law) to be seen below. Although interpretation tends to introduce subjective and cultural tonalities and values – which we will consider in Part II - foreign law always provides inspiration and stimulus.

In sum, as Turkey went through a process of total and global modernisation, westernisation, secularisation, democratisation and constitutionalism following the collapse of the Ottoman Empire and the founding of the Republic, efforts of reform rested solely on import from the major continental jurisdictions both as to form and content. Private law, administrative law, constitutional law, criminal law, civil and criminal procedures, commercial law, maritime law and the law of bankruptcy were thus reshaped. Other laws such as Labour Law and Social Security Law were passed later, again based on foreign models. Later still, significant developments in the fields of democracy, fundamental rights and freedoms and review of constitutionality found their way into Turkish law, the last by the 1961 Constitution in the preparation of which wide use was made of the West German and the Italian models. Its provisions on economic development were inspired by the 1949 Indian Constitution. The 1958 French Constitution and the American Constitution inspired the present 1982 Constitution. Thus we can speak of a 'synthetic legal system', constructed artificially, solely by legislation.

It is also worth remembering that historically, Turkish academics had most of their training in universities in the countries from where the receptions came. Academics so trained undertook the 'fitting' of models to the Turkish situation and the 'tuning' of them. Language training and translations were extensive. In addition, in the early years of the Republic, Swiss, Austrian and German academics also contributed to the new legal system thus greatly helping the imported system to take root. This was the consequence of a historical accident. Professors, such as Schwartz, König, Neumark and Hirsh, given sanctuary in Turkey before the Second World

[24] Örücü (1996) supra n 6 at 106.

War, held posts in Turkish universities. The presence of such German and Austrian professors in Turkey at the time of reception fuelled the spread of legal ideas in support of the received. In time, many of their Turkish assistant lecturers themselves became influential professors and so helped the internalisation of law, or to use Twining's terminology, 'internal diffusion'.

Since the reforms in the legal framework were accompanied and complemented by a series of social reform laws aimed at changing people, a most important feature of these far reaching radical reforms was that their impact was intended to be not just on the legal system, but also on the social system.[25] This means that the most significant import was 'modernity', and this was an import on a major scale.

Current 'receptions' in Turkey vis-a-vis European Community law are examples of weak 'imposed receptions', the qualifier 'weak' being attached to this analysis as the element of choice is still there.[26] Therefore, 'concerted parallel development', and 'reception' would be more appropriate terms of analysis for some of today's import.[27]

In Turkey, domestic integration and the centralised system are considered as *sine quo non* of each other even today, and the unification of diverse socio- and legal cultures through centrally imposed laws and integration are seen to go hand in hand. The legal system is still legalistic and positivist, that is, created top-down. Legal pluralism has never been on the agenda since the collapse of the Ottoman Empire. While trying to build a general theoretical framework for 'transfrontier mobility of law', I once designated the Turkish legal system as a '*purée*', pointing out the remarkable overriding forces such as elite dominance, the desire on the part of this *élite dirigeante* to westernise and modernise the society and to eliminate custom, and legalism, which moved the existing diverse elements into a compound, a legal system in the civilian tradition, making the Turkish experience an exception to the rule.[28] A comparatist would have expected the system to

[25] The social reforms were introduced by the eight reform laws (*İnkilap Kanunları*), establishing secular education and civil marriage, adopting the Latin alphabet and the international numerals, introducing the hat, closing the dervish convents, abolishing certain titles, and prohibiting the wearing of certain garments. These laws are still protected by the 1982 Constitution; their constitutionality cannot be challenged even today, nor can they be amended. See art 174 of the 1982 Constitution.

[26] See Örücü, E (2000) 'Turkey Facing the European Union – Old and New Harmonies' (25) *European Law Review* 57.

[27] See for a number of harmonisation packages introduced since 2002, Örücü, E (2004) supra note 7. The diffusion theory suggested by Twining as a method of analysis could apply to these new law reforms in Turkey facing the *acquis communautaire*, as in these borrowings, the 'export bias' is also obvious.

[28] Örücü, E (1995) 'A Theoretical Framework for Transfrontier Mobility of Law' in Jagtenberg,

become an overt mixed legal system, maybe even similar to Algeria. Yet, the old institutions were destroyed, and the new ones erected in their place mainly by legislative enactments. 'Optimistic normativism', that is using law as an instrument of 'social engineering', was the 'political belief'.[29] The modernising elite brought about development through legal enactment and enforcement of translocated laws from western countries. This allowed no scope for 'bottom-up' law-making. As would be expected, the discord between the official formal legal system and the existing socio-cultural systems was bound to create problems. Such issues will be considered in Part II. However, the absence of 'bottom-up' law-making in Turkey was and is compensated for by the role allocated to the High Courts at the level of civil (*Yargıtay*), administrative (*Danıştay*) and constitutional (*Anayasa Mahkemesi*) matters. Although the legal order cannot be said to have been nationally and organically grown at the outset, the external 'viruses' that were injected and therefore infected Turkish law may be said to have worked as positive 'irritants' so helping in the production of 'antibodies' to create a healthier body than one left to its own devices.[30]

I will now examine and attempt to illustrate the 'hyphenated' nature of laws in Turkey. I will also consider the factors that helped the creation of this synthetic legal system.

THE LEGAL SYSTEM AND THE SOURCE-LAWS

The elements of the present compound, all from the same legal-cultural tradition, are legal-culturally different from what was already there, and the socio-cultures they represent are also different from the indigenous ones. A new legal system was legislatively created and history was made irrelevant to law: the Turkish experience is an ahistorical episode.Thus, if continuity is needed in systems in transition, then the Turkish experience defies this rule: she made a clear cut with the past. Yet, if continuity is understood as continuity from 'the source law' (*kaynak kanun*), that is, a continued relationship with the models, then the diagnosis is quite different.[31] The claim that once transplanted, the cord tying the transplanted to its model is severed - which is the argument used for civil law influence in common law for instance – is not true for Turkey. In fact, in Turkey the cord cut

R, Örücü, E and de Roo, A (eds) *Transfrontier Mobility of Law* Kluwer Law International at 10.

29 Ajani (1998) supra n 12 at 68.

30 Compare with Teubner's views. See Teubner, G (1998) 'Legal Irritants: Good Faith in British Law or How Unifying Law Ends Up in New Divergencies' (61) *Modern Law Review* 11.

31 We will have to wait and see how the 2002 Civil Code and the 2005 Penal Code will be related to the source laws by the courts.

at the time of receptions was that with the national past. This cord was then re-attached to the new models. The new attachments are constantly reinforced. It has also been claimed that a borrowing once 'cut off from its roots' ceases to be part of that culture. Generally speaking, this is not the case in Turkey either, as the borrowings have never been severed from their roots. As will be observed below, these attachments are still being strengthened, so contributing to and maintaining the 'hyphenated' nature of the legal system, in spite of developing differences of interpretation due to context. The relationship between the historic models and the present Turkish law is interesting to trace.

The First Cord: Swiss-Turkish Law

Indeed in the early years following the receptions, Turkish private law was referred to as *'İsviçre-Türk Hukuku'* (Swiss-Turkish law). This alone justifies the designation 'hyphenated legal system'. There are many recent references to Swiss-Turkish law, thus indicating that the 'hyphenated' legal system is still in existence even more than 80 years after the first import. Obviously the ties are not as strong today as they were, but as will be seen, especially in times of developing principles, changing general policy or introducing far-reaching change into Turkish law, and notably in 'unification of precedents', the judiciary use such references either for justification or for comfort. Such references are frequent also in the usage of sections 1, 2, and 4 of the Civil Code. In addition, reference to 'the source law' is often made in dissenting opinions in support of views for opposing a majority decision. In doctrinal works the references have always been there. Both the doctrine and the judges refer frequently to von Tuhr, Merz, Andrew Schwartz, Karl Lorenz, Hedemann, Egger, Escher, the ZGB and the BGB. Nevertheless over the years, a Turkish Civil law, a Turkish Commercial law, and a Turkish Civil Procedure and other laws have developed, slowly diverging from 'the source laws'. However even today, the higher courts make use of the models when reaching decisions, though never base a decision solely on 'the source law'. 'The source law' is still seen as an aid to further modernisation, and as a stimulus.

In Developing Principles

Reference to Swiss-Turkish law is frequent for instance, in developing the principle of 'adapting contractual terms to changing circumstances' in private law contracts. Faced with extreme inflation and economic difficulties in the 1990's, the *Yargıtay* held the view that judges should have the power to interfere in contractual relationships and apply to private law contracts *clausula rebus sic standibus,* or the '*imprévision*' theory used normally in administrative contracts. The Court typically pronounces that if the balance between the parties is disrupted because of extraordinary circumstances and this becomes unbearable for one of the parties, then to bind them to the contractual obligations absolutely is not in keeping with notions of fairness, justice and objective good faith. Such burdens must be shared by all, even though in different proportions. This view applies especially to long-term contracts.

One of the most interesting of these cases deals with 'force majeure', the 'collapse of the foundation of contract', 'the intervention of the judge into the contract', and 'adapting the contract to changing circumstances' in 'real property sales contracts by instalments' with payments to be made in foreign currency. In this case,[32] the *Yargıtay* reiterated that the basis of contract law was *pacta sund servanda* and the freedom of contract, and then pointed to the necessity that there should be equality between the parties. The Court indicated that *pacta sund servanda* is limited by other principles of private law, the most important arising when the equilibrium of interests is distorted by supervening events. The *Yargıtay* stated that an insistence on performance may lead to a violation of section 2/2 of the Code (bad faith) and that, though an exceptional and secondary possibility, the judge can use his powers arising from section 1/1, and create rules for the facts before him to fill the gaps. The *Yargıtay* in this case referred to a Swiss Federal Court decision, pointing out that this principle could also apply to contracts which would have future results and contracts which do not terminate by performance. So in this case, since the instalments could be regarded as links in a chain covering a period of 72 months, the contract did not terminate by a single performance. Here justification was sought from 'the source law' and the Federal Court of that source when sections 1, 2 and 4 of the Civil Code were put into action and developments in the principle of adaptation were suggested.[33]

Later,[34] the rules of 'contractual adaptation' and thereby the '*imprévision*' theory were applied to bank credits indexed to foreign currency. The *Yargıtay* again reiterated that though freedom of contract and *pacta sund servanda* are the bases of Turkish contract law, the State has the Constitutional duty to protect the consumer and ensure the orderly and sound functioning of the money, credit, capital, goods and services market. Again, section 4 of the Civil Code was called in to help, and the *Yargıtay* stated: 'In order to

32 95/145;95/3339; 6.4.1995; 21 *YKD* 1995, 911. All the cases in this survey have been translated from Turkish by the author. These cases have also been used in Örücü (1999) supra n 5.
33 The Federal Court accepted the doctrine of 'adaptation' on 4.5.1952 at 916.
34 1996/11-762; 97/77; 12.2.1997; 23 *YKD* 1997, 679.

alleviate injustice, section 2/2 is normally used in Swiss-Turkish law. When the foundation of the contract collapses, "the source law" allows the judge to intervene. Nevertheless "adaptation" is a supplementary aid and expert evidence must be used.'[35]

Deciding on compensation for 'intangible damages' in another case, the *Yargıtay* considered 'Swiss-Turkish doctrine' and determined that the problem is viewed there in the context of 'neighbourhood law'. The decisions of the Swiss Federal Court were looked at before the opinion was expressed that intangible damages is the objective reduction in personal values and that this objective reduction also refers to other members of society.[36]

Even in the area of family law we see reference to Swiss law. In one case[37] the *Yargıtay* looked at Professor Tuor's textbook and the decisions of the Swiss Federal Court as well as Turkish doctrine, in determining what is an 'engagement' in order to decide on whether gifts beyond the ordinary should be returned upon the breaking of an engagement. The Court was careful to differentiate between the breaking up of an 'engagement', that is a promise to marry, in which case gifts beyond the ordinary should be returned, and of 'living together without a valid marriage act', in which case they need not; since both parties act outside legality, the law protects the possessor.

In Unification of Precedents

The *Yargıtay*, in a unification of precedents decision,[38] while dealing with 'arbitration agreements', first determined that a number of different systems were accepted by the laws of Switzerland, Germany, Austria and France,[39] and then said:

> Section 533 of the Turkish Code of Civil Procedure is differently arranged to "the source law", the Neuchatel Code of Civil Procedure section 488. Somehow, the words "unless otherwise contracted" in section 488/1 have not been incorporated into section 533. The translation leaves a gap. Neither does section 533 have any indication as to what would lead to an appeal. We therefore think that section

35 *Id* at 682.
36 96/3713; 96/4111; 8.4.1996; 22 *YKD* 1996, 1548.
37 98/10173; 98/12105; 24.11.1998; 25 *YKD*, 170.
38 93/4; 94/1; 28.1.1994; 20 *YKD* 1994, 519.
39 *Id* at 521-522.

> 533 should be interpreted anew, as the existing interpretations and practices do not give satisfactory results.[40]

Then the *Yargıtay* unified various decisions emanating from its chambers in the following way: 'During the discussions some judges have said that we cannot follow "the source law". The majority however, is of the view that we can. Thus, an arbitration award not in accordance with the law can be appealed against.'[41]

In another unification of precedents decision, this time in a very different area, that of natural paternity, illegitimacy and inheritance rights, the *Yargıtay*[42] unified the decisions of various of its chambers to the effect that when a natural child's paternity is determined by a court decision, that child becomes an illegitimate child and can inherit from the father according to the amended section 443 of the then Civil Code. The *Yargıtay*, after a comparative discussion of the position of natural, illegitimate and legitimate children in systems as far apart as Norway, Russia, France and England, looked specifically to the developments that have taken place in Switzerland as 'the source law', 'the jurisdiction from where we took our Civil Code',[43] and pointed to the reforms there in 1976, stating that the two types of suits for paternity have been abolished[44] and that no difference now exists between children who are acknowledged and those whose paternity has been determined by court decision. The *Yargıtay* then held: 'This is the path to be followed. Turkish law should be evaluated in keeping with contemporary and comparative developments.'[45]

Another area of interest is the 'hierarchy of the norms'. According to doctrine, if there is a gap between the Statute and a contract, parties may fill this by their free will. However, if there are imperative rules, then they cannot fill this gap. Since, after being amended in 1983, sections 1404-1406 of the Turkish Commercial Code were no longer imperative rules, according to the *Yargıtay*, parties could insert special rules into a contract and these rules take priority over the general rules in the Code.[46] The Court pointed out that in 'the source German Commercial Code' these provisions were suppletive and yet were received by Turkey at the time with adaptations to make them imperative, so making it impossible to change them by contract.

40 *Id* at p. 526.
41 *Id* at 528.
42 96/1; 97/1; 22.2.1997; 23 *YKD* 1997, 853.
43 *Id* at 856.
44 ZGB. sections 252, 261.
45 TCC section 1 and ZGB section 1.
46 95/1993; 95/3369; 14.4.1995; 21 *YKD* 1995, 1407.

However, there is no reasoning to be found to explain this departure.[47] The Court made references to the Italian and the German systems and stated that the system of Swiss-Turkish Law of Obligations is different to these in that there are neither general nor special rules on this matter,[48] and accordingly the will of the parties should be accepted.

In Dissenting Opinions

There is also reliance on 'the source law' where dissenting opinions seek support in opposing the majority decisions.

In a case revolving around whether the invalidation of the inheritance rights of a father could have an impact on the rights of his heir,[49] the dissenting opinion discussed Swiss law, although the decision itself did not. In this opinion reference was made to the work of Professor Escher of Zurich University (from a translation dated 1949) 'lending support to our view'.[50]

In another case[51] related to the determination of rent and interest, a dissenting opinion used Swiss and Turkish doctrine, Swiss and German laws, and the decisions of the Swiss Federal Court for support. The dissenting judges tried to limit the extensive use of section 2/2 of the Civil Code by the *Yargıtay,* saying that analogy and a claim of abuse of rights cannot be used to obstruct the reliance on the applicable provisions of the Code, since section 2/2 should have only a secondary and corrective role. One dissenting judge said: 'This view is supported by the BGB and ZGB as well as Swiss-Turkish law.'[52]

Again, in a case[53] revolving around the right to ask for interest in late payment for the expropriation price, dissenting opinions claimed that the issue should be regulated according to the understanding in 'the source law'. There were references to Turkish doctrinal writings on Swiss and German laws and to a translation of the works of von Tuhr. Citing principles of liability law (*neminem zoedere*) from Swiss and German laws, reference was made to the BGB when looking for a basis for additional damages as a result of devaluation. Further reference was made to Swiss Federal Court decisions: 'Swiss-Turkish law accepts that if inflation is higher than the rate of "moratory interest", then "additional damages" can

47 *Id* at 1409.
48 *Id* at 1411.
49 96/2-888; 97/306; 9.4.1997; 23 *YKD* 1997, 1687.
50 *Id* at 1699.
51 94/2;95/2; 24.11 1995; 22 *YKD* 1996, 165.
52 *Id* at 172.
53 96/5-144; 96/503; 19.6.1996; 23 *YKD* 1997, 168.

be demanded.'[54] As to proof, a decision of the Neuchatel Court of Appeal was cited, as translated by a Turkish Professor of Civil Procedure. This opinion indicates that in the area of property, expropriation, monetary debts, inflation and additional damages, section 2 of the Civil Code should be applied as supported by Professor Schwartz, who was one of the most influential and important of the foreign professors teaching in the İstanbul and Ankara University Law Faculties in the years following the receptions, and whose works are among the reference books still in use.

The Second Cord: German-Turkish Law

In 1994 the *Yargıtay* dealt with a case, in which sections 3 and 21 of the Commercial Code were applied. The Court had to determine what was a commercial act and whether delictual activities could be considered commercial acts in relation to insurance policies.[55] The *Yargıtay* said: 'In Turkish, German and Swiss laws, in order to consider the possibility of drawback interest for delictual acts, this delictual act should be regulated by the Commercial Code or be regarded as a commercial act both in view of the victim and the perpetrator.'[56] There was also some discussion of German 'source law' and doctrine on this issue in the dissenting opinions.

In a case[57] dealing with letters of guarantee, bills of lading and 'clear on board', and the resolution of the question as to whether the carrier is free of liability when the sender enters wrong information into the bill of lading, the *Yargıtay* indicated that the topic had been widely discussed in international law, and then referred to letters of guarantee (clear on board) in the French and the German Commercial Codes, showing that there is no agreement on the point. A dissenting opinion referred to German, Italian and French doctrine, and English doctrine and cases on misrepresentation. It was then suggested that:

> Since the applicable provision, section 1064/11 of the Turkish Commercial Code, does not exist in "the source German law" (HGB) and neither was it in the Turkish Government Draft Bill when it went to Parliament, then this must mean that the Judicial Committee added this in haste and it went through Parliament without discussion. It is obvious that the provision was written hurriedly. If regarded in this light, the rules of the Hamburg Convention on

[54] *Id* at 185.
[55] 94/2242; 94/7490; 10.11.1994; 21 *YKD* 1995, 425.
[56] *Id* at 428.
[57] 93/565; 94/3295; 21.4.1994; 20 *YKD* 1994, 1782.

Carriage of Goods by Sea could apply and section 1064/11 should be thus interpreted. This is also in accordance with legal opinion given by Turkish Maritime law experts.[58]

The Third Cord: Italian-Turkish Law

In the area of criminal law and criminal procedure, there are also references to 'the source law', the Italian (Penal Code) and German (Code of Criminal Procedure) laws. We can thus talk of Italian-Turkish and German-Turkish laws as other 'hyphenated' designations, although, contrary to the case in '*İsviçre-Türk Hukuku*', such hyphenated references are not made. As would be expected, in the area of criminal law and criminal procedure there are fewer references to 'the source laws'. These references are mostly in dissenting opinions rather than in the decisions themselves and are resorted to in order to challenge mistaken interpretation of the 1926 Turkish Criminal Code and the 1929 Code of Criminal Procedure. Mistakes in translation at the time of reception are pointed out and the *Yargıtay* is called upon to search for the true meanings in the original versions.

For instance, in a case concerning 'murder to facilitate the committing of another crime', the dissenting opinion said that the term 'crime' in sections 135, 150 and 163 of the Code of Criminal Procedure was a mistaken translation of the term 'act' in 'the source law', whereas the term 'action' used in section 257 was the correct translation.[59] It was indicated that when section 135 was amended in 1992, this mistake should have been corrected. After pointing to some other discrepancies, the dissenting judge said, 'as can be seen, as a result of giving wrong meanings to terms and concepts, the Turkish practice has become divorced from the laws of the legal systems that inspired it'.[60]

In a case[61] related to causing bodily harm to, and the maltreatment of members of the family, though there were no references to foreign sources in the decision, again the dissenting judge referred to mistakes in translation and interpretation. He criticised the established view of the *Yargıtay* that regards the term 'a number of persons' as more than three, and 'a few persons' as three. According to him these variations do not exist in the Italian 'source law', where the term '*plu persone*' is used to indicate more than two persons. The Turkish Code and the 'Majno' Annotations use sometimes one, sometimes another word to translate this term and

[58] *Id* at 1789.

[59] 97/1-76; 97/114; 13.5.1997; 23 *YKD* 1997, 1608 at 1615.

[60] *Id* at 1616.

[61] 96/8022; 96/9095; 3.12.1996; 23 *YKD* 1997, 617.

therefore there is some confusion. When sections 480 and 482 were being amended, the legislature followed the mistaken decisions of the *Yargıtay* and changed the term 'a number of persons' to 'three'. The dissenting judge said:

> While the law was being interpreted, "the source law" should have been consulted. It should not have been forgotten that the Turkish Criminal Code is the outcome of a reception and translation. Therefore, it is necessary to correct mistakes in translation by "corrective interpretation". The only acceptable departure from "the source laws" is where the legislature has shown reasons for this departure in debate in Parliament. Therefore, whenever necessary the Italian Code and reasoning must be used.[62]

Where the right to defence of the suspect is being determined, the *Yargıtay* was of the opinion that, reminding the suspect that he has the right to employ a lawyer and that he has the right to silence are essential elements of procedure, otherwise the right to defence is to be regarded as limited.[63] Two dissenting opinions, after stating that laws of all democratic states point in the same direction, referred to 'the source German Code of Criminal Procedure' sections 243 and 130 which have the same text as the Turkish sections 236 and 135. Both opinions extensively discussed decisions of the German Federal Court (BGH) and a decision of the Federal Court of Kern Roxin[64] with further references to foreign doctrine on criminal procedure. The *Yargıtay* was criticised for not applying the aforementioned sections in line with the German Federal Court practice and for not using its discretion in determining the value of such procedural niceties and taking them as absolutes.

In a case dealing with 'premeditated murder',[65] a dissenting opinion compared the Turkish *Yargıtay* to its French, German and Italian counterparts. It then pointed out that the word 'premeditated' was not defined in the Turkish Criminal Code and that because in the early years of the Republic it was the practice to interpret this Code according to the French Criminal Code rather than the Italian 'source law' - a linguistically easy but mistaken option according to him- a number of problems were created. The Zanardelli Code had a different system from the French. It was not possible to transfer the interpretation of one to the other. The 1810 French

62 *Id* at 620.

63 95/7; 95/302; 24.10.1995; 22 *YKD* 1996, 103.

64 *Id* at 109, 113-115.

65 94/1-167; 94/188; 27.6.1994, 20 *YKD* 1994, 1829.

Criminal Code was no longer in effect and the new Code had yet a different system and defined cases of premeditation as 'assassination'. The Italian criminal system left this determination to the judge.[66] According to this dissenting judge, the Turkish system seemed to sway between the French and the Italian systems by sometimes using the French conceptual structure 'calmness' (cool-headedness), and thus had internal inconsistencies. The *Yargıtay* should give a final definition of 'premeditation' and then use this definition as a criterion when viewing the decisions of the lower courts. The dissenting judge then referred to Spanish teaching and practice, which had also been influenced by the Italian, German and French laws, to show that they did follow this path.[67]

The Fourth Cord: French -Turkish Law

Another area worthy of mention, though not to be covered in this survey, is administrative law. The source French administrative law and the decisions of the *Conseil d'Etat* are integral parts of administrative law scholarship and teaching in Turkish Law Faculties. Young administrative law academics joining law faculties are expected to know or to learn French, if they aim to be good and creative researchers. From time to time *Danıştay* decisions also make reference to French doctrine and very occasionally to French cases, though the frequency of these references has decreased, and over the years a strong local administrative law scholarship has developed. The *Danıştay* is a very active court, which adjusts the techniques of judicial review to local problems effectively and, in the last decade, without reference to domestic and foreign doctrine or foreign judicial decisions.

CONCLUDING REMARKS

Laws of European origin, themselves the product of centuries long inter-receptions, displacements and translocations, had their full impact on Turkey in the past century. This blend gave Turkish law its civilian laic character. Zweigert and Kötz for instance, find this experience remarkable, since 'nowhere else in the world can one so well study how in the reception of a foreign law there is a natural interaction between the interpretation of the foreign text and the actual tradition and usages of the country which adopted it, with the consequent gradual development of a new law of an independent nature'.[68] Law developed after 1930 in Turkey is the

66 *Id* at 1833.
67 *Id* at 1834.
68 Zweigert and Kötz (1998) supra n 10 at 178.

continuation of the trend which was established between 1926-1930 and which in fact started as far back as in 1839. Developments today with the aim of further integration with Western Europe and the European Union, can be regarded as related to this steady line of development. So what was peculiar to this experience?

The first factor is that the Turkish Republic has never been a colony, which obviously attaches less stigma to incoming models.[69]

The second factor is that what was introduced was a way of life, not just a set of legal rules or even a legal system, so defying the 'mirror thesis'. What was borrowed was a means of modernity. The aim was to become European, legally, socially and culturally. This goal has symbolic value in Turkey, and has culminated in the desire to be accepted into the European Union as a full member and as a Western European state.

An overarching historical accident is the third factor. There were special conditions of this 'historical accident', which contributed to the Turkish experience. The Republic was established after the collapse of the Ottoman Empire and the war of independence. A firm decision was made for an independent, modern, viable Turkey and national unity was the driving force. The charismatic leader, Kemal Atatürk, had an exceptional vision. This was a 'paternalistic imposition of purpose'. The country was reduced in size inside compact borders. It had ten million people and an eighty percent illiteracy rate. Although the inclusion of the high rate of illiteracy among the factors contributing to the success of social reforms may sound bizarre: it actually helped in the process of changing from the old script to the Latin alphabet and the Roman numerals, since many were going to learn to read from scratch.

The official programme was geared to eliminate any kind of personal choice regarded by the formal legal system as undesirable and to this end cultural and legal pluralism was not acceptable. Thus this 'non socio- and non-legal culture bound' approach indifferent to legal history was the fourth factor.

Fifthly, the borrowing took place while the legal system was in the process of evolving and still incomplete. One could even query whether a fully developed, self-standing legal culture actually existed prior to these borrowings. The legal tradition was certainly 'weak' and widely

[69] Although Mattei says for Ethiopia that the strong and long-lasting colonisation by one single power meant that the flavour of the legal system did not change after colonisation. See Mattei, U (1995) 'The New Ethiopian Constitution: First Thoughts on Ethnical Federalism and the Reception of Western Institutions' in Grande, E (ed) (1995) *Transplants Innovation and Legal Traditions in the Horn of Africa* L'Harmattan Italia at 125.

open to foreign cultural intrusion.[70] In fact, some of the existing traditional institutions were themselves objects of earlier transplant. Therefore this was a case where, 'Between two totally different systems, an overall reception is easier than wide-ranging imitation of particular rules and institutions.'[71]

The borrowings owed more to extrinsic factors such as the political, economic and symbolic than to the intrinsic value of the borrowed institutions themselves, and therefore, cannot be seen as a 'transnational spread' or 'diffusion' of law with an 'export bias'. It was the desire to belong to and harmonise with a particular group, the western world, and ease of access, which were the important causal factors in the selectivity in this borrowing.[72] Yet, as there was no direct social contact between the models and the recipient, the culture of the masses, though changed, remained on the whole unrelated to the models and this in spite of domestic efforts to change the people, justifying the label 'a covert mixed legal system'.

In sum, in Turkey, at the level of law, the success of the import is not questionable; the mixed layers of modern law from various sources have been successfully adapted to the conditions of the recipient. We know that times of reception are also times for domestic creativity if the 'viruses', which then become 'irritants' and create their 'antibodies', are carefully and creatively nurtured. Has this happened in Turkey? Grief[73] discusses the concepts of 'corrective', 'habit forming factor' and 'contaminant', and Teubner,[74] 'legal irritants', 'assimilation' and 'healthy infusion'. These notions are worth assessing in the Turkish experience.

There will always be fears that in such a case as that of Turkey, the social and cultural systems and the legal system will not easily accord. However, the results of a number of surveys indicate that the transplanted legal system has indeed influenced even rural areas of Turkey. Starr and Pool[75] report that their data 'suggest that planned legal change over time

[70] Monateri, PG (1998) 'The "Weak" Law: Contaminations and Legal Cultures' in *Italian National Reports to the XVth International Congress of Comparative Law* Giuffrè editore 83 at 85.

[71] Sacco, R (1991) 'Legal Formants: A Dynamic Approach to Comparative Law (Installment ii of ii) (39) *American Journal of Comparative Law* 343 at 400.

[72] See Schauer, F (2000) 'The Politics and Incentives of Legal Transplantations' *Law and Development Paper* No: 2 CID Working Paper No: 44, available at: <http://www.cid.harvard.educidwp/044.htm>

[73] Grief, N (1998) 'The Pervasive Influence of European Community Law in the United Kingdom' in Watkin TG (ed) (1998) *The Europeanisation of Law* United Kingdom Comparative Law Series Vol: 18 110.

[74] Teubner, supra n 30.

[75] Starr, J and Pool, J (1974) 'The impact of a legal revolution in rural Turkey' (8) *Law and Society Review* 533. However, for a contrary assessment of 'effectiveness of the received law' in relation to 'effective economic development' in Turkey, see Berkowitz, D, Pistor K and Richard J-F (2000) 'Economic Development, Legality, and the Transplant Effect' *Law and Development Papers* No: 1, CID Working Paper No: 39 available at: <http://www.cid.harvard.

does indeed affect populations and institutions at the local level.' They give support to the view that a legal system of the modern type 'may be sufficiently independent of other social and cultural systems, that it may exist for long periods while maintaining a degree of dissonance with central cultural values.' Again, Starr and Pool submit, 'our data [...] suggest that the Turkish revolution is a revolution in more than form. [...] The use of the courts by citizens extends to areas formerly within the sphere of religious law alone - to such an extent that these are now among the most common kinds of cases.' [76]

According to Sacco, 'Borrowing and imitation is [...] of central importance to understanding the course of legal change', and 'the birth of a rule or institution is a rarer phenomenon than its imitation'.[77] This view also accords with Watson's view: 'The moving of a rule or a system of law from one country to another has now been shown to be the most fertile source of legal development since most changes in most systems are the result of borrowing.'[78] Monateri goes even further and says that practically every system has grown from 'contaminations' and the actual legal world is to be seen more as a world of 'contaminations' than a world split into different legal families.[79] Moreover the Turkish case provides additional evidence that there is not much that is original in law.[80] The originality is in the specific selectivity in the borrowing, in the ensuing mix and the homogenisation process in the courts.[81]

PART II. JUDICIAL NAVIGATION AS OFFICIAL LAW MEETS CULTURE IN TURKEY

THE CONCEPTUAL FRAMEWORK

This part will start with a summary of the conceptual framework to be used, then briefly consider some of the peculiarities of Turkish socio-culture – the underlay - and finally, look at how courts endeavour to tune the received law to meet the needs of society, thus completing the transposition process while at the same time configuring the legal framework to social needs,

educidwp/039.pdf>

[76] Starr and Pool (1974) supra n 75.

[77] Sacco, supra n 71 at 394, 397.

[78] Watson, A (1996) 'Aspects of reception of law' 44 *American Journal of Comparative Law* 345; Watson, A (1976) 'Legal Transplants and Law Reform' 92 *Law Quarterly Review* 94.

[79] Monateri, supra n 70 at 107.

[80] Grande, E. (1995)'Preface' in Grande supra n 69 at 14.

[81] The borrowing system realises a unique mixture of diverse patterns. See Monateri, supra n 70 at 106.

blending the underlay with the overlay. My main concern is to trace what happens when official Turkish law meets diverse cultures and diverse cultures meet such a law. I will consider a number of cases selected in three groups: when courts face culture contrary to the vision embodied in the official legal framework; when courts face culture which can be catered for within the legal framework, though not necessarily in keeping with it, and now also need revision because of the aspired European Union membership; and thirdly when courts face demands of further Europeanisation and human rights law, which may or may not fit in the official framework or - more important for our purposes here - the traditional values of the people.

Legal pluralism

Chiba, portraying the concept of legal pluralism, our first concept, as an 'effective attack on the common sense of orthodox jurisprudence' by rejecting the 'oneness of state law as law or universality of western law',[82] offers a model of official law as always interacting with unofficial law and legal postulates, and never existing in isolation. The State and its laws, society and its normative orders, and religion and world-views, are expected to work together to achieve a balanced and sustainable legal order. Yet, legal centralism reflects the ambition of the modern nation state for total legal control and by definition rejects polycentric law. Though, as Griffiths says, 'legal pluralism is the fact, legal centralism is a myth, an ideal, a claim, an illusion',[83] in the western world, the plural arrangement in a centralist legal system, the weaker version of legal pluralism, is the best on offer today. Catering for normative multiplicity, including normative dualism, without an overarching unitary normative framework does not seem to accord with a unitary western nation state, and definitely with the Turkish state. The stronger version of legal pluralism, where levels of law of equal value co-exist in the same territorial or social space as overlapping orders, is not favoured in the western world. The fit is always uncomfortable; the centralist forces of the unitary state do not live comfortably with so many rivals.

Rather than sociology or anthropology, how does law regard pluralism? 'The nation state originally was built on the idea of an identifiable culture', says Gessner, and though sub-cultural influence is of growing importance,

[82] Chiba, M (ed) (1986) *Asian indigenous law in interaction with received law*, KPI. Also see Chiba, M (1989) *Legal Pluralism: Towards a general theory through Japanese legal culture*, Tokai University Press.

[83] Griffiths, J (1986) 'What is legal pluralism?' (24) *Journal of Legal Pluralism and Unofficial Law*: 1-56.

'it can in most cases still be treated as a cultural unit'.[84] So what happens when this law meets diverse cultures? How can the modern unitary nation state recognise diversity, and cultural and religious norms developing independently of officially endorsed rules? Can the state control the whole of the law? Can cultural and social aspects of legal principles accept outside control? These questions are crucial ones for the Turkish legal system.

As we saw earlier, Turkey is a unitary nation state, which is the source of law and the legitimiser of sources of law. Here we have a monolithic, centralised, territorial and top-down model of law, which may or may not allow competing sources of law to exist. When it does not, it is regarded as intolerant, undemocratic, even despotic and self-referential. When it does however, this can only be a weak version of legal pluralism where the monolithic, top-down source of law is receptive to other sources, and therefore regarded as more tolerant, democratic, multi-cultural and reflecting an open society. Cultural pluralism becomes a serious issue when it appears to be a threat to the territorial integrity of a State, when nationalism inherent in culture groups is perceived as a threat to the monolithic values or dominant culture within that State.[85] Turkey is an example to show that law can be used as a creative tool for bringing about certain desired effects and sometimes even needs in society rather than rationally and naturally reflecting peoples' needs and desires.[86] Law can act as a harmonising agent with economic, social and cultural implications, but the legal system cannot escape becoming a 'covert' mixed legal system.

Transposition

Another concept pertinent for our inquiry is 'transposition'.[87] Although the term 'legal transplant'[88] has been the usual one applied to all import and

[84] Gessner supra n 3, 132.

[85] One of the factors related to the demise of the Ottoman Empire.

[86] This was the aim of the radical reform laws referred to earlier.

[87] Another of the concepts, 'hyphenated', as to the legal system and to the people, has been explored extensively above. This concept is not closely but tangentially related to the analysis in this article. Terminology used in classical statements of legal movements such as transplant, imposition and reception, have today been supplemented by a colourful vocabulary highlighting nuances in individual instances of this mobility such as grafting, implantation, re-potting, cross-fertilisation and so on. New notions and bases for analysis are being developed such as collective colonisation, contaminants, legal irritants, layered-law, hyphenated-law and competition of legal systems. Images such as contamination, inoculation, irritation, diffusion, infusion, seepage and infiltration are all appropriate in describing present day encounters, and the terms reception, imposed reception and concerted parallel development, the activities.

[88] See, Watson, A (1974) *Legal Transplants: An Approach to Comparative Law*, Scottish Academic Press footnote 53 at 30 where he also mentions imposed reception, solicited imposition,

export activities, I believe that the term 'transposition', as used in music, is more appropriate as it also involves 'tuning', that is the process of 'fit', the most important element for the workings of a legal system. The term 'transposition' is apt in instances of massive change based on competing models, in that here the pitch is changed. In musical transposition, each note takes the same relative place in the scale of the new key as in the old, the 'transposition' being made to suit the particular instrument or the voice-range of the singer. In law then, as each legal institution or rule introduced is used in the system of the recipient, transposition occurs to suit the particular socio-legal culture and needs of the recipient.

Legal developments of our day can be seen mostly as instances of transposition. In fact, there may be a number of transpositions, since, as seen in Turkey, no single model may have been used by any one recipient.[89] Without the appropriate transposition and tuning, a transplanted legal system not compatible with the culture in the receiving country will create only a virtual reality.[90] However, countries that adapt transplanted law can have more effective legality by further developing their formal sources and building effective legal systems with effective economic development. This receptivity can be enhanced by making significant adaptation in the foreign formal law to fit the pre-existing formal or informal legal order.

In historical terms, most of the tuning was carried out externally by imposers or exporters of law, by diffusion.[91] This is not a very sensitive kind of tuning, since it cannot consider the new pitch in its entirety, as the tuner is not an active player of the new instrument. It is internal tuning that is required and for that the tuners are usually the domestic judges. Below we will trace how Turkish judges cope with the tuning, transpose the received legal system and then navigate in order to deal with culture(s) and needs of the people that may or may not fit the official framework.

---

crypto-reception and inoculation. Also see for a more complete list, Örücü (1995) supra n 6 at 5. Here we see cross-pollination, engulfment, emulation, infiltration, infusion, digestion, salad bowl, melting pot and transposition. Also see, Örücü (2002) supra n 2. In addition, Monateri claims that the term 'legal transplant' utilised by Watson for 'scholarly purposes' is today taken over by 'purposive practical lawyers' involved in projects of 'exporting their own legal systems'. See, Monateri supra n 70 at 83. Transplants have also been classified into four groups: direct-receptive, direct-unreceptive, indirect-receptive, indirect-unreceptive, the indication being that even a 'transplant' from a 'transplant', that is indirect transplantation, rather than from an 'origin', that is direct transplantation, is possible.

89 Even what is called 'reciprocal influence' (a more acceptable term today among the comparatists) is actually a number of transpositions.

90 Smits, JM (1998) 'Systems Mixing and in Transition: Import and Export of Legal Models: The Dutch Experience', in Hondius Ewoud H (ed) *Nederlands Reports to the Fifteenth International Congress of Comparative Law,* Intersentia Rechtswetenschappen, 55.

91 Such was the case for instance in the British codifying of the common law for its introduction into the Indian Continent.

Navigation

This leads us to consider the concept 'navigation', the art and science of directing the movements of a vessel at sea towards its intended destination. It includes determining the position and course of the vessel by the principles of geometry and astronomy. The navigator uses intuition and traditional guidance in order to reach his intended destination. He steers by observing the general direction and force of the wind and the motion and force of the water. He uses information gained by the movements of the stars, the sun and the moon,[92] and above all, the compass. He takes soundings, calculates the impact of magnetism, the movements of the sea (as currents and tides), and the sideways drift (leeway).

The navigator must first determine his exact position. He must then determine the course to steer in order to travel from A to B. The pressures of water (currents and tides) and of wind from any direction always influence the sailing ship. Only a vessel in a known position and with known safe depth on still water and a fair stern wind can move along its course in a straight line. A sailing ship cannot sail directly into a head wind. The navigator steersman uses zigzag tacks to port and starboard across the wind in order to reach the intended point ahead. Similarly side winds must be calculated and a course closer to the wind taken to allow for leeway. He knows that the wind and sea pressures are but two of the influences. He must also adjust his steering according to the rise and fall of water levels.

Even when a ship is anchored, the tide causes her to swing. If the ship is tied to a buoy, the position of the buoy is not constant since it is anchored to the seabed on a length of chain and sea levels rise and fall causing some side-ways movement. The Magnetic North Pole is not a constant location either. Any swing away from it is a 'deviation'. This is caused by the magnetic fittings and components on a boat: some fittings will have no effect on the compass, others will. The amount of 'deviation' depends upon the direction of the 'ship's head'. The angle between the Magnetic North and the True North (Geographic North) at any time is the 'variation'. 'Variation' depends on the geographic location of the ship, and is measured as east or west.

The navigator uses charts (which are symbols) and a compass. He determines the course (the direction in which the ship is heading), calculates the ground track (the path followed), drift (the distance covered in a given time due to the movement of the tidal stream and wind) and leeway (side

[92] Gladwin, T (1964) 'Cultures and Logical Process' In Goodenough, W (ed) *Explorations in Cultural Anthropology: Essays in Honour of George Peter Murcock* , New York, McGraw-Hill.

wind altering progress so that another future position appears which is the estimated position, the result of travelling sideways and forwards). He takes bearings and notes the position line the bearings gives. He observes and adjusts and tries to keep on an even keel.

Replacing the above by legal and social realities we can regard the judge as both the navigator and the steersman, and his art of interpretation and working out solutions in hard cases and making decisions as to where to go, as navigation. By how much can the judge alter the course? What should be his points of reference when he takes bearings? Can he avoid collision of the legal framework and the traditions and mores of the people either by changing course or speed? What is the impact of the 'wind', the 'current' and the 'tide' on the course of legal change in Turkey?

A GENERAL OVERVIEW

We know that the technique, the form and the content of Turkish law and the values reflected therein, are all 'import'. The technique used is codification and the hierarchy of the norms, the accompanying elements deriving from the West, more specifically the civilian tradition. The official content, in many ways foreign to the Turkish *mentalité*, reflects values borrowed from the West with some modifications and do not fully reflect the values of the past traditional national spirit; yet this was intentional as the purpose was to change that *mentalité*. Because the original official vision did not fully take into consideration the winds, the currents, the tides and the starting point, and because the ship's speed, the course and the ship's position were plotted by simply measuring along the course line as if on a flat sea with the wind astern, today a heavy burden of adjustment falls upon the shoulders of Turkish academics and the judges as navigator and steersman. On the whole, the *Yargıtay*, the *Danıştay* and the *Anayasa Mahkemesi* cope well with this burden, trying to find a 'fit' between the official legal framework and the needs and mores of the people.

Though the Turkish Republic is heir to the Ottoman Empire and the 1839 *Tanzimat* (Reformation movement) may be regarded as the corner stone of Europeanisation for the Ottoman Empire, the Republic set up in 1924 after the collapse of the Empire is the most important starting point for our topic. The ideology underlying the Republic drew on 'some of the more extreme concepts of "modern" nationalism which were current in late-nineteenth-and early-twentieth-century Europe. Homogeneity – one language, one religion, one Volk – was considered to be the prerequisite of a strong and independent state'.[93]

Ascherson, quotes from Effie Voutira for whom the unreformed Ottoman State 'looked like a Kokoschka painting where the plurality and diversity of the different points of colour is such that there is no clearly discernible pattern, though the picture as a whole does have one [...]', especially when one stands back. 'By contrast, the modern world map looks more like a Modigliani painting, where all shapes and colours have clearly circumscribed boundaries and well defined surfaces with no ambiguity or overlap [...]'.[94] In Effie Voutira's sense, says Ascherson, the Turkish legal revolutions of the early twentieth century were therefore the overthrow of Kokoschka in favour of Modigliani. Nothing could have been more offensive to this scientific spirit of the Republic then the multi-ethnic, decentralised and in many ways tolerant Ottoman Empire. The reformers wanted those single, well-circumscribed blocks of primary colours.

In December 1999 on the occasion of Turkey's becoming a candidate to the European Union, the then Turkish Prime Minister Ecevit said that this official recognition was a landmark event not only for Europe, but also for the world and that full membership was 'Turkey's birthright by virtue of Turkey's historical development, its geography, and its present day attributes as well as the provisions of the 1963 Association Agreement'. Pointing out that 'the Turks have been Europeans for 600 years', he then added that Turks are not only European; they are Asian, Caucasian and Middle Eastern and European all at once.[95] This statement should be assessed in relation to the particular world-view -- which I call the vision -- the Turkish Republic is based on.[96]

As noted above in Part I, between 1926 - 1930 by the adoption and adaptation of Codes of foreign origin from Switzerland, Italy, Germany and France, the *élite dirigeante* constructed the legal framework and passed a series of social reform laws (*inkilap kanunlari*)[97] to supplement these Codes aimed at 'changing the people' and forging a new identity to fulfil the requirements of the vision.[98] This was a non-collaborating elite with a

[93] Ascherson, N (1995) *Black Sea* (Vintage) at 197.

[94] ibid

[95] Available at: <http://www.infa.gov.tr/grupa/ad/adc/candidacy.html>. In his speech he also cited the achievements.

[96] An appreciation of this vision is only possible by understanding and labelling the contents of the historical 'baggage' carried by the Turkish Republic.

[97] See supra n 25 for the list of these social reform laws.

[98] Maybe as every other revolution trying to forge an identity such as the French and the Russian, the Turkish revolution aimed at the basics: language reform, a new system of law, a new sense of national identity based on a newly created culture excluding the Ottoman heritage (the Islamic and Arabic elements)

vision for modernity, acting both as opinion maker and decision maker. All was achieved between 1924 and 1930 as the new Turkish Republic went through a process of total modernisation, westernisation, secularisation, democratisation and constitutionalism.

The ideological message, the original version of which is sometimes referred to as the tenets of 'Kemalism', was symbolised by 'Six Arrows': nationalism, laicism, republicanism, populism, statism and reformism.[99] Today this vision also includes westernisation, commitment to Kemal Atatürk nationalism, the rule of law, the welfare state, human rights and democracy. The above, all interlocked, constitute the official world-view. Over the years parts of this vision have found their way into the preambles of Constitutions. At present they are in the Preamble of the 1982 Constitution: 'the resolution to attain the contemporary level of civilisation as an honourable member of the family of world nations with equal rights', 'with sovereignty belonging unconditionally to the Turkish nation and to be used in its name not exceeding the limits of free democracy and the rule of law determined by its requirements as defined by this Constitution', and,

> no thought or consideration to be defended which is opposed to the Turkish national interests, the principle of the indivisible integrity of Turkish existence with its State and territory, Turkish historical and moral values, the nationalism, principles, reforms and modernisation of Atatürk, and that as demanded by the principle of laicism, sacred religious feelings being in no way permitted to interfere with State affairs and politics.

Furthermore, articles 1-3 of the Constitution, which are immutable, pose the characteristics of the Republic and reiterate that the State is a Republic, that it is democratic, laic and social, governed by the rule of law, respecting human rights within the concepts of public peace, national solidarity and justice, loyal to the nationalism of Kemal Atatürk, and based on the fundamental tenets set forth in the Preamble; the Republic is an indivisible whole comprising its territory and the nation; and its official language is Turkish. These articles and their immutable character are of the utmost importance for our purposes as they limit the manoeuvrability of the courts in their navigation to adjust the law - the overlay - to the needs and mores of the people - the underlay - and prevent the Turkish legal system from becoming an 'overt' mixed legal system.

[99] See for more on these and other developments Lord Kinross (1964) *Atatürk - The Birth of a Nation,* Weidenfeld and Nicolson.

From its inception the Turkish legal system tried to transform, the social, political, ideological, religious and economic systems it encountered. Though, historians and comparatists alike have hailed the Turkish experience as unique, since it represents the passage of a legal system from one legal culture to another, the interlocking of these systems may never be completed. As noted in Part I, the imported foreign sources are constantly referred to by courts and academics in developing the law, and yet the indigenous socio-culture is not related to the socio-cultures of the source laws.

In Turkey, there is assumed similarity of culture with the Turkic and Islamic States, alongside assumed similarity of culture with Europe; hence the statement of the Prime Minister referred to earlier. Turkey's legal system is based on the legal systems of European states, now most of them in the European Union. A minority of the population, living mainly in urban areas, is western in outlook and mentality: the Westernised-Turk. So for these educated, urbanised elite there is clear affinity of culture and outlook with West Europe and the Western way of life. Yet, a much larger part of the Turkish population is rural and has a traditional outlook, which is maintained even when this population moves into the cities. Some of these poorly educated, rural Anatolians have become wealthy and politically effective. In addition, in the cities, the gap between the rich and the poor is wide and the middle class has shrunk. Then there are those who, having started with a traditional rural existence, have worked in other countries in Europe for some time and having returned, fit neither into the first category, nor the second. In Turkey they are referred to as '*Alman-Türkler*' (German-Turks) or '*Almancılar*', irrespective of which country they may have been working in. It must also be remembered that though 98% of the population of Turkey is of the Islamic faith, they are not all of the same sect or school. The inherent problems are not difficult to contemplate, and the courts 'have a crucial role in moulding the diversities into a unity',[100] adjusting and homogenising the 'layers' of systems within this 'covert mix'.

Owing to the desire on the part of the elite to modernise, westernise and Europeanise the country and because all legal/cultural import from foreign models was voluntary, in the early period of the Republic there were fewer problems than now. For the fundamentalist Islamic sector however, all that is Western represents unwanted cultural elements and therefore there has always been reaction from that quarter. Today, there are also those who challenge the lack of democratic consultation by the elite in deciding on the models. In Turkey this dual reaction is always present. With the emergence

[100] Örücü (1996) supra n 6 at 95.

of democratic ideals and principles, and values of human rights, it becomes more and more difficult to achieve and maintain standardisation, and 'harmony in diversity' and further mixidness may have to be accepted. The question is: How far?

These days the most important changes in Turkish law result from the desire to integrate with European Union legislation, though Turkish people sometimes react to this new legal/cultural import made with the purpose of becoming a full member. In such an event, at the level of the legal system, no problem of accord should be expected, apart from bureaucracy, delays, lack of co-ordination, transparency and overlaps. At the level of the social and cultural systems no additional problems would be created for Turkey by a closer union with the European Union. Indeed, the solving of some of the social and cultural problems may be accelerated simply by Turkey's candidacy; yet, the existing problems will not go away swiftly or smoothly. However, the European Union may have problems of accommodating a 'hyphenated' socio-cultural fabric. It is only when Europe sees multiculturalism, multiple identities and religious toleration as central to its own identity that it can accommodate a socio-cultural fabric as diverse as that of Turkey.

As stated earlier, existing customs, usages and religious mores were not recognised as the basis of legal relationships in Turkey, and the radically reformist attempt to achieve a modern, western, laic and civilian democracy by creating a revolution, not only in the legal but in the socio-cultural fabric, became a prime example of 'social engineering through law'. The Turkish Republic being based on a vision, all her institutions were geared to the achievement of this vision, and the monolithic centralist legal system faces the same problems the European Union would face to accommodate the Turkish socio-cultural fabric.

Let us try to put the above in other words using the vocabulary of our navigation metaphor. The picture now becomes thus: If we regard Turkey as the sailing ship, the principles of Kemalism are the deep keel, keeping the ship on an even keel. However, there is always a swing. The ship's head is in the direction on the vision, the intended destination. We know that variation can occur. We know that variation is east or west. We also know that deviation can be caused by the contents of the ship, in this case the changing values in Turkey. The forces outside the ship are the forces of tidal streams, currents and winds as well as the heavenly bodies. The wind coming from the direction of the EU is a wind from the stern, in which case there is no sideways drift, but strong forward movement. If the wind is head-on there again will be no leeway, but the movement forward will be hampered or even stopped, in which case tacking or beating to windward will be necessary. A new course may have to be plotted. The crucial winds that can cause leeway and alter progress and direction are the side-winds, such as religion. Tidal levels vary. Sometimes it may be necessary to alter the ship's heading in order to counter a tidal stream, to keep the ship on an even keel and to make good an 'intended track', the destination. We have to remember though that all tidal information of times and heights are estimates and therefore approximate. How do navigators cope?

HOW DO THE COURTS STEER AND TUNE THE OFFICIAL LAW TO FIT SOCIETY?

It is important to note that parts of the vision of the Turkish Republic coincide with the demands of democracy, parts do not; parts of the vision clash with the indigenous culture and the aspirations of people, parts do not. In the outside world, the Council of Europe (especially the ECHR) and the European Union, represent some of the aspirations of the Western world today; and yet parts of the Turkish vision and most of the indigenous customs have to be given up to fit this world. There are additional outside forces such as religion, culture (tradition) and the past history, religious pressures from neighbouring countries, border disputes, the WTO, the IMF, and the globalising forces of the world economy. Obviously the legislature is involved in the process of tuning, but, as noted earlier, most of the burden falls on the shoulders of the judges.

Turkey is a country of paradoxes. As noted earlier, by choice, desire and design, the legal system was constructed, by borrowing from foreign legal systems. This legal system is secular and yet 98% of the people are Moslems. While the legal system has the aspiration to erase certain cultures and create a new culture, thereby assimilating people into a chosen image, when law meets cultures which it does not cater for, the judge either endeavours to eradicate or ignore them in keeping with the vision of the founding legislator, or, where he can, to accommodate them within the official framework.[101]

Culture and demands that clash with the vision and cannot be accommodated

Some aspects of the culture, such as religious marriage prior to or instead

[101] At this point it is worthwhile to remind ourselves that the *Yargıtay*, one of the most influential navigators, was enabled to make adjustments to the law by the flexible rules present in the 1926 Civil Code and now the 2002 Civil Code sections 1, 2 and 4, seen earlier. It is also worth repeating that the source of law is determined by the formal legal framework, and cultural values, custom and tradition become a source of law when recognised by courts.

of civil marriage, the wearing of the headscarf in the public sphere, and political parties upholding religion (*sheri'a*) or separationist views, clash with the officially protected vision and the courts cannot uphold these. The three issues above are related to laicism and the fourth to the unitary state with its nation and its territory, all protected by the Constitution, as seen earlier. Therefore, claims based on such issues not in keeping with the official law create major problems for the courts.

Religious marriage

Empirical research tells us[102] that there are seven types of traditional marriage in Turkey: *berdel* (two families agree and sons and daughters are exchanged in a double marriage), *beşik kertmesi* (two families agree upon the birth of two babies on their future marriage), *başlık paralı evlilik* (marriage takes place upon the payment of monies by the father of the prospective bride to the prospective husband), *kan bedelli evlilik* (made in order to put an end to blood fueds, one of the daughters of the family whose turn it is to carry out the next killing is given as a wife to the other family), *kuma evliliği* (a woman is married off to a man with more than one wife), *kayın evliliği* (a woman is married off to one of the brothers of her deceased husband upon the decision of the 'family council'), and *akraba evliliği* (marriage of a woman to a first degree relative). It has also been pointed out that, the realities of marriage in Turkey are quite outside the formally regulated one.[103] However in this inquiry, I am not looking into 'narratives' related to cultural pluralism but into what the courts (part of the official framework) can do to fit some of this alternative behaviour into the legal framework, that is, navigate within the framework without altering the ship's heading. We are dealing here, at best, with a weaker version of legal pluralism. None of the above types of traditional marriage would create a problem if formally concluded as civil marriages.

The official framework accepts only one type of marriage regulated in the Civil Code. Marriage has been secularised and is concluded upon the oral response of the two parties. A marriage certificate is given without which a religious ceremony cannot take place, and it is a criminal offence to undertake or perform such a ceremony without this certificate.[104] A religious

[102] From a piece of empirical research carried out by the CEDAW Committee on Turkey in 81 cities and interviewing 453 women cited by *Milliyet* Newspaper.

[103] See, Yılmaz, İ (2003) 'Non-recognition of Post-modern Turkish Socio-legal Reality and the Predicament of Women' (30:1) *British Journal of Middle Eastern Studies*: 25-41; and Yılmaz, İ (2005) *Muslim Laws, Politics and Society in Modern Nation States: Dynamic Legal Pluralism in England, Turkey and Pakistan*, Ashgate.

[104] This is today regulated by the 2005 Penal Code in section 230.

ceremony is not needed for the marriage to be binding. This was reiterated in the new 2002 Civil Code to indicate the secular nature of marriage in Turkey (section 143).

In earlier years, the *Yargıtay*, tried a number of ways to navigate round this. One way was to stress the acceptability of the civil marriage, even for those with religious objections to it, by stating: 'The fact that the marriage contract is formed by the accord of the consent of the parties is in keeping with both Islamic and Canonical laws. In these laws also, the marriage contract is not completed by an act of the religious man but by the declaration of the wills of the parties.'[105]

As to the children born into religious marriages, again, prior to the first Amnesty Act of 1933,[106] the *Yargıtay*, attempted to resolve the problem by way of interpretation (one tool of navigation): Children of such informal marriages were considered as legitimate by the Court when one of the parents died, by an analogous application of section 249 of the 1926 Civil Code, which said that children of couples who have made promises to marry each other, but were then unable to marry owing to the death or incapacity of one of them, could be declared legitimate by a court upon the application of the other party or of the child himself.

A judgement of the *Anayasa Mahkemesi* published in 2002 gives an authoritative answer to any question that might arise related to the acceptability of religious marriage as an alternative to civil marriage.[107] Section 237/4 of the then Penal Code criminalising religious marriage entered into without civil marriage and imposing a prison sentence of from two to six months on both the man and the woman, was challenged as violating several articles of the Constitution: article 2 (the principle of secularism), article 10 (equality), article 12 (the character and the scope of fundamental rights and freedoms) and article 24 (freedom to conduct religious services and ceremonies). The *Anayasa Mahkemesi*, referring to article 13 on the limitation of rights and freedoms, stated that section 237 had been inserted into the Penal Code in 1936 to give support to civil marriage, that without this section, polygamous marriages become possible and that, though such marriages have no legal consequence, being detrimental to the social order, they pose a threat to the concept of family. If couples enter such illegal unions, women cannot use their rights arising from marriage, children are illegitimate and lose their inheritance rights. Civil marriage must be

[105] 1965/3; 14.6.1965.

[106] Here I am not interested in 'legislative navigation', so will not deal with Amnesty Acts. For more information on this 'innovation' see Örücü, E (1987-88) 'Turkey: Reconciling Traditional Society and Secular Demands' 26 *Journal of Family Law*, 221-236.

[107] 1999/27; 1999/42; 24.11.1999; *Resmi Gazete*.No: 24743; 2 .5.2002.

strengthened to protect the family and the rights of women and children. The Court then went on to say that there is no violation of equality here as claimed, between those who live together with no marriage of any kind and those with only a religious marriage, since the first group do not wish their unions to be regarded as marriage. Equality before the law does not mean that everyone must be treated alike, differentiation based on article 13 is not unconstitutional. The Court, keeping to the 'intended track', saw the Civil Code as a fundamental building block of the bridge to a contemporary and laic legal system for the Turkish Republic, and said that civil marriage, being in the essence of that block, is specifically protected by article 174 of the Constitution. The most important function of laicism is to keep law and religion apart. In addition, as a religious marriage after the civil marriage is not banned, there is no violation of any fundamental right.

Nevertheless, in an effort to steer by taking into consideration the 'side-wind' and the 'headwind', and obviously with considerations of 'justice' in mind, the *Yargıtay* has tacked and extended the right to compensation for death in work-related accidents to the unmarried cohabiting woman (*nikahsız eş*), though be it on a different basis from the married woman. In fact, we have seen that neither the legal framework nor the courts regard couples living without an official secular marriage as being in a relationship to be protected by law. Therefore decisions of courts in this area, converting illegality into legality, are of the utmost importance for such couples. In the first case,[108] the childless surviving partner of an *imam nikahı*[109] union asked for material and moral compensation after the death of her partner in a work-related accident. The insurance company objected, though the lower court agreed. The *Yargıtay* decided on a percentage lower than that which would be the due of the married wife. In a similar later case,[110] there was a telling dissenting opinion by a female judge. Critical of the differentiation drawn between the two women, she said:

> Here "cohabiting couple" (*nikahsız eş*) refers to a traditional Anatolian relationship where couples live together as husband and wife, with close family ties and children. Therefore, the presence or absence of official wedlock should not be the criterion on which to treat the two women differently. The Social Security Agency will give a pension only to the officially married wife and this for life. This should be the only extra gain for the married woman. An

[108] 96/1606; 96/1661; 21.3.1996; 22 *Yargıtay Kararları Dergisi* 1996, 1291.

[109] *İmam nikahı* is a consensual marriage performed by an *imam* as a religious ceremony, which is only permissible in Turkey after a civil marriage ceremony.

[110] 97/3331; 97/4819; 8.7.1997; 23 *Yargıtay Kararları Dergisi* 1997, 1785.

> Anatolian village woman is already oppressed and faces the risk of being officially unmarried owing to tradition. She should not be further weakened when facing the law. This situation would only lead to mistrust of justice. The present circumstance is the outcome of the social structure. She should be given equal compensation.[111]

It appears that the *Yargıtay* can accommodate 'marriages' not accepted by the official system, when the matter at hand is not related to giving effect to the marriage but for instance, to the law of obligations where the Court does not have to go into the issue. Thus in a case related to the return of jewellery given at such a 'wedding' the Court referred to the female partner as the 'unofficial partner' (*gayriresmi eş*) and accepted the claim for compensation as the jewellery was no longer available for return.[112]

The Headscarf (The Türban cases)

Claims based on another Islamic practice, wearing the headscarf, remains unacceptable to the official law. In 1993 the name of a female trainee lawyer was removed from the Bar list because she came to court wearing a head cover and refused to remove it. According to the lower administrative court, as she was only a trainee and the matter solely a moral question, there was no violation of the respect due to the legal profession, though the regulations of the profession do impose certain conditions on appearance. The Danıştay however, saw no difference between a lawyer and a trainee, and regarded the issue as outside 'the right to religious freedom', saying: 'The behaviour of the trainee is contrary to the principles of a laic state governed by the rule of law, is incompatible with the profession of a lawyer and is an obstacle to her becoming and acting as a lawyer.'[113]

Headscarf cases have not lost their significance in Turkey, and continue to challenge the official legal framework. In fact this issue is one that the present government keeps on the agenda. However, the courts are bound by the vision within the official framework. A number of decisions have been given by the *Anayasa Mahkemesi* and the *Danıştay* on this issue. More important, the *Anayasa Mahkemesi* evaluates the headscarf (the *türban*) cases in educational establishments within the context of laicism. The first decision reached on this issue was in 1989, annulling the amendment to the

111 ibid

112 02/1153; 03/2380; 6.3.2003; 29 *Yargıtay Kararları Dergisi*, 2003, 1044.

113 92/3342, 93/2611, 5.7.1993.

law lifting the ban on the wearing of the *türban* in such institutions.[114] The Court opined that,

> [T]he fact that wearing of the headscarf, giving the person an appearance of being anachronistic, is gradually spreading, has obvious drawbacks for the Republican reforms and the principle of laicism. ... A laic legal order, laic education and laic administration cannot be thought of as separate from one another. ... Educational establishments cannot be set up contrary to the requirements of article 42 of the Constitution ... and higher education institutions are no exception. To separate students on religious affiliation, by symbols indicating which belief they support in classes, laboratories, clinics, policlinics and corridors, where students work together to reach the truth by being educated and applying scientific methods in a spirit of friendship and solidarity, would lead to conflict and hinder co-operation.

Later in 1991, in a second case[115] the *Anayasa Mahkemesi* decided that the regulation bringing 'freedom of attire' in higher education institutions did not apply to 'religious dress and covering the neck and hair with a scarf or *türban* due to religious belief', and that this regulation being unconstitutional should be annulled. According to the Court, any symbol representing religious belief should be kept out of educational institutions and allowing the wearing of the *türban* in the universities cannot accord with a laic scientific environment. The reasoning of the *Anayasa Mahkemesi* has also been accepted by the ECtHR[116] and the ban on the wearing of the *türban* in public institutions and educational establishments is regarded as essential to laicism which is seen as a *sine quo non* of democracy.

Referring to decisions of the *Danıştay* and the *Anayasa Mahkemesi,* and after extensive discussion of 'personality rights' and 'public interest', the *Yargıtay* held that the headscarf (the *türban*) cannot be worn in institutions of higher education, and therefore, the decision by the Principal of a

[114] This is usually referred to in Turkey as the 'First *Türban* Decision'. See, 1989/1; 1989/12; 7.3.1989; *Resmi Gazete* No: 20216; 5.7.1989. The appellant was the President of the Republic.

[115] Referred to in Turkey as the 'Second *Türban* Decision'. See, 1990/36; 1991/8; 9.4.1991 *Resmi Gazete* No: 20946; 31.7.1991. The appellant was the Sosyal Demokrat Halkçı Parti, the main opposition party.

[116] The Grand Chamber of the ECtHR, following the Chamber decision of 29.6.2004, decided in the *Leyla Şahin v. Turkey* on 10.11.2005 that such a ban can be regarded as 'necessary in a democratic society' and that those who agree to undertake university education are to be deemed as having agreed to accept the principles of laicism, one of the fundamental principles of the state. Turkey was found not to violate the Convention.

university not to allow female students to take exams with their heads covered did not constitute a violation of personality rights and was not a delictual act, as claimed.[117] In interpreting section 17 of the Law No: 2547 on Higher Education of 1990, the Court held that 'freedom of dress' was to be understood as 'within what was allowed by law' and although there were no provisions in any legislation banning the wearing of the headscarf, there were decisions by the *Anayasa Mahkemesi* and the *Danıştay*, courts that have the duty to interpret the law, law being a whole.

Then, in 2008, as the protector of the system and in view of the immutable concept of laicism in article 2 of the Constitution, the *Anayasa Mahkemesi* invalidated a constitutional amendment to articles 10 and 42 of the Constitution, by rejecting the addition by the Parliament of the clause, 'in the utilisation of all public services', to Article 10 on equality, and the sentence, 'no one shall be deprived of his/her right to higher education unless expressly prohibited by law', to Article 42 on education, introduced with the purpose of abolishing the ban on wearing headscarves for female university students.[118]

Closing of Political Parties (Religious/Leftist/Separationist)

There are a number of cases decided by the *Anayasa Mahkemesi* related to the permanent closing of political parties.[119] The majority of these cases are related to political parties that are politically left and/or advocate a separate homeland and/or autonomy for the Kurdish population. The Court bases its decisions on the Law on Political Parties. The political parties and their representatives base their cases partly on the two relevant articles of the ECHR, 11 and 17. The public prosecutor, and the Court following, rejects the claims based on the limitations introduced in 11/2 and 17/2.[120]

In two cases related to the closure of religious parties, the *Anayasa Mahkemesi* discussed laicism in relation to democracy.[121] In the 1998 case closing the *Refah Partisi* (the Welfare Party), both the public prosecutor

117 99/2625; 99/4428; 14.5.1999; 25 *Yargıtay Kararları Dergisi* ,1999, 1656.

118 2008/16; 2008/116; 5.6.2008 *Resmi Gazete* No:27032; 2210.2008. This decision has been assessed as, 'usurpation of power' by the Court. See Özbudun, E (2009) 'Judicial Review of Constitutional Amendments in Turkey' (15:4) *European Public Law*, 533-538.

119 1992/1; 1993/1; 14.7.1993 *Resmi Gazete* No: 21672; 18.8.1993; 1993/2; 1993/3; 30.11.1993 *Resmi Gazete* No: 22016; 9.8.1994; 1993/3; 1994/2; 16.8.1994 *Resmi Gazete* No: 21976; 30.6.1994; 1993/4; 1995/1; 19.7.1995 *Resmi Gazete* No: 23148; 2210.1997; 1995/1; 1996/1; 19.3.1996 *Resmi Gazete* No: 23149; 23.10.1997; 1996/1; 1997/1; 14.2.1997 *Resmi Gazete* No: 23384; 30.6.1998; 1998/2; 1998/1; 9.1.1998 *Resmi Gazete* No:23266, 22.2.1998.

120 However, most of such Turkish cases which ended up in Strasbourg were found for the political parties.

121 1996/3; 1997/3; 22.5.1997 *Resmi Gazete* No: 24067; 2.6.2000

and the defenders brought extensive discussion of various international instruments, the concept of laicism as understood by doctrine, and the law in some foreign jurisdictions. Freedom of expression was the major issue here and these cases tried to balance this freedom with the protection of the existing system in keeping with the official vision discussed earlier. In spite of such references however, in the case related to the closing of the *Fazilet Partisi* (the Virtue Party), although there was a call by the defending party for discussion of contemporary democracies where freedom, equality, pluralism and participation are regarded as fundamental and the rule of law is the basis, in the decision the matter was regarded as solely Turkish,[122] the ship sailing on the 'intended track'.

Culture and demands that can be accommodated within the legal framework

Some aspects of culture can be dealt with by the courts navigating between rules within the legal framework by satisfying the diverse cultural demands though not necessarily satisfying the demands of the EU and the ECHR. Some examples to be seen below are related to honour killings, rape in the family, equality between the spouses, a woman's surname, the abandoning of an illegitimate child to die, the status of blood brothers for insurance purposes, and 'the cow case'. These examples show how courts find it difficult to disregard localism and apply universalism, and thus use their discretion to appease localism – the underlay. There is no departure from the 'intended track' but tacking takes place in response to headwinds. Here we see the blending of the underlay and the overlay. This is the most significant category of navigation pointing to the 'covert mix' of the Turkish legal system.

Honour Killings

When courts face 'honour killings' or 'customary murders' among people from Eastern provinces where the honour of a woman is in the control of the male members of her family, they always deal with this problem within the framework of the Penal Code, received from the Italian legal system, but use the Code's facilities to reduce the penalty.[123] Thus in a typical case,

[122] 2000/86; 2000/50; 12/12/2000 *Resmi Gazete* No: 24268; 22.12.2000. Nevertheless the ECtHR found for Turkey in the *Refah* case based on the view that *shari'a* law and democracy are nor compatible. See the *Refah Partisi, Erbakan, Kazan and Tekdal and Others v. Turkey* Judgment Nos. 41340/98, 41342/98, 41343/98, 41344/98, Decision of 31.10.2000.

[123] The New Penal Code of 2005 deals with this issue in section 82/d and k, and categorically

the killing, usually committed by the youngest brother to take advantage of the then legal framework, was regarded as murder. Yet, as illustrated by the twenty-four court decisions examined between 1988 and 1999, the accused benefited from section 52 of the then Penal Code, which said that if a crime was committed under aggravating circumstances and provocation, this could be taken into account in sentencing; so could the demeanour of the accused. 'This coupled with the age of the boy or young man charged with the crime, often serves to decrease the sentence to virtually nothing',[124] though academic debate in Turkey always regarded such killings as the ultimate violation of women's human rights.

In 1997 a case involving a claim that section 462 of the then Penal Code was in violation of articles 5 (the State is under an obligation to remove all obstacles limiting fundamental rights and freedoms), 10 (Equality), 12 (Every person has inalienable and non-transferable fundamental rights and freedoms), 17 (Every person has the right to life, to protect and develop his/her material and moral being) and 19 (Every person has individual freedom and security) of the Constitution reached the *Anayasa Mahkemesi*.[125] The application was made by an Aggravated Felony Court dealing with an accused, who was convinced beyond doubt that his sister was in an illegitimate sexual relationship, and tried to kill both her and her lover. Section 462 foresaw a reduction of up to one eighth from a sentence of an accused if he/she was one of the spouses or one of the ascendants or sister or brother of the husband, wife, sister or a descendant of the victim.

Both the reasoning of the Felony Court and the *Anayasa Mahkemesi* bring an insight into the attitudes towards illegitimate sexual activity, including adultery, in Turkey. The Aggravated Felony Court stated that every person has the right to life and to the protection and development of life and can live his/her lifestyle by free will and choice; and the belief in 'cleaning' the name and honour (*namus*), and therefore is repugnant to general principles of law.

The *Anayasa Mahkemesi* however, limiting its inquiry into the killing or maiming of a sister by her brother, considered it within the ambit of serious provocation and did not find section 462 to be unconstitutional, stating that the legislature is free to decide which actions are to be considered as

---

states that the punishment for this offence is aggravated life sentence. This is an instance of the legislature responding to winds and tidal waves from the western world. Unfortunately, this issue has not gone away in spite of the new Penal Code of 2005 and has also become a problem in countries such as Germany, Sweden and the Netherlands where many traditional Turkish families live and work.

124 Arın, C (2001), 'Femicide in the Name of Honour in Turkey' (7) *Violence Against Women*, 824.

125 1997/45; 1998/48; 16.7.1998; *Resmi Gazete* 25297; 22.11.2003; 311

offences in society, what kind of and what length of sentence is appropriate and what are to be regarded as provocation and aggravating or mitigating circumstances. According to the Court, in using this discretion the legislature keeps in mind the sentencing policy, the social and cultural structure, and the ethical values of the country.[126]

A dissenting opinion was critical of the Court's decision in that the reduction in the sentence is related to who the victim is and therefore serious provocation seems to be the basis of the decision. This opinion stated that the personality of the victim cannot form the basis of accepting privileges for certain individuals; such a serious reduction sends a message that such an assault to the right to life is condoned in the name of protecting the name and honour of another. It is worthwhile noting that the decision of the *Anayasa Mahkemesi* was only published in November 2003, four years after the decision was reached. This delay tells us a lot about the ambivalent attitude of Turks, the Turkish judiciary and the Turkish legal system towards adulterous or illegitimate relationships.[127]

Other Family Matters

As far as rape in the family is concerned, the *Yargıtay* is now keen to use arguments of tradition and custom in order to increase sanctions. Thus in a case related to the rape of a 'niece', the Court held that: 'As in our traditions and customs related to our family structure the uncle has influence over his niece, his rape of her should be assessed under section 417 of the Penal Code', which should be qualified as 'aggravating circumstance'.[128]

However, in another case the *Yargıtay* pronounced the banning by a local administration of the payment of money by a bridegroom to the bride's father (*başlık parası*), to be illegal, and therefore not obeying the ban not an offence, saying that an administration could not ban a tradition or convert it into an offence. The Court held that, 'This centuries old tradition is a fact; the practice can only be banned by the legislator if regarded as against public policy.'[129] The Court added that in any event, to eradicate such a tradition should be a matter of education and not of law.

[126] Through the 2005 Penal Code, the Turkish legislature has made such offences punishable with an aggravated life sentence (sec. 82/d). Courts will now have to steer accordingly.

[127] See on the story of adultery in Turkey, Örücü, E (2006) 'The Story of Adultery in Turkey' in Bainham, Andrew (ed) *The International Survey of Family Law*, Jordan Publishing: 469-480.

[128] 03/2755; 04/747; 12.2.2004; 30 *Yargıtay Kararları Dergisi*, 2004, 1770.

[129] 1986/2-584; 1986/299; 26.5.1986, 12 *Yargıtay Kararları Dergisi* 1986, 1689.

Equality between the Spouses

A decision of the *Anayasa Mahkemesi* illustrates the general attitude to equality between spouses in Turkey -- a difficult issue. In this decision,[130] only published four years after it was delivered, the *Anayasa Mahkemesi* did not find section 153 (now 187) of the then Civil Code to be unconstitutional. A married woman, who wanted to use her maiden surname only, objected to section 153. The challenge was that this provision violated articles 10, 12, and 17 of the Constitution related to equality, fundamental rights and freedoms, personality rights and rights to development of personality. Following a very conservative interpretation of the family and the place of the woman in it, and referring to long established traditions, the *Anayasa Mahkemesi* saw no violation of any of the articles mentioned. However, in the dissenting opinion, the three judges saw a violation of article 10, 13 and 17 and the provision on equality and the Convention on the Elimination of All Forms of Discrimination Against Women, which Turkey ratified in 1985, and stated that the Constitution should be read in the light of International Conventions and contemporary developments. They referred to German family law, indicating that the spouses should be able to choose either of their surnames. Obviously, the fact that it took four years to publish its decision indicates how even the *Anayasa Mahkemesi* finds it extremely difficult to pass judgement in cases related to equality of the sexes in Turkey. It must be with this view in mind that the amended Civil Code has the same approach today.

We see that in Turkey, traditional values of family and lineage for men override claims to modernity. The principle of equality of the sexes, was specifically introduced into the Constitution in 2001 by a phrase in article 41, in addition to the existing 'equality before the law' principle in article 10. Now, added to the phrase, 'The family is the foundation of Turkish society', is the phrase 'and is based on equality between the spouses'. However, Turkish public policy considerations prohibit a man from taking his wife's surname. Thus a husband is not allowed to use the right given to a wife of having her family name added to that of her husband's (section 153). This prohibition effects even Turkish husbands of foreign wives in cases where the spouses live abroad and the law of that country allows the spouses to choose which surname they wish to be known by. This principle was pronounced in a case concerning a Turkish man who married a Swiss woman in Switzerland. The lower court was of the opinion that a correction of his surname in his Turkish personal status register was admissible since

130 1997/61; 1998/59; 29/9/1998; *Resmi Gazete*: 24937, 15/11/2002.

it had a 'foreign connecting factor'. The *Yargıtay* was quick to point out that the lower court's qualification was erroneous as there was no possibility in this case to resort to conflict of laws rules, and declared the Swiss rule to be totally against Turkish public policy.[131] It can be speculated that this new inequality of the sexes was not corrected in the amended version of section 153, because the assumption in male dominated Turkish society must have been that few men would want to choose their wife's surname – the impact of the underlay on the mixidness.

Abandoning an Illegitimate Child to Die

Another example is related to how the *Anayasa Mahkemesi* regarded section 475 of the then Penal Code, which created the offence and the punishment of the abandonment of a child or persons incapable of taking care of themselves.[132] The section accepted the abandonment of an illegitimate child not older than five days as a mitigating circumstance, in order to protect the '*namus*' (honour and good name) of the perpetrator, the wife, the mother, the daughter, the grand daughter or the sister. The sentence to be administered could be reduced by up to one third. The claim in the case was that the reasons for reduction violates feelings of justice and equity, threatens the life of an illegitimate child, and encourages the commission of a crime with less stigma; to treat the abandonment and even abandonment to death of an illegitimate child cannot be regarded as less onerous than of a legitimate child and that there was a violation of articles 10, 17, 41 and 138 of the Constitution.

The *Anayasa Mahkemesi* held that,

> When a child born out of wedlock is abandoned within five days of birth, the reason for the reduction in sentencing is the negative effect this birth has on the mother and the family and consequently the saving of the honour. [...] In reality, considering an act as an offence is related to the pressure of society. Today a person's fright, astonishment, anger, excitement, sadness, aggressiveness and similar psychological states are regarded as important. Section 475 should be assessed in this light. [...] Although article 138 states that judges decide eventually according to their conscience, this is within the framework of laws; and the Constitution.

131 18.HD; 1997/288; 1997/1496; 25/2/1997; 23 *Yargıtay Kararları Dergisi*, 1997, 1118.

132 1997/60; 1998/53; 22.9.1998; *Resmi Gazete*: 23770; 29/9/1999.

There were two dissenting opinions, both of interest. One said that people live in society, its pressure is always felt and crime is committed related to this effect of the society on the individual; the societal causes of crime. The responsibility of the individual is shared between the individual and society. The opinion pointed out that it was true that in Turkish society to 'save honour and good name' was accepted as part of traditional and social values and was very important and that it was this that was taken into consideration in section 475. The same mitigating circumstances that were in section 592 of the Italian Penal Code, the source law, were abrogated in 1981. Section 453, related to murdering such a child, which also allowed mitigating circumstances, was amended in 1991 and the reduction of sentence is now only applicable to the mother. Therefore section 475 should also be regarded in this light. This dissenting opinion suggested the annulment of the article for those other than the mother, there being a violation of articles 2 (rule of law), 38 (crime and punishment) and 41 (protection of the family).

The second dissenting opinion approached the subject from the point of view of equality in the right to life between a legitimate and an illegitimate child, stating that section 474 covered abandonment of a legitimate child and considered such abandonment as an aggravating circumstance. Since both children should be protected by law equally, this was a violation of article 10 on equality. Whatever the reason, this difference meant that the right to life of an illegitimate child was less worthy of protection than that of a legitimate child which also violated article 17 since the right to life is inviolable and no other value or tradition could justify its violation. Accordingly, if Turkey wanted to reach contemporary levels of civilisation, as expressed both in the Preface and article 174 of the Constitution, then there was no place for such a provision in Turkish law – a view supporting further suppression of the underlay.

There is no such section in the 2005 Penal Code. In fact section 82/e punishes such an offence with an aggravated life sentence. Thus, this could be regarded as a further alienation of the law from the people. The winds and the tidal stream from the ECHR and the EU are the forces here.[133]

Blood Brother's Rights

In another case a life insurance policy was taken out for the benefit of a 'blood brother'. The official law makes no reference to this customary

[133] Some of the changes brought to the Penal Code applicable to cases covered in Section(b) of art. 82, means that in future, similar cases would have to be dealt with under Section (c) below.

relationship. However, the *Yargıtay* said that according to Turkish folklore and customs this institution is valued, that it is a 'private pact' which creates a relationship like brotherhood or bosom friendship, and that since the 'blood brother' should be considered to have a moral interest in the continuation of the life of the other, he therefore should be accepted as the beneficiary.[134]

Special Nature of Hac[135]

Some religious and traditional values are given additional weight by the *Yargıtay*. When baggage, carrying gifts brought back from the *Hac*, was lost in transit, though article 22 of the Montreal Protocol amending the Warsaw/Hague Protocol was to be applied, the *Yargıtay* held that, 'When the special nature of this journey and the spiritual value of the gifts to be given to relatives and friends are taken into account, it emerges that the claimant should be given "moral" compensation and not solely "material" compensation.'[136]

The Cow Case

A most remarkable case serves as an example of interlocking of the social, religious and the legal culture by the innovative dexterity of the *Yargıtay* as navigator. This decision of the *Yargıtay* reached in 1979,[137] is a good illustration of the covert nature of this mixed legal system. The case concerned the sexual involvement of an under-age village boy with a neighbour's cow. The owner of the cow, rather than suing for bestiality under the Criminal Code, sued to recover damages from the father of the boy under the Civil Code. He claimed that according to religious sources, which he cited, his cow had become untouchable and could not be sold or its meat and milk consumed. The case was dismissed by the lower court for lack of legal ground, since religious law is not a recognised source of Turkish law. The owner of the cow appealed. The *Yargıtay* overturned the decision of the lower court, saying that,

> Although religious rules or sentiments could not form the basis of any claim, if the complainant could prove by expert evidence that there were local religious or moral beliefs or customs to the effect

134 95/3856; 95/4829; 9.6.1995, 21 *Yargıtay Kararları Dergisi* 1995, 1412 at p. 1414.

135 *Hac* is the religious pilgrimage to Mecca.

136 01/5985; 01/8861; 12.2.200;1 (2003) 29 *Yargıtay Kararları Dergisi* 2003, 43.

137 79/1644; 79/14383; 21.12.1979. I have used this example on many occasions in my work.

> that the meat and the milk of such an animal could not be consumed, then the animal would be considered to have lost its market value, in which case, by the application of the '*noxal*' rule of Roman law, the cow should be given to the father of the boy and the claimant should be given the market value of the cow by the father.

The formula is a fine example of how the *Yargıtay* avoids openly facing religious issues and resolves disputes within the formal legal system. The case shows how the 'layers' of systems may be interlocked and that the judges of the *Yargıtay* are such innovative navigators.[138]

Outside pressures that clash with the framework or the culture

There is now pressure from the outside world stemming from Turkish aspirations to EU membership, which may lead to results not necessarily supported by all the Turkish people, such as the abolishing of the death penalty, and some which clash with the official vision, such as making it difficult to close political parties, and enabling re-trials after successful ECtHR appeals. Following such pressures the legislation has been changed but some of these changes challenge the indigenous socio-culture further than the official legal framework ever did. Below are some examples to show how the courts navigated before the changes and how changes have taken place.

Since 1987 when Turkey accepted the right of individuals to apply to the ECtHR, there have been more than 4000 such applications from Turkey to the Commission of the ECHR. When legislation has been found wanting, and this is quite rare, amendments have been undertaken and further changes have been brought in. The problems seem to lie in the application and implementation of the law and court decisions. Most of the applications are related to criminal law and criminal procedure, especially to execution without trial, death in prison and torture. There have been cases related to the right to life, to torture, to the period spent in custody,

[138] There was a second very similar case in 1998, where the lower court decided that the pursuer had no case as there was no 'medical objection' to the utilisation of the meat and the milk of such an animal, the *Yargıtay* overturning the decision, declared that when there is no codal provision applicable to a matter then, according to section 1 Civil Code, tradition and custom are to be resorted to, and that, 'Since facts are not in dispute in this case, tradition and custom have to be investigated in line with the claim, and if custom, tradition, religious and moral beliefs and conceptions are in line with the claim, then the existence of damages cannot be questioned. The pursuer should be asked whether he wishes to surrender the animal to the defendant in return for the market price, and if not, then reasonable compensation must be decided upon.' 98/2632; 98/3249; 24.3.1998; 24 *Yargıtay Kararları Dergisi*, 1998, 834. These are the only two cases I have come upon on this subject!

to judicial independence, and to cases taking an unreasonably long time to finalise. Moreover, there are other areas of concern, some of which are difficult to resolve in view of the characteristics and principles of the vision of the Republic discussed earlier. These cases are related to freedom of religion and conscience, freedom of expression, closure of political parties, the right to complain and the freedom to seek rights, and property rights, specifically expropriations. Without a fundamental upheaval of the system, including amendment of the Constitution in very significant ways, or very progressive, creative and active courts taking into consideration decisions of the ECtHR and decisions of courts in other jurisdictions in human rights cases, this problem may remain. Here 'cultural exceptionalism' overrides 'globalising uniformity', at times giving a stronger voice to the underlay.

However, in one case related to Law No: 4307 of 1997 on Primary Education, extending education in primary schools from five to eight years, the claim was that this was contrary to a number of articles of the Constitution, and articles 9 and 10 ECHR and article 2 of its Protocol 1, as it would impede religious education. The appellant, the *Refah Partisi* (the main opposition party), made reference to foreign doctrine and decisions of the ECtHR on democracy, pluralism, equality, tolerance, fundamental rights and freedoms, conditions of social peace and laicism. There were references to a number of International Conventions, the ECHR, and foreign jurisdictions. The *Anayasa Mahkemesi,* deciding solely within the framework of the Turkish Constitution held:

> On the other hand, though not a direct basis for constitutional control, the ECHR has value and effect as a supplementary norm and its Article 9 related to freedom of religion and conscience is in essence parallel to Article 24 of the Turkish Constitution. There is no violation of Protocol 1 Article 2, since there is no limitation or prohibition on the choice parents have on the child's religious education.[139]

In this case nothing was found to be unconstitutional. The Court was indeed aware of the 'wind from astern', and that its position would be supported by outside demands, 'the tidal wave' from Europe.

[139] 1997/62; 1998/52; 16.9.1998 *Resmi Gazete* No: 24206; 30.10.2000; and *AMKD*: 36, 2001, 198.

The Position of the Wife

A woman living apart from her husband, sued for divorce, because of serious incompatibility.[140] Her husband objected as the case should have been brought before the court of his residence (*kocanın ikametgah mahkemesi*), which was accepted by the then Turkish Civil Code as the residence of the wife and the court of this residence as the competent court in divorce cases brought by either spouse. The challenge was that this created an inequality for the wife and violated her freedom of establishment. The claim was that there was a violation of articles 10, 13 and 23 of the Constitution.

The *Anayasa Mahkemesi* stated that although every person is free to choose his/her own abode, one person cannot have more than one (section 19 Civil Code); the family is a unit accepted by society, and various laws regulate this unit for its continuity, proper functioning and solidarity. Consequently, some individual rights have been transferred to the family in keeping with the structure of this relationship and the section concerned is related to the family having one residence. The Court found that public interest justified this regulation and that the article related to freedom of establishment could be limited as all rights can be for public interest, public morality, public health and any other special ground mentioned in the pertinent article, as long as these limitations are proper in a democratic society. There were no dissenting opinions. Thus tradition trumped human rights.

Although the above case shows the conservative approach to family relationships in keeping with the majority of the values of the populace, again further Europeanisation meant that this or a similar provision did not find a place in the new 2002 Civil Code. The traditional understanding of the 'family unit' is further challenged and the judge has now to steer under the pressure of the 'tidal streams' and 'winds' that push the 'ship' from astern in the direction of the 'charted route' of the Republic.

In yet another case, a wife became a guarantor to her husband and a debtor to third parties in her husband's interest without asking permission from the judge. The claim was that this provision (section 169 of the then Civil Code), which appears to be protecting the rights of a wife, actually treats her as a minor since the husband in the same position does not need permission, and the insinuation is that she is a second-class citizen, and therefore, there is a violation of articles 10 and 12 of the Constitution. The *Anayasa Mahkemesi* said that, 'the aim of this provision is to protect the wife from entering under obligations unwittingly as she may not know the

140 1993/23; 1993/55; 2/12/1993; *Resmi Gazete*: 23917, 25/12/1999.

consequences, the scope and the aim of this debt. She may enter such an obligation under the husband's influence.'[141] This limitation was found to protect the unity of the family and in the public interest.

There were dissenting opinions to the effect that this unequal treatment of the woman violated the Convention on the Elimination of All Forms of Discrimination Against Women, any discrimination based on sex is illegal; national provisions should be viewed in the light of this Convention, not just the Turkish Constitution; the Turkish Civil Code is based on the Swiss Code of 1907 (in effect in 1912) and it may have been meant to protect the wife; but in our day this is not acceptable; this protection presumes that the woman is less intelligent and less capable; and her legal capacity has been limited by this provision; it assumes that she cannot foresee the consequences of her actions, and this cannot be acceptable.

This section of the Civil Code has now been changed, equalised and modernised by the legislator navigating with the western 'wind' blowing astern. However, it can be claimed that it is now detrimental to illiterate women who would sign any piece of paper under the threat of their husbands, and therefore, does not accord with Turkish realities as they stand at present.[142] Perhaps courts, with more sensitive instruments, are better coastal navigators than the legislator.

The *Yargıtay* for instance, was extremely cautious in the application of the then section 134 of the Civil Code, which was amended in 1988 introducing divorce by mutual consent. The *Yargıtay* has not changes its approach in view of the new section 166. The Court believes that divorces apparently based upon mutual consent may not be so; women who are the weaker partners in Turkish marriages, may be forced by their husbands to accept divorce under threat of, for example, taking the children from them. Thus the judge must hear both parties himself personally, be convinced that they are expressing their wills freely, and endorse as acceptable the arrangements made by the parties for the financial consequences of the divorce and the children. In addition, the Court refrains from recognising a divorce decree obtained abroad if the foreign judge has not ensured the existence of these conditions. Here we see the Court acting as the protector of women and children and taking into consideration the realities of Turkish society, the underlay.

[141] 1997/27;1998/43; 30/6/1998; *Resmi Gazete*: 23934; 15/1/2000; and 1999/47; 1999/46; 28.12.1999; *Resmi Gazete*: 23989; 10/3/2000.

[142] Maybe the changes in the Swiss Civil Code should have been followed. There this provision was removed from the Swiss Code in 1984; now a ratification of such a contract is demanded in relation to either party, in keeping with the equality principle.

The publication of the decision of the *Anayasa Mahkemesi* annulling the then section 159 of the Civil Code, which stated that a wife needs her husband's permission to work outside the home, was delayed for two years. The decision reached in 1990 was only published in 1992. The delay was due to the difficulty in the composing of the reasoning through which the Court tried to satisfy all sides, and perhaps to hold back the introduction of the change. What is worthy of note in relation to our study here is that the *Anayasa Mahkemesi,* having found this section unconstitutional and drawn Parliament's attention to other such sections in the Civil Code in need of removal, has tried hard not to be misunderstood by the target audience at home. After a very thorough and progressive comparative survey and with full reference to contemporary foreign and international developments, the *Anayasa Mahkemesi* nevertheless felt that it should end its opinion with a statement reflecting a very traditional view. It said that this decision should not be taken to mean that the Court condoned a new life style for the family in which a working wife could neglect her family duties towards her husband and children; if she intended to work, the Court would like to see her making arrangements for these domestic duties to be performed by another person.

It is remarkable that the New Civil Code of 2002 has inserted a new section 192 'The profession and job of spouses' replacing the annulled section 159, to the effect that, 'Each spouse is free to choose a profession or a job without seeking permission of the other. However, in the choice and performance of a profession or a job, the peace and interest of the marriage union must be considered'. It would be interesting to observe how the judges will navigate round this point, and balance the inside and the outside forces.

Rights of the Child

A child of the parties to a divorce has now to be heard before custody is allocated following a divorce. To give voice to the child is a new concept for Turkish society and in such decisions, the *Yargıtay* refers to article 12 of the UN Convention on the Rights of the Child and article 6 of the European Convention on the Implementation of the Rights of the Child, both 'side winds',[143] disregarding the values of the underlay.

[143] 2004/3580; 2004/4216; 5.4.2004; 30 *Yargıtay Kararları Dergisi,* 2004, 1201.

Paternity

Section 310 of the 1926 Civil Code concerned the court's decision on paternity upon the demand of a woman in cases where a man had promised marriage to the woman, or sexual intercourse had constituted an offence or an abuse of position. As various methods of deciding on 'paternity with all its consequences' had been quashed by the *Yargıtay*, the lower court brought this case to the *Anayasa Mahkemesi*, saying: '"Natural fatherhood" in section 297 only gives the right to demand compensation whereas "paternity with all its consequences" (section 310), gives the child quite different rights, and from the point of view of the innocent child this differentiation creates inequality.'

The *Anayasa Mahkemesi* held that,

> In cases where the conditions of section 310 are not met there can be no decision on "paternity with all its consequences". This provision is for the protection of the family and to discourage other types of cohabitation; this is in the public interest and morality, and the provision does not violate article 10 of the Constitution. This regulation is also in keeping with the necessities of a democratic society and therefore not contrary to articles 12 and 13. Article 41 is for the protection of the child, the woman and the family. The reasoning of this section specifically mentions that the family to be protected and to be established as an institution in society is the family as envisaged by the Civil Code. One of the aims therefore is to prevent free unions and encourage the formation of the family. This provision is not contrary to these aims.[144]

There were no dissenting opinions.

However, we now see that there is no distinction left between legitimate and illegitimate children or between cases that determine paternity in the new 2002 Civil Code. This is an intriguing development. On the one hand it accords with the values upheld by the ECHR and on the other with those of some at home who want to have children born out of *imam nikahı* relationships to be equated to those born in wedlock. Thus it has a paradoxical consequence, which gives the navigators a freer hand to indirectly uphold a culture which otherwise clashes with one of the values of the official framework: laicism.

[144] 1993/37; 1993/56; 7.12.1993; *Resmi Gazete*: 23918; 26.12.1999.

Freedom of expression

In an area regarded as sacrosanct (and also covered by the Preamble of the Constitution), a human right -- that of freedom of expression -- is limited in view of the protected values. To incite people to hatred and animosity based on religious and racial differences was a punishable offence in the then Penal Code sections 312 and 59. This is still the case in the new Penal Code of 2005. Thus in a case where laicism was attacked and living under Islamic *shari'a* was promoted, the *Yargıtay* relied on the Constitution saying that though article 24 guarantees freedom of religion and conscience, article 14 states that this freedom cannot be used with the aim of creating discrimination of language, race, religion and sect. The Court also referred to the principle of freedom of religion and conscience as it appears in the judgments of the ECtHR and to limitations for the purposes of territorial integrity of the nation, public order, national security, preventing crime and securing the authority and effectiveness of the judicial power. The Court stated that the Constitution accepts 'the laicist Republic' as the *sine-qua-non* of democracy and that democratic regimes have the right to protect themselves. It is interesting to note that the *Yargıtay* also says that, though section 312 may be seen as being anti-democratic, judges do not have the competence to differentiate between legislation on the criterion of 'good law' and 'bad law', as 'only the Constitutional authorities can resolve such political discussions',[145] the ultimate limitation for judges.

CONCLUDING REMARKS

As I have stated elsewhere[146] the formal legal system in Turkey performs a balancing act. At times it tries to maintain a firm stance, at other times it allows the traditionalist views to be heard. This is mostly achieved by the navigational skills of the judge. The cases considered in Part II indicate that when elements from two interpretive models combine, one drawing its understanding from culture, tradition and religion and the other from official law, they might be able to tap into each other and mesh, bringing 'cultural conversation' and creating a 'fit' in a wider narrative. In Turkey there is no competition between the rules, as the official legal system does not permit this, but at times there is contradiction. It is the courts that try to create

[145] 98/10296; 98/11672; 23.9.1998; 24 *Yargıtay Kararları Dergisi*, 1998, 1724. In addition, when religion is used for anti-laic purposes and division and animosity in the populace by way of the press, again, section 312 is resorted to. See 2002/9667; 20 02/10406; 7.11.2002; 29 *Y Yargıtay Kararları Dergisi* , 2003, 634

[146] Örücü (1996) supra n 6, 110-111.

harmony. In the Turkish experience the concepts and values introduced in the early years of the Republic were to a large extent incompatible with the indigenous system, and the deeper values and purposes of the two were not commensurable. One way out was to establish a global purpose, and hope that a bridge could be built by the courts between traditional culture and western style expression of the norms and standards. This created the covert mixed legal system.

GENERAL CONCLUSION

In a modern unitary nation state of the western type, the accommodation of cultural diversity and multiple normative orders can only be brought about by the judge, who is the tuner, or navigator and steersman of the law, by using discretion and creative interpretation, and not by the legislators whose main demarcation lines are clearly drawn, for instance, within Turkey by the Constitution and the immutable laws, and within Europe and within the European Union by the demands of human rights and 'ever closer integration'. Turkish courts will become even more important as navigators and tuners in the coming years, in their efforts to keep the ship in shape and on course.

As noted, the 'modern layer' of the Turkish legal system is the ultimate and predominant one reflecting the 'hyphenated' nature of the law and embodying the mixing layers of the system. This modern layer is synthetic and eclectic and this mixed nature of the modern layer has been kept alive, examples of which have been seen in Part I. In fact one can talk of the 'mixed modern layer' or 'modern layers' rather than the 'modern layer' of law. The interaction between the 'modern layers' is of utmost importance for the functioning of the legal system, even more important than that between the modern layers and the underlying layers, such as the traditional and religious. The maintenance of the 'hyphenated' nature of the legal system is also important in not allowing the received legal institutions to be profoundly transformed upon transfer. A weak pluralism is enveloped in the monolithic legal system. This system reflects various legal cultures married to each other, blending the alien socio-cultures reflected in the official framework with the re-constructed local socio-culture(s). No one of the layers is in competition. All live under and within the top-down model in a covert mixedness.

So, if we 'approach law as the outcome of a rather complex competitive relationship between different layers of law',[147] or even between different

[147] Grande (1995) supra n 80 at 7.

layers of systems, be they legal, sociological, cultural or religious, what is the outcome in Turkey? We know that the legal evolution has been through a succession of imports from abroad. We also know that the Turkish legislature is intent on keeping the legal and the social fabric under centralised control. So, are the various systems successfully intertwining? It has been said that, 'Law and other such systems exist in a world where they are each the background or environment of each other'.[148] Is this so for Turkey, or have 'they become increasingly isolated from each other as they become more and more self-referential'?[149] Although the Turkish legal system is self-referential, in the sense that it is concerned with the law as envisaged by the formal legal system and does not enrich itself beyond necessity by constructive discourse with other systems in society, it is at the same time not self-referential, in the sense that it still consults 'the source laws', and now tries to fit into the European Union requirements, thus taking advantage of and strengthening its 'hyphenated' nature. The judges also try to blend all this with the underlay as seen above.

I have not set out in this contribution to assess the 'health' of this 'hyphenated' and 'synthetic' legal system. In fact, the means of diagnosing the 'health' of a legal system is an unsettled issue: measuring 'effectiveness', 'efficiency', 'sustainability' of reforms, 'effective economic development' and the 'use made of the law', have all been suggested - a most unsatisfactory term often used being 'it works' or 'shows results'.

If continuity and harmony are in the essence of well functioning systems, then, internalisation of norms and standards by the people in the recipient system is crucial. Internalisation is also crucial if there are to be fruitful developments. Though the synthetic '*purée*' of Turkish law and its 'synthetic' and 'hyphenated' nature together with the 'hyphenated' nature of her socio-culture are here to stay, as seen, the formal legal system in Turkey at times tries to maintain a firm stance; at other times it allows traditionalist views to be heard. Yet, the overall picture is quite static. Whatever the future developments and the shape of the mixture, both the legal and the socio-cultural systems will remain 'hyphenated' and mixed.

In sum, from its inception, the synthetic Turkish legal system did not totally mix with, but tried to transform, domestic systems, be they social, political, ideological, religious or economic. Turkish law is not internally homogenous and its roots lie wide. However, the intertwining of the 'hyphenated' legal and social systems of Turkey is not complete. Whether it will ever become so is open to conjecture. The final question must be: Does

148 Bankowski, Z and Christodoulidis, E (1998) 'The European Union as an Essentially Contested Project' (4) *European Law Journal* 341 at 348.

149 Id.

such a 'synthetic' and 'hyphenated' legal system with a hyphenated socio-culture, deserve a special place in transplant theories and in the analysis of mixed legal systems, and a reconsideration, while the theoretical borders of analysis are being redrawn? Can this legal system be an illustration to reinforce the hypothesis that 'mixed legal systems are at new frontiers'?

Customary Law v Common Law Marriages: a Hybrid Approach in South Africa

MARISSA HERBST AND WILLEMIEN DU PLESSIS

INTRODUCTION

The conflict between customary law and common law is a theme that permeates the history of colonialism in Africa. In the English speaking colonies customary law was, according to Allott, recognised as a result of treaties, the economic benefit of allowing traditional leaders to handle traditional disputes instead of government courts, the idea that English law was too advanced to be understood by traditional communities and the fear of conflict.[1] The so-called 'repugnancy' test was introduced.[2] Hooker states that '(r)epugnancy is a term used to indicate that customary law will not be admitted "if repugnant to justice, morality, or good conscience".'[3]

A similar approach to customary law initially was followed in the Cape. With the introduction of the Black Administration Act 38 of 1927, formal provision was made that Blacks could conclude common law[4] marriages but customary marriages[5] were not recognised[6] owing to their polygamous nature.[7] The only favourable provision of the Act in reference to customary

1 Allott, AN (1970) *New Essays in African Law* Butterworths at 12-13.

2 See Hooker, MB (1975) *Legal pluralism: an introduction to colonial and neo-colonial laws* Clarendon Press at 129-135; Allott supra n 1 at 158-181.

3 Hooker supra n 2 at 130.

4 Marriages concluded in terms of predecessors to the Marriage Law Amendment Act 17 of 1921 and subsequent amendment acts as well as the Marriage Act 25 of 1961.

5 See para 2 below.

6 Section 22(6).

7 *Seedat's Executors v The Master (Natal)* 1917 AD 302, Dlamini, CRM (1989) 'The New Marriage Legislation Affecting Blacks in South Africa' *Journal of South African Law* 408 at 410; Labuschagne, JMT (1991) 'Erkenning van die inheemse huwelik: [Recognition of the

marriages was that a court could not find that the tradition of *lobola* (bridewealth) was against natural justice and public policy (the so-called repugnancy clause).[8] The existence of customary marriages was, however, taken into account when disputes arose. Limited recognition was given to wives from customary marriages in actions dealing with the negligent causation of the death of the breadwinner.[9] In some instances the courts resolved that a marriage concluded in terms of the Marriage Act 25 of 1961 could not undo a customary marriage.[10]

The non-recognition of customary marriages sometimes led to severe hardship in that children were not regarded as legitimate and that wives of customary marriages were not given the same status as wives from civil marriages in matters of intestate succession and maintenance.[11]

The South African Law Reform Commission wrote several Discussion Papers and made proposals regarding the recognition of customary marriages. The Commission attempted to reconcile customary and civil law traditions in proposed legislation.[12]

With the introduction of the Interim Constitution (Constitution of the Republic of South Africa 200 of 1993) and the final Constitution of the Republic of South Africa, 1996 (hereafter Constitution) a new dispensation was introduced. Not only does section 112 of the Constitution state that customary law must be applied where applicable, subject to the Constitution, but section 15(3) states that nothing prevents legislation from recognising, inter alia, marriages concluded 'under any tradition, or a system of religious, personal or family law.' Section 9 of the Constitution further regulates that everyone should have the right to equal protection of the law.

The Recognition of Customary Marriages Act 120 of 1998 (Recognition Act) was enacted in terms of section 15(3) of the Constitution.[13] As the name of the Act indicates, the purpose of the Act is to recognise customary

---

customary marriage] Zimnat Insurance Co Ltd v Chawanda 1991 2 SA 825 (ZS)' (54) *Journal of Contemporary Roman Dutch Law* 843 at 844, Prinsloo, MW (1990) 'Regspluralisme, 'n menseregte-akte en die interne aanwysingsreg' [Legal Pluralism: a Human Rights Bill and the Internal Rules of Choice of Law] (23) *De Jure* at 357-363.

[8] Section 11(1) Black Administration Act 38 of 1927. *See* also Rubin, L (1965) 'The Adaptation of Customary Family Law in South Africa' in Kuper H and Kuper L (eds) *African Law: Adaptation and Development* University of California Press at 198-215.

[9] Section 31 Black Laws Amendment Act 76 of 1963.

[10] Section 22(7) Black Administration Act.

[11] Kaganas F and Murray C (1991) 'Law and Women's Rights in South Africa: An Overview' (16) *Acta Juridica* at 1-38.

[12] South African Law Reform Commission 1997 available at <http://wwwserver.law.wits.ac.za/salc/discussn/dp74.html>.

[13] The Act was put into operation on 15 November 2000.

marriages and, by implication, polygamy. The question is, however, if the Act succeeds in this purpose and if, indeed, full recognition is given to traditional marriages or whether a new marriage regime was created?

The purpose of this article is to compare customary law marriages before and after the enactment of the Recognition Act in order to determine the Constitutional and common law influences on the Act.[14] First, a historical overview will be given of the recognition of customary law and customary marriages and then a comparison will be made between customary marriages before and after the introduction of the Recognition Act in order to come to a conclusion.

RECOGNITION OF CUSTOMARY MARRIAGES - HISTORICAL OVERVIEW

African customary law in the modern sense of the word (i.e., with Western influence):[15]

> denotes all those legal systems originating from African societies as part of the culture of particular tribes or groups that have been maintained, supplemented, amended and or superseded in part by:
> (a) changing community views and the demands of the changing world;
> (b) contact with societies with other legal systems;
> (c) contact with and the influence of other legal systems; and
> (d) the direct and indirect influence of foreign (non-indigenous) government structures.

Customary law is used in contrast with common law. Common law[16] is not used in its traditional Anglo-American sense, but refers to South African law based on Roman Dutch Law and English law as amended by legislation.[17]

[14] The paper is partially based on an unpublished LLM dissertation by Herbst, M (2005) Die Bestaanbaarheid van Gewoonteregtelike Huwelike in die Lig van die Grondwet [The Existence of Customary Marriages in View of the Constitution] North-West University.

[15] Olivier, NJJ et al (1996) *Indigenous Law* Butterworths at 186. See also Allott, AN (1960) *Essays in African Law*: with special reference to the law of Ghana Butterworths at 61-64; Allott supra n 1 at 145-157.

[16] South African law is also referred to as civil law - but then again not in the European tradition - it is used as a synonym for common law – see note 18.

[17] South African law is a mixed legal jurisdiction based on Roman Dutch law and English law. The South African private law is not codified and is regarded as customary law. Customary law in this paper, however, refers to African Customary or Indigenous law. See also Allott (1960) supra n 15 at 14-16; Rubin supra n 8 at 196-198.

According to South African common law before 2002, a marriage was regarded as a voluntary institution between one man and one woman to the exclusion of anyone else[18] while African customary marriages were regarded as potentially polygamous. Legislation, however, stated that a court may not find that *lobolo*[19] is in conflict with public policy.[20]

After the introduction of the 1994 Constitution, the South African Law Reform Commission investigated the possible recognition of customary marriages. The dilemma was whether common law or customary law should be the point of departure. A bill was proposed that eventually formed the basis for the Recognition Act.

The Commission attempted to codify customary law, taking into account the right to equality, dignity and freedom. Sections 9,[21] 15(3),[22] 30[23] and 31[24] of the Constitution place an indirect obligation on government to recognise customary marriages in the same manner as common law marriages. However, the recognition of customary marriages as well as the exercise of cultural rights may not be in conflict with any other provision in the Bill of Rights.[25] There are rules in customary law which at first glance from a western perspective may be in conflict with the Bill of Rights, for example with the right to equality, which complicated the dilemma of the Law Reform Commisson even further.[26] The eventual Recognition Act was a compromise negotiated at workshops held countrywide.

The Constitution is the supreme law of South Africa and any law or conduct inconsistent therewith is invalid.[27] There is a Constitutional obligation on the courts to develop customary law in order to promote the Bill of Rights.[28] Before the Constitution, customary rules were only recognised if they were not in conflict with natural justice or public policy. Since 1994, the rules of natural justice and public policy were substituted by the rules contained in the Constitution.[29] In *Alexkor Ltd v Richtersveld*

18 In 2006 a Civil Union Act 17 of 2006 was approved, recognising marriages between persons of the same sex.

19 Payment of bride-wealth. Also, *inter alia,* referred to as *bogadi, bohali, xuma, lumalo, thaka, ikhazi, magadi and emabheka* – see also section 1 Recognition of Customary Marriages Act 120 of 1998.

20 Section 11(1) Black Administration Act 38 of 1927; section 54A of the Magistrates' Court Act 32 of 1944 and section 1 of the Law of Evidence Amendment Act 45 of 1988.

21 Equality clause.

22 Freedom of religion, belief and opinion.

23 Language and culture.

24 Cultural, religious and linguistic communities.

25 Sections 15(3)(b), 30 and 31(2).

26 See also the Promotion of Equality and Prevention of Unfair Discrimination Act 4 of 2000.

27 Section 2 Constitution.

28 Section 39 Constitution.

29 Section 211(3) of the Constitution: 'The courts must apply customary law when that

Community,[30] the Constitutional Court confirmed that customary law is part and parcel of South African law and that it should be regarded as such.

The debate on the recognition of customary law within a human rights dispensation is based on the idea that customary law *per se* is in conflict with the Constitution, and especially of the equality clause. The supporters of this idea argue that the nature of customary law and human rights differs. Customary law is based on the idea of community and communal rights while human rights are of an individual nature. It is, however, not true that individuals adhering to a system of customary law only have rights pertaining to the group. Individual rights also are recognised although these rights must be exercised within the group. Customary law is continuously adapting to changing circumstances unique to Africa and, especially, South Africa.[31]

CUSTOMARY LAW v COMMON LAW

For many years parliament and the courts found it difficult to refer to marriages concluded in terms of customary law as 'marriages' and the term 'customary union' was preferred due to it polygamous nature.[32] However, in this paper the term 'customary marriages' is preferred as the correct terminology referring also to pre-2000 marriages. In order to determine the nature of customary marriages, pre and post 2000 a comparison will be made pertaining to polygamy, requirements of a valid marriage, matrimonial property regime, dissolution of a marriage and the status of women in such marriages.

law is applicable, subject to the Constitution and any legislation that specifically deals with customary law.'

30 2003 12 BCLR 1301(KH) para. 51.

31 See in this regard Bennett, TW (1995) *Human Rights and Customary Law under the South African Constitution* Juta at 28; De Koker, JY (1996) 'Die Bestaanbaarheid van Lobolo in die Nuwe Suid-Afrikaanse Regsbedeling' [The Existence of Lobolo in the New South African Legal Dispensation] (21) *Journal of Juridicial Science* 75 at 79-80; Nhlapo, TR (1991)'The African Family and Women's Rights: Friends or Foes?'(16) *Acta Juridica* 135 at 138, Bekker, JC (1991) 'Interaction between Constitutional Reform and Family Law' (16) *Acta Juridica* at 1-17; Maithufi, IP (1998) 'The Effect of the 1996 Constitution on the Customary Law of Succession and Marriage in South Africa: Some Observations' (31*De Jure* at 285-293; Nicholson, CMA (2003)'The Realisation of Human Rights within the Context of African Customary Marriages' (66) *Journal of Contemporary Roman Dutch Law* at 373-388 and Vorster, LP (2001) 'South African Customary Law and Ethnicity: Challenges for South Africa' (24) *South African Journal of Ethnology* at 119-124.

32 *Seedat's Executors* supra n 7; Dlamini supra n 7 at 410; Prinsloo supra n 7 at 357-363; Bennett, TW (1994) 'The Equality Clause and Customary Law' (10) *South African Journal of Human Rights* at 122-127.

Poligamy

As has been stated before, the colonial authorities did not recognise a customary marriage due to its polygamous nature. The nature of customary marriages was not well understood and polygamy was seen as a form of slavery.[33] *Lobolo*[34] was regarded as payment for the wife.

In terms of customary law a man may marry more than one wife -- a woman may not marry more than one husband.[35] There is no restriction on the number of wives a husband may have, except that he should be able to maintain all of his wives and that *lobolo* should be paid for each one.[36]

Different family units are created. Each spouse in a multiple household has her own status and authority, forms a separate unit and has a form of independence.[37] The status and 'rank' of the house depend largely on the woman's social prestige, her relationship to the other households and the status of her children in relation to intestate succession.[38] A distinction is made between a single household and a complex polygamous system.[39]

Section 2(3) recognises all polygamous marriages concluded before the commencement of the Recognition Act as marriages. Similarly, section 2(4) provides for the conclusion of polygamous marriages after the commencement of the Act. However, these marriages must comply with the requirements of the Recognition Act. In terms of customary law, the husband did not need to consult his wives when he decided to conclude another marriage. The Recognition Act protects the rights of the first wife or wives in that the husband has to apply to court to change the matrimonial property regime of the first marriage and to approve a written contract regulating the future matrimonial property regime.[40]

[33] Du Plessis, W (1993) 'Poligamie, buite-egtelikheid en intestate erfreg: [Polygamy, Illegitimacy and Law of Intestate Succession] *Dhansay v Davids* 1991 4 SA 200 (K)' (56) *Journal of Contemporary Roman Dutch Law* 149 at 151.

[34] See more information on *lobolo* below.

[35] Marriages between women are sometimes recognised by customary law – *see* Oomen, B (2000) 'Traditional Woman-to-Woman Marriages, and the Recognition of Customary Marriages Act' (63) *Journal of Contemporary Roman Dutch Law* at 274-282.

[36] In Islamic law, for example, a man may not marry more than four wives -- Pearl, A (1987) *A Textbook on Muslim Personal Law* (2nd ed) Croom Helm at 514.

[37] Olivier et al supra n 15 at 57-58; Bennett, TW (1991) *A sourcebook of African customary law for Southern Africa* Juta at 232-237 and Maithufi, IP (1992) 'Do We have a New Type of Voidable Marriage?' (55) *Journal of Contemporary Roman Dutch Law* at 628-630.

[38] Bennett supra n 37 at 401-405, Olivier NJJ et al (1998) *Inheemse Reg* [Indigenous Law] Butterworths at 44-45.

[39] Bekker, JC (1982) *Seymour's Customary Law in Southern Africa* (4th ed) Juta at 126.

[40] Section 7(6). *See* Herbst supra n 14 at 95-96.

Requirements for a Valid Marriage

There were various requirements for a valid customary marriage, namely consensus between the parties, a formal ceremony to transfer the bride to the other family and the payment of *lobolo*.[41] These requirements will be referred to briefly.

Consensus

The customary law initially was not concerned with consensus between the two marrying parties. The marriage was regarded as a union between two families rather than two individuals.[42] An essential requirement was that the family councils had to be in agreement as to the identity of the two parties. The family councils could take into account the preferences of the two marrying individuals. The courts, however, changed this requirement by insisting that both individuals to the marriage (at the time of the union) should agree to the marriage, resulting in subsequent legislation and courts prohibiting forced marriages. In the former Transkei and KwaZulu-Natal, women who had reached the age of majority could undertake their own marriage negotiations and the permission of the fathers or family elders were not necessary.[43]

In terms of some of the customary law systems it is possible to abduct a girl to another family household in order to force the girl's family to give permission for the marriage. This is known as *ukuthwala*. More often than not, the girl agreed to the abduction, but the former Transkei and KwaZulu-Natal banned the practice as it was not always possible to ascertain if the girl indeed did agree to be abducted.[44]

The Recognition Act explicitly requires permission of both individuals to the marriage.[45] The purpose is to prevent forced marriages similar to those that occurred in the former Transkei and KwaZulu-Natal. The Recognition

[41] See in this regard Olivier et al supra n 15 at 20.

[42] *Mabena v Letsoalo* 1998 2 SA 1068 (T).

[43] Sections 42 and 116(1)(b) of the KwaZulu-Natal Codes on Zulu Law; *see* also *Zimande v Sibeko* 1948 NAC (K) 21.

[44] Olivier et al supra n 38 at 11, Bohler-Müller, N (2001) 'Cultural Practises and Social Justice in a Constitutional Dispensation: Some (More) Thoughts on Gender Equality in South Africa' (22)*Obiter* at 142-152; Herbst supra n 15 at 64. In terms of the Constitution, such action would be in conflict with sections 9, 10 and 12 of the Constitution, namely the right to equality, the right to dignity and the right to freedom and security of a person.

[45] Section 3(2)(a). See also Bekker, JC (2001) 'Requirements for Validity of Customary Marriages' (24) *South African Journal of Ethnology* 41 at 44; Maithufi, IP and Bekker, JC (2002) 'The Recognition of Customary Marriages Act of 1998 and its Impact on Family Law in South Africa' (35) *CILSA* 182 at 185; South African Law Reform Commission supra n 12.

Act does not define what should be regarded as permission but only states that permission of the individual is needed as a minimum requirement. The Recognition Act therefore amends the traditional position in that now the individuals decide on the conclusion of the marriage and not the families.[46]

Age requirement

Customary law does not have a specific age requirement but the Recognition Act includes an age requirement to allow the individuals to the marriage to take an informed decision with regard to the consequences of the marriage.[47] In terms of customary law, puberty and initiation ceremonies are prerequisites to the acceptance of someone as an adult in the community. Puberty was regarded as the minimum requirement for marriage, as the ultimate goal of a marriage was regarded as procreation.[48]

The Recognition Act provides that both parties should be at least 18 years of age.[49] The age requirement is based on the requirement stated in the *African Charter on Human and Peoples' Rights* of 1981.[50] If a person under the age of 18 wants to conclude a marriage, he or she needs permission from the Minister of Internal Affairs as well as his or her parents. In this regard, the requirements of the 1961 Marriage Act was incorporated into the Recognition Act.[51]

Lobolo

Lobolo is defined in the Recognition Act as 'property in cash or kind ... which a prospective husband or head of his family undertakes to give to the head

46 Bennett, TW (2004) *Customary Law In South Africa* Juta at 202; South African Law Reform Commission supra n 12, Mqeke, RB (2003) *Customary Law and the New Millennium* Lovedale Press at 87.

47 Olivier et al supra n 38 at 6.

48 See also Labuschagne supra n 7 at 545-549, De Koker supra n 31 at 82-83.

49 Section 3(1)(a)(i).

50 Article 6 of the Protocol to the African Charter on Human and Peoples' Rights on the Rights of Women in Africa, of 13 September 2000 (entered into force 25 November 2005).

51 South African Law Commission supra note 12. The South African Law Reform Commission attempts to give effect to section 28(2) of the Constitution that states that the best interest of the child should be the ultimate goal to be achieved - see also section 5 of the Recognition of Customary Marriages Act 120 of 1998. In terms of the Guardianship Act 192 of 1993 children under the age of 21 years must obtain their parents' permission to marry. According to section 24 of the Marriages Act 25 of 1961 this permission should be in writing. Section 26(1) of the Act determines that a boy under the age of 18 and a girl under the age of 15 should obtain permission from the Minister of Internal Affairs. See also Bennett supra n 46 at 206-207.

of a prospective wife's family in consideration of a customary marriage.'[52] *Lobolo* could consist of cattle, other animals or any other property as agreed to by the parties. In modern times cash is the preferred *lobolo*.[53] The validity of a customary marriage is based on the agreement to pay *lobolo*. It is not necessary to pay *lobolo* prior to a marriage but it may be paid during the existence of a marriage.[54] Communities have different practices pertaining to the payment and nature of *lobolo* which should be taken into account in disputes pertaining to customary marriages. In 1995 in *Thibela v Minister van Wet en Orde*[55] the court again confirmed that *lobolo* is not against the rules of natural justice or public policy.[56]

Although the Recognition Act includes a definition of *lobolo* it does not state that it is a requirement for a valid marriage.[57] Section 3(1)(b) only states that marriages must be 'negotiated and entered into or celebrated in accordance to customary law.' The South African Law Reform Commission proposed that the parties should decide if they wish to negotiate and insist

[52] Section 1.

[53] See also Sachs, A and Welch, GH (1990) *Liberating the law: creating popular justice in Mozambique* Zed at 86-110 on *lobolo* in Mozambique. The Mozambican government did not interfere with *lobolo* and the authors state the following at 98: 'It is precisely in a situation of major social and cultural transformation that the usefulness and limitations of the law as an instrument of social control and social change become most evident. In the case of *lobolo* the strategy of the law was neither to recognize nor to penalize, but rather deliberately to ignore the institution. The State denounced but did not suppress it [...] The courts said in effect that *lobolo* was a social transaction that might have meaning for the parties involved and even for the community to which they belong, but that it had no legal significance as far as state institutions were concerned [...] they could never use it as the basis for founding a legal claim.' Communities continued to deal with *lobolo* issues outside the courts.

[54] The courts regarded the full payment of *lobolo* as a requirement for a valid customary union –creating injustice in some instances - see *Mtembu v Letsela* 1998 2 SA 675 (T); see also Van der Linde, A (1998) 'Inheemse reg: Intestate erfreg. [Indigenous Law: Law of Intestate Succession] *Mtembu v Letsela* 1998 2 SA 675 (T)' (31)*De Jure* 380-384) and Van Heerden, F (1998) 'Die Intestate Erfopvolgingsreg van 'n Swart Vrou in 'n Gebruiklike Huwelik [The Law of Intestate Succession of a Black Woman in a Customary Marriage] - *Mtembu v Letsela* 1997 2 SA 936 (T)' (61) *Journal of Contemporary Roman Dutch Law* at 522-532. The Constitutional Court specifically stated in *Bhe v Magistrate, Khayelitsha* supra note 31, at para [5] that it is not a requirement that the *lobolo* should be paid in full before a marriage is concluded. An agreement to pay *lobolo* is sufficient.

[55] 1995 3 SA 147 (T).

[56] 149F-J; 150H. The claimant instituted a claim for damages and loss of maintenance based on the unlawful causation of the death of the breadwinner. The deceased paid *lobolo* for the claimant and her illegitimate son. *See* also Knoetse, E (1998) 'Inheritance in terms of a Putative Marriage: A Transkeian Case Visited' (19) *Obiter* at 166-175.

[57] In Tanzania it was regarded that the declaration that *lobolo* was not a requirement for a valid customary marriage, undermined the practice. It was, however, also established in various research projects that it was virtually impossible to abolish the practice of *lobolo* - see in this regard Rwezaura, BA (1990) 'The Integration of Marriage Laws in Africa with Special Reference to Tanzania' in Abun-Nasr, JM, Spellenberg, U and Wanitzek, U (eds) (1990) *Law, Society and National Identity in Africa* H Buske at 141-142.

on the payment of *lobolo* and that it should not be a formal requirement for customary marriages.[58] *Lobolo* is not a requirement for any other recognised marriage in South Africa.

Transfer of the Bride

A customary marriage was only valid once the bride was formally transferred to the family of the prospective husband. She is then formally regarded as part of the husband's family. The release of the bride from her own family relationship to incorporation into her husband's family is celebrated with extensive public rituals and ceremonies. The courts initially had difficulty in determining whether the ceremony should be regarded as a requirement of a customary marriage, but gradually it was accepted as such.[59]

The Recognition Act does not regulate the transfer of the bride but it could be regarded as a custom referred to in section 3(6) of the Act. If a specific custom is in conflict with the Constitution, the courts would most probably deal with it on an *ad hoc* basis as was the case in in *Mabuza v Mbata.*[60] In this case the question was whether the *ukumekeza* custom was a requirement for a valid customary marriage. In terms of this custom, a woman is expected to cry when formally transferred to the family of the husband. She has to appear semi-naked in front of her prospective family - if she does not cry she could be beaten until she does.[61] Hlophe J found that the custom is not necessarily a prerequisite for a Swazi marriage and that dispensation thereof cannot be regarded as a fatal flaw in the marriage ceremony. He also stated that marriage practices evolve as customary law does, and that he should consider whether practices are in conflict with the Constitution or not -- for example in this case the right to human dignity.[62] He must then develop customary law to ensure that it is not in conflict with the Constitution.

58 South African Law Reform Commission supra n 12; see also De Koker supra n 31 at 80-81, Maithufi and Bekker supra n 46, at 186-187; De Koker, JY (2001) 'Proving the Existence of an African Customary Marriage' (9) *Journal of South African Law* 257 at 268-270. See also Bennett supra n 46 at 234-236 and Mofokeng LL (2005) 'The Lobolo Agreement as the "Silent" Prequisite for the Validity of a Customary Marriage in terms of the Recognition of Customary Marriages Act' (68) *Journal of Contemporary Roman Dutch Law* at 277-288.

59 Olivier, NJJ, Olivier, WH and Olivier, NJJ (1989) *Privaatreg van die Bantoetaalsprekendes* [Private Law of Bantu-speaking peoples] Butterworths 52-53; Bennett supra n 37 at 213.

60 2003 4 SA 218 (KH).

61 Para. [22].

62 The constitutionality of the practice was, however, not in dispute but the question whether the parties were married or not and whether a divorce order could be granted - see 226C-E.

Marriage ceremonies are not described in the Marriage Act 25 of 1961, except for the formal questions that a marriage officer should ask with regard to consensus of the parties.[63]

Absence of a Common Law Marriage

Prior to 1988 a man could enter into a common law marriage with someone other than his customary wife during subsistence of a customary marriage. The customary marriage would have been regarded as dissolved and only the common law marriage would receive recognition.[64] Section 1 of the Marriage and Matrimonial Property Law Amendment Act 3 of 1988 amended this position by stating that a spouse should first dissolve his or her customary marriage before entering into a common law marriage. There was no obligation on the husband to pay maintenance to his customary wives.

Section 3(2) of the Recognition Act explicitly states that none of the parties to a customary marriage will be allowed to conclude a marriage in terms of the 1961 Marriage Act. Section 10(1), however, provides that two parties in a monogamous customary marriage may conclude a common law marriage but not vice versa. It is clear that the intention of section 10 is to further monogamous marriages rather than polygamous marriages. There is no sanction involved if parties do not adhere to sections 3(2) or 10(1) of the Act and it is uncertain if the subsequent marriage will be voidable or void.[65]

The Recognition Act is not retrospective in nature and therefore all marriages concluded before 1 November 2000 are regulated in terms of customary law.[66] Any practice of such a customary marriage that any of the parties might regard as being in conflict with the Constitution will have to be dealt with on an *ad hoc* basis.

[63] Sections 29-30.

[64] Bennett supra n 37 at 239-241. It was uncertain what the influence of section 22 of the Black Administration Act 38 of 1927 would be on common law marriages. In *Ndhlovu v Ndhlovu* 1937 NAC (N&T) 80 the court found that a subsequent marriage would be invalid while the court in *Malaza v Mndaweni* 1975 BAC (C) 45 found that the common law marriage would be voidable. See also Olivier, Olivier and Olivier supra n 59 at 227. The customary wife and children were protected in terms of section 22(7) of the Black Administration Act 38 of 1927 in relation to inheritance.

[65] Van Schalkwyk, LN (2000) 'Kommentaar op die Wet op Erkenning van Gebruiklike Huwelike 120 van 1998' [Commentary on the Recognition of Customary Marriages Act 120 of 1998] (63) *Journal of Contemporary Roman Dutch Law* 479 at 480-481.

[66] Bennett supra n 37 at 239.

Registration

Before commencement of the Recognition Act it was not necessary to register customary marriages except in KwaZulu-Natal.[67] Parties could apply to register marriages in the former Transkei but it had no effect on the validity of the marriage.[68]

The South African Law Reform Commission was of the opinion that registration would be necessary to provide proof of the marriage to third parties as well as to determine the matrimonial property system.[69] Section 4 of the Recognition Act places an obligation on parties to register their marriages but omission to do so has no effect on the validity of the marriage.[70]

Prohibited Degrees of Relationship

Each community had their own rules pertaining to the prohibited degrees of relationship. One such rule was, for example, that people should not marry within the same tribe, but since tribes are no longer small entities, the chance of blood relations marrying one another is no longer perceived to be a problem. Other rules similar to common law developed.[71] Incest, however, could be reversed with a cleansing ceremony.[72]

The Recognition Act states that with regard to prohibited degrees of relationship the customary rules apply.[73]

Matrimonial Property System

In terms of customary law, a single household is an undivided economic unit under the control of the head of the family if a man is married to one wife. In the case of a polygamous marriage, a distinction is made between family property controlled by the family head and house property controlled by the members of a specific household.[74]

[67] Sections 44-50 of the KwaZulu-Natal Codes on Zulu Law.

[68] Bekker supra n 45 at 43; West, A (2002) 'Proprietary Consequences of Marriages in Customary law and the Contractual Capacity of Spouses so Married' (14:418) *De Rebus* at 58; Bennett supra n 37 at 218.

[69] South African Law Reform Commission supra n 12.

[70] Section 4(a).

[71] Bekker supra n 39 at 123-124; Schapera, I.(1994) *A Handbook of Tswana Law and Custom* F Cass at 127, Bekker, JC (1983) *Marriage, Money, Property and the Law* Butterworths 6.

[72] Bennett supra n 37 at 207.

[73] Section 3(6); Bekker supra n 45 at 87.

[74] Olivier et al supra n 38 at 57-58.

According to the KwaZulu-Natal Codes of Zulu Law, house property belongs to the specific house but is still under the control of the family head. The house property must, however, be utilised for the benefit of the members of the specific household. The family head must maintain the daily needs of his wife (wives) and children. Family property includes all the property in the family excluding house property and personal property. Personal property includes, for example, clothes and other smaller items of personal nature or gifts that were received. Women had control over their personal property only.[75]

Section 7(1) of the Recognition Act provides that customary law regulates the matrimonial property regime of marriages concluded before commencement of the Act. The matrimonial property regime of marriages concluded after 1 November 2000 is regulated by section 7(2) of the Recognition Act. The Recognition Act abolishes the customary law matrimonial property system by determining that customary marriages are marriages concluded in community of property and of profit and loss between the spouses, except when a pre-nuptial contract is concluded to regulate otherwise. The matrimonial property regime must be regulated anew if a man wants to marry another wife. A court application must be made in this regard. In effect, aspects of the Marriage Act 25 of 1961 and the Matrimonial Property Act 88 of 1984 substitute the customary matrimonial property regime.[76] Spouses may decide to change their matrimonial property regimes and women may apply for maintenance in the case of dissolution of the marriage.[77]

Dissolution of the Marriage

Initially a customary marriage was only dissolved at the death of the husband. The marriage could, however, continue if the woman was transferred to one of the brothers of the deceased to sire an heir. If a woman returned to her father's household owing to ill-treatment by her husband or any other valid reason, a husband may *phutuma* (fetch) his wife by paying a fine to his wife's father. If she is not 'phuthuma' within a reasonable time, it could have been accepted that the husband did not want to continue with the marriage. These rules developed into rules that constitute divorce. If the wife refuses to return to her husband, he could reclaim some of the *lobolo* paid. If the husband does not want his wife, he could, if he has reason to do so, send her back to her father. If the divorce was initiated by the wife,

[75] See Bennett supra n 37 at 232-237 and Maithufi supra n 37 at 628-630.

[76] Bennett supra n 46 at 261-262; Maithufi and Bekker supra n 46 at 187-190.

[77] Section 7(4); see also Van Schalkwyk supra n 65 at 489-490.

the father had to repay some of the *lobolo*. Once the *lobolo* is repaid, the marriage was regarded as dissolved.[78]

Numerous grounds for the dissolution of customary marriages developed through the ages. However, men may rely on more reasons for divorce than the wife. If a wife leaves her husband, she may only leave with her personal property and is not allowed to take any portion of the family property even if she contributed thereto. Her only obligation is to raise her children at her father's homestead.[79] The marriage was informally dissolved.

The grounds for divorce in terms of customary law relates to the idea of irretrievable breakdown of the marriage.[80] Section 8 of the Recognition Act therefore refers to irretrievable breakdown of the marriage as the main ground for divorce. Parties may also rely on other grounds set out in the Marriage Act 25 of 1961, such as insanity and presumption of death. The marriage can only be dissolved by court order. It excludes the role of the father of the woman who may still order her back to her husband's homestead. The courts decide when there is irretrievable breakdown of the marriage and also what would be just and equitable in each instance.[81]

A husband may not claim *lobolo* if the dissolution of the marriage was due to his fault only. If the wife's actions led to divorce, her father has to repay the *lobolo* but may deduct some money or keep some of the cattle as legitimate deductions.[82]

The Recognition Act does not regulate the repayment of *lobolo*, nor does it place any obligation to do so and the customary rules most probably will apply.

Status

Before 2000, women married in accordance with customary law (outside KwaZulu-Natal) were regarded as perpetual minors. Section 11(3) of the Black Administration Act 38 of 1927 and section 38 of the Transkei Marriage Act 21 of 1978 entrenched this position. It was perceived to give recognition to the customary law position of women.[83] Section 11A was introduced in

[78] Olivier et al supra n 38 at 67-77.

[79] Maithufi and Bekker supra n 45 at 261.

[80] Bennett supra n 37 at 246-249, Maithufi and Bekker supra n 45 at 262-264.

[81] Maithufi and Bekker id at 261-262

[82] Id at 261; Schapera supra n 71 at 62.

[83] It is disputed if this was indeed the customary position of women - *see* in this regard Balatseng, D (1996) 'Equality and women under customary law' 36(335) *Woord en Daad/Word and Action* at 9-11, Dlamini, CRM (1991) 'The role of customary law in meeting social needs' (16) *Acta Juridica* at 71-85.

the 1980s to allow these women at least to obtain immovable property either in ownership or leasehold. The age of majority in KwaZulu-Natal was 21 years for men and women.[84]

Section 6 of the Recognition Act determines that a woman has full status and capacity in addition to any other rights she may have in terms of customary law. It is stated explicitly that she has the right to conclude contracts, to litigate, and to acquire assets and to dispose of them. Equal status infers that the man is no longer the sole head of the family and decisions should be taken jointly. The age of majority is established in terms of the Age of Majority Act 57 of 1972.[85] Section 6 confers upon women the rights and powers of women in terms of customary law and therefore the ranking of women in terms of customary marriages may still prevail.[86] The unequal position pertaining to customary wives that was created by legislation is thus abolished by the Recognition Act. Mothokoa,[87] however, argues that equality is still not a reality for women in the rural areas and that despite the Recognition Act their lives continue in a traditional setting.

CONCLUSION

Customary marriages are formally recognised by the Recognition of Customary Marriages Act. The question was whether the traditional customary marriage was recognised or whether a different form of marriage emerged.

The Constitution had a huge influence on the development of both the common law and customary law of South Africa. In the decision to draft legislation recognising customary marriages, the South African Law Reform Commission had to take the provisions of the Constitution into account. Equality issues had to be addressed.

If one reflects again on the history of the recognition of customary law, customary law was recognised because it suited the colonial authorities to do so. The recognition was, however, made subject to the so-called repugnancy clause that was later refined to public policy and natural justice. Customary marriages were not recognised as they were regarded to be in conflict with public policy due to their polygamous nature. It became, however, clear

[84] Vorster, LP, Dlamini-Ndwandwe, N and Molapo, MJ (2001) 'Consequences of the dissolution of customary marriages' (24) *South African Journal of Ethnology* at 63-67.

[85] Section 9. Section 13 repeals the provisions dealing marital power in the Transkei Marriage Act 21 of 1978 and the KwaZulu-Natal Codes of Zulu Law.

[86] Bekker supra n 45 at 48-50.

[87] Mothokoa, M (2004) 'New families, new property, new laws: the practical effects of the Recognition of Customary Marriages Act' (20) *South African Journal of Human Rights* 616-641; Hellum, A 'Human rights and Gender Relations in Postcolonial Africa: Options and limits for the subjects of legal pluralism' <eli.warwick.ac.uk/global/issue/2001-1/hellum.html>.

that these 'marriages', or unions as they were called, existed and had to be regulated in some way or another. It was then stated that courts may not find that *lobolo* is against public policy. The courts and parliament did give indirect recognition to customary unions when disputes had to be dealt with -- also in relation to successsion. But this recognition or regulation was *ad hoc* and not carried out in a consistent manner.

The Constitution of the Republic of South Africa recognises customary law but again only if the rules are not in conflict with the Constitution. Although far removed from colonial rule, a new limitation, namely the Bill of Rights, was placed on the recognition of customary laws by the new rulers.

In the pre-1994 dispensation, judges and magistrates, mostly white males, gave content to the public policy from their own perspective. Their own ideas and upbringing influence their decisions and in most instances the common law was seen to be superior to the customary law.[88] Since 1994 judges have to give content to the Bill of Rights -- a new dispensation with a judiciary reflecting the diversity of South Africans. This time, however, the measuring instrument is more concrete and the playing field levelled. The Bill of Rights dictate the public policy and judgements. In a more sophisticated way, again, another legal system dictates the contents and interpretation of African customary law as Hlophe J states:[89]

> (I)f one accepts that African Customary Law is recognised in terms of the Constitution and relevant legislation to give effect to the Constitution, such as the Recognition of Customary Marriages Act No 120 of 1998 referred to above, there is no reason, in my view, why the courts should be slow at developing African Customary Law. Unfortunately one still finds dicta referring to the notorious repugnancy clause as though one were still dealing with a pre-1994 situation. Such dicta, in my view, are unfortunate. The proper approach is to accept that the Constitution is the supreme law of the Republic. Thus any custom which is inconsistent with the Constitution cannot withstand constitutional scrutiny. In line with this approach, my view is that it is not necessary at all to say African Customary Law should not be opposed to the principles of public policy or natural justice. To say that is fundamentally flawed as it reduces African Law (which is practised by the vast majority in this country) to foreign law – in Africa!

[88] See also Cowen DV (1963) 'African legal studies - a survey of the field and the role of the United States' in Baade HW and Everett, RP (eds) *African Law New Law for New Nations* Oceana at 19.

[89] *Mabuza v Mbata* supra n 60 at para [30].

Customary law is not static and develops continuously.[90] The development of customary law cannot be forced into a specific format that will fit into a individualistic human rights dispensation but should be reconciled with the Bill of Rights, taking into account the communal nature of customary law.[91] The Recognition Act only succeeds marginally in this regard.

Customary marriages are recognised in terms of the Recognition Act. For the first time official recognition is given to polygamous marriages, but only to a limited extent. The marriage regime is amended to align it with the Bill of Rights and the existing common law marriage system. The Recognition Act's requirements is a mixture of statutory rules as well as customary law. [92] The only elements of traditional marriages that remained are the reference to the conclusion and negotiation of the marriage, the prohibited degrees of relationship, the reference to *lobolo*[93] and the role of the traditional leader in the mediation of marriage disputes.[94] The matrimonial property regime is similar to that of the Matrimonial Property Law Act and the rules of dissolution are similar to those contained in the Divorce Act 70 of 1979. One traditional element that is still included is that the traditional leader may act as mediator in marital disputes and dissolution.[95]

Customary marriages can no longer be regarded as 'traditional customary marriages', but what has developed is a hybrid approach between common law and customary law, making the South African system perhaps more complex as a mixed legal jurisdiction -- now not only a mixture of Roman Dutch and English law, but a mixed legal jurisdiction of Roman Dutch, English and African Customary Law within a Constitutional dispensation.[96]

[90] Du Plessis, L (2002) 'Legal and Constitutional Means Designed to Facilitate the Integration of Diverse Cultures in South Africa: a Provisional Assessment' (13) *Stellenbosch Law Review* at 376; see also Sachs and Welch supra n 53 at 130 who states that 'Traditional law in Mozambique, as traditional law in all African countries, has a dynamic and vitality of its own. It is not composed of rigid, compartmentalized and impersonal norms. Reflecting its character as part of the symbolic life of the people, of the community life of social interaction and mutual aid, of respect for the ancestors and for the elderly, traditional law is, in addition to being law, part of our culture.'

[91] Maithufi & Bekker supra n 45 at 261. The Constitution is based on negotiation. The Constitution does not reflect western values only as people from all cultures participated in the discussions.

[92] Bekker supra n 45 at 50.

[93] Bennett supra n 46 at 199, Bekker 'Requirements' supra note 45 at 46.

[94] See also Bekker, JC (2003) 'The official status of customary law – ten years later' (26) *Anthropology Southern Africa* 124 at 129-130.

[95] Section 8(5).

[96] See also Tetley, W 'Mixed Jurisdictions: Common Law vs Civil Law (Codified and Uncodified)' <www.unidroit.org/english/publications/review/articles/1999-3.htm> par 5 who is of the same opinion. See <www.droitcivil.uottawa.ca/word-legal-systems/eng-

From a western and constitutional perspective the improvement of women's position is lauded, but traditionalists still argue that the Recognition Act interferes with traditional practices and customs. Traditionalists are of the opinion that individuals should choose whether they would like to submit themselves to customary law or not and that parliament should not interfere with how a customary marriage should be regulated.[97] Bekker[98] states in this respect that

> society will (not) change by legal decree. The living law will probably for a long time to come differ from the law on paper. The so-called common law may in fact distort customary law and practice to the extent that the enacted version becomes meaningless in society.

In considering whether traditional communities will adhere to the Recognition Act or if they will continue traditional practices even if their marriages will not be recognised, the following remark of Allott[99] should be remembered:

> Social change is desirable; law can be a potent tool in aiding that change. But it is a precision tool, and one which like the carpenter's chisel, is easily blunted in unskilled hands.

tableau.php> for an alphabetical list of the world's legal jurisdictions as well as their foundations. Mixed legal jurisdictions also are identified.

97 Maithufi and Bekker supra n 46 at 196.

98 Bekker supra n 94 at 130.

99 As quoted by Mqeke R (1999) '"Rainbow jurisprudence" and the institution of marriage with emphasis on the Recognition of Customary Marriages Act 120 of 1998' (23) *Obiter* at 52. Hellum supra n 87 argues that not all women have a similar experience of laws such as the Recognition Act. The level of education and the living conditions of a person could make a huge difference. However, empirical research is necessary to determine the long term effect (or not) of the Recognition Act.

Mixing South African Common and Customary Law of Intestate Succession: "Potjiekos" in the Making

CHISTA RAUTERBACH*

INTRODUCTORY REMARKS: THE CONTEXT

It is no secret that colonialism had a considerable impact on the existence and development of law in South Africa. Modern South African law comprises a conglomeration of metaphorical transplanted laws, chiefly a mixture of Roman-Dutch law and English common law,[1] intermingled with indigenous laws, which are referred to as customary law.[2]

* Sections of the research on which this article is based, were made possible by the financial support of the National Research Foundation. However, the author takes full responsibility for any possible errors and opinions.

1 One of the features of the South African legal system is the fact that it is largely uncodified. Every lawyer knows that he or she has to consult various sources to find the law. These sources include legislation, precedent, Roman-Dutch law, custom, customary law, modern legal textbooks and the Constitution. According to Girvin SD (1996) 'The Architects of the Mixed Legal System' in Zimmermann, R, and Visser, D (eds) *Southern Cross: Civil And Common Law In South Africa* Juta at 95, the mixed legal system in South Africa owes a great deal to the earlier judges of South Africa.

2 In terms of the Recognition of Customary Marriages Act 120 of 1988 'customary law' is defined as the 'customs and usages traditionally observed among the indigenous African people' and in terms of the Black Administration Act 38 of 1927 the term 'Black', which refers to 'African', includes 'any person who is a member of any aboriginal race or tribe of Africa'. The Law of Evidence Amendment Act 45 of 1988 defines 'indigenous law' as the 'Black law or customs as applied by the Black tribes in the Republic or in territories which formerly formed part of the Republic' and the South African Law Reform Commission defines customary law as the 'various laws observed by communities indigenous to the country'. Although customary law and indigenous law are used as synonyms in South African law, the first is preferred, since it is also the expression used in the Constitution of the Republic of South Africa, 1996, (the Constitution). Nowadays the term 'Black' is also offensive and the term

In spite of customary law's being the law of the original inhabitants of this country,[3] there has never been parity in the weight accorded to the transplanted laws and the indigenous laws. During the First Worldwide Congress on Mixed Jurisdictions in 2002, Visser commented as follows:[4]

> [Customary law] has always been treated as a stepchild in the South African legal order and this has obviously disadvantaged the many people who substantively live in accordance with autochthonous law for certain or all purposes.

The unequal relationship between the transplanted and indigenous laws was evident as early as in 1652, when the Dutch East India Company established a refreshment station in the Cape. The law applicable to the settlers was Roman-Dutch law, which was the official law of the Netherlands at that stage. Of course, the Dutch government was then confronted with the existence of an indigenous people on Cape soil, whose customs and usages were totally different from those it was accustomed to, but there is no evidence that any account was taken of these customs and usages.[5]

It was only after the second British occupation, in 1806, that customary law received some form of recognition. The British confirmed Roman-Dutch law as the basic law of the land[6] and followed a policy of non-interference with the customs and usages of indigenous people, provided that these customs and usages were not repugnant to public policy and the principles of natural justice.[7] During this time the various territories which were

'African' is preferred.

[3] This statement is controversial, since the history books show that the original inhabitants were Koi and San. The other Africans are immigrants from the north of Africa (at least north of the Zambezi River). They and the European immigrants (the colonists) met, the Europeans moving east and north, the Africans southwards. Both had a part in eradicating the khoi and Hottentots. The Europeans and Africans were more or less simultaneous immigrants, each occupying their tract of land. They met and collided in the vicinity of the Kei- and Great Fishrivers. Later, when the whites immigrated inland, northwards over the Orange River and across the Drakensberg and the Vaal River, they fought each other in numerous ongoing wars in order to gain supremacy and territory. For detailed discussions of the early history of South Africa, see Muller, CFJ (1990) *Vyfhonderd Jaar Suid-Afrikaanse Geskiedenis* Juta.

[4] Visser, D (2003-4) 'Cultural Forces in the Making of Mixed Legal Systems' (13) *Tulane Law Review* 74.

[5] Van Niekerk, GJ (2006) 'Legal Pluralism' in Bekker, JC, Rautenbach, C, and Goolam, NMI (eds) *Introduction to Legal Pluralism in South Africa* Butterworths at 6-7.

[6] Under the 1806 Treaty of Capitulation, whereby the Netherlands ceded the Cape to Britain. See Bennett, TW (2006) 'The Conflict of Laws' in Bekker, JC, Rautenbach, C, and Goolam, NMI (eds) *Introduction to Legal Pluralism in South Africa* Butterworths at 17.

[7] There were four reasons why the English colonials partially recognised customary law. These were: (a) economic considerations; (b) fear of discontent; (c) their treaties with certain chieftains; and (d) the belief that English law was too progressive to apply to the indigenous

eventually to become South Africa[8] regulated the application of customary law by means of their own legislation.[9] In 1927, the various territorial laws were finally consolidated in the controversial Black Administration Act,[10] which used to provide (and to some extent still provides) for the management of the affairs of certain black persons. Although subject to severe criticism, portions of this Act are still in operation today.[11]

Section 11(1) of the Black Administration Act gave universal recognition to customary law for the first time, although customary law's application was limited to the customary courts and special courts established to deal with matters 'between Natives involving questions of customs followed by Natives'.[12] When the special courts were abolished in the eighties, this section was repealed by section 54A(1) of the Magistrate's Court Act[13] which extended the application of customary law by any court where people from indigenous communities were involved. Section 54A(1) was repealed and section 1(1) of the Law of Evidence Amendment Act[14] ensued. In terms of the latter any court may take judicial notice of customary law if it is readily ascertainable and not opposed to the principles of public policy and natural

---

communities. See Allott, AN (1970) *New Essays in African Law* Butterworths at 12-13; Olivier, NNJ (2004) 'Recognition of Customary Law' in Joubert, WA, *et al* (eds) *The Law of South Africa* (32) Butterworths 12; Bennett, TW (1996) 'African Land: A History of Dispossession' in Zimmermann, R, and Visser, D (eds) *Southern Cross: Civil and Common Law in South Africa* Oxford University Press at 67. The Privy Council echoed the sentiments of the English government. In *Oke Lanipekun Laoye v Amao Ojetunde* 1944 AC 170 it declared: 'The policy of the British Government in this and other respects is to use for purposes of the administration of the country, the native laws and customs in so far as possible and in so far as they have not been varied or suspended by Statutes or ordinances. The courts which have been established by the British Government have the duty of enforcing these native laws and customs, so far as they are not barbarous, as part of the law of the land.'

8 Eg, the British Colonies (the former Cape and Natal), the Boer Republics (the former Transvaal and Orange Free State) and various indigenous kingdoms (inter alia, the Zulu and Basuto).

9 For a general discussion of the earlier position of customary law in South Africa, see, inter alia, Whitfield, GMB (1948) *South African Native Law* Juta at 1-39; Van Niekerk supra 5 at 6-7, and Bennett, TW (2004) *Customary Law in South Africa* Juta at 34-49.

10 Act 38 of 1927. Initially it was named the Bantu Administration Act.

11 Especially those sections dealing with land registration and tenure, customary courts, the operation of Code of Zulu law and the definitions.

12 See Olivier, NNJ, Olivier, NNJ, and Olivier, WH (1989) *Die Privaatreg van die Suid-Afrikaanse Bantoetaalsprekendes* Butterworths at 610-611 for the wording of the relevant section.

13 Act 32 of 1988. See Olivier, NNJ, Olivier, NNJ, and Olivier, WH *Die Privaatreg van die Suid-Afrikaanse Bantoetaalsprekendes* supra 12 at 611 for the wording of the relevant section.

14 Act 45 of 1988. This section read as follows: 'Any court may take judicial notice of the law of a foreign state and of indigenous law in so far as such law can be ascertained readily and with sufficient certainty: Provided that indigenous law shall not be opposed to the principles of public policy and natural justice: Provided further that it shall not be lawful for any court to declare that the custom of lobola or bogadi or other similar custom is repugnant to such principles.' See Olivier, NNJ 'Recognition of Customary Law' supra note 7 at 24-28, for a discussion of the guidelines for exercise of the court's discretion in terms of section 1(1).

justice. Notwithstanding this Act, customary law was occasionally treated as a subordinate system of law which was often brushed aside to apply the common law (Roman-Dutch law), which was seen as the general law of the land.[15]

Although section 1(1) of the Law of Evidence Amendment Act is still in operation, it can safely be accepted that the South African Constitutions[16] have removed any doubt as to the status of customary law in the South African legal system: it is a part of modern South African law on a par with (and not subordinate to) the common law (Roman-Dutch law).[17] In *Alexkor Ltd v Richtersveld Community*[18] it was stated:

While in the past indigenous law was seen through the common law lens, it must now be seen as an integral part of our law. Like all law it depends for its ultimate force and validity on the Constitution. Its validity must now be determined by reference not to common-law, but to the Constitution.

Customary law generally deals with private relationships and therefore operates in the private sphere only.[19] It pertains to limited areas of law,

15 Bennett supra n 9 at 43. Conflicting views as to which system of law enjoys precedence were expressed in a number of cases. See Olivier, NNJ (1986) 'Regspluralisme in Suider-Afrika' Unpublished LLD thesis at 72-74 (on file in the University of Pretoria Library) for a discussion of the various viewpoints.

16 The interim Constitution (Constitution of the Republic of South Africa 200 of 1993) made provision for the indirect recognition of customary law by recognising 'traditional authority which observes a system of indigenous law' (section 181(1)) and by providing for the application of customary law in the courts in terms of Principle XIII. The new Constitution (supra note 2) is more explicit and provides for the application of customary law by the courts when applicable. It is, however, subject to the Constitution and other legislation – see section 211(3). For a general discussion, see Rautenbach, C (2003) 'Comments on the Status of Customary Law'(14) *Stellenbosch Law Review* 107-114.

17 *Bhe v Magistrate, Khayelitsha (Commission for Gender Equality as Amicus Curiae); Shibi v Sithole; South African Human Rights Commission v President of the Republic of South Africa* 2005 1 SA 580 (CC) (*Bhe v Magistrate, Khayelitsha)* para 40 and 148. See also, the similar view of Bennett supra 9 at 43.

18 2003 12 BCLR 1301 (CC) para 51. See also, *Pharmaceutical Manufacturers Association of SA: In re Ex Parte President of the Republic of South Africa* 2000 2 SA 674 (CC); 2000 3 BCLR 241 (CC) para 44; *Mabuza v Mbatha* 2003 4 SA 218 (C); 2003 7 BCLR 743 (C) para 32; *Bhe v Magistrate, Khayelitsha* para 43.

19 The traditional public/private divide in western legal systems is unknown to customary law. Even the customary court system deals with the relationship between the offender and his or her community. For a general discussion of the operation of customary courts in South Africa, see Rautenbach, C (2005) 'Therapeutic Jurisprudence in the Customary Courts of South Africa: Traditional Authority Courts as Therapeutic Agents' (22) *South African Journal of Human Rights* 323-335.

such as family law,[20] law of property,[21] law of delict,[22] traditional leadership and the courts[23] and, finally, intestate succession laws which form part of the main matter of this article.[24]

The law of succession is one area of customary law which has been subject to severe criticism over the years, especially since the inception of South Africa's new constitutional dispensation and the concomitant development of people's awareness of their human rights and freedoms. The distinctive feature of customary law that is most at odds with current western values is the rule of male primogeniture relating to the law of succession, which conflicts with the western notion of equality between sexes. It is therefore not surprising that this feature has been challenged, at regular intervals in the courts[25] and in the literature[26] especially on constitutional grounds. The matter has more or less reached a logical conclusion with the recent decision of the Constitutional Court in *Bhe v The Magistrate, Khayelitsha*,[27] and subsequent legislative developments, and one

[20] Dealing with the legal principles applicable to marriage and dissolution of marriage, see Jansen, R-M (2006) 'Family Law' in Bekker, JC, Rautenbach, C, and Goolam, NMI (eds) *Introduction to Legal Pluralism in South Africa* Butterworths at 29-52.

[21] Dealing with legal principles applicable to property rights, see Bekker, JC, and Maithufi, IP (2006) 'Law of Property' in id at 53-77.

[22] Dealing with legal principles applicable to delictual claims, see Knoetze, E, Labuschagne, JMT, and Van den Heever, JA (2006) 'Law of Delict' in id at 79-89.

[23] Dealing with the characteristic indigenous authority system of the traditional communities, including the principles applicable to traditional leaders and traditional courts, see Bekker, JC, and Boonzaaier, CC (2006) 'Traditional Leadership and Governance' in id at 113-129; and Koyana, DS, Bekker, JC, and Mqeke, RB (2006) 'Traditional Authority Courts' in id at 131-146.

[24] Although the term 'succession' is used, it must be borne in mind that 'succession' and 'inheritance' in fact mean two different things; inheritance means the transfer of rights in property and succession means the transfer of rights, duties and power pertaining to the deceased's status. See Bennett supra 9 at 334. See Rautenbach, C, Du Plessis, W, and Venter, AM (2006) 'Law of Succession and Inheritance' in Bekker, Rautenbach, and Goolam supra n 20 at 93-111 for a general discussion of the principles applicable to the customary law of succession.

[25] Eg, the *Mthembu*-trio, namely; *Mthembu v Letsela* 1997 2 SA 936 (T); *Mthembu v Letsela* 1998 2 SA 675 (T) and *Mthembu v Letsela* 2000 3 SA 867 (SCA); *Bhe v Magistrate, Khayelitsha*.

[26] Mqeke, RB (2003) *Customary Law and the New Millennium* Lovedale Press at 112-113; Bennett supra n 9 at 337-362.

[27] Three cases came before the Constitutional Court and were heard together because all of them concerned customary succession laws. The first two, *Bhe v The Magistrate, Khayelitsha* 2004 (2) SA 544 (C) and *Shibi* (7292/01 (T) 19 November 2003, unreported), came before the Court for confirmation while the third, an application for direct access, was brought jointly by the South African Human Rights Commission and the Women's Legal Centre Trust. The decision of the Constitutional Court and its predecessors elicited numerous responses from legal writers. See, amongst others, Knoetze, E (2004) 'End of the Road for the Customary Law of Succession?' (67) *Journal of Contemporary Roman-Dutch Law* 515-524; Banda, T (2005) 'The Constitutional Court's Approach to Customary Law in *Bhe v Magistrate, Khayelitsha*: Has the Baby been Thrown out with the Bath Water?' *Responsa Meridiana* 5-18; Maithufi,

of the questions that remain is whether or not these changes amounts to a harmonisation and integration of customary law, or are tantamount to an abolition of customary law.

In the discussion at hand I shall make a few remarks on the legal reform of the customary law of succession in South Africa. This will be done in the context of and in comparison with the South African common law (Roman-Dutch law). As it is impossible to deal with all the relevant aspects, I shall limit the discussion to Allott's observations on the unification of laws in the light of the activities of the South African Law Reform Commission and the recent decision of the Constitutional Court in *Bhe v The Magistrate, Khayelitsha*. Following this, I shall conclude the discussion with a few remarks on the influence of the common and constitutional law on the customary law of succession (in its current form) - or the interference of the former with the latter - in a mixed legal system such as that of South Africa.

COMMENTS ON THE DEVELOPMENT OF THE CUSTOMARY LAW OF SUCCESSION

Harmonisation, integration and unification

In the sixties, Allott[28] made the observation that the unification of laws on the African continent proceeded along three lines; harmonisation, integration and unification. By harmonisation he meant 'the removal of discord, the reconciliation of contradictory elements, between the rules and effects of two legal systems which continue in force as self-sufficient bodies of law'.[29] Integration, according to him, is a further step; it is 'the making of a new legal system by the combining of separate legal systems into a self-consistent whole'. The combined legal systems are no longer autonomous, but they retain 'a life of their own as sources' of law.[30] He said that the final step is unification, which entails the 'creation of a new, uniform, legal

IP, and Moloi, GMB (2004)'Customary Law of Succession: *Bhe v Magistrate, Khayelitsha* Case No 9489/02 (C)' (67) *Journal of Contemporary Roman-Dutch Law* 507-515; Rautenbach, C, Du Plessis, W and Pienaar, G (2006) 'Is Primogeniture Extinct like the Dodo, or is there any Prospect of it Rising from the Ashes? Comments on the Evolution of Customary Succession Laws in South Africa' (22) *South African Journal of Human Rights* 99-118.

28 Allott, AN (1965) 'Towards the Unification of Laws in Africa' (14) *International and Comparative Law Quarterly* 366-389.

29 The existing legal systems stay in force, but the incompatible results of applying one or the other of the two systems are eliminated. See id at 377.

30 This method amounts to a fusion of laws. There is an 'outline' law which regulates a specific area of law, eg succession, but which allows for the continued existence, within that structure, of different types of succession, namely common law and customary law. See id at 377.

system entirely replacing the pre-existing legal systems, which no longer exist' as autonomous systems or as bodies of laws. The unified legal system may, however, still draw its rules from the systems it has replaced.[31]

Reflecting on developments on the African continent, he pointed out that harmonisation, integration and unification may be brought about by the indirect intervention of judges and the direct intervention of the legislator.[32] He foresees that the reconciliation of juridical concepts, rules and institutions, which may vary between two legal systems, could present a technical problem, but is of the opinion that one has to find 'an alternative new law which reconciles and unifies the old', even if they are as different as unwritten customary law on the one hand and sophisticated written common law on the other.[33]

In South Africa the legal development of the customary law of succession is taking place either by means of the indirect intervention of the judiciary or the direct intervention of the legislator.

Indirect intervention of the judiciary

Allott's explanation can be applied more or less ed to recent developments in the South African customary law of succession. As stated above, the current position of the customary law of succession has been occasioned by a judgement of the Constitutional Court.[34] It is important to understand that different intestate succession rules applied to different people, depending on a person's skin colour. Section 23 of the Black Administration Act[35] contained conflict rules indicating the circumstances when the customary law of succession is applicable to a deceased estate, usually in cases when the deceased was a member of an indigenous community, whilst the Intestate Succession Act[36] applied to deceased estates where the customary law is not applicable. Using race as a determining factor to decide which law is applicable gives rise, more often than not, to accusations of unfair discrimination and the discussions surrounding these issues are always laden with tension and involve emotional arguments. It is therefore not

[31] Id at 377-388.

[32] Id at 386.

[33] Id at 386-387.

[34] *Bhe v The Magistrate, Khayelitsha.*

[35] The repealed section 23 contained rules pertaining to customary succession and indicated when the customary law and when the common law had to be applied. Section 23 was declared invalid by the Constitutional Court in *Bhe v The Magistrate, Khayelitsha* and was also repealed on 12 April 2006 by the Repeal of the Black Administration Act and Amendment of Certain Laws Act 28 of 2005.

[36] Act 81 of 1987.

surprising that the legal consequences flowing from the different application rules have often formed the subject matter ofcourt cases.[37] In October 2004 the Constitutional Court in *Bhe v The Magistrate, Khayelitsha* struck down section 23 in the Black Administration Act and the customary rule of male primogeniture as being unconstitutional and, since this judgement brought about what may be called a unification of laws by means of integration, it can be seen as an indirect intervention of judges. In order to understand the conclusion reached by Justice Langa, who delivered the majority judgement, it is necessary to provide a brief explanation of the development of the common and customary succession laws in South Africa.

Until recently, legislative initiatives to develop succession laws in South Africa were confined to the common law (Roman-Dutch law). The common law of intestate succession used to be a 'rather complex legal mosaic',[38] but today the rules are set out in the Intestate Succession Act[39] which produced a much simpler, more logical and equitable product in this area of law. The Act follows the modern notion of drawing the circle of intestate beneficiaries as small as possible; a notion which does not necessarily correspond with the indigenous communities' idea of extended families.[40]

Not much was done to keep the customary law of succession in line with socio-economic changes and the human rights regime. It has escaped major legislative reform and was uncodified to a large degree.[41] Its application used to be regulated in terms of the ill-fated Black Administration Act in which section 23 (the conflict rule) prescribed the conditions determining when a deceased's estate had to devolve according to the customary law of succession and when not. The succession rules themselves are uncodified and differ from community to community. To complicate matters even further, there are *official*[42] and *living* (unofficial) versions of customary

37 See, eg, the court cases where the differences in the administration of estates depending on the colour of a person were successfully challenged as discussed by Rautenbach, C (2004) 'The Administration of Black Estates: Life Before and After 5 December 2002' (67) *Journal of Contemporary Roman-Dutch Law* 216-228; and Kotzé, L, and Rautenbach, C (2007) 'Bereddering van Intestate Boedels van Swart Persone: Van Toeka tot Nou' (70) *Journal of Contemporary Roman-Dutch Law* 43-64.

38 In the words of Kahn in Corbett, MM, Hofmeyr, GYS, and Kahn, E (2001) *The Law of Succession in South Africa* Juta at 566.

39 For a discussion of the historical development, see Van der Merwe, NJ, Rowland, CJ, and Cronjé, MB (1990) *Die Suid-Afrikaanse Erfreg* 21-89 Van der Walt Publishers.

40 De Waal, MJ 'The Law of Succession and the Bill of Rights' available at <http://www.mylexisnexis.co.za>.

41 In the KwaZulu-Natal province, the customary law of succession is regulated in terms of the KwaZulu Act on the Code of Zulu Law 16 of 1985 and the Natal Code of Zulu Law Proc R151 of 1987 published in Government Gazette 10966 of 9 October 1987. These two statutes are collectively known as the Codes of Zulu law.

42 Also referred to as the textbook version.

intestate succession laws, which often ential that expert evidence has to be led regarding the existence or non-existence of a succession rule in a particular indigenous community.[43]

Another problem is the judiciaries' awareness of the constitutionally entrenched cultural rights, which makes them careful not to infringe on the rights of indigenous communities by adapting their laws to typically western norms and values. As examples, one can refer to the *Mthembu v Letsela*[44] cases, where a mother unsuccessfully approached the courts three times to contest the rule of male primogeniture in order to save her family's home from her husband's father. The Court was reluctant to declare the rule of male primogeniture unconstitutional, because of the male heir's concomitant maintenance duty.[45] The matter did not advance to the highest courts[46] of South Africa but in 2005, the rule of male primogeniture was again, and this time successfully, challenged in the Constitutional Court in *Bhe v The Magistrate, Khayelitsha.*

The Constitutional Court also tested the constitutionality of section 23 of the Black Administration Act and found it to be unconstitutional on the basis that it discriminates on grounds of race, colour and ethnic origin. The Court described it as 'a comprehensive exclusionary system of administration imposed on Africans', 'specifically crafted to fit in with notions of separation and exclusion of Africans from the people of "European" descent' with the result of ossifying customary law.[47] The violation of equality and human dignity caused by section 23 were so serious that it could not be justified.[48] Accordingly it was struck down.[49]

The Court's striking down of section 23 did not render the customary law of succession inapplicable. The latter was still relevant in terms of the

[43] See Bennett supra n 9 at 337-45 for a discussion of the two versions of customary law of succession. See also, Bekker, JC, and Maithufi, IP (1992) 'The Dichotomy between "official customary law" and "non-official customary law"' (17) *Journal of Juridical Science* 47-60; *Mabena v Letsoalo* 1998 2 SA 1068 (T) 1074 H-I.

[44] See supra n 24.

[45] See *Mthembu v Letsela* 1997 2 SA 936 (T). Justice Le Roux pointed out that 'the devolution of the deceased's property onto the male heir involves a concomitant duty of support and protection of the woman or women to whom he was married by customary law and of the children procreated under that system and belonging to a particular house. [...] I find it difficult to equate this form of differentiation between men and women with the concept of "unfair discrimination" as used in section 8 of the [1993] Constitution (945-947)'. He compared this form of differentiation between men and women with other methods of differentiation, such as the provision of separate toilet facilities.

[46] Supreme Court of Appeal or the Constitutional Court.

[47] See paras 61 and 72.

[48] In terms of section 36 of the Constitution.

[49] See para 72.

general imperative to apply customary law when appropriate.[50] This meant that the constitutionality of the customary rule of male primogeniture still had to be assessed, but after careful consideration it suffered the same fate at the hands of the Court, which found the rule to be out of pace with changing social conditions and values and contradictory to the notion of equality. It was accordingly struck down.[51] By striking down the rule of male primogeniture, the Court brushed aside the application of customary law of intestate succession with one stroke of its pen.

The customary law of succession can now be applied only if so chosen by means of freedom of testation,[52] a freedom which is fairly unpopular and unknown to most indigenous communities.[53] If a deceased opts for the customary law of succession in his or her will, this act could give rise to interesting issues. What would happen to the eldest male's concomitant duty to support? Would the dependants be able to compel him on the basis of his customary duty to support them or would they have a common-law claim for maintenance against the estate of the deceased?[54] The Court also averred that the rules in the Intestate Succession Act should not be seen as fixed rules; the beneficiaries should be allowed to conclude a family agreement[55] which could be in accordance with the customary rules of intestate succession.[56] Although this is true, it is doubtful whether beneficiaries would yield their potential possession of property just to satisfy the customary succession rules.

It is not so much the Court's striking down of section 23 and the rule of male primogeniture that deserves our attention. What is significant is the path the Court followed to fill the *lacuna* created by its invalidation of the customary law of succession. The Court acknowledged the fact

[50] See section 211 of the Constitution.

[51] See paras 81-100.

[52] This is also the option proposed by the Master of the High Court. See the Information Leaflet distributed by the Department of Justice and Constitutional Development entitled 'Customary Law: The Way Forward'.

[53] There is also the notion that wills (or testate inheritance) were not known in customary law of succession. However, it was accepted that a family head could make certain allocations of property to houses and individuals and that his deathbed wishes should be respected. These remarks serve to indicate that the idea of wills may well have been known to customary law, albeit not in the Western legal sense. See Rautenbach, C, Du Plessis, W, and Venter, AM 'Law of Succession and Inheritance' supra n 24 at 93.

[54] In terms of the common law, a needy child has a claim against a deceased parent's estate. See Corbett, Hofmeyr and Kahn supra n 38 at 41-42 for a discussion of the principles pertaining to redistribution agreements.

[55] Such an agreement is nothing other than the redistribution agreement available to the common law beneficiaries. See Wiechers, NJ, and Vorster, I (2006) *Administration of Estates* Butterworths at 1.9, 5.15-5.18.

[56] See para 130.

that there is a considerable number of people whose lives are governed by customary law and whose affairs need to be regulated in terms of an appropriate norm.[57] The remedies the Court considered were:[58] (a) to simply strike down the impugned provisions (section 23, its regulations[59] and the customary rule of male primogeniture) and then to leave it to the legislature to deal with the gap; (b) to suspend the declaration of invalidity of the impugned provisions for a specified period; (c) to develop the customary rules of succession in accordance with the Bill of Rights; (d) to replace the impugned provisions with a modified Intestate Succession Act, governing all intestate estates (including those of polyganous unions) in South Africa.[60]

The Court opted for the latter remedy and decided to modify the Intestate Succession Act to apply to all estates, irrespective of the skin colour of a deceased.[61] In its order the Court also formulated a number of rules to govern instances where a deceased is survived by more than one spouse, thus providing for polyganous households.[62]

Although the customary law of succession in its current form was replaced by the Intestate Succession Act, which is western in nature, the Court made sure that it did not prevent future development of the customary law of succession by means of future enactment of legislation.[63] The court order resulted in the emergence of a unique uniform code[64] for intestate succession made up of essentially western elements, mixed with unique indigenous elements, which applies to all South Africans, irrespective of race or colour. Against this background it is not entirely wrong to conclude that the Constitutional Court arranged the intestate succession laws of South Africa into a systematic code, and that in so doing it codified the succession laws into one code, the Intestate Succession Act, which applies to

[57] See para 107.

[58] See para 105.

[59] Regulations for the Administration and Distribution of the Estates of Deceased Blacks (R.200) published in *Government Gazette* 10601 of 6 February 1987.

[60] Section 1 of the Intestate Succession Act had to be modified to include estates that have formerly been governed by section 23 of the Black Administration Act. See para 136 for the order of the Constitutional Court.

[61] See para 136.6.

[62] See para 136.7. Polygany is another controversial subject which has been discussed by Herbst, M, and Du Plessis, W (2007) 'Customary law v Common law marriages: a hybrid approach in South Africa' *Second Worldwide Congress on Mixed Jurisdictions*, 27-30 June 2007, Edinburgh. See this issue of the *JCL* at ....

[63] See para 124 where the court declared: 'This will ensure that their interests [women and children] are protected until Parliament enacts a comprehensive scheme that will reflect the necessary development of the customary law of succession.'

[64] Knoetze, supra n 27 at 524 refers to it as a '(partial) unification of the customary and common law'.

all persons irrespective of their race or colour. The judgement of the Court seems to satisfy Allott's definition of *integration* rather than *harmonisation*. The effect of the judgement appears to have been the creation of a new separate system of intestate succession, but with the former succession laws retaining 'a life of their own as sources of rules'. In other words, there was a fusion of laws into an 'outline' law which regulates the area of succession, but which allows for the continued existence of common law and the customary law of succession in certain circumstances.[65]

The Court's decision to strike down customary law instead of developing it in accordance with constitutional rights and values could be queried. The Court pointed out that there was not enough evidence before it to allow it to determine the true content of *living* customary law and to develop it. The Court held that their difficulty lay not so much in the recognition of the notion of *living* customary law as in the determination and testing of its content.[66] The difficulty in determining *living* customary law may be the downfall of customary law in many instances. It is often easier to opt for the application of the common law rather than to try to determine what the applicable customary rules are.[67] The question can also be posed whether or not the abolition of a customary rule such as the rule of male primogeniture can be regarded as *development*, as required by section 39(2) of the Constitution, or is in fact merely a *rejection* of customary law rules.

The decision of the Constitutional Court was followed up by two statutes which can be labelled as the 'direct intervention of the legislator'.

Direct intervention of the legislator

In making its order and commenting on the future development of the customary law of succession, the Constitutional Court had in mind the earlier recommendations made by the South African Law Reform Commission regarding the legislative reform of the customary law of intestate succession.[68] It also foresaw that its order, namely to include the customary law of succession under the umbrella of the Intestate Succession Act, would act as an interim measure until the legislature deals with the customary law of succession in a new or amended statute.

[65] See above section on 'Harmonisation, integration and unification'.

[66] See para 109.

[67] See eg, the discussion by Lehnert, W (2005) 'The Role of the Courts in the Conflict Between African Customary Law and Human Rights' (21) *South African Journal of Human Rights* 241-277.

[68] See para 121.

The Commission's recommendations amounted to the enactment of a unified code of succession which would result in the codification of the customary law of succession. Codification is the reduction or arranging of laws into a systematic code.[69] This does not necessarily entail the codification of an entire legal system, but could involve the codification of certain areas (in this instance, succession laws) by means of piecemeal legislation. In a mostly uncodified legal system such as that of South Africa, except for open-minded court judgements,[70] piecemeal legislation is the only way to effect legal reform.[71]

In 1998 the South African Law Reform Commission commenced with its investigation into the harmonisation of the common and customary law. They published various *Issue Papers*[72] in this regard, to illicit responses from the general public. *Issue Paper 12*,[73] dealing with the customary law of succession, posed various questions concerning the substance of customary law in the area of succession, and was regarded as being important. However, before the investigation could reach a conclusion the Department of Justice and Constitutional Development responded to the mounting pressure for action by developing and submitting to Parliament in 1998 the Customary Law of Succession Amendment Bill. The Bill was the result of the government's attempts to harmonise the common and

[69] See Murray, JAH *et al* (eds) (1978) *The Oxford English Dictionary* Oxford University Press, under the lemma 'codification' and Soanes, C, and Stevenson, A (eds) (2005) *Oxford Dictionary of English* Oxford University Press, under the lemma 'codify'.

[70] In *Bhe v The Magistrate, Khayelitsha* the court refused to leave the customary law of intestate succession to be developed by the courts on an *ad hoc* basis. It held as follows (para 112): 'The problem with development by the courts on a case by case basis is that changes will be very slow; uncertainties regarding the real rules of customary law will be prolonged and there may well be different solutions to similar problems. The lack of uniformity and the uncertainties it causes is obvious if one has regard to the fact that in some cases, courts have applied the common law system of devolution of intestate estates. Magistrates and courts responsible for the administration of intestate estates would also tend to adhere to formal rules of customary law as laid down in decisions such as *Mthembu* [see note 24] and its predecessors.'

[71] A third method of legal development is by means of custom. In *Van Breda v Jacobs* 1921 AD 330 the court held that the requirements for proving assertion of a custom are the following: (a) the custom must have been in existence for a long period; (b) the relevant community must generally observe the custom; (c) the custom must be reasonable; and (d) the content of the custom must be certain and clear. See also, Kerr, AJ (1999) 'Role of Courts in Developing Customary Law' (20) Obiter at 50.

[72] Eg, South African Law Reform Commission (1996) *Issue Paper 4 on The Application of Customary Law: Conflict of Personal Laws* Project 90; South African Law Reform Commission (1997) *Issue Paper 3 on the Harmonisation of the Common Law and the Indigenous Law (Customary Marriages)* Project 90; and South African Law Reform Commission (1998) *Issue Paper 12 on the Harmonisation of the Common Law and the Indigenous Law: Succession in Customary Law* Project 90.

[73] Id.

customary law, and also to resolve some of the problems caused by the dual marriage system. The purpose of the Bill was to extend the common law of testate and intestate succession embodied in the Wills Act[74] and the Intestate Succession Act to all persons, to repeal section 23 of the Black Administration Act and to enact new provisions that would be consistent with the provisions of the 1996 Constitution.[75] However, the Bill was met with so much hostility from traditional leaders that its enactment was not pursued further. It is ironic that the order of the Constitutional Court in *Bhe v The Magistrate, Khayelitsha* in practice gave effect to this Bill four years later without the house of traditional leaders making use of its opportunity to make submissions.[76] The Commission's investigation was revived in 1999, and *Discussion Document* 93 was published as a result in 2000. *Discussion Document* 93 contains various recommendations and a draft Bill similar to the one proposed in 1998. The Commission's initial approach was to revisit the whole of customary law with a view to proposing a comprehensive statute codifying the relevant aspects of the customary law. However, they soon realised that it would be a very difficult task and decided to consider a second option, which was to determine which areas of customary law of succession raised serious constitutional issues that needed to be addressed. The Commission acknowledged that many customary rules of succession are in conflict with the western notion of equality and out of step with social practice and that they should be replaced or developed in order to give more secure rights to a deceased's immediate family.[77]

In accordance with the decision of the Constitutional Court and the recommendations of the South African Law Reform Commission, the legislature published the Reform of Customary Law of Succession and Regulation of Related Matters Bill (B10-2008) in 2008. The Bill was transformed into an Act entitled the Reform of Customary Law of Succession and Regulations of Related Matters Act 11 of 2009. The Act was assented to on 19 April 2009 but to date the commencement of the Act has not been published. As it now stands, the Act has important implications for the customary law of succession. The purpose of the Act is stated in its long title as being to modify the devolution of intestate property in relation to persons subject to customary law. The preamble of the Act elaborates

74 Act 7 of 1953.

75 Preamble to and memorandum of the Law of Succession Bill.

76 They were invited by the registrar of the Constitutional Court to do so. See *Bhe v The Magistrate, Khayelitsha* para 4.

77 South African Law Reform Commission (2000) *Discussion Paper 93 on Customary Law: Succession* xvi, 38-40, 70-73. For a discussion of the Commission's proposals, see Rautenbach, C, and Du Plessis, W (2003) 'South African Law Commission's Proposals for Customary Law of Succession: Retrogression or Progression?' (36) *De Jure* 20-31.

further on the purpose of the Act, stating that widows and certain children need protection under the customary law of succession, that social circumstances have changed, and that the customary law of succession does not provide adequate protection for the welfare of family members. The Act furthermore affirms that the Intestate Succession Act will be applicable to all intestate estates, irrespective of the fact that a person is subject to customary law. It is noteworthy that the Act extends the meaning of certain typical common-law concepts (such as descendant and spouse) to include beneficiaries who do not normally qualify as such in terms of the common law. For example, a descendant is defined in section 1 to include:

> a person who is a descendant in terms of the Intestate Succession Act;[78]
> a person who was accepted by the deceased as his or her own child in terms of customary law;
> a woman from a substitute marriage;[79]
> a woman from a woman to woman marriage.[80]

The Act claims to be a modification of the Intestate Succession Act. However, the common-law division between testate and intestate succession is not always kept in mind. For example, section 4 of the Act gives freedom of testation to females regarding house property and also extends the meaning of children referred to in the will of a female to include more than just her biological children. The Act is silent on its retroactivity and will thus apply only to estates where the deceased died after the commencement of the Act. Also, the Act will apply only to intestate customary estates and will alter the character of the customary law of succession by "replacing" it in essence with the Intestate Succession Act. Not only is the customary law of succession influenced by common-law principles but also the common law of succession will be influenced by customary-law principles. This development may be regarded as a healthy shift in the direction of harmonising the laws of South Africa.

[78] The Intestate Succession Act does not define "descendant" but the common-law understanding of descendant is that descendants include the blood relations in the descending line. However, the Act does make provision for an extension of the concept to adopted children who are regarded as the descendants of the adoptive parents (in s 1 of the Act).

[79] A substitute marriage consists of a marriage between the deceased and another woman in accordance with customary law for the purpose of providing children on behalf of his wife.

[80] A woman to woman marriage consists of a marriage between a deceased woman and another woman under customary law for the purpose of providing children for the deceased woman's house.

A statutory modification of the Intestate Succession Act can be seen as a convenient solution for most of the problems in the customary law of succession. However, using a statute which used to serve the common law of intestate succession might be seen as a take-over by the common law instead of a harmonisation between the common and customary law. From the outset, the purpose of the South African Law Reform Commission was to *harmonise* the common and customary laws of South Africa. The dictionary meaning of 'harmonisation' is 'reduction to harmony or agreement; reconciliation'[81] and to 'produce harmony' or to 'make consistent'.[82] Also Allott's description of harmonisation[83] makes it clear that harmonisation[84] does not mean the abolition or take-over of one legal system (customary law), by replacing it with another legal system (common law), and implies that care should be taken that the one is not perceived to be or is in reality dominant over the other.

Du Bois[85] points out that there are fundamental differences between the common and customary laws of South Africa which may hamper efforts to harmonise these systems. These differences include the facts that: (a) the legal range of customary law is narrower than that of the common law; (b) customary law is based on the ethos of reconciliation and solidarity, rather than vindication and individuality, which are salient features of the common law; (c) a single unified system of customary law does not exist, whilst the common law (although largely uncodified) consists of unified legal rules; and (d) customary law is 'living' law which depends for the most part on social practices, whilst the common law can be found in written authorities (old authorities, statutes, judicial decisions and custom). In taking these differences into consideration one should guard against the temptation to simply use the common law in areas subject to customary law. If harmonisation, integration or unification is the way to go, there should be *agreement* and *consistency*, even if it is necessary to sacrifice South Africa's common-law heritage in order to develop a new legal system.

81 Murray *et al* supra n 69, under the lemma 'harmonization'.

82 Soanes and Stevenson supra n 69, under the lemma 'harmonize'.

83 See para 2.1.

84 See above 'Introductory Remarks: The Context' for the topics included in customary law.

85 Du Bois, F (2004) 'Introduction: History, System and Sources' in Van der Merwe, CG, and Du Plessis, JE (eds) *Introduction to the Law of South Africa* Kluwer at 49.

CONCLUDING REMARKS: 'POTJIEKOS'[86]

Thus far the idea of mixed legal systems has mainly concentrated on 'mixing' the common and civil law in certain legal orders, one of them being that of South Africa.[87] In their 1996 publication, Zimmermann and Visser[88] prophesied that customary law's newly acquired status[89] might lead to the 'africanisation of the Roman-Dutch law in twenty-first century South Africa'. When the recent developments in the field of the common and customary law of succession are considered, their prediction seems to be spot on. The Constitutional Court's[90] use of the Intestate Succession Act as an interim measure brought about uniformity in the South African laws of succession. Although the Act was initially the product of modified Roman-Dutch law, it is now infused with indigenous elements to apply to all South Africans. The desire of the Court to grant immediate relief to litigants that appear before it is understandable. However, one should be careful not to confirm allegations that the common law is being used to undermine the survival of customary law in spite of constitutional guarantees as to its continued existence on a par with the common law of South Africa.[91]

The Constitutional Court's robust approach to fulfilling its developmental function with respect to changing the common and customary law has contributed to the judiciaries' current label of 'judicial law-making', which is in contrast with the courts previously being labelled

[86] Potjiekos ('pot food') is uniquely South African, and is a friendly food to be enjoyed by rich or poor, young and old, city-dwellers and country folk. It is the ideal food to serve to a crowd of friends. It is traditionally made around an open fire, preferably in the company of good friends, and with a mixture of meats and vegetables, packed in layers. When it is served, all of the food has a delicious meaty flavour. The word 'potjiekos' in the title of this section and in the title of this contribution refers to South Africa's mixed legal system, consisting of common, civil and customary law layers which blend with each other as the pot simmers along. Available at <http://www.3men.com/Potjiekos.htm>.

[87] Reid, KGC (2003-4) 'The Idea of Mixed Legal Systems' (13) *Tulane Law Review* 5-40; Zimmermann, R, and Visser, D (1996) 'South African Law as a Mixed Legal System' in Zimmermann and Visser (eds) *Southern Cross: Civil and Common Law in South Africa* Juta at 2. True to the nature of legal academics, they have attempted to define and characterise the phenomenon of mixed legal systems. See eg, Palmer's explanation of the three core characteristics of a mixed legal system, namely: (a) it is a hybrid system consisting of common law and civil law elements which forms the main building blocks of the mixed system; (b) the duality of the mixed system is obvious and qualitative and is recognised as such by the observers within and outside such a system; and (c) within a mixed legal system, private law is predominantly civil law and public law is predominantly common law. Palmer, VV (2001) 'Introduction and Comparative Overview' in Palmer *Mixed Jurisdictions Worldwide: The Third Legal Family* Cambridge University Press at 1-80, 7-11.

[88] Zimmermann, R, and Visser, D, (eds) (1996) *Southern Cross: Civil and Common Law in South Africa* Juta at 6, 12-15.

[89] In terms of the interim Constitution and later the final Constitution.

[90] *Bhe v Magistrate, Khayelitsha.*

[91] See the criticisms raised by Banda supra n 27 at 14-17.

as mere organs of the executive. This also signifies South Africa's transition from parliamentary sovereignty to its being a constitutional state.

Although the Constitutional Court took measures to develop the customary law of succession by integrating it with the Intestate Succession Act, it held the view that the legislature is in the best position to 'make the adjustments needed to rectify the defects identified in the customary law of succession'.[92] This point of view has been criticised in that it does not take heed of some of the effects of codification, namely that it would change the flexible and dynamic nature of customary law.[93] Vorster also cautioned against thoughtless codification of customary law by saying:[94]

> Codification entails a complete enactment, a substitute for all the former law. To achieve success, it should be [...] effective and it should be generally accepted by the people whose lives it envisages regulating. If these minimum requirements are not met, the contemplated reform may meet [sic] with rejection, and even conflict. It may also lead to social perturbation when the new codified law is not understood properly by the very people it seeks to serve.

These are some of the viewpoints and warnings the South African Law Reform Commission which the legislature needs to heed when legislating in the area of succession.

The debate pertaining to the content and future of the South African law (with its mixture of common, civil and customary law) is not new.[95] Although the Roman-Dutch law in reality denied all forms of discrimination and sought to protect rights and freedoms, legal history shows that it was transformed into a tool with the purpose of doing quite the opposite, and it thus obtained the reputation of being the law of the oppressors.[96] It will be difficult, if not impossible, to escape this label, and one has to endorse the words of Du Bois,[97] that 'there is no turning back'.

During his address on the future of Roman-Dutch law in Southern Africa (especially in Lesotho) Justice Mahomed indicated that the influence

92 *Bhe v Magistrate, Khayelitsha* para 115. This was also the viewpoint of previous decisions, eg, *Mthembu v Letsela* 2000 3 SA 867 (SCA) 883 H-J.

93 Banda supra n 27 at 17.

94 Vorster, L (1998) 'Legislative Reform of Indigenous Marriage Laws' (38) *Codicillus* at 38-39.

95 Legal academics have been debating the issues for a long time. See, eg, Du Plessis, W (1991) 'Afrika en Rome: Regsgeskiedenis by die Kruispad' inaugural lecture delivered on 27 September, North-West University, South Africa.

96 Du Bois supra n 82 at 15-16.

97 Id at 18.

of Roman-Dutch law and customary law works both ways. Roman-Dutch law will undoubtedly influence the values and content of customary law, and the values and content of Roman-Dutch law will, in turn, be influenced by customary law. He foresaw that the dualism of Roman-Dutch and customary law on Southern African soil might gradually break down into a more integrated system and declared, *inter alia*, that:[98]

> Southern Africa will be poorer without the sound discipline, effectiveness and historical experience of Roman-Dutch law [...] [and] will also be poorer without the spiritualising, humanistic and bonding values of Customary law.

It is also important to remember that the law reflects the mores of society, but changes slowly, so that it is inclined to reflect the mores of society as they were in the past rather than in the present. Perhaps one could argue that we have groups of people in South Africa with conflicting mores, some of which are archaic, and that the differences are likely to be elided in the near future under the pressure of globalisation, for instance. In that case it would seem to be attractive to accept the existence of different legal regimes in different groups of the population for the time being. But as none of these groups is discrete (the process of globalisation being well advanced in some areas) there would so often be cases where dispute would arise as to which regime should be applicable that it would not be practical to accommodate a number of different systems simultaneously. We therefore need to abide by one single system - that much is obvious - and debate should be about the mores that inform the system rather than about whether or not we should have a plurality of systems.

By putting all of the different laws into one big pot, letting it simmer and infuse all of the ingredients with all the different flavours, we might eventually have a wonderfully integrated 'potjiekos' mix, distinctly South African, to be enjoyed by all.[99]

Seen against this background, there is much value in the view of Justice Sachs that, what is developing in South Africa should be called South African law.[100] He comments as follows: 'Roman Dutch law will survive in the future by fusing itself with African law, shedding its name, and becoming an integral part of a new South African law.'

[98] Mahomed, I (1985) 'The Future of Roman-Dutch Law in Southern Africa, Particularly in Lesotho' (2) *Lesotho Law Journal* at 363. See also, Du Bois supra n 82 at 18-19.

[99] This process, if it is going to happen at all, will definitely not happen in a short period of time and it is unlikely that we will see it happen in our time.

[100] Sachs, A (1990) *Protecting Human Rights in a New South Africa* Oxford University Press at 91.

Oriental and Occidental Laws in Harmony: The Case of Trusts in Sri Lanka

ANTON COORAY

INTRODUCTION

Sri Lanka's legal system is a rich mix of native laws and two great received legal traditions, the Roman-Dutch law and English law. The recorded history of Sri Lanka begins with the arrival of Vijaya, an exiled North Indian prince, and his entourage about 500 BC. The community that Vijaya founded in Sri Lanka flourished and established its own language Sinhalese and developed its own distinct culture and traditions, which was undoubtedly influenced by Indian law and custom.[1] The Sinhalese came under the benevolent influence of Buddhism brought to them by the Great Indian Emperor Asoka's son.

By the time the Portuguese landed in Colombo in 1505, the Sinhalese community had established an almost exclusive presence in the interior of the island, known as the Kandyan Kingdom -- the upcountry. There they had developed their own law, the Kandyan law, which shows an Indian ancestry and Buddhist influence.

Probably in the third century BC, South Indians began to arrive in Sri Lanka in large numbers either as invaders or settlers and established their presence mainly in Northern Sri Lanka. They brought along with them their Hindu religion, South Indian culture and their Tamil language and in the course of time developed their own customary law -- the Thesawalamei, which today applies to Tamils settled in the North of Sri Lanka.

[1] See Derrett JDM (1956)'The Origins of the Laws of the Kandyans' (XIV) University of Ceylon Review 105.

Today, the Sinhalese constitute over 74% of the local population and about 90% of them are Buddhists. The Tamils account for around 14% of the population and a large majority of them are Hindus. There is a third ethnic community in Sri Lanka, the Muslims, who account for about 8% of the population. The establishment of the Muslim community has been traced to Arab traders, known as Moors, who settled in Sri Lanka. In later years Indian Muslims who settled in Sri Lanka integrated into the Moor community. Malays, who arrived from South East Asia during the time of Dutch occupation of Sri Lanka, are the other important section of the Muslims of Sri Lanka. There might be a small minority of Sinhalese or Tamils who have embraced Islam. Whatever racial origin a Muslim may have, all Muslims are united by their religion -- Islam, which is not only a religion but also a well-established code of law. [2]

It is in this backdrop of the three major customary laws that the influence of the Portuguese (1505-1656), the Dutch (1656-1796) and the British (1796-1948) must be viewed. The Portuguese made no attempt to introduce their law to the coastal areas of Sri Lanka which they controlled and only succeeded in introducing their religion, Roman Catholicism. The Dutch, who too could not extend their authority beyond coastal areas, not only introduced their version of Christianity, they also introduced their laws and their judicial and administrative system.

With the Dutch occupation in 1656, Sri Lanka came under the influence of Roman-Dutch Law. Just as place names like Hulftsdorf, Bloemendaal and Wolfendaal continue to feature on the Island's map, Roman-Dutch law has withstood many a tide of legal and political change to remain as the foundation of Sri Lanka's general or common law.

The surrender of the Dutch possessions in Sri Lanka in the twilight years of the Eighteenth Century was a blessing in disguise for the future of Roman-Dutch law: The British administration, which undertook to continue to apply existing laws,[3] extended the application of Roman-

[2] See the judgment of Justice M Jameel, a prominent Muslim judge, in the Supreme Court case of *Ramupillai v Minister of Public Administration* [1991] 1 Sri Lanka Law Reports 11, where he said at 45-46 that a 'Muslim' is a person who has 'received' or 'embraced' or 'follows' Islam. He said 'Taken in its literal Dictionary meaning, Muslim will denote the religion and not the race of the individual' and that 'the Muslims (that is to say followers of Islam, be they Ceylon Moors, Ceylon Malays, Singhalese Tamils or of any other race or Nationality) in Sri Lanka are governed by the Muslim Law.'

[3] The Proclamation of 23rd September 1799 stated that 'the temporary Administration of Justice and Police in the Settlements of the Island [...] should, as nearly as circumstances will permit, be exercised by us, in conformity to the laws and Institutions that subsisted under the ancient Government of the United Provinces, subject to such deviations in consequence of sudden and unforeseen emergencies, or to such expedients and useful alterations as may render a departure therefrom, either absolutely necessary and unavoidable, or evidently

Dutch law beyond the Dutch-controlled coastal areas when in 1815 British sovereignty was extended to the whole of Sri Lanka.

The British not only extended their authority to the whole of Sri Lanka, but also established a modern system of judicial and civil administration. They respected the prevailing laws, namely Roman-Dutch law and the customary laws, which they pledged to continue to apply. However, laws prevailing at the time of British occupation were applied through courts of law modelled on the British system by judges trained in the English legal tradition. These judges were not impressively familiar with Roman-Dutch law, or even the local customary laws which had not been comprehensively codified or at least well documented with sufficient clarity.[4] Perhaps because of unfamiliarity with the existing laws, or more probably dissatisfaction with their state, the British administration introduced English law to cover large areas of law -- especially constitutional law, criminal law, evidence, criminal and civil procedure and commercial law. Even in areas like property and family law -- areas largely governed by Roman-Dutch law and the customary laws--the introduction of English law through legislation and judicial decisions has made significant changes in order to modernise the law.[5]

Roman-Dutch law, though enjoying a territorial expansion, did not experience the same fortune in relation to its substantive reach. Under the British rule it began to be replaced or modified by English law, just as place names like Amsterdam, Rotterdam and Middelburg gave way to local names in Northern Sri Lanka. English law succeeded in establishing a greater presence in Sri Lanka by infiltrating the common law. This it did firstly through legislation by replacing Roman-Dutch law in many important areas[6] and secondly through judicial law-making by modifying or even repealing Roman-Dutch law.[7]

---

beneficial and desirable'.

[4] The British administration took active steps to compile native laws for codification. The Mohameden Code and the Code of Thesawalamai were compiled in the early years of British rule and formed the basis for legislation of later years, which modified or improved the original codes to meet the changing needs of the society. The British had no success in codifying Kandyan law, but compilations of Kandyan law by several civil servants such as D'Oyly, Sawers and Turner have served the nation well. See Nadaraja T (1972) *The Legal System of Sri Lanka in its Historical Setting* EJ Brill 183-188.

[5] See generally Cooray, A (1996) 'Sri Lanka: Oriental and Occidental Laws in Harmony' in Ötücü, E, Attwooll, E and Coyle, S (eds) *Studies in Legal Systems: Mixed and Mixing* Kluwer International 71-88 and Cooray, A (1995) 'Asian Customary Laws through Western Eyes: A Comparison of Sri Lankan and Hong Kong Colonial Experience' in Knalfa, LA and Binnie, SWS (eds) *Law, Society, and the State: Essays in Modern Legal History* University of Toronto Press 145-177.

[6] The most obvious examples are in the areas of criminal law and commercial law.

[7] During the early period of British rule, when the judiciary played an important part

The reception of the concept of trusts into Sri Lanka provides an excellent example of judicial and legislative incorporation of English law. More importantly, it illustrates how Sri Lanka has evolved as a mixed legal system, enabling the quintessentially English concept of trust to operate side by side with Roman-Dutch law without touching the sensitivities of religion and custom.

Trusts, in the sense we know it, was unknown to Roman Dutch law, although attempts have been made to find some Roman-Dutch origins especially in *fidei commissum*. Trusts, an equitable remedy evolved to mitigate the harshness of or to supply omissions in the common law, did not sit easily with Roman-Dutch property law which did not recognise equitable ownership of property. This did not prevent the reception of trusts in Sri Lanka, first through judicial decisions and then through legislation. Indeed, as we will see later, the concept of equitable ownership had all but in name found its way into the Sri Lankan law.

The reception of trusts in Sri Lanka was not by way of an offensive intrusion into the Roman-Dutch based common law of Sri Lanka, but as a welcome device to resolve disputes which Roman-Dutch law was seen to be ill-equipped to handle. In that process of judicial law-making we witness the application of English and Roman-Dutch legal principles to different aspects of a legal dispute before the court, amply justifying the description of the Sri Lankan legal system as a genuine mixed legal system.

It was not only the Roman-Dutch background that judges and the legislature had to contend with in introducing the concept of trust. They had also to take account of the range of customary laws, commonly referred to in the Sri Lankan legal literature as personal laws or special laws. These special laws operate as the first law of application, in the sense that the common law becomes applicable only where a special law--Thesawalamai, Muslim law or Kandyan law--is silent. While in that sense common law is subordinate to special laws, legislation occupies a place superior to both the common law and special laws. Therefore, provisions of the Trusts Ordinance of 1917 and other trust related legislation are applicable in derogation not only of the Roman-Dutch based common law

in ascertaining the scope of substantive principles of law drawn from Roman-Dutch law and customary laws which they were mandated to apply, there is a manifest bias towards English law with which the judges were familiar. Judges were selective in applying Roman-Dutch law, insisting that not the whole of Roman-Dutch law but only so much of it as had been received and applied consistently in Sri Lanka as was suitable to local needs and circumstances would apply. In the process of this selective application, courts instead of applying Roman-Dutch law pure and simple, adapted it to suit changing local needs, and where Roman-Dutch law was wanting or unsatisfactory, resorted to English law. See Nadaraja supra n 4 at 241-247.

but also Sri Lanka's own customary laws. For that reason, the draftsmen of the Ordinance took great care to provide for the preservation of some aspects of religious laws in Sri Lanka to exist side by side with the English law based provisions of the Trust Ordinance.

Of three main customary laws, there was no need to make special provision for the Thesawalamai or Kandyan law, as the concept of trust was alien to them. In contrast, Muslim law had its own rules relating to religious trusts. Similarly, Hindu law too has its own idea of religious trusts, and, although Hindu law is not as such a source of law in Sri Lanka, any Indian Hindu religious practices regularly followed in Sri Lanka have binding legal force as local customs.[8]

The Trust Ordinance in its chapter on charitable trusts expressly provides that in determining any questions relating to the existence of a trust, the devolution of trusteeship or the administration of trust, or, in settling any scheme of management for a religious trust, the court must have regard to 'the religious law and custom of the community concerned'.[9] While in relation to religious charitable trusts the Trust Ordinance is the primary source of law, religious law and custom continue to play an important role not only in determining the meaning and scope of charity but also in relation to regulating the management of religious trusts.

The Trusts Ordinance governs only trust matters: any matters that are ancillary to the determination of a trust matter will be governed by Roman-Dutch law or any relevant custom or special law. For instance if a question arises in relation to the capacity of parties, the common law or applicable special law will apply except where the Trusts Ordinance makes special provision.

The law of trusts is mainly contained in a codifying statute, the Trusts Ordinance of 1917, which is modelled on the Indian Trusts Act of 1882. In this paper I will briefly examine the process of reception of trusts in Sri Lanka and the role of the judiciary and the legislature in facilitating such reception. This paper focuses more particularly on two issues:

1. Does Sri Lankan trusts law recognise the English distinction between legal and equitable ownership, a distinction not known

[8] For instance before the introduction of the Trusts Ordinance in 1917, courts had given effect to local customs derived from Indian Hindu religious practices in disputes relating to trusteeship of Hindu Temples. See *Ramanathan Kurukkal* (1911) 15 New Law Reports 216. *Murugasu v Aruliah* (1913) New Law Reports 217 is a case where there was no evidence that an Indian customary Hindu law relating to Hindu temple administration had been received and acted upon in Sri Lanka.

[9] Trusts Ordinance of 1917, s106.

to the Roman-Dutch law which provides the foundation of Sri Lanka's common law.

2. To what extent has Sri Lanka's trusts law accommodated local custom and religion, while exerting a significant influence on the administration of religious trusts?

JUDICIAL RECEPTION OF TRUSTS INTO SRI LANKA

By the time the Trusts Ordinance was enacted in 1917 the concept of trust had already been judicially received, judges having a free hand to import the concept of trusts so long as that was not inconsistent with the promise of the British administration to continue in force laws prevalent at the time of the British occupation.[10]

The Charter of Justice of 1801, which was proclaimed when Sri Lanka became a Crown Colony just four years into British occupation of the Maritime Provinces of Sri Lanka, replaced the then existing Dutch courts with a system of courts based on the English model. It provided that the court at the apex, the Supreme Court, was also a court of equity with the power to administer justice according to the rules and proceedings of the High Court of Chancery in Great Britain, as nearly as may be. Thus the way was paved for the Supreme Court to import the greatest ever invention of equity--the trusts--into Sri Lanka, where the dominant Roman-Dutch jurisprudence did not draw a distinction between legal and equitable ownership of property. If the Charter of Justice of 1801 appeared to confer equitable jurisdiction on the Supreme Court alone, local judges proved such interpretation to be wrong: In 1827 the Court of Appeal held that provincial courts could also exercise equitable jurisdiction by granting an injunction and ordering specific performance.[11] Thus, any court of civil jurisdiction could exercise equitable jurisdiction, including most notably in relation to trusts.

The Charter of Justice of 1833, which replaced the Charter of Justice of 1801, and subsequent statutes relating to the constitution of courts did not refer to any equitable jurisdiction. However, this was not for the

[10] A view was expressed by the Supreme Court of Sri Lanka in the 1969 case of *De Costa v the Bank of Ceylon* 72 New Law Reports 457 that the Proclamation of 1799, when it declared that the laws subsisting under the Dutch government in Sri Lanka would continue subject to modifications and alteration to be effected by 'lawful authority,' intended to authorise the legislature and the executive and not the judiciary to alter or modify the Roman-Dutch law. However, the reality is that Sri Lankan judges not only modified Roman-Dutch law, but sometimes simply ignored Roman-Dutch law and resorted to English law.

[11] *Mathes Pulle v Rodrigo* (1827) Ram 119. Cooray LJM (1971) *The Reception in Ceylon of the English Trust* Lake House Printers, provides an excellent analysis of the Trusts Ordinance.

reason that the legislature intended to deny courts of law any equitable jurisdiction. In fact, as will be seen later, courts continued not only to exercise an equitable jurisdiction making copious references to English precedent,[12] but, more importantly for the present purposes, in the years leading to the enactment of the Trusts Ordinance in 1917, to apply trust principles simply by assuming that trusts was part of the law of Sri Lanka. The judicial recognition of trusts was well assisted by several local statutes which implicitly recognised the applicability of equitable principles. For instance the Prescription Ordinance of 1834 provided for a limitation period for trusts, and the Trustees Ordinance of 1871 had a number of provisions relating to the administration of trusts.

Judges were aware of their duty to apply Roman-Dutch law that subsisted under the Dutch administration[13] and whenever they applied English law in preference to Roman-Dutch law they gave reasons for so doing. An obvious excuse was that there was no Roman-Dutch principle relevant to a matter before the court. In *Ramalingam v Mohideen*[14] a person who had hired the complainant's car had refused to pay the hire on the ground that the car broke down soon after the start of the journey and he had to use alternative means of travel. The Supreme Court was unable to find a Roman-Dutch authority dealing with breach of contract by refusal to pay a lump sum contract price. English law, on the other hand, had a solution in *Cutter v Powell*[15] which had set out the principle that where there was a contract to do work for a lump sum, the price of it could not be recovered until the work is completed. The Supreme Court had no hesitation in filling the gap in the local contract law saying that the *Cutter v Powell* was 'a reasonable principle' to apply in Sri Lanka.

English law was introduced even where there was a relevant Roman-Dutch principle, if the court considered that English law would be useful to refine it. For instance in the 1903 case of *De Zilva v Cassim* the Supreme Court recognised the Roman-Dutch principle that no one is allowed to avail himself of his own fraud, a principle recognised in English law too.[16] The facts indicated, however, that the intended illegal purpose, namely to defraud creditors, had not in fact been carried out. Middleton J stated that he could not find any Roman-Dutch principle that covered such a situation

12 As in *Perera v Perera* (1907) 10 New Law Reports 230.

13 By virtue of the Proclamation of 23 September 1799, giving effect to the rule in *Campbell v Hall*. See supra n 3.

14 (1921) 23 New Law Reports 409.

15 6 Term Reports 320

16 *De Zilva v Cassim* (1903) 7 New Law Reports 230.

and turned to English trusts law, according to which a resulting trust would arise where the intention to defraud has not been carried into effect.[17]

In the early years of the British rule, judges took great pains to draw analogies between trusts and *fidei commissum* in order to facilitate the reception of trusts. Having found the justification, what the courts did in fact was to import the English law of trusts rather than to apply the Roman-Dutch principles. In *Samuel Silva v Warnakulasuriya de Silva*[18] the Supreme Court held that a trust had been created and it had to be interpreted according to the principles of *fidei commissum*. However, it went on to apply principles of trusts law.[19] In *Ibrahim Saibo v Oriental Banking Corporation* [20] (A) had transferred his property to the plaintiffs gratuitously in order to defraud his creditors. There was an agreement between (A) and the plaintiffs that the property would be transferred back to (A), once the debt was compounded. While A was yet insolvent the plaintiffs claimed that they were the absolute owners of the property. The Supreme Court approved the decision of Berwick J of the District Court where he had applied the principle of 'implied trusts' (presumed intention resulting trust as we know it today) and held that the plaintiffs held the property in trust for (A). The result was that (A)'s creditors were entitled to receive his beneficial interest towards the satisfaction of the outstanding debt.

Berwick J justified his resort to the English terminology of 'implied trusts' on the ground that the Roman-Dutch law on implied contract was in substance the same as implied trusts. Berwick DJ said:

> With respect to the objection that the doctrine of implied trusts is no part of the Dutch Law, it is quite true that we have no technical terms corresponding to implied or resulting or constructive trusts, but we have the things themselves; and the only reason we have not the terms arises from the difference in the system of administration of law and equity being such that there is no occasion for them. But it is to be remembered that English trusts are the very offspring of the Roman Law, enlarged and developed from the Roman *fidei commissa* (which were only testamentary), so as to embrace trusts created by parties *inter vivos* and ultimately embracing trusts created by implication of law, which are analogous to what, ages before, were

17 Citing *Symes v Hughes* LR 9 Eq 475 and *May on Fraudulent and Voluntary Disposition of Property*.
18 (1910) 5 Weer 16.
19 See Cooray supra n 11 at 23.
20 See *Ibrahim Saibo v Oriental Banking Corporation* (1874) 3 New Law Reports 148.

known to the Civil Law as obligations arising *ex quasi contractu,* such as the *condictio indebiti'.*[21]

In later years, the courts asserted that since trust principles had found their way into Sri Lanka by a series of cases, it was not necessary to trace the origin of trusts in Roman-Dutch law.[22] In *Soysa v Cecilia,*[23] a case decided after the introduction of the Trusts Ordinance of 1917, Bertram CJ, having observed that condition and modus were ways of imposing limitations on property in the hands of an administrator, said: 'But we have received into our legal system a principle which is of a more far-reaching character and of more convenient application, that of the trust, a principle which our system had assimilated long before the enactment of the Trusts Ordinance.'[24] In some other cases English trusts principles were applied without any reference to how and when they had been incorporated into the law of Sri Lanka.

The question whether the origin of trusts could be traced to *fidei commissum* became no longer relevant when the Trusts Ordinance of 1917 explicitly stated that a trust does not include a *fidei commissum.*[25] Most significantly, *fidei commissum* was finally abolished in 1981 thereby making way for the permanent and exclusive presence of trusts in Sri Lanka.[26]

INCORPORATION OF TRUSTS BY LEGISLATION

The courts had a limited role in incorporating trust principles into the law of Sri Lanka primarily because they could do so only in the context of litigation involving issues that needed to be resolved by reference to trust principles. The true extent to which judges had this opportunity is uncertain in the absence of comprehensive law reporting in the early years of British rule.

Before the enactment of the Trusts Ordinance in 1917, even where a trust principle was relied upon by courts, there was no certainty as to the precise content and scope of such principle. This was mainly because English

21 Id at 150-151.

22 See *Carimjee v The MunicipalCouncil* (1905) 1 Balasingham Reports 75, discussed in Cooray supra n 11 at 24.

23 (1921) 23 New Law Reports 74.

24 Id at 77.

25 Trusts Ordinance section 3(b). It is interesting to note that in South Africa too the current view is that a trust, and particularly a testamentary trust, does not take effect by way of a *fidei commissum.* See *Braun v Blann & Botha NNO* 1984(2) SA 850 (A). See generally Cameron E et al (eds) (2007) [2002] *Honore's South African Law of Trusts* Juta (5th edn) at 54-57.

26 The Abolition of Fidei Commissa, Entails, Settlements and Restraints on Alienation Law No 80 of 1981, s.3.

legislation relating to trusts had not been extended to Sri Lanka. The courts, however, did not hesitate to extend the content of such English legislation to Sri Lanka to cure uncertainties in the local law. In a case decided in 1909 Middleton J, having observed that the English Trustee Act 1893 was not part of Sri Lankan law, said: 'We should apply to questions arising on the subject the best principles we can derive from Imperial legislation (where it does not specifically apply) and English judicial decisions because the law relating to trustees is decidedly of English origin'.[27]

It was this uncertainty of the scope of the law of trusts that led to the enactment of the Trusts Ordinance of 1917. The Attorney-General said in 1916, when introducing the Trusts Bill, that the 'introduction of the English law of trusts into the Roman-Dutch law of the colony, which is its common law. [...] has been gradual, partial, and it is not very clear to what extent it has gone'. He said that 'it would not be easy to define the law of trusts in the Colony.[28]

The enactment of the Trusts Ordinance was so significant that a Supreme Court judge observed in 1927, rather incorrectly, that 'the whole subject of trusts as known to the English law is foreign to our law and the Ordinance No 9 of 1917 may be said to have first introduced the law of trusts into our legal system'.[29]

The Long title of the Ordinance describes the Ordinance as one enacted to define and amend the law relating to trusts. As the purpose of the Ordinance was not to repeal the existing law, it could be argued that pre-1917 case law is still relevant and continues to be in force so far as such decisions are not inconsistent with statutory provisions. It may also be possible to refer to pre-1917 cases to illustrate and supplement the Ordinance. This is especially because the Trusts Ordinance has only 117 sections and has no Schedules or subordinate legislation.

It is the Indian Trusts Act of 1882 that provided the model for the Sri Lankan statute, with two main exceptions:

1. The Indian Act specifically excludes from its application (1) rules of Mohammaden law as to Wakf and (2) public or private religious or charitable endowments. On the other hand, the Sri Lankan Ordinance contains a chapter dealing with charitable trusts.[30] Section 106 provides that in charitable trust matters the

[27] *Mohamado v Ussen* (1909) 1 Current Law Recorder 53.

[28] (1916) Ceylon Hansard 247-248.

[29] *Chetty v Finlay* (1927) 29 New Law Reports 66, 70-71.

[30] It must be noted that English law relating to charitable trusts may become relevant in India under tax statutes which grant tax relief for charitable donations and which use the

courts must have regard not only to the trust instrument if any, but also to (1) the religious law and custom of the community concerned and (2) to the local custom or practice with reference to the particular trust concerned. Thus unlike in India, where the nature and scope of charity is left to be determined with reference to general and customary law of India, the starting point for charitable trusts in Sri Lanka is the Trusts Ordinance, which will be applied in the context of applicable religious or customary principles.[31]

2. The Sri Lankan Ordinance contains a *casus omissus* section, namely section 2, which enables courts of Sri Lanka to draw on English equitable principles where the Ordinance is wanting. Although the Indian Act has no such section, it has not prevented Indian courts from applying English law so long as they are not inconsistent with the Act.[32]

INTEGRATION OF THE ENGLISH CONCEPT OF TRUST INTO THE SRI LANKAN LAW

The Trusts ordinance is a fairly comprehensive code and deals with express trusts, implied trusts, charitable trusts, powers and obligations of trustees, rights and liabilities of beneficiaries, and administration of trusts. In the following pages we will briefly examine the interaction of the English law of trusts in Sri Lanka with the common law and special laws. To examine the first relationship we will focus on the distinction between legal and equitable ownership. To examine the second relationship we will focus on charitable trusts.

Law and Equity

Law and equity, while they have had different historical beginnings, are today seen as complimentary rather than competing systems. At the time the Trusts Ordinance was introduced it was well appreciated that Roman-Dutch law, just as the Indian law, did not recognise the distinction between legal and equitable property rights. As a result, the draftsmen followed the Indian Trusts Act, which drew no distinction between legal and equitable

traditional English definition of charitable trusts. See for instance *Trustees of Tribune Press v The CIT* (1939) 43 CWN 1065 (PC).

31 See *Kumarasamy Kurrukal v Karthigesa Kurrukal* (1923) 26 New Law Reports 33 and *Fernando v Sivasubramanium* (1959) 61 New Law Reports 241.

32 *Dev Lakshmi v Vishwakant* (1971) 73 Bombay Law Reports 594.

ownership. While the historical origins and development of law and equity may be forgotten and the distinction between legal and equitable rights in the property law area may not be as clearly marked as it once was, the basis of English trusts law continues to lie in the separation of legal and equitable ownership.[33]

While Indian and Sri Lankan judges have repeatedly said that the distinction between equitable and legal ownership forms no part of their legal system, courts have gone on to recognise and enforce several aspects of equitable ownership. For instance in *Richard Taylor v Sri Krishna Chandra*[34] it was said that trusts in India could be recognised and enforced without relying on a legal-equitable division. The Privy Council held in the case of *A Krishna v Kumara K Deb*[35] that trusts law could operate without relying on the distinction between legal and equitable ownership of property because the Supreme Court of India was a court of law and equity.

A careful examination of the case law shows that the idea of equitable ownership has to a large extent become part of trusts law in Sri Lanka. For instance, in a series of cases the Supreme Court has recognised that an equitable lease would prevail over a forfeiture clause in a legal lease.[36]

The Trusts Ordinance contains two specific provisions that appear to suggest that a beneficiary has no equitable interest in the trust property. The interpretation section defines 'the beneficial interest' as 'his right against the owner of the trust property'. Section 8 provides that 'the subject matter of a trust must be property transferable to the beneficiary. It must not be a merely beneficial interest under a subsisting trust'. While these two sections appear to indicate that a beneficiary has less than an equitable interest, Indian courts have narrowly interpreted the corresponding provisions in the Indian Trusts Act. In *Pestonji v Jalbhoy*[37] it was held that what the Indian equivalent of section 8 prohibits is the creation of a trust over the beneficiary's right to proceed against the trustees. It was held that a beneficiary may create a trust of his beneficial interest, meaning the benefit he receives as beneficiary under an existing trust.[38] This decision

33 Alternative foundations of trusts have been suggested, but none enough to replace the separation of legal and equitable ownership.

34 32 Mad 443.

35 (1869) 4 *Bombay Law Reporter Oudh Cases* 270.

36 These cases include *Perera v Thaliff* (1904) 8 New law Reports 118, *Perera v Perera* (1907)10 New Law Reports 230 and *Sanoon v Theyvandera-Rajah* (1963) 65 New Law Reports 574.

37 1934 AIR Bombay 64.

38 The Privy Council in the case of *Valliyammai v Majeed* (1947) 48 New Law Report 289, 292-3 referred to an argument based on the Prevention of Frauds Ordinance which assumed that the beneficial owner under a trust of land acquires a proprietary interest, and, not merely a right to proceed against the trustee. Their Lordships considered that such an assumption would involve that the Law of Sri Lanka recognizes the distinction between

emphasises that a beneficiary has not only a right against the trustee for maladministration, for instance to receive what he is entitled to receive under the trust, but also a proprietary interest in what he is entitled to receive under a trust.

There are other provisions that give substance to the beneficiary's interest. For instance, a beneficiary may not only compel a trustee to perform his duties and restrain him from committing any breach of trust, he may follow and trace trust property in the hands of strangers.[39] Thus, unlike in South Africa, the beneficiary not only has a right *in personam* against the trustee but has a right *in rem*, which must necessarily mean that the beneficiary has an equitable interest, which he can enforce against anyone other than a bona fide purchaser for value.[40]

The rule in *Saunders v Vautier*,[41] which is the best illustration of the beneficiary's proprietary interest in the trust property, is incorporated in the Trusts Ordinance through section 58. This section permits beneficiaries to direct the trustee to collapse the trust and transfer the trust property to them. This section together with section 60 clearly shows that the beneficiary's right is not a mere right against the trustee for due performance of his trust duties.

Another illustration of how Sri Lankan law protects the beneficiary's equitable interest comes from the area of property law. The Partition Ordinance of 1863, in order to ensure finality of a partition decree, states that a partition decree wipes out any property interest which is not specifically preserved by it. Section 9 of the Partition Ordinance provides that the decree is 'good and conclusive against all persons whomsoever, whatever right or title they have or claim to have in the said property'. In *Marikar v Marikar*[42] Bertram CJ held that a partition decree wipes out only legal rights that are not expressly preserved in the decree, and does not affect equitable interests. Bertram CJ's view impliedly supports the view that a beneficiary has equitable title, different from legal title.[43]

---

legal and equitable estates in land. Their Lordships found it unnecessary to decide that question, as they were able to dispose of the case with reference to the Trusts Ordinance, having concluded that the Prevention of Frauds Ordinance had no direct application to the facts of the case.

39 See section 65 etc in Chapter III 'Of the Duties and Liabilities of Trustees'

40 *Seelachchy v Visuanathan*(1922) 23 New Law Reports 97 recognised the equitable interest of a wife in relation to community property which she could enforce in rem, other than against a bona fide purchaser for value.

41 See *Sriskandan v Abilin Nona* (1961) 63 New Law Reports 217, 223 and *The Missionary Society Corporation v Jayawardene* (1918) 20 New Law Reports 359.

42 (1920) 22 New Law Reports 137.

43 The Partition Act of 1951 which replaced the Partition Ordinance of 1863 provides that a partition decree wipes out not only legal rights but any encumbrance on the land including

The above discussion shows that while the legislature and the judiciary seem to profess that the English distinction between legal and equitable ownership is not of significance to the operation of the concept of trust in Sri Lanka and India, in reality many important aspects of that division have become part of our law. What Varada Chariar J said in the 1942 case of *Punjab Province v Daulat Singh*[44] is equally true of Sri Lanka: 'On an analysis of the legal incidents involved, it will be found that for all practical purposes there is little or no difference between a beneficiary under the English law and a beneficiary under the Indian Trusts Act, so far as the substance is concerned'. This view is reinforced by the elementary fact that a trust seeks to protect the interests of the beneficiary the law does not recognize, especially in implied trusts. Sri Lankan courts have on many occasions protected the interests of an intended beneficiary where such interests had not been formally declared, by holding that formality requirements affect legal transactions but not trusts.[45]

It is clear that the division of legal and equitable ownership between the trustee and the beneficiary has an immediate relevance to incompletely constituted trusts. Where a person wishes to set up a trust by making a gratuitous transfer of the trust property to another on trust, the trust will not be completely constituted until legal title in the trust property is transferred to the intended trustee. The validity of the transfer is governed by the common law relating to transfer of gifts. The common law rule relating to gifts is that a promise of a gift is not specifically enforceable: Equity will not assist a volunteer. In other words, where the donor has done everything necessary to transfer the property to the intended donee, legal ownership continues to remain in the donor. This rather harsh principle laid down in *Milroy v Lord*,[46] has been softened in a series of cases by resort to constructive trusts. The *Re Rose*[47] principle recognises that where the donor has done everything within his power to divest himself of property, the equitable interest passes to the donee, and the donor becomes a mere legal owner. Thus comes into being a constructive trust, which makes the intended donee the 'true owner'.[48] This principle took a great leap forward

a trust.

44 All India Reports 1942 FC 38, at 43.

45 See for instance *Narayanan Chetty v James Finlay* (1927) 29 New Law Reports 66.

46 (1862) 4 De GF & J 264.

47 [1952] Ch 499.

48 Evershed MR famously said in *Re Rose* [1952]Ch 499 at 510: 'If a man executes a document transferring all his equitable interest, say, in shares, that document, operating, and intended to operate, as a transfer, will give rise to and take effect as a trust; for the assignor will then be a trustee of the legal estate in the shares for the person in whose favour he has made an assignment of this beneficial interest'. See Martin, JE (2005) *Hanbury and Martin Modern Equity* (17th ed by Martin JE) Sweet & Maxwell 4-011.

when the English Court of Appeal held in *Pennington v Payne*,[49] that even where the donor has *not* done everything within his power to transfer the property to the donee, equity will intervene if the stage has been reached where it would be unconscionable for the donor to resile from his promise of a gift.

In Sri Lanka, Roman-Dutch law governs formation of contracts, except in relation to contracts that are expressly intended to be governed by English law, such as sale of goods contracts. Therefore, in the generality of contract disputes valuable consideration in the English sense has no relevance. What Roman-Dutch law requires is *justa cuasa* (just cause or serious intention) and not valuable consideration: any promise of a gift made with a serious mind and accepted by the donee is enforceable. Thus, in Sri Lanka, where a person has entered into a binding agreement with another to make a gift, the donee has a common law right to seek specific performance.[50] To that extent, the donee does not have to rely on a claim of equitable ownership and a consequential constructive trust to benefit from the failed promise of trust. However, where a promise of a gift has been made (on trust or not) but there is no valid contract of gift between the donor and the donee, the only way in which the donee could found a claim is through the *Re rose* principle or the newer *Pennignton v Wayne* principle of unconscionability.[51] If Sri Lankan law is to benefit from these principles it is necessary for the courts to construe liberally the rights of the beneficiary. This is an area not specifically dealt with in the Trusts Ordinance or the general law of Sri Lanka.

LJM Cooray takes a pragmatic approach to the divide between equity and law. He argues that:

> [T]he distinction between law and equity and its consequences which flow from this distinction are not relevant in the law of Ceylon. The beneficiary under a trust in England has an equitable interest. The whole concept of the trust in Ceylon resembles and was copied from the English concept. But the content of the law of trusts in Ceylon, including the beneficiary's rights are statutory and to be found in the sections of the Trusts Ordinance.[52]

49 [2002] 1 WLR 2075.

50 See Weeramantry CG (1999) [1967] *The Law of Contract* Lawman (India) at para 984 'Want of Mutuality'.

51 Martin supra 48 at 4-012.

52 See Cooray supra n 11 at 187-189.

He admits that such an approach may not suit an analytical jurist who would want to analyse the interest of the beneficiary and the trustee in conceptual terms.

Such a pragmatic approach might be suitable when one deals with fairly straightforward disputes between the beneficiary and the trustee, which can be resolved by a simple application of the provisions of the Trusts Ordinance. However, if the law of trusts is to become an evolving law rich enough to meet novel situations and challenges, it is essential that we give full effect to trusts' underlying concepts.

Charitable Trusts

The Trusts Ordinance deviates from its model, the Indian Trusts Act of 1882, when it deals with religious and charitable trusts. The Indian Trusts Act excluded from its scope religious or charitable endowments, leaving that area to be governed by Muslim law and Hindu law. The reason for this is that Hindus and Muslims, the dominant communities in India, have a long established tradition of making donations for the upkeep of temples and mosques and other religious purposes. These endowments were managed in accordance with ancient religious practices. The Colonial administration was careful not to be seen as interfering with native religion and custom and intervened only to regulate the administration of such institutions, which in substance had much in common with English trusts.

The British administration in Sri Lanka took a different approach to the regulation of religious and charitable trusts in 1917. It brought religious trusts within the general scope of the Trusts Ordinance. The statement of objects and reasons appended to the Trusts Bill stated that:

> The originating cause of this Ordinance is the unsatisfactory condition of the law relating to religious trusts, more particularly as far as it concerns the Hindu religious trusts. The defects in this department of the law which principally occasion inconvenience are:
>
> 1. the informal nature of the constitution of many of these trusts ;
> 2. the uncertainty of the law as to the recognition in our courts of the customary religious law of the community concerned ;
> 3. the uncertainty as to the person in whom the title to the temple or other religious foundation in question is vested;
> 4. the absence of any proper control over trustees and their accounts.

While the Trusts Ordinance applies to all trusts in Sri Lanka, it made certain important concessions to religious communities.

Chapter 10 of the Trusts Ordinance deals with charitable trusts. The chapter starts with section 99, which adopts Lord Macnaghten's classification[53] of charitable purposes, with a slight modification in order to give a wider scope to religious trusts. Section 99(1) (with the modification in favour of religious trusts italicised) reads as follows:

> The expression "charitable trusts" includes any trust for the benefit of the public or any section of the public within or without Ceylon of any of the following categories:
> 1. for the relief of poverty;
> 2. for the advancement of education and knowledge;
> 3. for the advancement of religion *or the maintenance of religious rites and practices*; or
> 4. for any other purposes beneficial or of interest to mankind not falling within the preceding categories.

The italicised words were intended to accommodate local religious practices some of which might not have satisfied the requirement of public benefit as understood in England. This has enabled courts of Sri Lanka to uphold trusts to observe an annual Muslim festival,[54] and to keep a lamp burning in a Buddhist temple.[55]

Section 100 provides that 'the court has the same power for the establishment, regulation, protection and adaptation of all charitable trusts as are exercised for the time being with reference to charitable trusts within the meaning of English law by the High Court of Justice in England'. At the same time, the Ordinance expressly provides that in determining any question relating to the constitution of any trust, the devolution of trusteeship and the administration of a trust, or in settling a scheme of arrangement for a religious trust, the court must have regard to the religious law and custom of the community concerned, and to the local custom or practice with reference to the particular religious trust concerned.[56]

Hindu temple charities illustrate the difference between the Indian and Sri Lankan response to local religious laws and practices. The practice in India has been for the well-wisher to dedicate a property for a religious purpose such as by building a temple and installing an idol. When a

53 In *Commissioners for Special Purposes of Income Tax v Pemsel* [1891] AC 531 at 583.

54 *Mohamadu v Meera Kandu* (1923) 24 New Law Reports 390.

55 *Ratgama Pannasekara Nayaka Thero v Caldera* (1956) 58 New Law Reports 331.

56 See s106 of the Trusts Ordinance.

property is dedicated, ownership of property passes for the religious purpose. A problem arose in relation to endowments to install an idol or establish a temple where generally there was no body of persons to receive the property. It came to be accepted that in such a situation the property would vest in the idol, which was regarded as a juristic person, and would be managed for the religious purposes by the manager or other person responsible for administration.[57] Thus the manager, who in the English sense would be the trustee, did not have legal ownership of the property.[58]

In Sri Lanka the Hindu religious practice had to be in tune with the Trusts Ordinance, which required the trustee to have legal ownership of trust property.[59] In *Kumaraswamy Kurukkal v Karthigesu Kurukkal*[60] members of a Brahmin family built a Hindu temple, with public donations, and dedicated it. They executed an instrument providing for the administration of the temple designating S and T as the founder administrators. T transferred his interest in the temple to his son by way of donation and the son sued T for declaration of title as owner of the temple. T pleaded that the temple was a charitable trust. The Supreme Court agreed that the temple was intended as a religious charity but there was a formal defect in creating the charitable trust, in that no instrument of trust was executed.

Bertram CJ conceded that according to Hindu religious law prevalent in India, the temple becomes the property of the deity to whom it is dedicated, with the manager of the temple serving as trustee, but pointed out that religious law and custom must yield to legislation. He said:

> We are no doubt authorized in these questions to have regard to the religious law and custom of the community concerned, but [...] we cannot subordinate to any such law or custom our own express law. According to our own law as declared and defined by the Trusts Ordinance, the *dominium* of the property remains vested in the legal owners.

Thus the Supreme Court upheld the charitable trust not on the basis that the temple became the property of the deity, as in India, the trust was

57 See *Vidya Viruthi v Bala Swami* Law Reports 48 Indian Appeals 302.

58 *Prosunna v Golap* Law Reports 2 Indian Appeals 145 (PC).

59 The Trusts Ordinance defines a trust as 'an obligation annexed to the ownership of property' in the sense that the owner of the property is under an obligation to hold it for the benefit of another.

60 (1923) 26 New Law Reports 33.

upheld on the basis that the founders remained legal owners but bound as de facto trustees.[61] In another case[62] Bertram CJ said:

> When a person who is the owner of property purports to transfer it to a Temple, the effect of his so doing is to constitute himself a trustee of the Temple. The document of dedication is in fact a declaration of trust and the dominium remains with the dedicator and passes on his death to his heirs subject to the trust. [63]

While in India the nature of a charitable trust is determined by the local religious law alone, in Sri Lanka the nature of a charitable trust is determined in accordance with the provisions of the Trusts Ordinance construed in the context of local religious practices and customs. While both in India and Sri Lanka, a Hindu religious trust of a temple would in reality operate through a manager, the conceptual basis is different. The Trusts Ordinance thus provides a harmonious co-existence of statute law which is based on English law and religious laws which are rooted in local usage.

An important aspect of religious trusts in India is that to create a religious trust of immovable property *inter vivos* there is no requirement of writing and registration.[64] For instance, there is no requirement that there should be express words of gift or trust where property is dedicated to a deity. All that is needed is evidence that the donor set aside a property to be dedicated for the religious purpose.[65] This flexible rule is somewhat unruly. For instance in the case of *Howard v Pestonji* [66] two brothers solemnly declared that the temple they erected on their land was for community worship, but the property continued to be under their control. Upon insolvency, the property was held to be their private property and not property held on a religious trust.

[61] Section 107 of the Trusts Ordinance that Bertram CJ relied on is headed 'de facto trusts'.

[62] *Karthigasu Ambalavaner v. Subramaniar Kathiravelu* (1924) 27 New Law Reports 15 at 21.

[63] See also *Murugesoe v Chelliah* (1954) 57 New Law Reports 463, 468 where it was reaffirmed that unlike a deity in India, a temple in Sri Lanka was not a juristic person and that the dedication of a temple was considered a declaration of trust and the donor was regarded as the trustee.

[64] Section 5 of the Indian Trusts Act requires formal constitution of trust. The Act, however, does not apply to religious and charitable trusts.

[65] *Prosonno v Prosonno* Indian Law Reports 25 Calcutta 112.

[66] Discussed in Mukherji BK (1983) *The Hindu Law of Religious and Charitable Trusts* (5th ed) Eastern Law House at 372.

The Trusts Ordinance of Sri Lanka, while it applies to religious and charitable trusts, relaxes its rule relating to formal constitution of trusts.[67] Section 107 states as follows:

> In dealing with any property alleged to be subject to a charitable trust, the court shall not be debarred from exercising any of its powers by the absence of evidence of the formal constitution of the trust, if it shall be of opinion from all the circumstances of the case that a trust in fact exists, or ought to be deemed to exist.

It has been held that section 107 gives power to courts to define terms of a trust where it appears that a charitable trust is intended. *Kumaraswamy Kurukkal v Kathiragesu Kurukkal*,[68] which is discussed above, is a good illustration of the application of that section. *Suppramanium v Erampakurukkal*[69] is a case where the settlor who wished to dedicate property to build a religious institution declared himself trustee with a co-trustee but did not formally transfer the property to the co-trustee. The Supreme Court refused to hold that a valid charitable trust can be created by transferring the property to a trustee without compliance with the necessary formalities. However, since the settlor had made a self-declaration of trust, the failure to transfer property to the co-trustee did not stand in the way of a valid trust.

It must be noted that the exemption from formality rules is consistent with the then prevailing English law. Gareth Jones in his classic work on the history of the law of charity shows how in the early years judges were magnanimous in giving effect to charitable trusts and how the judicial attitude gradually turned into one of careful scrutiny.[70]

There might be instances where English concept of a charitable trust may be in conflict with the religious laws. Such a well recorded conflict came to light in the Indian case of *Abul Fata v Rassonmony*[71] which concerned a family wakf. A wakf in Muslim law is a dedication of property to god in perpetuity for the benefit of mankind. There was however a prevalent view that a wakf could be created for the benefit of one's family without any public benefit. In *Abul Fata* case the Privy Council held that while a

[67] Section 5 of the Trusts Ordinance which prescribes formalities for the creation of trusts is declared to be subject to section 107.

[68] (1923) 26 New Law Reports 33.

[69] (1922) 23 New Law Reports 417.

[70] Gareth J (1986) *History of the Law of Charity 1532-1827* Gaunt & Sons at 60-65 'The Perfection of Imperfect Instruments 1545-1700' and at 135-138 'The Perfection of Imperfect Instruments 1700-1827'.

[71] (1894) Law Reports 22 Indian Appeals 76.

wakf may be validly created for the benefit of the family with a substantial residual benefit to the public, a wakf which in substance is nothing but a family settlement would offend the rule against perpetuity.

There was much public dissatisfaction with this ruling and the Indian legislature had to intervene and overrule the Privy Council decision. In 1913 the Mussalman Wakf Validating Act was passed to uphold the validity of family wakfs. That Act defines a wakf as 'the permanent dedication by a person professing the Mussalman faith of any property for any purpose recognised by the Mussalman law as religious, pious or charitable'. The effect of this law is to recognise family wakfs not only as religious trusts but also as charitable trusts. Such trusts do not attract the common law principle of perpetuity. Tax legislation, however, would not recognise family wakfs as charities for the purpose of tax relief as they do not satisfy the public benefit requirement that tax statutes invariably impose.

The Muslim Intestate Succession and Wakf Ordinance of 1931 of Sri Lanka provided that 'charitable trust' includes 'any trust or wakf for the benefit of the Muslim public or any section of it' for any of the four '*Pemsel*' categories. When in 1956 a new Muslim Mosques and Charitable Trusts or Wakfs Ordinance was passed the definition of wakfs was altered by giving the '*Pemsel*' categories a Muslim flavour. Category 4 'for any other purposes beneficial or of interest to mankind in general' became 'any purpose beneficial to Muslims or any section thereof and any other purpose recognized by Muslim law as religious, charitable or pious'. This change would probably bring the Sri Lankan law in line with the Indian law, which recognises family wakfs.[72] However, family wakfs will not enjoy tax relief because Sri Lankan tax legislation too would insist on public benefit in addition to charitable purpose. [73]

It is interesting to note that after the enactment of the Wakfs Ordinance of 1931, the Trusts Ordinance was amended to provide that Chapter 10 of the Ordinance on charitable trusts does not apply to religious trusts regulated by the Wakfs Ordinance in so far as it is inconsistent with the provisions of the Wakfs Ordinance'.[74] In *Bhai Beebi v Naeem*[75] the Court of Appeal examined Indian authorities on the meaning and scope of wakfs. While the principles enunciated in Indian cases were useful to understand

72 A view has been expressed that Indian law which recognises family trusts is based on the Hanafi law and does not apply in Sri Lanka because Muslims in Sri Lanka belong to the Sahfei sect. See Jaldeen MS (1993) *The Muslim Law of Succession Inheritance and Wakf in Sri Lanka* Aitken Spence at 293.

73 See for instance *Caffoor (Trustees of the Abdul Gaffoor Trust) v Income Tax Commissioner (Colombo)* [1961] AC 584 (PC) where what appears to be a private wakf was held not to satisfy the public benefit requirement.

74 See s109 of the Trusts Ordinance.

75 [1981] 2 Sri Lanka Law Reports 335.

the concept, the Court of Appeal felt that wakfs operate in Sri Lanka in the context of charitable trusts, in the sense that provisions in the Trusts Ordinance apply to wakfs. What does not apply to a wakf is any provision in the chapter on charitable trusts, which is inconsistent with the Wakfs Ordinance. There was no inconsistency between Chapter 10 of the Trusts Ordinance and the Wakfs Ordinance; the definition of wakf in the Wakfs Ordinance of 1931 was very similar to the definition of charitable trusts in the Trusts Ordinance. The Court of Appeal decided that when a property is dedicated for a Muslim charitable purpose, such as for the purpose of a Muslim burial ground, legal title to the property remains in the dedicator (the *wakif*) but he becomes a trustee holding the property in trust for the benefit of the objects of the dedication. Where no provision is made for the appointment of trustees, the *wakif* is trustee and the devolution of trusteeship would be as in the case of Hindu religious trusts.

CONCLUSION

The Trusts Ordinance was introduced at a time the judiciary had warmly welcomed the English law of trusts into Sri Lanka in order to supply omissions in the common law and the customary laws. Both Roman-Dutch law and the customary laws, namely the Muslim law and Hindu law, had institutions which closely resembled trust. The entry of trusts, therefore, necessarily occasioned conflicts.

The conflict with Roman-Dutch law related to the theoretical basis of trusts, particularly whether the separation of legal and equitable ownership was of the essence of trusts. The Privy Council said in the case of *Sitti Kadija v De Saram*, quoting RW Lee[76] that 'the distinction between the legal and the equitable estate is of the essence of the trust; the idea is foreign to *fidei commissum*.' We have seen that, despite claims that the Trusts Ordinance was intended not to be burdened with the idea of equitable interest, courts of Sri Lanka had relied on the idea of equitable interest not only in relation to trusts but also in relation to other property issues.

The conflict between English law of trusts and religious and customary laws arose from the fact that Muslim law and Hindu law had developed their own ideas of trusts in their religious context, which were not easily reconcilable with the English concept of trusts. We saw how courts of Sri Lanka gave effect to the Trusts Ordinance in relation to Muslim and Hindu trusts, avoiding any friction between the local practices and the imported English law. The Trusts Ordinance made inroads into traditional religious practices, not so much to oppress, but to regulate religious charities in accordance with the Trusts Ordinance.

76 Lee RW (1931) *An Introduction to Roman-Dutch Law* (3rd ed) Clarendon Press at 372

There are examples of positive contribution that the English concept of trust made to special laws. *Seelachchy v Visuanathan,* [77] where the court gave effect to the Thesawalamai concept of community of property between husband and wife, provides a good illustration. Community of property requires that any property acquired by a spouse becomes part of the community of property. However, unless the acquiring spouse transfers a share of it to the other in compliance with formalities, the legal title remains with the acquiring spouse. This meant that the acquiring spouse could dispose of that property thereby prejudicing the other party's interest. Bertram CJ held that the other spouse acquires an 'equitable right' to have that property declared part of the community and held that section 99 of the Trusts Ordinance covered the situation by imposing a constructive trust.[78]

While Hindu and Muslim religious trusts are regulated by the Trusts Ordinance, trusts relating to the administration of Buddhists Temples are regulated by a separate statute, the Buddhist Temporalities Ordinance of 1981. That Ordinance contains provisions relating to the administration of Buddhist temples through the medium of a trust under the Public Trustee's supervision. Kandyan law, the law applicable to Sinhalese people resident in the Kandyan Provinces, does not know of trusts and therefore Kandyan Sinhalese will have to use English law of trusts, as set out in the Trusts Ordinance, if they wish to create a trust. The problem with Kandyan law in relation to trusts is that gifts are revocable under Kandyan law. As a general rule trusts are irrevocable and the settlor has no control over the administration of the trust. While there was judicial opinion that a donation was irrevocable if such was the express intention of the donor,[79] it was thought necessary to make statutory provision that it would be unlawful to revoke a gift which creates a charitable trust or passes property to the trustee of a Buddhist temple. [80]

It remains to be said that a trust created by a person governed by a special law will be bound by his special law only where there is anything in it which relates to the trust, such as a religious trust. It would also be possible for him to create a trust, expressly providing that the trust will not be governed by the special law, which would otherwise apply. While there is no case law on this point, an analogy may be drawn from cases where courts have recognised the right of Muslims and Kandyan Sinhalese to create

77 (1922) 23 New Law Reports 97.

78 Section 99 provides that 'where [...] the person having possession of the property has not the whole beneficial interest therein, he must hold the property for the benefit of the persons having such interest, or the residue thereof (as the case may be), to the extent necessary to satisfy their just demands.'

79 See *Kirihenaya v Jotiya* (1922) 24 New Law Reports 149.

80 See The Kandyan Law Declaration and Amendment Ordinance No 39 of 1956 section 5.

a *fidei commissum* (since abolished) although the institution was unknown to either special law,[81] and where the legislature has recognised the need to enable people governed by a special law to enter into transactions under the common law. For instance it is lawful for Kandyans to marry under the General Marriage Ordinance rather than the Kandyan Marriage and Divorce Ordinance.[82]

In Sri Lanka, as in many other English-speaking countries, English law has been welcomed for its modernity and versatility. Sri Lanka has not, however, received English law in order to entirely undermine the role played by Roman-Dutch law and the local laws and customs. What the introduction of trusts law into Sri Lanka shows is how the arrival of a great legal tradition, through codification at that, can still respect the established legal traditions in the host jurisdiction, and operate side by side with them.

81 See *Assistant Government Agent, Kandy v Kalu Banda* (1921) 23 NLR 26 (for Kandyan Law) and *Weerasekera v Peiris* (1933) 34 NLR 281,PC (for Muslims).

82 See *Sophia Hamine v Appuhamy* (1922) New Law Reports 353

'All this together make up our *Common* Law': Legal Hybridity in England and Ireland, 1704-1804

SEÁN PATRICK DONLAN

> *All this together make up our Common Law; and though it runs thro' different Channels, yet every part of it (even that in the Spiritual courts) may claim the name of the Common Law of England. For the whole is a composition of the Feudal, Civil and Canon Laws; and its Definitions, Divisions and Maxims are drawn out of one of those three Laws. – Thomas Wood, A new institute of the imperial or civil law (1704) at viii*

No legal tradition is a purely native growth.[1] Significant and explicit legal hybridity was, in fact, the norm across Europe before the nineteenth century. There were multiple—often transnational, or pre-national and trans-territorial—contemporaneous legal traditions co-existing in the same geographical space and at the same time, though often affecting different individuals. This 'plurality of laws', of legal orders recognisable as such to modern eyes, blurred seamlessly into the less formally institutionalised, but meaningful, 'normative pluralism' from which more formal laws often emerged and competed.[2] Especially before modern legal positivism,

[1] Örücü, E 'A general view of "Legal Families" and of "Mixing Systems"' in Örücü and Nelken, D (2007) *Comparative law: A Handbook* Hart Publishing. See also Palmer, VV (2007) 'Mixed Legal Systems ... and the Myth of Pure Laws' (67) *Louisiana Law Review* 1205.

[2] Confusingly, this 'plurality of laws' is usually referred to as 'legal pluralism' by comparatists and legal historians. But 'legal pluralism' is also used by legal anthropologists and sociologists to include both state ('official') law and other meaningful non-state norms ('unofficial laws'). Cf. Griffiths, J 'The idea of sociology of law and its relation to law and society' in Freeman, M (ed) (2005) *Law and Sociology: Current Legal Issues – Volume 8* Oxford University Press at 63-4.

centralisation, and nationalism, such norms are appropriately included within the juridical sphere. The boundaries between such formal and informal 'legalities' were especially porous.[3] As a consequence, both the plurality of laws and normative pluralism deserve greater attention in historical and comparative analysis. Indeed, Esin Örücü and Vernon Palmer, the most important modern comparatists writing on mixed legal systems or traditions, have each made similar suggestions for expanding legal research beyond the European hybrids or 'classical mixed jurisdictions'.[4] Both have also noted the considerable difficulties involved in such study.

This assay into comparative legal history has a somewhat narrower aim. It stays largely within Europe, highlighting the historical hybridity of the Anglo-American legal traditions.[5] It reviews, all too briefly, the complex genealogy of English law before the *Code Civil* (1804) through the rich, and admittedly partial, primary literature of eighteenth-century Anglophone jurists. Given such sources, its focus is also inevitably on the plurality of English laws rather than normative pluralism. The essay is part of a wider project in comparative law and legal history on legal hybridity and diffusion, the mixtures and movements of laws.[6] It might be seen as a small step towards the application of the 'family trees' model suggested by Örücü.[7] A final theme is to note that (i) present discussions can profit from the study of the pluralism of the past and that (ii) legal history can also benefit from the rich conceptual vocabulary developed in the study of mixed legal traditions.[8] Given the limitations of space, however, this paper merely hints at these possibilities. Modern scholarship on mixed jurisdictions, Scottish materials, and secondary sources on legal history are cited sparingly.

[3] See Tomlins, CL 'The Many Legalities of Colonialization: A Manifesto of Destiny for Early American Legal History' in Tomlins and Mann, BH (eds) (2001) *The Many Legalities of Early America* Unviersity of North Carolina Press at 2-3.

[4] See Örücü, 'Developing comparative law' in Örücü and Nelken, supra n 1 at 61. See also Palmer, (2008) 'Two Rival Theories of Mixed Legal Systems' (3) *Journal of Comparative Law* 7 and Örücü, (2008) 'What is a Mixed Legal System: Exclusion or Expansion?' (3) *Journal of Comparative Law* 34. These articles are included in (2008) 12:1 *Electronic Journal of Comparative Law*. (www.ejcl.org/121/abs121-16.html and www.ejcl.org/121/abs121-15.html respectively). See also this volume.

[5] Cf Makdisi, JA (1999) 'The Islamic Origins of the Common Law' (77) *North Carolina Law Review* 1635.

[6] On diffusion, see Twining, W 'Globalisation and Comparative Law' in Örücü and Nelken, supra n 1.

[7] 'Family Trees for Legal Systems: Towards a Contemporary Approach' in Van Hoecke, M (ed.) (2004) *Epistemology and Methodology of Comparative Law* Hart Publishing at 363.

[8] See Donlan, 'Histories of Hybridity: A Primer, a Plea, and a Plan (of Sorts)' in Cashin-Ritaine, E and Donlan (eds) (forthcoming 2010) *The Emergence of Hybrid Legal Systems: Their Implications for the Comparative Lawyer* Swiss Institute of Comparative Law.

The failure to acknowledge legal hybridity and diffusion both distorts the past and obscures our understanding of the present. This neglect is arguably most significant in the Anglo-American legal traditions.[9] The creation of genuinely common or general national laws, a legal 'system' centred on the state, and the elimination of competing jurisdictions was a very long historical process throughout Europe. In its open nature and use of transnational, pan-European bodies of law and legal doctrine, England was actually little different from its continental cousins. But this fact has often been obscured by English law's *comparative* independence from the European *iura communa* and a long-standing belief in Anglo-exceptionalism. English law was always part of a wider European jurisprudential-juridical legal culture. Over centuries, its jurists were in constant communication with, and selectively incorporated significant elements of, continental law. But the English 'common law' also competed with its own *iura propria*, its local and lesser jurisdictions, as well as other normative traditions. All were essential to modern—and plural—Anglo-American legal traditions. And a wide variety of legal sources or authorities, including many from beyond the law, were persuasive in legislation and adjudication. The 'common law' only achieved its hegemony over the course of centuries by borrowing from and absorbing its rival jurisdictions, both foreign and domestic. In sum, it 'is not the sole source of English law, though in the long run it turned out to be its principal unifying factor.'[10]

OUR LAWS ARE AS MIXED AS OUR LANGUAGE

For centuries, Roman military and political dominance extended throughout most of Europe. Much of Britain, too, was colonised by Rome from 78-409 AD. Indeed, Richard Burn (1709-85)—DCL, noted legal writer, justice of the peace, and subsequently chancellor of Carlisle—wrote that 'some of the most eminent Roman lawyers, as Papinian, Paulius, and Ulpian [...] did sit in the seat of judgment in this nation.'[11] Later conquests were of ever greater consequence. John Ayliffe (1676-1732), LLD, published on civil and canon law, wrote a history of Oxford, and served as a proctor in the University's chancellor's court. He noted that the '[c]hanges of Government' due to 'the *Romans*, *Saxons*, *Danes*, and *Normans* [... meant] that now our Laws

[9] 'However mixed his system is in fact the English lawyer does not think of it as such.' McKnight, J (1977) 'Some Historical Observations on Mixed Systems of Law' (22) *Juridical Review* (ns) 177 at 178.

[10] Martinez-Torrón, J (1998) *Anglo-American law and canon law: canonical roots of the common law tradition* at 183.

[11] Burn, R (1767) *Ecclesiastical Law* (2nd edn) H Woodfall and W Strahan at v-vi.

are a Mixture of all these Laws put together'.[12] The arrival of the Anglo-Saxons in the fifth and sixth centuries was especially important, not least on the self-image—and legal fantasies—of later generations. Even they arguably 'incorporated various Roman concepts, practices and rules into their own regal customs.'[13] Christianity was a still more critical conduit for Romanist learning. Both English law and society remained diverse, including the absorption of successive waves of Vikings in the ninth and tenth centuries. At its borders, too, England was surrounded by Celts with their own aboriginal laws. Conquest and the forceful 'migration of laws' subsequently played a role in the English conquest of Wales and Ireland and later in English colonies. As a result of these different influences, John Reeves (1752-1829), the greatest English legal historian of the eighteenth century, remarked that '[t]he common law is of a various and motley origin.'[14]

The Franco-Normans, Norsemen who had settled in France, added administrative *nous* to England's centralised kingship. While its folk-law was broadly similar to their own, the inter-regnal transfer to the Normans effected significant changes. For centuries, England was ruled by French-speaking monarchs with claims to the French throne. England's distinctive legal creations (central and Eyre courts, the writ, and the jury) are generally credited to the Normandy-born Henry II (1133-89). The laws, too, were expressed in a variety of languages. Latin, English, and 'Law French' remained important for centuries; where appropriate, Celtic languages were also used.[15] And, an anonymous eighteenth-century writer noted,

[12] Ayliffe, J (1734) *New Pandect of Roman Civil Law* [...] Printed for T Osborne at xlvii. Cf Edward Wynne's (1767) *Eunomus: or dialogues concerning the laws and constitution of England.* '[C]onsider in the course of history, the variety of invasions this island has sustained, most of them in their turns productive of laws; consider a happier view, the mixed body of the English legislature; men various in their talents, their education, their pursuits and connections; many of them improved by an experience and knowledge of other countries; consider all this, and it will be no wonder that the law we live under is as compound as the atmosphere in which we breathe: that the political maxims of other states are adopted and made to conform to the genius of this: and by a kind of legislative commerce, the defects of our natural growth (if such occur) are improved by the importation of foreign productions.' Ibid., 111-12. Printed for B White and Son.

[13] Winkler, JF (1992) 'Roman Law in Anglo-Saxon England' (13) *Journal of Legal History* 101 at 108. Cf Sherman, CP (1914) 'The Romanization of English law' (23) *Yale Law Journal* 318.

[14] (1783) *A History of the English Law from the Saxons to the End of the Reign of Edward the First* T Wright at 2.

[15] See 'FO' (1701) *The Law French Dictionary Alphabetically Digested* Printed for I Cleave and J Hartley; Kelham, R (1779) *A Dictionary of the Norman or Old French Language* Printed for E Brooke.

> the probability is, as *Lord Bacon* has expressed it, that our Laws are as mixed as our language, compounded of British, Roman, Saxon, Danish, and Norman customs; and as our language is so much the richer, so the Laws are the more complete.[16]

Formally at least, this linguistic pluralism lasted into the eighteenth century when it was altered by legislation. Through a long series of wars, especially the 'Hundred Years War (1337-1453), England slowly lost its continental possessions. But the Calais Pale fell only in the mid-sixteenth century; the Channel Islands remained England's. Claims to the French throne were not formally abandoned until the end of the eighteenth century.

The eleventh-century rediscovery of Justinian's (482/3-565) *Digest* (c533) brought a revival of the *Corpus Iuris Civilis*. The importance of 'the Common Civil Law of the *Romans'* was not lost on eighteenth-century English jurists.[17] Thomas Bever (c1725-91), DCL and professor of civil law at Oxford at mid-century, was judge of the cinque ports and chancellor of the dioceses of Lincoln and Bangor. He noted that, with the rediscovery, Roman law 'became, almost instantaneously, the supplement, not only of the European feudal constitutions; but was also dignified with the title of the universal law of the great community of mankind, over the whole face of the globe.'[18] A class of professional lawyers and elaborate written doctrine developed. Indeed, 'the Books of the *Civil* Law were receiv'd into all Parts of the Western Empire, and were adorn'd with excellent Glosses and Commentaries, which were made with great Harmony and Agreement unto each other.'[19]

The early development of centralised royal courts meant that England was not a weak borrowing system. The turn to neo-Roman models was thus less dramatic and reception more inhibited, than elsewhere in Europe. But, as on the continent, English folklaw blurred seamlessly into feudal institutions. The Oxford professor of common law Robert Chambers (1737-1803) argued that England was 'like all other European nations, [...] for some centuries after the Conquest regulated by the feudal subordination and consequently governed by the feudal law'.[20] Francis

[16] (1791) *A Law Grammar; or, an Introduction to the Theory and Practice of English Jurisprudence* Printed for CGL, J Robinson, T Whieldon, W Clarke, and Ogilvy and Speare at 17.

[17] (1923) *A Dissertation on the Law of Nature, the Law of Nations, and the Civil Law in General Together with some Observations on the Roman Civil Law* [...] Printed for J Roberts at 51. The appendix or '*Libri juridici*' is forty-two pages long.

[18] Bever, T (1766) *A Discourse on the Study of Jurisprudence and the Civil Law* Clarendon Press at 20.

[19] Ayliffe, supra n 12 at xxxix.

[20] Chambers, R (1999) *A Course of Lectures on the English Law Delivered at the University of*

Stoughton Sullivan (1719-66) was a barrister, advocate and a judge in the ecclesiastical courts and the court of admiralty of Ireland. Also professor of both civil and common law at the University of Dublin, he was repeating a cliché in writing that feudalism was 'a kind of *jus gentium*' or universal law throughout Europe.[21] Indeed, the feudal law was absorbed into the learned laws. Richard Wooddeson (c1745-1822), Oxford lecturer in moral philosophy and subsequently professor of common law, wrote how, as a result of the Sicilian king Frederick II (1194-1250), the feudal law 'under the title of *Feudorum Confuetudines*, [was] subjoined to the *Corpus Juris Civlis*, by a discordant kind of alliance.'[22]

It is difficult to overstate the Church's philosophical and practical-political importance to European history. Its responsibilities extended far beyond theology. In law, its institutions bequeathed a *Roman-canonical* influence throughout Europe: professional, judge-centred courts emphasising writing and permitting appeals. Henry II's famous dispute with Thomas Becket (1118-70), the archbishop of Canterbury, was part of wider debates on the boundaries of church and state. Canon law and the ecclesiastical courts were important in England into the nineteenth century. '[A]ll Christian States and Princes have admitted the *Canon-Law* more or less, without Distinction of Religion, and do still retain some Part of it.'[23] Arthur Browne (1756?-1805), LLD, was regius professor of both civil law and (occasionally) Greek in Dublin, an advocate in the ecclesiastical and admiralty courts of Ireland, a polemicist, and a member of the Irish Parliament before the Act of Union 1800.[24] 'Churchmen', he wrote, were 'our first Jurists'.[25] This was true beyond the ecclesiastical courts. The kings' advisors, and consequently judiciary, were frequently clergy trained in the 'learned laws'.

European jurists created a *ius commune*, a body of doctrine or 'law' common across the frontiers of the continent, in contrast to particular laws specific to a place. They acted as teachers and scholars, and served as advisors, diplomats, record-keepers, administrators, and judges across the continent, paving the way for receptions of the canon and civil

Oxford 1767-1773 (composed with Samuel Johnson) Wisconsin, Curley, TM (ed.) at 112.

21 (2004) [1776] *Lectures on the Constitution and Laws of England* (2nd edn) Lawbook Exchange, Donlan SP (ed.) at 19.

22 *Elements of Jurisprudence* […] Printed for T Payne and Son at 83. See also Idem. (1792-93) *A Systematical View of the Laws of England* […] Printed for T Payne

23 Ayliffe, J (1726) *Parergon Juris Canonici Anglicano: or, a Commentary by way of Supplement to the Canons and Constitutions of the Church of England* D Leach at xix.

24 See Donlan (2009) '"The Debt is Forgotten": A Compendious View of Arthur Browne, 1756?-1805' (13) *Electronic Journal of Comparative Law* (www.ejcl.org/133/abs133-3.html).

25 Browne, A (1797) *A Compendious View of the Civil Law and of the Law of the Admiralty* A Strahan at i.39.

laws. Lawyers throughout Europe 'applied a mixed legal system whose components were on the one hand local statutes and customs and on the other hand the law books of Justinian and the Canon Law.'[26] Over centuries, this vulgarised Germanic-Romanist *mixité* displaced local laws. 'Every constitution of modern Europe [was] founded upon an union' of the civil, feudal, and canon laws.[27] Common lawyers, too, drew on the *ius commune*. Indeed, it has been argued that,

> [i]n the realm of basic principles, organizing ideas, techniques of argumentation, and habits of thought, the parallels are sufficiently great that one might want to call the common law simply a variant, admittedly an eccentric variant, of the multitude of legal systems that ultimately derive from the *ius commune*.[28]

The nineteenth-century English legal historian FW Maitland (1850-1906) argued that the term 'common law' was itself borrowed by analogy from the '*ius commune*' of the canonists to distinguish general from particular laws.[29]

While Bever bemoaned that later writers did not produce more scholarship, he believed England 'never [...] failed to produce a succession of great and able Civilians, who have done the highest honor to their profession, both as advocates and statesmen.'[30] As on the continent, English legal education in the civil and canon laws was conducted in the universities. Oxford and Cambridge taught the learned laws from an early date.[31] University education in the *lex proprium* was, across Europe, a much later development.[32] The *Corpus Iuris Canonici* was, it was argued, 'introduced into *England* during the reign of king *Stephen*, AD 1149 by the industry of *Roger Vacarius*, who read public lectures upon their use and excellency in the university of Oxford.'[33] If the Lombard Vacarius (c1120-c1200) could

26 Coing, H (1973) 'The Roman Law as Ius Commune on the Continent' (89) *Law Quarterly Review* 505 at 510.
27 Bever, T (1781) *History of the Legal Polity of the Roman State and of the Rise, Progress and Extent of Roman laws* Printed for W Strahan and T Cadell at xii.
28 Donahue, C, Jr (1992) 'Ius Commune, Canon Law, and Common Law in England' (66) *Tulane Law Review* 1745 at 1748.
29 Maitland, FW (1898) *Roman Canon Law in the Church of England: Six Essays* Methuen & Co at 4.
30 Bever supra n 27 at x.
31 De Zulueta, F and Stein, P (1990) *The Teaching of Roman Law in England around 1200* Selden Society.
32 Note, however, the importance of the oral doctrine or 'common learning' of the judge-jurists of the English Inns. Baker, J (2001) *The Law's Two Bodies: some Evidential Problems in English legal history* Oxford University Press.
33 *A Law Grammar* supra n 16 at 131.

not have taught at Oxford, his *Liber pauperum* (c1170s) was an important channel for continental thought into the following century.[34] English, Welsh, and Irish civilians were educated both at home and abroad. Their training in pan-European bodies of law made them especially useful as diplomats and advisors. Long after the Reformation, Oxford still conferred degrees, Browne noted, '*in utroque Jure tam Civili quam Canonico.*'[35]

Within England, the common law had important advantages over its rivals. Its effectiveness as a forum and its greater guarantee of enforcement meant it began to absorb competing courts. Like the *ius commune*, it also served as subsidiary law and was received in England's other jurisdictions. Genuine custom was, in effect, colonised and conquered by the common law. Common law courts eventually acted as superior courts. By the fifteenth century, however, the royal courts were increasingly criticised for their rigidity. As a result, additional courts rooted in the king's prerogative powers arose. Most important was the fifteenth-century development of the 'Equity' courts. The king's Chancellor, acting on his behalf, was permitted to decide petitioners' claims 'equitably', i.e. according to justice and conscience. Eventually the Court of Chancery developed for this purpose. Sir Jeffray Gilbert (1674-1726), judge of the Irish king's bench and chief baron of the Irish exchequer, noted that from a 'very small and inconsiderable beginning, [the equity courts] hath not only curbed the jurisdictions of the common law, but hath introduced a new process, and a new manner of trial totally before unheard of.'[36] Chancery was especially open to the influence of the learned laws. 'Almost all of the chancellors, from Becket to Wolsey [...] were ecclesiasticks, well skilled in the Roman laws.'[37] According to Charles Barton (1767/8-1843), barrister and legal writer, they 'naturally entertained a predilection for the civil, as connected with the canon or ecclesiastical law; they consequently adopted its rules and principles in their mode of dispensing justice'.[38] Procedures as well as substantive elements were borrowed.

[34] Southern, RW (1984) 'From Schools to University' in Catto, JI (ed.) *The History of the University of Oxford: Volume I – the Early Oxford Schools* Oxford University Press at 9.

[35] Browne, A (1803) *A Compendious View of the Ecclesiastical Law of Ireland* (2nd edn) RE Mercier at 123n.

[36] (1756) *Two Treatises on the Proceeding in Equity: and the Jurisdiction of that Court* Printed for Richard Watts at 24 (published posthumously). Volume one was called *Forum Romanum: or, the Roman Tribunal.*

[37] Burn supra n 11 at v-vi.

[38] (1796) *Historical Treatise of a Suit in Equity* [...] Printed for P Byrne at 19.

AN INSTITUTE OF THE LAWS OF ENGLAND

An even more distinctively Anglo-civilian body of law and lawyers developed. Samuel Hallifax (1733-90), LLD, professor of civil law at Cambridge, and bishop of St Asaph, wrote on law and religion. He noted this sectorial civilian influence:

> the Imperial law, to this day, obtains, under different restrictions, in the Courts of Bishops and their officers, the Courts Military, the Courts of Admiralty, and the Courts of the two Universities; in all which it has been received either by the consent of Parliament, and so is become a part of the Statute or Written law; or by immemorial usage and custom, and thus constitutes an inferior branch of the Common or Unwritten law.[39]

This use of the *ius commune* occurred, in part, because it was believed that 'courts of different regions should observe and adhere to an uniformity of decisions' across Europe.[40] These courts were in addition, of course, to the ecclesiastical courts. The civilians' 'Doctors' Commons' provided a place for practitioners to dine and socialise. A voluntary society like the English Inns, it probably dates from the late fifteenth century.[41] Doctors' Commons did not have a teaching function or control entry into the profession, but its members had a monopoly in the civilian and ecclesiastical courts.[42] An almanac from 1777 listed fourteen public offices.[43] Many of the civilian advocates were also members of the Inns. They were, like their continental contemporaries, 'mixed jurists'.

The existence of these jurisdictions did not, of necessity, generate conflict. For some time, 'Common lawyers seemed to have regarded canon law and civil law as comparable bodies of law maintained and passed down

39 (1774) *An Analysis of the Roman Civil Law compared with the Laws of England* J Archdeacon at xx.

40 Wooddeson, R (1792-3) *A Systematical View of the Laws of England* [...] Printed for T Payne at 138 (discussing admiralty).

41 Squibb, GD (1977) *Doctors' Commons: a History of the College of Advocates and Doctors of Law* Oxford University Press; Logan, FD (1988) 'Doctor's Commons in the early Sixteenth Century: a Society of Many Talents' (61) *Historical Research* 151.

42 Andrew Coltée Ducarel (1713-85), DCL, commissary of Canterbury, and fellow of the Society of Antiquaries, wrote a 'Summary account of the Society of Doctors Commons' in 1753. He presented the work to Sir George Lee (1700?-58), DCL, MP, dean of arches, and judge of the prerogative court of Canterbury. It was included (1931) as Appendix One in (15) *London Topographical Record* 21.

43 (1977) *Browne's General Law-list* [...] (2nd edn) Printed for the Author at 153-6. Also included is a list of the doctors and proctors of Doctors Commons. Ibid. at 147-52.

by their counterpart professions in much the same way.'[44] Many civilians, including the 'legal humanists', sought to use their learning to reform English law.[45] The civilians 'were the first [...] to attempt an exposition of English law on truly systematic lines.'[46] They were similarly critical of the exceptionalism and insularity of the legal history of the common lawyers. And English law was, in fact, supplemented by continental and canonical legal methods, maxims, courts and procedures, as well as specific doctrines. They were '*adopted*, or used by way of *illustration*' or 'to regulate inconvenient usages or other defects.'[47] Such borrowing occurred through both formal and informal legislative, doctrinal, and judicial receptions. This was, Bever wrote, 'a very innocent, nay, a very laudable plagiarism'.[48]

Thomas Wood (1661-1722) was an Oxford DCL and briefly assessor of the vice-chancellor's court there. He was also called to the bar at Gray's Inn. He wrote that 'the most ancient of [common law] writers, would look very naked, if every *Roman* Lawyer should pluck away his Feathers.'[49] The most important legal literature of the early common law showed considerable Roman erudition. Indeed,

> [f]rom the reign of *Stephen* to that of *Edward* the third, the Civil Law prevailed very much, and even the Judges and Professors of the Common Law had frequent recourse to it, when the Common Law was silent or defective; as plainly appears from the works, of *Bracton, Thornton*, and *Fleta*, who have transcribed one after another, in many places, the very words of Justinian's Institutes.[50]

If English borrowing was not as extensive as in other parts of Europe, Halifax wrote that 'certain parts and principles of the Imperial law have been incorporated into our own, [is] a fact too incontestable to be denied.'[51] Indeed, he claimed that 'great improvements' were made by such 'ingraftments'.[52] The sixteenth century even saw 'a Reception of the

44 Seipp, DJ (1993) 'The Reception of Canon Law and Civil Law in the Common Law Courts before 1600' (13) *Oxford Journal of Legal Studies* 388 at 412.

45 Terrill, RJ (1981) 'Humanism and Rhetoric in Legal Education: the Contribution of Sir John Dodderidge (1555-1628)' (2) *Journal of Legal History* 30.

46 Rodgers, CP (1984) 'Legal Humanism and English law – the Contribution of the Civilians' (19) *Irish Jurist* (ns) 115 at 120.

47 Browne supra n 25 at i.12n19.

48 Bever supra n 18 at 25.

49 (1704) *A New Institute of the Imperial or Civil Law* WB at ix.

50 *A Law Grammar* supra n 16 at 129-30.

51 Hallifax supra n 39 at xvi.

52 Id. at xxi.

continental *lex mercatoria* in England.'[53]

Both legal records and law reports were common in Europe's secular and spiritual courts.[54] But being handwritten and elliptical, they were often of little use in future adjudication. Reports were unofficial, rarely contained more than the judgment reached and the parties involved, and generally lacked an explanation of the court's motives or reasoning. As with Roman edicts, English writs provided some legal continuity. But especially before printing, there were few authentic texts of either legislation or jurisprudence. Even English judicial 'opinions were not sources of law, but simply evidence of what the law was. Legal learning and reasoning transcended single instances.'[55] The decisions of juries were less useful still for the development of a meaningful jurisprudence. But lacking the texts and elaborate written commentary of the learned law, common lawyers increasingly relied on the reports generated in adjudication. Already by the time of *Les comentaries ou les reportes de Edmunde Plowden* (1571), the common law '[h]ad come to depend on judicial decisions, interpreted in the context of the facts which gave rise to them.'[56] Such case 'law' was effectively doctrine, though of a particularly important sort. It was binding in the instant case and persuasive for future decisions. As in Europe, precedents possessed authority on the basis of fairness and as 'best evidence' of the law.[57]

Slowly, very slowly, the plurality of European laws would give way to nation-states and common national laws.[58] A series of horrific confessional wars resulted in the formal recognition of states and the elaboration of a more complex 'law of nations'. European princes were now sovereign both internally and externally. Philosophically, the Reformers' emphasis on divine law-making served as a model for state absolutism and legal positivism. Catholic thought also remained important. The canon law continued almost without alteration in protestant kingdoms. In England, a 'kind of National Canon law, composed of legatine and provincial constitutions, and adapted only to the exigencies of this church and

[53] Stein, P (1988) [1977] 'Continental Influences on English legal thought, 1600-1900' in Stein, P (Gonville, P) *The Character and Influence of the Roman Civil Law: Historical essays* Hambledon Press at 218.

[54] Wijffels, A (ed.) (1997) *Case Law in the Making: the Techniques and Methods of Judicial Records and Law Reports – Volume One: Essays* Dunckler & Humblot.

[55] Baker, J (1990) *An Introduction to English Legal History* (3rd edn) Oxford University Press at 227.

[56] Baker, J (1989) 'Records, Reports and the Origins of Case-law in England' in Baker, J (ed.) (1989) *Judicial Records, Law Reports, and the Growth of Case Law* Dunckler & Humblot at 42.

[57] See Stein, P (1988) [1985] 'Civil Law Reports and the Case of San Marino' in supra n 53 at 118-9.

[58] Glenn, HP (2005) *On Common Laws* Oxford University Press.

kingdom' was created.[59] And, with the growth of internal state power, the expansion of the English common law continued. By the sixteenth century, Wales was already firmly within the orbit of English law; in the following century, it finally displaced native Irish law and the mixed 'March' laws at its borders. Scotland had, of course, long been independent and drew heavily on the *ius commune*. The union of the English and Scottish crowns (1605) and parliaments (1707) suggested a legal union, but the common lawyers successfully prevented it.[60] Instead, Scots law would increasingly come under the influence of English law.

Within England, too, the common law began to absorb other jurisdictions. This exposed internal divisions within English law, as the relationship between common lawyers and prerogative lawyers and civilians deteriorated in the seventeenth century.[61] As Browne later noted of the equity courts, '[t]he charge of encroachment on [...] legal jurisdictions, was prompted by ignorance, or instigated by party'.[62] Parliamentarians aligned themselves with the apologetics of the common law and the 'ancient constitution'; common lawyers associated themselves with rising parliamentary power. This internecine rivalry is exemplified in Sir Edward Coke's (1552-1634) clashes with Sir Francis Bacon (1561-1626). Like many English lawyers who found their way to print, Bacon attended university. There, he was exposed to the civil law and later studied it privately. He also attended Gray's Inn. His *Maxims of the law* (1597) was '[a] rapproachment between the traditional common law notion of maxim and the civilian theory of *regulae'* enshrined, among other places, in Justinian's *Digest* (*De diversis regulsis iuris antique*).[63] Bacon's suggestions for legal reform also included an early modern codification or 'digest' of the law. It was, he wrote, 'rather a matter of order and explanation, than of alteration.'[64] His suggestions were frequently reprinted in the following centuries.

The hostility between Anglo-civilians and common lawyers was not without humour. George Ruggle's (c1575-1621/2) *Ignoramus* (1615), performed by students of the civil law, was especially critical of its common law rivals.[65] King James I loved it; Lord Coke did not. Indeed, Coke 'could

[59] Blackstone, W (1765) *Commentaries on the Laws of England: Book the First* Clarendon Press at 82.

[60] Levack, BP (1975) 'The Proposed Union of English Law and Scots Law in the Seventeenth Century' (20) *Juridical Review* (ns) 97.

[61] Moccia, L (1981) 'English Law Attitudes to the "Civil Law"' (2) *Journal of Legal History* 157.

[62] Browne supra n 25 at i.40-1.

[63] Stein, P (1966) *Regulae Iuris: from Juristic Rules to Legal Maxims* Edinburgh University Press at 170.

[64] Eg, Bacon, F [1616-17] 'A proposal for compiling and amendment of our laws' in Bacon, F (1737) *Law tracts* [...] Printed for E Nutt, R Nutt, and R Gosling.

[65] Tucker, EFJ (1977) 'Ruggle's Ignoramus and Humanist Criticism of the Language of the

not endure any thing connected with the civil law.'[66] Ironically, the period was one in which civilians were especially accomplished. The Italian expatriate Alberico Gentili (1552-1608) was a noted writer on the law of nations and was later admitted to Gray's Inn. Arthur Duck's (1580-1648) *De usu authoritate juris civilis Romananorum* was published posthumously in 1653, translated and reprinted into French and German. Richard Zouche (1590-1661), it has been written, 'was [...] the last of his kind: an English civil lawyer whose writings acquired a durable European reputation.'[67] Like the works of his contemporaries, John Cowell's (1554-1611) *Institutiones juris Anglicani* (1605) pressed the common law into a civilian framework. He had received an LLD from Cambridge and served as professor of civil law and justice of the peace there. His *Interpreter* (1607), a law dictionary, ignited considerable controversy. Definitions in the work claimed extensive powers for the crown. While the king himself suppressed the work, the dictionary was useful enough to be republished in the eighteenth century.[68]

Debates about the power of monarchy came to a head in the seventeenth century, overlapping with jurisdictional disputes. The association of the Anglo-civilians with royal absolutism was long-lasting.[69] In the late eighteenth century, Browne wrote that '[t]he contest of prevalence [...] has long since ceased, but this contest, conducted on political rather than philosophical grounds, engendered a cloud of heat and prejudice, which long obscured a fair comparison of their merits.'[70] The effective victory of parliament and common lawyers over, respectively, the king and civilian and prerogative lawyers had profound effects. Bever noted that, as a result, 'the Roman or civil law [... was] too often carelessly thrown aside as obsolete and useless; and even represented as dangerous to the civil polity of the nation.'[71] Indeed,

> some ignorant people have been induced to think the civilians a tribe of dangerous intruders, who, if not resisted, would spread slavery, popery, and foreign power, over the whole kingdom. Under the influence of these vain and ridiculous terrors, they have supposed

Common Law' (30) *Renaissance Quarterly* 341. The title character was named after a grand jury endorsement.

66 Browne supra n 25 at ii.84n16.

67 Levack, BP 'Law' in Tyacke, N (ed.) (1997) *The History of the University of Oxford: Volume IV – Seventeenth-Century Oxford* Oxford University Press at 563.

68 Eg, (1727) *A Law Dictionary: or the Interpreter of Words and Terms Used in either the Common or Statute Laws of Great Britain, and in Tenures and in Jocular Customs* E and R Nutt.

69 Levack, BP (1973) *The Civil Lawyers in England 1603-1641* Clarendon Press.

70 Browne supra n 25 at i.21.

71 Bever supra n 27 at ii-iii.

> the whole body of the civil law to be the work of the absolute princes of Rome; and have therefore too hastily concluded, that any encouragement given to the study of it must involve our English liberties in ruin.[72]

Sullivan, educated as a civilian, made the same links in the eighteenth century.[73] This internal legal rivalry was deeply entangled with competing professional interests and political ideologies. Common law purists reacted with hostility to, as they saw it, civilian pollutionists.

THE STUDY OF THE LAW OF NATURE AND NATIONS

Pan-European movements in moral and legal philosophy meant that the law of nature and nations were areas of particular civilian influence. John Taylor (c1704-66) was a Cambridge LLD, a classical scholar and civilian advocate, ecclesiastic, and subsequently chancellor of Lincoln. He suggested that '[t]he *Jus Gentium*, or Law of Nations, in the Conception of the Roman Lawyers, differed little from the Law of Nature' and 'it may not be altogether improper to consider the Law of Nature as a Text, and the Civil Law as a Comment.'[74] In response to the political and philosophical crises of the early seventeenth century, some natural lawyers suggested the possibility of constructing a rational system of law on the basis of deduction. Even in England,

> [i]n purely formal terms, arguments from the writing of Natural Lawyers—of foreign Natural Lawyers at that—provided a legally acceptable foundation for the overturning of long-standing Common Law rules. [...] Nowhere is there a hint that Pufendorf's principles are any less valid as sources of legal argument than are the earlier decisions of the English courts.[75]

Natural law could, it seemed, be redacted into written, positive law. In the following century, Sir James Mackintosh (1765-1832), polemicist, barrister, lecturer at Lincoln's Inn, and MP, noted that 'the law of nations, [had],

[72] Bever supra n 18 at 29. See Jolowicz, HF (1949) 'Some English Civilians' (2) *Current Legal Problems* 139.

[73] '[T]he common lawyers and parliament perceived the design, and foresaw the consequences that might follow. Their opposition was steady and successful'. Sullivan supra n 21 at 181-82.

[74] Taylor, J (1755) *Elements of the Civil Law* Cambridge at 128, 133. A second edition (1769) and an abridged (1773) *Summary of the Roman law* [...] Printed for T Payne, were later published.

[75] Ibbetson, DJ (2001) 'Natural Law and Common Law' (5) *Edinburgh Law Review* 4 at 9.

in many of its parts, acquired among our European nations much of the precision and certainty of positive law' through the works of the continental natural lawyers.[76]

Contemporaneously, 'institutional' writings became important.[77] These were based on the simple, comprehensive structure of Justinian's *Institutes*, 'an epitome of the Digest' and 'shew[ed] an easy way to the obtaining a knowledge of the *Civil law*'.[78] They were generally written in the vernacular rather than in Latin and sought to rationalise existing laws or harmonise them into a common national law. Wood wrote *Institutes* of both civil and common law. While not the first, he noted in his 'An Institute of the Laws of England' that he

> *Entertained Hopes that Now It might not be Impossible to Sort, or to put in some Order, this heap of Good Learning; and that a General and Methodical Distribution, Preparatory to a more Large and Accurate Study of our Laws, might now be made [....]*[79]

Sir Matthew Hale (1609-76) and Gilbert each adopted variations on the institutional approach.[80] Other Englishmen drew on more contemporary continental developments. Sir Henry Finch (1558-1625), for example, utilised Ramist logic to organise English law in his *Nomotexnia* (c1585).[81] Throughout Europe and America, modern natural law and institutional writings provided a standard by which laws could be reformed or unified. Each weakened the *ius commune*, simplified education in the national laws, and, on the continent, prepared the way for later codifications.

This plurality of laws continued after the Interregnum and the 'Glorious Revolution' of 1688. But, by the end of the seventeenth century, the common law had clear priority over other internal laws and institutions. The prerogative courts were either restrained or, in the case of the courts of star chamber and requests, eliminated.[82] Common law and equity courts

[76] (1799) *Discourse on the Study of the Law of Nature and Nations* Printed for T Cadell, Jr and W Davies at 5.

[77] Luig, K (1972) 'The Institutes of National Law in the Seventeenth and Eighteenth Centuries' (17) *Juridical Review* (ns) 193. Coke borrowed the title, but little else, for his (1628-44) *Institutes*.

[78] Cunningham, T (1771) *A New and Complete Law Dictionary* [...] (2nd edn) His Majesty's law printers, under 'CIV'.

[79] (1720) *An Institute of the Laws of England; or, the Laws of England in their Natural Order* [...] E Nutt and R Goslin at ii.

[80] In Hale's (1713) *History and Analysis of the Common Law of England* (posthumously published) J Nutt, and Gilbert's unpublished treatise on English law (c1700) respectively.

[81] Prest, W (1977) 'The Dialectical Origins of Finch's Law' (36) *Cambridge Law Journal* 326.

82 The court of star chamber has long been a victim of whiggish history, but English

began to converge. The civilian jurisdictions, Hale wrote, were 'but *Leges sub graviori Lege*, and the Common Laws of this Kingdom have ever obtain'd and retain'd the Superintendency over them'.[83] Edward Bullingbrooke (?), LLD, was vicar-general of Armagh, and advocate in the Irish ecclesiastical and civilian courts. Of the former, he wrote that they were 'inferior branches of the customary law of the land, and may properly be called the king's ecclesiastical laws'.[84] The common law had established a clear priority over other jurisdictions. Common law judges even began to sit alongside the civilians in the admiralty courts and on the court of Delegates. These changes also made Roman and continental law less threatening and

> Civil law was openly and explicitly considered a source of jurisprudence for the common law—a philosophizing jurisprudence distinct from doctrine and thus different from jurisprudence as it existed on the continent. In this guise, the civil law and related national law gradually found a nonspecialized place in English legal thought that did not threaten English law or liberty and therefore could be broadly acknowledged and appreciated.[85]

Bever, for example, cited John Locke's (1632-1704) recommendation to read Hugo Grotius (1583-64) and Samuel Pufendorf (1632-94), 'the ornaments of the last century, [...] the fathers of modern jurisprudence.'[86]

Taylor's *Elements of the civil law* (1755) was a popular work on 'the *Common Law* of the *Romans*'.[87] It was 'meant to serve for an Introduction to the Study of the Civil Law; or rather, to contain the Principles of Law in general.'[88] In this equation of Roman law with perennial principles, its use appeared unavoidable. Similarly, the translator of Claude Joseph De Ferrière's (1680?-1748?) *History of the Roman or Civil law* (1724) claimed that it was a 'Treasure, [...] the most perfect Collection of Natural Reason and Equity, applied to all the various Transactions and Intercourses between

criminal law owes much to it in areas like conspiracy, contempt of court, perjury, fraud, and defamation. Barnes, TG (1961) 'Star Chamber Mythology' (5) *American Journal of Legal History* 1.

83 Hale supra n 80 at 44.

84 (1770) *Ecclesiastical Law; or, the Statutes, Constitutions, Canons, Rubricks, and Articles, of the Church of Ireland* Boulter Grierson at x. Bullingbrooke published an abridgement of Irish statutes and a work on the justices of the peace.

85 Hamburger, PA (1989) 'The development of the nineteenth-century consensus theory of contract' (7) *Law and History Review* 241 at 258.

86 Bever supra n 18 at 35 (footnote b). See Id. at 35-6.

87 Taylor supra n 74 at 145.

88 Id. at v.

Man and Man'.[89] This was not a view reserved to the Anglo-civilians. The popular author Giles Jacob (c1686-1744) wrote that 'no other Laws are esteem'd comparable to it for its Equity.'[90] Noted common lawyers like Sir John Holt (1642-1710), chief justice of king's bench, made similar remarks. 'Insomuch as the law of all nations are doubtless raised out of the ruins of the civil law [...]' he wrote, 'it must be assumed that the principles of our law are borrowed from the civil law'.[91] In discussing the law of nations, Chambers called on Grotius and Pufendorf, as well as Christian Wolff (1679-1754), Jean-Jacques Burlamaqui (1694-1748) and Emmerich de Vattel (1714-67).[92]

Although Wood, among others, had argued for university study of the common law, William Blackstone (1723-80) was the first such lecturer.[93] This jurist, legislator, and judge had, in fact, previously sought the Oxford professorship in civil law and had some familiarity with civilian doctrine. It has even been suggested that he 'was essentially a civilian and an academic'![94] His *Commentaries on the laws of England* (1765-9), based on his lectures, certainly borrowed institutional elements.[95] As a consequence, the clarity and comprehensiveness of the work served a code-like function and ironically helped insulate English law from further borrowing. It would be especially important in America given the scarcity of law reports. Referring to the civil law as 'a collection of written reason', Blackstone echoed his generation's belief in its place as an 'ornament to the scholar, the divine, the statesman, and even the common lawyer'.[96] In encouraging the study of English law, he wrote that

[89] (1724) *The History of the Roman or Civil law* [...] Printed for D Browne and F Clay, John Beaver (tr.) at A3. This included, without footnotes, a section on England from Duck's [1643] *De Usu Authoritate Juris Civilis Romananorum.*

[90] (1721) *A Treatise of Laws: or, a General Introduction to the Common, Civil, and Canon Law* Printed for T Woodward and J Peele at 244. Jacob wrote books on manorial law, statute law, public law, and a law dictionary. He also published (1725) *A Student's Companion: or, the Reason of the Laws of England* E Nutt, R Nutt, and R Gosling, and (1718) *Lex Mercatoria: or, the Merchant's Companion* E Nutt and R Gossling.

[91] *Lane v Sir Robert Cotton* (1701) 12 Mod Rep 482.

[92] Chambers supra n 20 at 83-94.

[93] (1708) *Some Thoughts Concerning the Study of the Laws of England in the Two Universities* J Morphew.

[94] Simpson, AWB [1981] 'The Rise and Fall of the Legal Treatise' in (1986) *Legal Theory and Legal History* Hambledon & London at 296.

[95] Cairns, JW (1984) 'Blackstone: an English Institutist: Legal Literature and the Rise of the Nation State' (4) *Oxford Journal of Legal Studies* 318; Watson, A (1988) 'The Structure of Blackstone's Commentaries' (97) *Yale Law Journal* 795.

[96] Blackstone supra n 59 at 5.

> These originals should be traced to their fountains, as well as our distance will permit; to the customs of the Britons and Germans, as recorded by Caesar and Tacitus; to the codes of the northern nations on the continent, and more especially to those of our own Saxon princes; to the rules of the Roman law, either left here in the days of Papinian, or imported by Vacarius and his followers; but, above all, to that inexhaustible reservoir of legal antiquities and learning, the feodal law, or, as Spelman has entitled it, the law of nations in our western orb. These primary rules and fundamental principles should be weighed and compared with the precepts of the law of nature, and the practice of other countries; should be explained by reasons, illustrated by examples, and confirmed by undoubted authorities; their history should be deduced, their changes and revolutions observed, and it should be shewn how far they are connected with, or have at any time been affected by the civil transactions of the kingdom.[97]

This from a whiggish and insular common lawyer.

Continental natural jurisprudence played an influential, if limited, role in every enlightened English lawyer's thought. In teaching English law, Wooddeson adopted the 'same threefold division which the Institutes of Justinian have taught us, and which appear [...] the most clear, and analytically just'.[98] In insisting that legal studies be rooted in moral philosophy, he wrote that

> it was not till within the two last centuries, that the fundamental principles of moral jurisprudence were duly investigated and embraced. Within that period the writings of Hooker, Cumberland, and Butler among our own countrymen; and among foreigners those of Grotius, Winkler, Pufendorf, Burlamaqui, Bynkershoëk, Barbeyrac, and Vattel have been received with very general and merited applause.[99]

The first Cambridge professor of common law, Edward Christian (c1758-1823), similarly reflected civilian influence. His elliptical *Syllabus; or, the heads of lectures ...* (1797), included a chapter on 'Civil and canon law' as well as a number of chapters on ecclesiastical matters.[100] At Oxford,

97 Id. at 35-36.

98 Wooddeson supra n 40 at 111.

99 Id. at 4.

100 (1797) *A Syllabus; or, the Heads of Lectures ...* Printed for J Butterworth, T Cadell, Jr, W

Robert Eden's (1701-1759) *Jurisprudentia philological sive elementa juris civilis, secundum methodum et seriem Institutionum Justininani* [...] (1744) was popular with students for decades.

English translations of continental texts were also common in the eighteenth century. Numerous others were accessible through Latin. George Harris (c1721-96), DCL, published a critical translation of the first book of Justinian's *Institutes*.[101] Early in the century, Wood translated part of the work of Jean Domat (1625-96).[102] Grotius and Pufendorf, too, were frequently translated.[103] The Scot George Turnball (1698-1748), translated Johann Gottlieb Heineccius (1683-1741).[104] Charles de Secondat, baron de Montesquieu's (1689-1755) *L'Esprit des lois* (1748) was extremely popular, both in French and through the English translation of Thomas Nugent (1700?-72). Among many other continental authors, the Irishman also translated the works of Burlamaqui.[105] The writings of Vattel, Frederick II of Prussia's (1712-86) code, and Cesare Beccaria's (1738-94) *Dei delitti e delle pene* (1764) were all translated at mid-century.[106] Gaetano Filangieri's (1752-88) treatise on the 'science of legislation' was translated in part in 1791. The complete extant text was available in English in 1806.[107]

THE DECLINE AND FALL OF THE ROMAN EMPIRE

Numerous eighteenth-century Anglophone authors were writing in this tradition, blending pan-European legal and moral philosophy. Many Scots were influential, including Gershom Carmichael (1672-1729) and Francis Hutcheson (1694-1746), the Irish 'father of the Scottish enlightenment'.[108]

Davies, and J Deighton at 5.

101 (1749) *D Justiniani Institutionum Liber Primus* Printed for J Millan.

102 Domat's (1680-94) *Les Loix Civiles dans leur Ordre Naturel, suives du Droit Public* was translated as (1705) *A Treatise of the First Principles of Laws in General* WB. Another translation, that of William Strahan (?-1748), was entitled (1722) *The Civil Law in its Natural Order* Bettenham.

103 See Stein, P (1980) *Legal Evolution: the Story of an Idea* Cambridge University Press at 3. A life of the Dutchman was translated from the French: de Burigny, JL (1765) *The life of the truly eminent and learned Hugo Grotius* Printed for A Millar, J Whiston, B White, and L Davis.

104 (1763) *A Methodical System of Universal Law* [...] Printed for G Keith, Turnbull, G (tr.).

105 (1748) *Principles of Natural Law* [...] J Nourse and (1752) *Principles of Politic law* [...] J Nourse.

106 Vattel, E (1759) *Law of Nations; or Principles of the Law of Nature Applied to the Conduct and Affairs of Nations and Sovereigns* J Coote; (1761) *The Frederician Code; or, a Body of Laws for the Dominions of the King of Prussia* (2 vols, translated from the French) A Donaldson and J Reid; (1767) *An essay on crimes and punishments* (with a commentary attributed to Voltaire) J Almon.

107 (1791) *Analysis of the Science of Legislation* [...] Printed for GGJ and J Robinson, Kendall, W (tr.) and (1806) *The Science of Legislation* Emery and Adams, Clayton, R (tr., 1745-1828).

108 Carmichael published translations of Pufendorf with extensive commentary in 1718 and 1724. Hutcheson's (1747) *Short introduction to moral philosophy* R Foulis, was published

One of England's best-known moral philosophers, Thomas Rutherford's (1712-71) most important publication was an institutional work based on Grotius.[109] Edward Gibbon (1737-94) relied, in part, on Heineccius for the famous forty-fourth chapter (on Roman jurisprudence) of his *The decline and fall of the Roman empire* in six volumes (1776-88). William Paley's (1743-1805) *Principles of moral and political philosophy* (1788) was also extremely popular. Paley, DD, served as chancellor of the diocese of Carlisle and a justice of the peace; his work discusses moral obligations, property, contracts, crimes, and 'civil government'. Alexander Crowcher Schomberg (1756-92), poet and jurist, wrote on Roman and maritime law.[110] Robert (Plumer) Ward (1765-1846) studied at Oxford and in France. He practiced briefly as a barrister, wrote a work on the law of nations, was subsequently an MP, served as a sheriff, and wrote novels.[111]

It is difficult to plot the 'penetration and resistance' of civilian influence. Eighteenth-century lawyers were themselves of different minds. It was generally conceded that common lawyers were 'indebted to [civilians] chiefly for systematical schemes'.[112] Ayliffe wrote that the common law 'originally gave no methodical Account of Things purely rational, as of Obligations, Contracts, Crimes, Trespasses, Last Wills and Testaments, and the like.'[113] Wooddeson 'quoted rules for the interpreting of laws, which seem' he said 'evidently taken from the Civilians.'[114] Indeed, the *ius commune* and the canon law were both important, as '[v]irtually all of the thirty-six Latin-language maxims on law and on statutory interpretation extracted by Thomas Wood from Sir Edward Coke's Reports and Institutes are readily traced to these sources, or directly to Justinian's codification.'[115] Wood's argument about continental influence was strong:

> [I]f there is that wide difference between the Common and Civil Laws in their forms of Pleading and manner of Tryal, this is only

posthumously.

[109] (1754-56) *Institutes of Natural Law being the Substance of a Course of Lectures on Grotius de jure belli et pacis* […] J Bentham.

[110] (1785) *An Historical and Chronological View of Roman law* Oxford University Press, subsequently translated into French, and (1786) *A Treatise on the Maritime Laws of Rhodes* Oxford University Press.

[111] (1795) *An Enquiry into the Foundation and History of the Law of Nations* […] *to the Age of Grotius* P Wogan, P Byrne, W Jones, and J Rice.

[112] Chambers supra n 20 at 119. Bever noted the 'peculiarly scientifical cast of the civil law', supra n 11 at 24.

[113] Ayliffe supra n 12 at xlvii.

[114] Wooddeson supra n 40 at 85.

[115] Baade, H (1994) 'The Casus Omissus: a Pre-History of Statutory Analogy' (20) *Syracuse Journal of International Law and Commerce* 45 at 92.

> the stile, practice, and course of the Courts. I contend that there is a mixture in the *Principles, Maxims* and *Reasons* of these two Laws; and indeed the Laws of all Countries are mixed with the Civil Law, which have arrived to any degree of perfection. [...] True it is that the Common and Civil Laws had not the same Root or Stock; yet by Inoculating and Grafting, the Body and Branches do seem at this day to be almost of a Piece.[116]

Wood explicitly borrowed John Selden's (1584-1654) famous image of English law as the ship of the Argonauts, in which it remains essentially the same while constantly changing. He continued by adding, '[u]pon a Review, I think it may be maintain'd, that a great part of the Civil Law, is part of the Law of *England*, and interwoven with it throughout.'[117]

In the eighteenth century, the distance between judicial methodologies on either side of the English Channel was not so great as it was to become.[118] In England, '[t]he theory was that the court should look to the reason of the precedent, the principle behind the rule.'[119] They were not, strictly speaking, binding. In fact:

> *Judicial decisions*, or determinations of the courts of justice [...] altho' by virtue of the laws of this realm they bind as a law between the parties thereto, as to the particular case in question, until reversed by writ of error; yet do not make a law properly so called (for that only the king and parliament can do): yet they have a great weight and authority in expounding, declaring, and publishing what the law of this kingdom is; especially when such decisions hold a consonancy and congruity with resolutions and decisions of former times.[120]

Wood noted, however, that English law reports 'are as highly valued as the *Responsa Prudentum* amongst the Romans to be found in the *Digest*, which are *Authoritative*.'[121] Indeed, Ayliffe criticises the growing importance of past decisions as effectively making 'every Judge [...] a Law-giver, by drawing the Law *de Similibus ad Similia*, as he fancies'.[122]

116 Wood supra n 49 at xi-xii.
117 Id. at xii.
118 Gorla, G and Moccia, L (1981) 'A "Revisiting" of the Comparison between "Continental Law" and "English Law" (16th-19th Century)' (2) *Journal of Legal History* 143.
119 Lobban, M (1991) *The common law and English jurisprudence 1760-1850* Oxford University Press at 86.
120 Burn supra n 11 at xxv.
121 Wood supra n 79 at 16.
122 Ayliffe supra n 12 at 8.

In eighteenth-century England, reception was, at least in one area, a common theme. As Browne put it, 'the debt of our code to the civil, is most conspicuously shewn in the branch of title arising from contract.'[123] William Murray, Lord Mansfield (1705-93), perhaps the most famous British lawyer of the century, was both criticised and celebrated for borrowing from the civil law and *lex mercatoria*.[124] The Scots' jurisprudence contributed to the incorporation of the principles of the law merchant and the law of nations into English commercial law.[125] In this, he was not entirely novel. Mansfield followed Holt, among others, in arguing in *Pillan v Van Mierop* that '[t]he law of merchants and the law of the land is the same'.[126] Sir John Eardley Wilmot's (1709-92) opinion in the same case even more explicitly relied on civilian authorities. The Welsh legal comparativist William Jones (1746-94) argued, in fact, for the basic similarity of much of English and Roman law. A graduate of Oxford and the Middle Temple, he wrote that 'a perfect harmony subsists on this interesting branch of jurisprudence in the codes of nations most eminent for legal writers, particularly of the ROMANS and the ENGLISH.'[127] The work of the French jurist Robert Joseph Pothier (1699-1772) on obligations was utilised extensively in England, both in the original and the early nineteenth century translation. His English translator cites Jones' suggestion that 'the greatest portion of which is law at *Westminster* as well as at *Orleans*'.[128]

The Anglo-civilians still practiced, published, and played an important role in public life. If out of necessity, they wished only 'to live in perfect amity with her sister profession'.[129] Sir George Hay (1715-78), DCL, became an MP, the king's advocate-general, and vicar-general to the archbishop of Canterbury. There were also numerous practical works on admiralty and the ecclesiastical courts.[130] Both still played important roles. The

[123] Browne supra n 25 at i. 35. See gen. Ibbetson (1999) *A Historical Introduction to the Law of Obligations* Oxford University Press.

[124] For the previous century, see Coquillette, DR (1981) 'Legal Ideology and Incorporation II: Sir Thomas Ridley, Charles Molloy, and the Literary Battle for the Law Merchant, 1607-1676' (61) *Boston University Law Review* 315. Molloy's (1645/6-90) (1676) *De Jure Maritime et Navali: or a Treatise of Affairs Maritime, and of Commerce* was repeatedly reprinted in the eighteenth century.

[125] Rodgers, CP(1987) 'Continental Literature and the Development of the Common Law by the King's Bench: c1750-1800' in Piergiovanni, V (ed.) *The Courts and the Development of Commercial Law* Dunckler & Humblot.

[126] 3 Burr 1669.

[127] Jones, W (1781) *On the Law of Bailments* J Nichols at 11.

[128] (1802) *A Treatise on Obligations Considered in a Moral and Legal View* Martin & Ogden in the preface (citing Jones).

[129] Bever supra n 18 at 29.

[130] Eg, Cockburn, W (1753) *The clerk's assistant in the practice of the ecclesiastical courts ...* Printed for R Main; Watts, R (1757) *The practice of the court of admiralty in England and Ireland*

admiralty court was, Browne wrote, governed by 'those parts of the civil law which treat of maritime affairs, blended with other maritime laws; the whole corrected, altered, and amended, by acts of parliament and common usage.'[131] He acknowledged debts to Mansfield and to the 'eminent judge who now presides in the English high court of admiralty', Sir William Scott, Lord Stowell (1745-1836), DCL.[132] A graduate of the Middle Temple, Stowell was advocate-general, MP, judge of the high court of admiralty, and privy councillor. Into the following century, his reputation would rival Mansfield's. An Irish almanac of 1794 noted that the ecclesiastical courts took

> cognizance, and give sentence on Ordinations, institution of Clerks to Benefices, celebration of Divine Service, and all that relate to Churches, Matrimonial Rights, Divorces, Bastardy, Probate and Administration of Wills, Simony, Blasphemy, Adultries, Incests, Fornications, and Defamation.[133]

With Burn and Browne, Edmund Gibson (c1669-1748), bishop of Lincoln and later London, and Thomas Oughton (1660-?), proctor and registrar of the court of delegates, each published important works on ecclesiastical law.[134]

With many contemporaries, Mansfield recommended that English law students study continental texts.[135] Many of the Anglo-civilians retained links to the universities, though legal education there was not thriving and 'study had declined.'[136] But this was truer still of the Inns of the period. Professorships of civil law, as with others, were often nominal appointments and commitment to teaching varied extensively. Some were noteworthy. Oxford's French Laurence (1757-1809), a protégé of Edmund Burke (c1730-97), participated in the impeachment of Warren Hastings (1732-1818), and was one of the Irishman's literary executors. He was also an MP and a judge

Printed for R Watts.

131 Browne supra n 25 at ii.34.

132 Id. at ii.43.

133 (1794) *The City and County Calendar or Irish Court Registry for the Year of Our lord 1794* [...] N Kelly. A list of courts, judges, and advocates is included in *Ibid.* at 135-8. Cf (1794) *The Treble Almanac* [...] Printed for S Watson and T Stewart at 61-2.

134 The (1713) *Codex Juris Ecclesiastici Anglicani* J Baskett and (1728) *Ordo Judiciorum* J Hooke respectively.

135 (1797) *A Treatise on the Study of the Law: Containing, Directions to Students, Written by those Celebrated Lawyers, Orators, and Statesmen; the Lords Mansfield, Ashburton, and Thurlow* [...] Printed for Harrison, Cluse, and Co. at 49.

136 Bever supra n 18 at 28.

of the court of admiralty of the cinque ports. Even the young Burke had noted, at mid-century, the hybrid nature of English law:

> the truth is, the present system of our laws, like our language and our learning, is a very mixed and heterogeneous mass, in some respects our own; in more borrowed from the policy of foreign nations, and compounded, altered, and variously modified, according to the various necessities which the manners, the religion, and the commerce of the people have at different times imposed.[137]

The Irishman, a student of both Trinity College, Dublin and the Middle Temple, made similar remarks throughout his career.[138] Arthur Browne, Burke's friend and correspondent, wrote more specifically that 'much of the civil law ... was incorporated with our own, though by long use the debt is forgotten, and we are apt to consider it as part of our original stock.'[139] And, like Browne, other Anglo- and Hiberno-civilians were important to law and politics. Joseph Jowett (1751-1813), LLD, of Cambridge gained attention for his comparison of the Roman and English law. Dublin's Patrick Duigenan (1734/5-1816), LLD, was a particularly boorish protestant bigot, but served at various times in the metropolitan court of Armagh, the consistorial court of Dublin, the diocesan courts of Meath and Elphin, and as judge of the Irish prerogative court.[140]

The eventual victory of the common lawyers and the either/or nature of much comparative law has seriously distorted the complexity of England's legal past. 'Legal history is winner's history'.[141] Many ideas and institutions seen to exemplify the 'common law' are quite recent developments, not least the modern Anglo-American advocate-led adversarial criminal trial. For centuries, criminal cases were dominated by the judges and juries heard numerous cases very rapidly. The introduction of counsel in the eighteenth century, however, altered trial dynamics considerably.[142] The

[137] Burke, E [c1757] 'Fragment.—An Essay Towards an History of the Law of England' in Langford, P (gen ed) (1997) *The Writings and Speeches of Edmund Burke* (10 vols) Oxford University Press at i.325.

[138] See Donlan (2003) '"A Very Mixed and Heterogeneous Mass": Edmund Burke and English Jurisprudence, 1757-62' (4) *University of Limerick Law Review* 79 and (2001) '"Beneficence Acting by a Rule": Edmund Burke on Law, History, and Manners' (36) *Irish Jurist* (ns) 227.

[139] Browne supra n 25 at i.12-13.

[140] See generally the anonymously published (1804) *Sketches of the Lives and Characters of Eminent English Civilians* G Kearsley, by Charles Coote (c1760-1835), DCL and judge of the court of delegates.

[141] Helmholz, RH (1987) *Canon law and the law of England* Hambledon Press at 1.

[142] Beattie, JM (1991) 'Scales of Justice: Defense Counsel and the English Criminal Trial in the Eighteenth and Nineteenth Centuries' (9) *Law and History Review* 221.

lawyer-centred oral and adversarial trial before a jury brought about the complex law of evidence, the 'beyond-reasonable-doubt' standard, and the rhetorical excesses that still mark Anglo-American law. In fact,

> [t]he broad similarity between the historic common law criminal procedure and the modern Continental procedure should serve to remind us that adversary procedure cannot be defended as part of our historic common law bequest. The criminal lawyer and the complex procedures that have grown up to serve him and to contain him are historical upstarts.[143]

Similarly, principles like the presumption of innocence and the privilege of self-incrimination also have European origins.[144]

There were also England's *iura propria*, its numerous jurisdictions beyond or below the 'superior' courts.[145] If we only use Chambers' account, the courts of justice at mid-century (c1767-73) included: parliament, the privy council, the lords and the court of the lord high steward, chancery, king's bench, common pleas, exchequer, exchequer chamber (of various sorts), circuit or assize courts, the session of justices of the peace (quarter sessions), county courts, the sheriff's torn court, the manorial courts of leet and baron, coroner's court, the courts of weights and measures, and the fair courts of piepowder.[146] Even this list is not comprehensive. There existed, too, counties palantine, providing varying levels of legal autonomy, as well as the Isle of Man and the Channel islands. Numerous 'courts of requests' created by statute served as small claims courts, as did a wide variety of borough courts. Many of these were administered in a summary manner by men untrained in the law, common or otherwise. There was considerable discretion and little precedent. Frequently lacking a record of their activities, the equitable 'law' they applied was ephemeral. Here especially, the 'often contradictory systems of normative ordering' that existed could easily trespass on the motivations and decisions of the courts.[147]

143 Langbein, JH (1977-78) 'The Criminal Trial before the Lawyers' (45) *University of Chicago Law Review* 263.

144 Pennington, K (2001) 'Innocent Until Proven Guilty: the Origins of a Legal Maxim' in Maffei, D (ed) *A Ennio Cotese: Tomo III* Il Cigno Galileo Galilei; and Macnair, MRT (1990) 'The Early Development of the Privilege Against Self-Incrimination' *Oxford Journal of Legal Studies* 66.

145 For Ireland, see Brown, M and Donlan, 'The Laws in Ireland, 1789-1850: A Brief Introduction' in Brown and Donlan (eds) (forthcoming 2010) *Law and the Irish, 1689-1848: Power, Privilege and Practice* Ashgate.

146 Chambers supra n 20 at 217-26.

147 King, P (1989) 'Gleaners, farmers and the failure of legal sanctions in England 1750-1850' (125) *Past and Present* 116 at 146.

A VERY MIXED AND HETEROGENEOUS MASS

Esin Örücü has made fine distinctions, and employed colourful culinary metaphors, in analysing the balance of elements in specific mixed legal traditions: e.g., 'mixing bowls', 'salad bowls', 'salad plates', purées, etc.[148] But for both English and continental legal traditions in the nineteenth century, 'sausage-making' may be more apt. Considerable change came to Europe's legal ideas and institutions in the aftermath of the revolution in France. The hybridity that had characterised its *ancien régimes* was significantly altered by the legal unity of the modern state and nationalism.[149] The focus on legal positivism, on law-making and legal clarity, was linked to the new powers of the state and demands for popular accountability. In continental law, this was expressed in legislation, often codes, and exegetical interpretation. In English law, it corresponded with British parliamentary supremacy and the rise of statute law. Law reporting improved. A clearer appellate hierarchy of courts was established with professional Law Lords at their head. Precedent hardened into *stare decisis.* A new focus on substantive, rather than procedural, law emerged. And, along with the Act of Union of Britain and Ireland in 1800, the final absorption or 'suffusion' of England's civilian, ecclesiastical, and equity jurisdictions occurred. In this internal convergence and national divergence, we might argue that the various elements of English law were ground and pressed into a single casing.

The metaphor of 'sausage-making' obviously brings to mind the comment, attributed to Bismark, that 'the less the people know about how sausages and laws are made, the better they sleep'. This admonition cannot, however, apply to comparatists. Legal history is essential to their work. The legal hybridity and diffusion of European legal history has significant implications for modern law, challenging the conjoined ideas of legal centralism and monism, nationalism, and positivism.[150] Europe's multifarious legal traditions were forever in motion towards new permutations and equilibria. If the triumphalist dominance of its 'common

[148] For the conceptual complexity and sophistication of these discussions, see Örücü, E (1996)'Mixed and Mixing Systems: a Conceptual Search' in Örücü, E, Attwooll, E and Coyle, S (eds) *Studies in Legal Systems: Mixed and Mixing* Kluwer Law International.

[149] 'The new, unified national laws were not suppletive; they were binding, and purported to obliterate local particularity.' Glenn (1987) 'Persuasive Authority' (32) *McGill Law Journal/ Revue de Droit de McGill* 261 at 279.

[150] 'This awareness should also make us more sensitive to hybridity worldwide. 'Scholars who study the one could learn from those who study the other, and vice versa.' Heirbaut, D (2008) 'Europe and the people without legal history: on the need for a general history of non-European law' (68) *Tijdschrift voor Rechtsgeschiendenis* 269 at 277.

law' often obscures English legal hybridity and diffusion, this kaleidoscopic motion was, and is, no less true of the Anglo-American legal traditions.

Mixed Jurisdictions: Lessons for European Harmonisation?

JAN M SMITS

INTRODUCTION

There are several reasons for the renewed interest in mixed jurisdictions.[1] Apart from the general academic climate, becoming more and more favourable towards comparative law,[2] and the interest of jurists in the mixed systems themselves,[3] mixed jurisdictions are often said to offer an example for the future European harmonisation of private law. The idea itself seems appealing enough: if a new private law for the European Union is to come about, it will necessarily have to be a mixture of both the civil law and the common law traditions and therefore it may be useful to look at the experience of mixed jurisdictions such as Scotland, South Africa, Quebec and Louisiana.[4] In this contribution, the thesis is discussed with a special focus on the specific *lessons* we may learn in Europe from the experience of mixed jurisdictions.

[1] For an elaborate overview of this renewed interest and the reasons for it: Reid, KGC (2003) 'The Idea of Mixed Legal Systems' (78) *Tulane Law Review* 5 at 17 ff. Also see Du Plessis, J (2006) 'Comparative Law and the Study of Mixed Legal Systems' in: Reimann, M and Zimmermann, R (eds) *The Oxford Handbook of Comparative Law* OUP 477 ff.

[2] For instance see the interest in mixed systems expressed in Reimann, M and Zimmermann, R (eds) (2006) *The Oxford Handbook of Comparative Law*, Smits, JM (ed) (2006) *Elgar Encyclopedia of Comparative Law* and Örücü, E and Nelken, D (eds) (2007) *Comparative Law: A Handbook* Hart.

[3] Cf. e.g. Palmer, VV (ed) (2001) *Mixed Jurisdictions Worldwide: The Third Legal Family* CUP, and Zimmermann, R and Visser, D and Reid, K (eds) (2004) *Mixed Legal Systems in Comparative Perspective* OUP.

[4] Cf. Smits, JM (2002) *The Making of European Private Law* Intersentia; id, (2001) 'Introduction: Mixed Legal Systems and European Private Law' in Smits, JM (ed) *The Contribution of Mixed Legal Systems to European Private Law* Intersentia 1 ff.

After a short discussion of the standard view of the experiences mixed systems have to offer the European Union (section 2), this article identifies the specific framework in which the experience of mixed systems is useful for the European harmonisation process (section 3). Subsequently, the main part of this article consists of a discussion of three debated aspects of this experience (sections 4-6).

THE STANDARD VIEW

The idea of mixed jurisdictions as models for a future European private law is not new. Already in 1924, the French comparative lawyer Lévy-Ullmann noted that 'Scots law gives us a picture of what will be some day [...] the law of the civilised nations, namely a combination between the Anglo-Saxon and the continental system.'[5] It is no surprise that, with the present efforts to create a more common private law for the European Union, this idea has found new grounds among comparative lawyers.[6] If a possible connection between the civil law and common law is already established in mixed systems, these systems may provide a 'wealth of experience'[7] of how these two legal traditions may be accommodated in the framework of the European Union.

There is a good reason why this traditional view of looking at mixed systems has attracted so much interest. The view is usually put in such general terms that it is difficult *not* to agree with it: it leaves open the question, 'What type of experience can one draw from in looking at mixed jurisdictions? Is it that the legal method used by mixed jurisdictions jurists is superior to that of jurists in either civil law or common law countries? Is it the substantive law that may offer fruitful insights? Or is it more the *negative* experience of mixed systems we can learn from in Europe? The latter may be the right conclusion if one focuses on what the process of 'critical picking and choosing'[8] from both legal traditions led to in some areas of Scots and South-African laws. In particular among Scots lawyers, it

[5] Lévy-Ullmann, H (2006) 'The Law of Scotland' (37) *Juridical Review* 390. Cf. MacQueen, HL (2000) 'Scots Law and the Road to the New Ius Commune' *Ius Commune Lectures on European Private Law* 1, METRO, 2.

[6] Zweigert, K and Kötz, H (1998) *Introduction to Comparative Law* 3rd ed. OUP 204; MacQueen, supra n 5.

[7] Reid, K and Zimmermann, R (2000) 'The Development of Legal Doctrine in a Mixed System' in Reid, K and Zimmermann, R (eds) *A History of Private Law in Scotland* OUP 2000, Vol. 1, 3.

[8] Lord Cooper of Culross (1957) 'The Importance of Comparative Law in Scotland', in his *Selected Papers 1922-1954*, 145.

is debated whether Scots law is not more of a muddle than an optimal mix of the best ingredients of the two great legal traditions.[9]

This open-endedness of the idea of mixed systems as a model for Europe makes it an attractive view for several strands of thought in the debate about European harmonisation of private law. Those who are in favour of a top-down approach by way of enacting a European Civil Code can for example point at similarities in substance between several sets of principles of private law (or even the future Common Frame of Reference as envisaged by the European Commission[10]). Apparently, the drafters of some of these instruments were partly inspired by Scots law.[11] But the idea also appeals to those who favour a bottom up approach towards legal harmonisation: they can point at the importance of a legal system growing in an organic way, as Scots and South African laws have done to a large extent in the past. It will become clear in the next section of this article that this bottom up perspective fits in best with attaching importance to the experiences of mixed jurisdictions.

The above should make us realise that when we try to draw lessons from the development of mixed systems, we are to turn away from generalities and ask in more detail what we can learn *exactly* from the experiences of mixed systems. This, however, does suggest a specific view of the harmonisation process. This view is set out in the next section.

EUROPEAN HARMONISATION: WHERE DOES THE EXPERIENCE OF MIXED SYSTEMS FIT IN?

There is no lack of opinions on how to establish a more uniform private law for the European Union.[12] It is clear that not all of these take the same stance towards the experience to be drawn from mixed jurisdictions. If one does not believe in the feasibility of European legal convergence or disputes the

[9] Cf. Rodger, A (1996) 'Thinking about Scots Law' (1) *Edinburgh Law Review* 3; Whitty, N (1996) 'The civilian tradition and debates on Scots law' *Tydskrif vir die Suid-Afrikaanse Reg* 227 and 442 and in particular, Evans-Jones, R (1998) 'Receptions of Law, Mixed Legal Systems and the Myth of the Genius of Scots Private Law' (114) *Law Quarterly Review* 228 ff.

[10] See Communication from the Commission to the European Parliament and the Council, *A More Coherent Contract Law – An Action Plan*, COM (2003) 68 final, *OJ EC* 2003, C 63/01.

[11] See for such similarities MacQueen, supra n 5. In particular the PECL and the PETL were inspired by Scots law, See Lando, O and Beale, H (eds) (2000) *Principles of European Contract Law, Parts I and II* Kluwer; Lando, O, Clive, E, Prüm, A and Zimmermann, R (eds) (2003) *Principles of European Contract Law, Part III* Kluwer; Hayton, DT, Kortmann, SCJJ and Verhagen, HLE (eds) (1999) *Principles of European Trust Law* Kluwer.

[12] For a short overview: Smits, J (2007)'Convergence of Private Law in Europe: Towards a New Ius Commune' in Örücü, E and Nelken, D (eds) *Comparative Law: a Handbook* Hart 219 ff.

unifying effect of legal transplants,[13] one considers things differently than if one thinks highly of centralist European intervention to protect the weaker party in the European marketplace.[14] Also the drafting of coherent sets of European principles[15] seems to be at odds with attaching importance to the organic legal development mixed jurisdictions are known for.

The view of European harmonisation most compatible with attaching importance to the experience of mixed systems seems to be the one that takes jurisdictional competition as a starting point. In the original version of jurisdictional competition as put forward by the American author Charles Tiebout,[16] each jurisdiction is governed by the preferences of its citizens. As preferences among citizens may differ, competition among several jurisdictions is likely to emerge: consumers and firms will leave the jurisdiction they dislike ('vote with their feet') in favour of the jurisdiction they find more attractive. This means that national governments are stimulated to make their jurisdiction as attractive as possible.

Jurisdictional competition is said to have two advantages over centralist lawmaking. First, it allows experiment: looking at other countries' solutions to legal problems shows whether or not these solutions function in any way. In this respect States can indeed be seen as 'experimenting laboratories'.[17] It is likely that these types of experiments will lead to innovation: countries that see how certain legal rules and solutions are successful abroad will be tempted to adopt these for their own citizens. Second, jurisdictional competition allows the satisfaction of diverging preferences. Centralist lawmaking would reduce this. But unlike the case in the original Tiebout thesis, jurisdictional competition need not take the form of people actually moving *physically* to another jurisdiction. Competition among legal systems can also take place in a less expensive way, namely by a *choice of law* for a

[13] Legrand, P (1997) 'The Impossibility of Legal Transplants' (4) *Maastricht Journal of European and Comparative Law* 111 ff.

[14] Mattei, U (2003) 'Hard Code Now! A Critique and a Plea for Responsibility in the European Debate over Codification' in id, *The European Codification Process: Cut and Paste* 107 ff.

[15] Study Group on a European Civil Code (2006) *Principles of European Law* Sellier.

[16] Tiebout, C (1956) 'A Pure Theory of Local Expenditures' (64) *Journal of Political Economy* 416 ff. Also see Ogus, A (1999) 'Competition between national legal systems: a contribution of economic analysis to comparative law' (48) *International and Comparative Law Quarterly* 405 ff. and Wagner, G (2005) 'The Virtues of Diversity in European Private Law' in Smits, J (ed) *The Need for a European Contract Law* Europa Law Publishing 5 ff.

[17] Brandeis, L, in *New State Ice Co. v. Liebmann*, 285 U.S. 262: 'To stay experimentation in things social and economic is a grave responsibility. Denial of the right to experiment may be fraught with serious consequences to the Nation. It is one of the happy incidents of the federal system that a single courageous State may, if its citizens choose, serve as a laboratory; and try novel social and economic experiments without risk to the rest of the country.' Cf. Hayek, FA (1968) 'Der Wettbewerb als Entdeckungsverfahren', *Kieler Vorträge N.S. 56*.

specific jurisdiction (such as English law or the law of the state of Delaware). In contract and company law, this choice of law can be usually made by the parties.[18] And in so far as national legislators or courts decide to take over law of foreign origin – as happened on a large scale in mixed systems – this also fits in with the Tiebout thesis: the preferences satisfied are then simply those of the national legislators, courts and other '*Rechtshonoratioren*.'[19]

There is still one other aspect in which the theory of Tiebout should be amended to fit the experience of the mixed jurisdictions. Both in the original Tiebout thesis and in the variant in which not so much the citizens as the law itself moves, it is the *entire* legal system that is chosen as the relevant law. But it is paradigmatic for mixed systems that they take over only *parts* of the law existing elsewhere, subsequently adapting these parts to their own needs. Typically, areas such as procedural law and trust law are taken from the common law tradition, whereas others (like property law) are based more on the civil law. This important characteristic of mixed jurisdictions is formulated well by Derek van der Merwe:[20]

> [T]he legal practitioner in a "mixed" (or "hybrid") legal system is an instinctive eclectic: he or she will seek authority in the grand manner, the process of distilling legal wisdom largely uninhibited by rigid doctrinal boundaries. Such a state of mind is conducive to an unfussy flexibility in the application of the law.

In my view, the theoretical framework of jurisdictional competition explains best the development of mixed jurisdictions. I am also a fierce proponent of the idea that the private law of the European Union should develop along the same lines.[21] It is here that we can learn from mixed systems: they offer experience on how courts and legislators are able to make use of materials of both the civil and the common law tradition.[22] At the same time, we should not forget that this selection process – how to make the right choices out of a plurality of different sources – is not

[18] In the European Union within the limits set by the Convention on the law applicable to contractual obligations (Rome 1980), *OJ EC* 1998, C 27/34 and by the *Centros* case (ECJ 9 March 1999, Case C-212/97, *ECR* 1999-I, 1459).

[19] Cf. Rheinstein, M (1970) 'Die Rechtshonoratioren und ihr Einfluss auf Charakter und Funktion der Rechtsordnungen' *Rabels Zeitschrift* Mohr Siebeck1 ff.

[20] Van der Merwe, D (1996) 'Property in Mixed Legal Systems: South Africa' in Van Maanen, G and Van der Walt, A (eds) *Property Law on the Threshold of the 21st Century* 356 ff.

[21] Smits, JM (2006) 'European private law: a plea for a spontaneous legal order' in Curtin, DM, Smits, JM et al, *European Integration and Law* Intersentia 55 ff.

[22] Also see Reid, supra 1 at 26: the experience lies not so much in new substantive law, but in lessons for 'selection, combination, and rationalization of existing rules drawn from a variety of sources.'

unproblematic. In the following sections, three different problems are discussed.

HOW TO FIND THE 'BEST' RULES?

One of the most problematic aspects of lawmaking in mixed jurisdictions is that the supposedly superior way of creating a legal system – by critically picking and choosing the 'best rules' from a plurality of sources – is not properly applied in practice. Both Scots and South-African laws are examples of where sometimes the wrong choices were made by the courts, thus posing a threat to the quality of these legal systems.[23]

The main reason for this problem seems to be that mixed systems often show a bias towards one legal tradition or the other. Both in Scotland and South Africa, there have been strong 'purist' tendencies to preserve and reinforce the civil law element at the expense of common law influence.[24] One well-known example from South-African law is the case *Regal v. African Superslate (Pty.) Ltd.*,[25] in which the Appellate Division of the Supreme Court replaced the doctrine of nuisance (that had been well-established for over 80 years) by the fragmentary Roman-Dutch law on rights of neighbours. In doing so, the court considered it a pity that there were so few rules in the relevant Roman-Dutch law, but that they would then simply have to be developed. But also the opposite happened: in some areas of Scots law (notably in the law on unjust enrichment[26]), there was common law influence precisely because little was known about the civil law approach: with better access to civil law materials, the law would probably have looked quite different.

Can we draw any lessons from this for the European harmonisation process? One lesson seems to be that any bias towards one legal system or the other should be avoided. At the same time, we should submit that this is not unproblematic within the European Union. Unlike the case in mixed systems, there is no natural tendency among national courts and legislators in Europe to look abroad for comparative inspiration, even though this has improved over the last decade.[27] One cannot really blame the national

[23] Cf. Rodger, A (1997)'The Use of the Civil Law in Scottish Courts' in Carey Miller, D and Zimmermann, R (eds) *The Civilian Tradition and Scots Law* Duncker & Humblot at 225. Also see Du Plessis, J (1998) 'The Promises and Pitfalls of Mixed Legal Systems: the South African and Scottish Experiences' (9) *Stellenbosch Law Review* 338.

[24] See in more detail Smits (2002) supra n 4 at 125 ff.

[25] 1963 1 *SA* 102 (AD).

[26] Evans-Jones, supra n 9 at 236 ff.

[27] See in more detail Smits, JM (2006) 'Comparative Law and Its Influence on National Legal Systems' in Reimann, M and Zimmermann, R (eds) *The Oxford Handbook of Comparative Law* OUP 513 ff.

institutions for this: the necessary prerequisite for better comparatively informed national judiciaries and legislators is the emergence of a transnational academic dialogue.[28] This dialogue has not developed yet but as soon as it has, substantive arguments in favour and against certain outcomes will be similar across the European Union. This does not mean national legislation or outcomes of concrete cases will be the same: when it comes to weighing the relevant arguments, every legal system has to make its own choice. In the *McFarlane* case, Lord Steyn put it like this: 'The discipline of comparative law does not aim at a poll of solutions adopted in different countries. It has the different and inestimable value of sharpening our focus on the weight of competing considerations.'[29]

HOW TO KEEP THE LAW COHERENT?

A second problem related to lawmaking in mixed jurisdictions, is how to keep the law coherent. When choosing from different sources – as mixed jurisdictions have done in the past extensively – a lack of coordination in selecting the proper rules may cause the law to become incoherent. Any legal system is in need of some mechanism by which the law is made coherent. In civil law systems, both the national legislator and legal science have a key role in ensuring this coherence, whereas in the common law this is mainly achieved by the system of precedent. Mixed systems have sometimes fallen pray to a lack of such coordination in their formative stage. Thus, in South-African law and Scots law, the exact place of *stare decisis* and the role of academia were for a long time not clear.[30]

At the same time, this problem of coherence should not be exaggerated. In the law of obligations, the civil law and common law approaches often do not contradict but rather supplement each other. The South-African law of delict is a wonderful example of this: it accepts the general liability for wrongful acts in delict, while at the same time it recognises the importance of identifying specific manifestations of delictual behaviour. The generalising civil law approach thus goes hand in hand with the

[28] Cf. Zimmermann, R (1997) 'The Civil Law in European Codes' in Carey Miller, D and Zimmermann, R (eds) *The Civilian Tradition and Scots Law* Duncker & Humblot 293: 'the essential prerequisite for a truly European private law would appear to be the emergence of an "organically progressive" legal science, which would have to transcend the national boundaries and to revitalize a common tradition.' Also see Glenn, HP (2003) 'Mixing It Up' (78) *Tulane Law Review* 79 ff.

[29] *McFarlane v. Tayside Health Board*, 2000 SC (HL) 15 per Lord Steyn.

[30] Cf. Visser, D (1997) 'Placing the Civilian Influence in Scotland: A Roman-Dutch Perspective' in Carey Miller, D and Zimmermann, R (eds) *The Civilian Tradition and Scots Law* Duncker & Humblot 49, who mentions a constant 'concern for coherence' in South-African law.

simultaneous recognition of specific torts as we know it from the common law.[31] Such co-existence can also be found in the field of contract law and in the field of trusts and covenants. Acceptance of truly alien elements is far more exceptional. One recent example is the Scots case of *Sharp v. Thomson*,[32] in which the House of Lords imported a common law idea into the essentially Romanist system of Scots property law.

Also at the European level, the problem of incoherence resulting from consulting different sources should not be overstated. A transnational legal debate does not mean that rules from one jurisdiction can simply be imported into another. Instead, the debate should take place at the level of *arguments*. The only useful convergence of private law does not consist in a search for uniform rules or outcomes, but in identifying common sets of arguments to be weighed in different ways in the various national jurisdictions.[33] This fits in well with the experience of the 'real' common law: English common law, as it spread out over the world, is a good example of this type of argumentative community. When deciding a case, common law courts tend to look at the arguments used by their foreign colleagues, but this does not mean that the rules or outcomes are the same everywhere. Thus, in the New Zealand case of *Invercargill City Council v. Hamlin*[34] (a negligence case), the Privy Council denied that there was only *one* common law. Lord Lloyd of Berwick held that 'the ability of the common law to adapt itself to the differing circumstances of the countries in which it has taken root, is not a weakness, but one of its great strengths'.[35] It led the Court to apply a concept of negligence in New Zealand that was essentially different from the one in England. What is important here is that these varying views are based on a different weighing of similar arguments.

Of course, this does not mean that there is no need for any coordination at all if one adheres to a harmonisation process from the bottom up. In areas of the law where coherence is unlikely to result from the activities of courts and academia alone – like in parts of property and insolvency law – some coordination by the legislator is certainly needed: spontaneous orders have their limits.[36] But legislative activity need not take the form of

31 See e.g. Neethling, J (2001) 'Tort Law in South Africa: The Mixing of the General and the Particular' in Smits (2001) supra n 4 at 81 ff.

32 1997 SC (HL) 66. Cf. Reid, K (2000) 'Property Law: Sources and Doctrine', in: Reid, K and Zimmermann, R (eds) *A History of Private Law in Scotland, Vol. 2* OUP, 196.

33 This is elaborated in Smits, JM (2008) 'Contract Law in the European Union: Convergence or Not?' in ***Proceedings of the 4th European Jurists' Forum***, Manz, 45ff.

34 *Invercargill City Council v. Hamlin*, [1996] 2 *W.L.R.* 367.

35 Id at 376 per Lord Lloyd.

36 Cf. Kanning, AJ (2007) 'The Emergence of a European Private Law: Lessons From 19th Century Germany' (27) *Oxford Journal of Legal Studies* 193 ff.

classic statutory intervention. One alternative is to draft optional sets of (internally coherent) rules that exist next to the national codes.[37]

HOW TO ENSURE A CONTINUOUS COMPARATIVE INSPIRATION?

One of the things surprising for an outsider to the debate about mixed jurisdictions is the lack of consensus on how to define such a jurisdiction. There is no generally accepted criterion by which to decide what constitutes a mixed system.[38] Thus, it is not clear what the degree of mixture should be, whether this mixture should concern only substantive law or also methodology, how the mixture is structured,[39] or how long the mixture must have been there. It is equally uncertain whether the qualification of a mixed system mainly concerns the way the jurisdiction was formed in the past or also applies to certain contemporary characteristics of that system. In my view, the latter question refers to one of the most important debates: can we still speak of a mixed jurisdiction if it is no longer open to the influences of both the civil law and the common law tradition? Such a legal system has become autonomous and one no longer needs to look abroad for inspiration. But the mere fact that there is no *need* for it, does not mean it is not *useful* to do so. In my view, the definition of a mixed jurisdiction is therefore decided primarily by the *process* that the jurisdiction makes use of in making and applying the law. If this process is led by the *continuous* desire to look for comparative inspiration, resulting in a jurisdiction that effectively consists of elements of both the civil and the common law, we can speak of a mixed jurisdiction.

The history of most mixed jurisdictions shows that the more autonomous the jurisdiction becomes, the less courts and the legislators look abroad.[40] This is unfortunate. If one adopts my view of what forms the core of a mixed system, it even means such a jurisdiction is no longer mixed. The

[37] See the suggestion to introduce an optional code in the field of contract law: Communication from the Commission to the European Parliament and the Council, *A More Coherent Contract Law – An Action Plan*, COM (2003) 68 final, *OJ EC* 2003, C 63/01.

[38] See on this debate e.g. Örücü, E, Attwool, E and Coyle, S (eds) (1996) *Studies in Legal Systems: Mixed and Mixing* Kluwer, and Du Plessis, supra n 1 at 478 ff.

[39] T.B. Smith, for instance, uses a narrow definition of a mixed legal system, namely one in which the 'civilian or Romanistic foundations have been overlaid by Anglo-American jurisprudence'. See Smith, TB (1962) *Studies Critical and Comparative* W. Green and Son Ltd at ix.

[40] Cf. McDiarmid, C (1999) 'Scots law: the turning of the tide' *Juridical Review* 156 ff.; MacQueen, HL (2003) 'Mixing it? Comparative Law in the Scottish Courts' (6) *European Review of Private Law* 735 ff. For South Africa, see Zimmermann, R (1995) 'Roman Law in a Mixed Legal System' in Evans-Jones, R (ed), *The Civil Law Tradition in Scotland* OUP 55 ff.

way to prevent this process from taking place is to allow the competition between the various legal traditions to be continuous. As William Tetley explained, [41] the long time survival of a mixed system is contingent upon the presence of at least two different cultures or even languages within the relevant jurisdiction. Only if the importance of *both* traditions ('two "nations" in a single State'[42]) is emphasised, the mixed system will flourish. This finding is in line with the fact that Scots law blossomed up again with the Act of Union of 1707, in which the civil law was protected. The same is true for South Africa, where civil law was on the rise again after the creation of the Union of South Africa in 1910. There is no need to explain that this phenomenon fits in well with the theoretical framework of jurisdictional competition.

What lessons are to be drawn from this for the European harmonisation process? The experience of mixed jurisdictions confirms the importance of separate jurisdictions claiming to be attractive suppliers of law on the European market: the advantages of a mixed system are exploited most if there is a permanent competition among rules of several origins. The requirements William Tetley[43] defines for a mixed system to be successful are all fulfilled at the European level: next to the existence of various (legal) cultures and languages, Tetley explains that also the co-existence of several legislatures and court systems within the jurisdiction helps to promote and preserve its mixed character. In addition, it is important that legal education reflects the various legal traditions. The present political structure of the European Union guarantees that all these requirements can be fulfilled, although there remains the practical problem of ensuring there is enough information available about other jurisdictions. Again, the only possible way to deal with this problem of information is to promote a European legal debate.

CONCLUSION

This contribution did not seek to draw lessons from the *substantive* private law of mixed jurisdictions for future European developments.[44] Instead, its focus was on what lessons can be drawn from how mixed systems develop as successful or unsuccessful mixes of civil law and common law. The core

[41] Tetley, W (2003) 'Nationalism in a Mixed Jurisdiction and the Importance of Language' (78) *Tulane LR* 175 ff. Also see Wasserstein Fassberg, C (2003) 'Language and Style in a Mixed System' (78) *Tulane Law Review* 151 ff.

[42] Tetley, id at 190.

[43] id at 186 ff.

[44] Cf. Kötz, H (2003) 'The Value of Mixed Legal Systems' (78) *Tulane Law Review* 435 ff.

of the view expressed in the above is that a mixed jurisdiction should be constantly looking for what are the 'best' rules and institutions and should not be led by any 'nationalist' considerations in doing so. To me, there is no doubt that the future of private law in the European Union also lies in this process of finding comparative inspiration in arguments used elsewhere. In this respect, the new *ius commune* will always be in the making: it is much more a continuous process than an end product in which national legal systems have been replaced by some harmonising instrument. Just as mixed systems may benefit from the powerful defence of both the civil law and the common law tradition, Europe can benefit from the vast experience of individual member states on how to make and apply the law.

It seems appropriate to end with a quotation by the famous T.B. Smith. When in the 1960's Lord Denning called for English and Scots law to become one,[45] Smith replied as follows: 'You honour me with your proposal, Sir, but I will not marry you. We have much in common, but perhaps not as much as you think. We should remain friends and share ideas [...].'[46] Let this view also be the right one for the European Union.

45 Lord Denning (1961) *Borrowing from Scotland* (26th David Murray Lecture) Glasgow 40.
46 Smith, TB (1961) *British Justice: the Scottish Contribution* Stevens and Sons Ltd at 228.

Beyond the Usual Suspects: Application of the Mixed Jurisdiction Methodology to Public International and International Trade Law

COLIN B. PICKER

INTRODUCTION

Comparativists sometimes study other comparable legal systems, hoping to discern lessons that may then be applied to their own legal systems. Thus, an American may become an expert on the English legal system, and then seek to apply some aspects of that system within America. Such an effort is generally thought to be legitimate, as both America and England are Common Law jurisdictions. Mixed Jurisdictions are similarly studied, often with the hope that lessons learned from those studies may be applied to other comparable legal systems – typically other Mixed Jurisdictions. Thus, a scholar from Sri Lanka may study the Scottish private law with a view to employing some lesson from that study within Sri Lanka – a sister-Mixed Jurisdiction. An American studying Mixed Jurisdictions, however, perhaps should come from Louisiana, otherwise any applications of the Mixed Jurisdiction jurisprudence to that scholar's home legal system may be considered somewhat suspect. But, as this Article will show, lessons derived from the study of Mixed Jurisdictions may, and should, be applied more broadly.

In this Article, I will argue that a narrow application of the lessons from the Mixed Jurisdictions is misplaced. This is not to say that all that is applicable or relevant to Mixed Jurisdictions may be considered outside of the Mixed Jurisdictions, but rather that with some imagination and courage, the tremendous wealth of ideas being generated within Mixed

Jurisdiction scholarship may have considerably wider application than is presently being considered. There may be a little bit of Mixed Jurisdiction in many legal systems. By way of illustration, an example of just how far a field the study might go, this Article will show that the characteristics of Mixed Jurisdictions may even be found within international law, and more specifically within certain parts of the field that has come to be known as international trade law. If within those fields, then within all legal systems, for they are applicable to all legal systems. Thus, perhaps the Mixed Jurisdictions jurisprudence truly will have greater application than is presently thought to be the case.

Of course, the comparative analysis that will be attempted in this Article relies on the traditional comparative law classifications. Those classifications, of course, fail to truly reflect the complexities involved, but such classifications are necessary for comparative analysis to proceed.[1] Needless to say, at all times the inherent simplification must be kept in mind and reconsidered throughout the comparative process. Additionally, the classifications described here are discussed in terms of the classical characteristics – even as many of those characteristics are fading within the different described systems, and even as in many respects those different systems are converging.[2]

INTERNATIONAL LAW – AKIN TO A MIXED JURISDICTION?

While it may be argued that all legal systems are 'mixed', the ones classified as Mixed Jurisdictions are mixed in a similarly specific manner and to a certain comparable degree.[3] That similarity allows for useful and legitimate comparative work among those systems. But those characteristics may also be identified to a significant extent in other legal systems, and as such those Mixed Jurisdictions can then be employed for useful comparative work with other legal systems – in this case, with international law.

1 See Fassberg, C (2003) 'Language and Style in a Mixed System' (78) *Tul. L. Rev.* 151 at 171.

2 See Glendon, MA, Carroza, P & Picker, C (2007) *Comparative Legal Traditions: Text, Materials And Cases On Western Law* 3rd ed, Thomson West Publishing at 241 and 799.

3 Reid, KGC (2003) 'The Idea of Mixed Legal Systems' (78) *Tul. L. Rev.* 5 at 19; Visser, D (2003)'Cultural Forces in the Making of Mixed Legal System' (78) *Tul. L. Rev.* 41 at 46. For an overview of Mixed Jurisdictions, *see* Glendon et al, supra n 2 at Chapter 19.

The General Characteristics of a Mixed Jurisdiction as Applied to International Law

Vernon Valentine Palmer has argued that there are three overarching characteristics and then a whole host of lesser more specific characteristics to this 'new' legal family. The three overarching characteristics are that:

> (1) The 'basic building blocks' of a Mixed Jurisdiction are from the Civil and Common Law Traditions;
> (2) The dual character, Civil Law and Common Law, is objectively apparent; and
> (3) In a Mixed Jurisdiction, the Public Law tends to be Common Law in style, while the Private Law tends to be Civil Law.[4]

Palmer has additionally identified other more specific characteristics, that will also be considered later in this Article. Of course, it must be remembered that not all the legal systems that have been considered to be Mixed Jurisdictions satisfy all of these criteria – an important point when international law is viewed under a Mixed Jurisdiction lens. Nonetheless, can these general characteristics be found within international law?

The 'basic building blocks' of a Mixed Jurisdiction are from the Civil Law and Common Law Traditions

This criteria is used to distinguish those other mixed systems of the world that would consequently have little in common with those mixed systems that have been derived from the Common and Civil Law traditions. Though '[i]t goes without saying that some Mixed Jurisdictions are also derived partly from non-occidental legal traditions: the North African countries, Iran, Egypt, Syria, Iraq, and Indonesia, for instance.'[5]

Given the western pedigree of international law, it would appear that this criterion should be easily satisfied. Nonetheless, the issue bears consideration and careful explication. While the term 'international law' was coined by a jurist from the Common Law world, Jeremy Bentham,[6] for the most part it was Civil Law trained jurists that created modern

[4] Palmer, VV (2000) *Mixed Jurisdictions Worldwide: The Third Legal Family* Cambridge Univ. Press at 7–9.

[5] Tetley, W (2003) 'Nationalism In A Mixed Jurisdiction And The Importance Of Language (South Africa, Israel, And Quebec/Canada)' (78) *Tulane L. Rev.* 175 at 183.

[6] See Janis, MW (1984) 'Jeremy Bentham and the Fashioning of "International Law"' (78) *Am. J. Int'L L.* 405 at 408.

international law.[7] Thus from its earliest, international law was born among early Civilian ideas, with the predictable result that it reflected those very ideas.[8] Of course, the jurists responsible for creating the ideas and institutions of international law could, as a theoretical matter, back then and now, have developed the new international law in isolation from their domestic legal environment. But people do not, and can not do that. The jurists necessarily borrowed and adopted existing institutions, ideas and mechanisms from their existing Civil Law legal systems – sometimes subconsciously, and perhaps even when they may have explicitly tried to reject Civil Law notions.[9] It was only natural then that they would create international law in the 'image' of Civil Law. The impact of the Common Law world on international law would, in contrast, have to wait until the twentieth century. In particular, during the last sixty years, since the end of the Second World War, the influence of the Common Law world and its legal culture was most pronounced. In that time, international law has absorbed various Common Law ideas and institutions, ones that might very well have been anathema to its original Civil Law character.

This geopolitical ordering of international law has been further reinforced as a result of the fact that the vast bulk of the day-to-day operations of international law take place within the domestic legal institutions[10] – the vast majority of which are systems within either the Civil or Common Law traditions.[11] True, despite that borrowing from the Civil and the Common Law, international law has some unique aspects, reflecting the fact that its primary subjects are states, but then each of the Mixed Jurisdictions also include significant unique features.[12]

[7] Such as Hugo Grotius (1583-1645) Francisco de Vitoria (1486-1546), Alberico Gentili (1552-1608), Francisco Suarez (1548-1617) and Samuel Pufendorf (1632-94). See also Merryman, JH & Clark, DS (1978) *Comparative Law: Western European and Latin American Legal Systems* Bobbs Merill at 3. But see, e.g., Yasuaki, O (2000) 'The History of International Law: Universality and Particularity - The Birth Of International Law As The Law Of International Society' (94) *Am. Soc'y Int'l L. Proc.* 44 (arguing that international law only came into being once the Western notion of international law was applied to Africa, through colonisation, and once China accepted the Western international law at the end of the nineteenth century).

[8] See Butler, W (ed) (1980) *International Law in Comparative Perspective* Brill at 15 ('since the age of Grotius, when the law of Rome was the basic element in almost the whole of the law of Europe and was universally regarded as the standard by which justice should be measured.').

[9] See *e.g.*, Bederman, DJ (1996) 'Reception of the Classical Tradition in International Law: Grotius' De Jure Belli Ac Pacis' (10) *Emory Int'l L. Rev.* 1 at 20-21.

[10] Janis MW & Noyes, JE (2006) *International Law: Cases And Commentary* 3rd edn Thomson West Publishing at 180.

[11] See Glendon, supra 2 at 68-72 (global distribution of the Civil Law) and 320-324 (global distribution of the Common Law).

[12] Visser, supra n 3 at 47; Örücü, E (2003) 'The Judge and Jurist in Scotland: On the Verge of a second Renaissance' (78) *Tul. L. Rev* 89 at 90-91. See also Barnes, WR (2005) 'Contemplating

The Dual Character of International Law is Objectively Apparent

This characteristic of Mixed Jurisdictions really constitutes two separate and distinct requirements. The first is that there be a 'dual' character, in other words that the system is not solidly or predominantly part of just either the Common Law or the Civil Law. The second is that the dual character be objectively apparent. Employing an objective standard necessarily suggests that a subjective standard is inappropriate. Thus, just because a country might argue that its legal system includes this dual character, that assertion will not alone prove to be sufficient to satisfy this criteria.

The first requirement, that international law has a dual character must overcome the wide spread view that Civil Law has served as the most significant influence on international law.[13] Civil Law jurists were its main creators.[14] Indeed, today many still believe that international law is essentially a Civil Law system.[15] This is understandable given that Civil Law is the predominant legal tradition within the Western Legal Tradition. More countries employ a legal system within the Civil Law tradition than within the Common Law.[16] More people in the world live under Civil Law than under the Common Law.[17] It thus makes sense that Civil Law *should* have been the dominant influence on international law.

Demographics and history, however, are *today* insufficient to maintain the predominantly Civil Law character of international law. The world today is a different place than it was four hundred years ago, indeed even from what it was forty years ago. It is almost as though the Civil Law tradition imbued throughout traditional international law is under assault from the legal imperialism of the Common Law countries – primarily

a Civil Law Paradigm for a Future International Commercial Code' (65) *La. L. Rev.* 677 at 684. 'All but three of the one hundred ninety-one nations of the world have some form of either civil law or common law.' (footnote omitted))

13 Nagle, LE (2000) 'Maximizing Legal Education: The International Component' (29) *Stetson L. Rev.* 1091 at 1092 ('It is the civil-law traditions that have most widely influenced international law, international organizations').

14 See Merryman & Clark, supra n 7 at 3.

15 'The study of civil law concepts is particularly helpful to the common law lawyer working with public international law, which is largely based on civil law and natural law principles.' Schadbach, K (1998) 'The Benefits of Comparative Law: A Civil European View' (16) *B.U. Int'l L.J.* 331, 385.

16 One study found that 51 nations utilise common law, whereas 115 countries have civil law systems. See Barnes, supra n 12 at 684.

17 See Barnes, supra n 12 at 685-685 ('Common law (exclusive of any Civil Law), whether in "pure" or "mixed" form, is utilized by some fifty-one nations, or 26.7% of all nations of the world. These nations account for 34.81% of the world's population. [. . .] Civil law (exclusive of any Common Law), whether in "pure" or "mixed" form, is utilized by some 115 nations, or 60.21% of all nations of the world. These nations account for 59.01% of the world's population.' (footnotes omitted))

from the United States and the United Kingdom. It has been suggested that international law is moving away from the 'civil-style approach' and towards a common law, almost as though it were being subjected to an 'Americanisation.'[18]

While international law is not yet 'Americanised', nonetheless at this time there is sufficient Common Law influence alongside the Civil Law influence so that international law can fairly be characterised as a dual system.

But, it is not sufficient that we characterise it as a dual system, but that the second half of this criteria should be satisfied - that the dual character be objectively obvious. For a domestic system this proposition is less problematic inasmuch as the character or legal tradition of the legal system is something that is frequently considered and so the 'obvious' will be noticed! For international law, such an examination is less likely and hence even the obvious may be missed. This myopia is a consequence of the usual view that international law is sui generis and that international law scholars are not usually thinking along comparative lines when considering the field as a whole. As such the issue of membership in a legal family, let alone whether it has a dual character, typically will not come up. This Article, however, by subjecting international law to a comparative analysis, lifts the veil obscuring the natures, obvious or not, of international law.

Once the comparative analysis is undertaken and the evidence even marginally mustered, as is undertaken in this Article, it is indeed objectively clear that the Civil and Common Law are the significant contributors of the style and character of international law. Furthermore, it is also clear that neither predominates in influence or in representation throughout international law today. As such, the two traditions, Common Law and Civil Law, are the two primary parts of international law. Thus, when viewed correctly, international law is obviously a dual system of Civil and Common Law.

In a Mixed Jurisdiction, the Public Law Tends to be Common Law-Like, While the Private Law Tends to be Civil Law-Like

One of the most awkward factors for international law is the fascinating observation that Mixed Jurisdictions' private law tends to be Civil Law-like and their public law tends to be Common Law-like.[19] This characteristic is, as an initial matter, difficult to consider for international law because the

[18] See Bhala, R (2000) 'Five Theoretical Themes in the World Trade Organization Adjudicatory System' (6) *ILSA J. Int'l & Comp. L.* 437 at 442.
[19] Palmer supra n 4, at 8-10.

international law that we tend to discuss is already considered public law, indeed it is referred to as 'Public International Law'. In contrast, 'Private International Law' traditionally covered what in the United States is called 'conflicts of laws'.[20] Despite this difficulty, it is nonetheless possible, if admittedly occasionally contrived, to view international law in a few different ways that show that there is an emerging pattern of Common Law-like attributes within a so-called public side and Civil Law-like attributes within a so-called private side of international law.

While novel, perhaps the best and most accurate way to handle this issue is to divide international law itself into a public and private-type framework. By analogy to domestic systems, the international institutions are accorded the role of the government or public body while the states, the subjects of international law, are accorded the role that private parties, individuals, are accorded within a domestic legal system. Thus, the law governing the actions of international law institutions would be the public law component of international law. The international law regulating interstate or transnational behaviours would then constitute the 'private' law component of international law. Applying this framework we can indeed see a division such as occurs within Mixed Jurisdictions. Within this designated international 'public law', we can see that the behaviour of international institutions and their interaction with the state members tend to reflect Common Law conceptions of public law. Those conceptions include independence of the judiciary; separation of powers; methods of selection of judges (from practice, not via a judge school); and with respect to international law's direct application to the new subjects of international law, individuals in human rights contexts, free speech, due process of law, and freedom from arbitrary arrest.[21] These are all traditionally considered to be Common Law style public law norms, and all shared by the Mixed Jurisdictions.[22] In contrast, the interstate international law obligations, what this analogy is designating as the 'private law' part of international law, are usually a result of treaty obligations, interpreted according to the Civil Law-like Vienna Convention on Treaties.[23] Admittedly, this is a crude approximation to the public-private law split within domestic legal systems and it deserves more attention than that briefly provided here, but it nonetheless provides some basis for the contention that international law is similar to Mixed Jurisdictions in this regard.

20 See Janis and Noyes, supra n 10 at 767

21 Palmer supra n 4 at 9-10.

22 Id.

23 Treaties are often interpreted in a Civil Law style, *see* Schadbach supra n 15 at 386, n. 321.

Admittedly, this issue, the public-private law division among Civil-Common Law norms, is complex and not as easily applicable to the so-called public international law. [24] Perhaps the issue is that international law is still in the early stages of development in comparison to domestic legal systems and until international law is more firmly involved in private law matters, such as may be the case in the area of contracts, this criteria is simply not as amenable to consideration.[25] Or perhaps this issue is simply not relevant to international law – where individuals have relatively little role and where the states are not really easily analogised to private parties. If so, then that failure should not prejudice any determination of whether or not international law is akin to a Mixed Jurisdiction. Indeed, other jurists have noted that this last criterion may not even be a necessary Mixed Jurisdiction characteristic.[26]

International Law and the Specific Characteristics of Mixed Jurisdictions

Surprisingly, more easily considered than the general characteristics of Mixed Jurisdictions are the similar specific characteristics of Mixed Jurisdictions and their applicability to international law. This relatively straightforward analysis may reflect the underlying similarity of the nuts and bolts of international law and of the Mixed Jurisdictions. Employing Palmer's criteria, the question is whether international law has the following specific Mixed Jurisdiction shared characteristics:

1. Similar Origins of the Mixed aspect of the Jurisdiction
2. Similar Judicial Character
3. Similar Linguistic Issues
4. Similar Approach to Precedent and Legal Sources
5. Similar Reception of the Common Law
6. Similar Creativity
7. Similar Reception of Anglo-American Procedure

[24] Indeed, so-called public international law now involves private parties and their private relations. Increasingly private parties are having direct involvement with international law, through human rights or international contract laws and so on. Thus, tort-like actions may now fall under international law – though a public component must also be involved. *See, e.g., Kadic v. Karadzic*, 70 F.3rd 232, 245 (2nd Cir. 1995), cert denied 518 U.S. 1005 (1996). Private contracts between parties of different nationalities may also be covered by treaty law. See, e.g., *United Nations Conference on Contracts for the International Sale of Goods*, Vienna, Austria, Mar. 10-Apr. 11, 1980, Final Act, U.N. Doc. A/CONF.97/18 (Apr. 10, 1980) (CISG); *The Convention on the Carriage of Goods by Sea*, Mar. 31, 1978, 17 I.L.M. 608 (Hamburg Rules).

25 Much contract and commercial law is subject to international law regulation - through such international law as the CISG.

26 Visser supra n 3 at 47

8.Similar Style of Commercial Law.[27]

As the analysis below suggests, the application is not exact, with international law lacking some of the characteristics – but then not every Mixed Jurisdiction has all of these characteristics.

The Similar Origins of Mixed Jurisdictions

Mixed Jurisdiction systems were typically 'mixed' as a result of conquest (typically, a Civil Law system coloniser defeated by a Common Law system coloniser) or through a Civil Law system gradually suffering such intense contact with the Common Law that it eventually adopted Common Law characteristics.[28] The development of modern international law is similar. Modern international law was originally heavily influenced by the Civil Law environment in which it was born in the sixteenth and seventeenth centuries. But, for international law a story could legitimately be told that like the Mixed Jurisdictions, the Common Law 'conquest' of international law followed the defeat or destruction of the influence of the Civil Law countries on international law following the First and Second World Wars, and the concomitant rise in the Anglo-American Common Law influence on international law. That development has accentuated in this modern period of international institution building, institutions that are frequently employing Common Law ideas and mechanisms, no doubt as a result of the powerful influence and involvement of the Common Law United States. Even the EU's potential Civil Law counterweight in the development of international law is somewhat offset by the EU's own very powerful Common Law member – the United Kingdom.[29]

Furthermore, the origin and formation of a Mixed Jurisdiction is often fraught with internal disputes between those trying to preserve the original Civil Law system and those permitting or pushing the Common Law into the system – with language and culture playing a part in the conflict.[30] Nor does the battle ever stop – for that same battle is present to some degree in

[27] See Palmer supra n 4 at 76-80.

[28] See id at 18-19. Most were created as a result of conquest, Scotland was formed as a result of the intensive interaction between it and its southern neighbour. See MacQueen, HL (2001) 'Mixed Jurisdictions and Convergence: Scotland' (29) *Int'l J. Leg. Inf.* 309 at 309; Tetley, W (2000) 'Mixed Jurisdictions: Common Law v. Civil Law (Codified and Uncodified'(60) *La. L. Rev.* 677 at 688. The unusual member of the Mixed Jurisdictions is Israel which purposively adopted Civil Law aspects after it became independent. See Fassberg supra n 1 at 155-58. Palmer supra n 4 at 5.

[29] Perhaps the involvement of Ireland and the United Kingdom in the EU will eventually turn the EU into a Mixed Jurisdiction. See Tetley (2003) supra n 5 at 206.

[30] Palmer supra n 4 at 18

every Mixed Jurisdiction to this day. The participants include the 'purists' ('keep the Common Law out'), the 'pragmatists' ('if a Common Law idea works, let us use it'), and the 'pollutionists' (arguing to use Common Law as 'it is better law' or 'it is what I know').[31] International law has experienced and is presently experiencing these same 'turf' battles.[32] International law 'purists' decry the growth of powerful international law courts, *stare decisis*, and so on – in other words those aspects of the Common Law system invading the traditional Civil Law.[33] On the other hand, 'pragmatists' in international law look to solve the problems of the day, especially when the issue appears novel to international law or the international law institution is new, often by employing Common Law techniques and norms.[34] Perhaps it is that the 'pollutionists' in international law tend to be Common Law practitioners/jurists transplanted into the international law world and bringing their traditions in the name of what they might consider to be the 'better' system or sometimes through simple ignorance of the Civil Law aspects of international law, sometimes without even realising that the Common Law may be perceived as an alien invasion. This last is especially the case when new international law institutions or norms are created and powerful Common Law countries seek application of their traditions, believing them to offer the better law.[35]

In these ways, and others not explored due to space limitation in this Article, international law shows substantial similarity in its origin to that of the Mixed Jurisdictions.

Similar Judicial Character

The Mixed Jurisdiction judicial character, like other public law aspects of Mixed Jurisdictions, tends to be closer in style to the Common Law.[36] The

[31] Id at 31-32.

[32] Indeed, it may be that some of the criticism of the idea presented in this Article will be motivated by those seeking to preserve a Civil Law-like international law in the face of the continuing Common Law incursions.

[33] See generally Bhala, R (1999) 'The Myth About Stare Decisis and International Trade Law (Part One of a Trilogy)' (14) *Am. U. Int'l L. Rev.* 845 (providing a detailed discussion of the origin, myths, and arguments concerning the use of precedence/stare decisis in international law in general).

[34] Id. See also Bhala, R (2001) 'The Power of the Past: Towards De Jure Stare Decisis in WTO Adjudication (Part Three of a Trilogy)' (33) *Geo. Wash. Int'l L. Rev.* 873 (providing just the sort of pragmatic response suggested above).

[35] See e.g., Langer, M (2005) 'The Rise of Managerial Judging in International Criminal Law' (53) *Am. J. Comp. L.* 835 at 856-58 (the procedural rules for the International Criminal Tribunal for Yugoslavia were drafted reflecting adversarial notions as a result, in significant part, of the role of the United States).

[36] Palmer supra n 4 at 36.

judiciaries of the Mixed Jurisdictions tend to employ generalised courts that are centralised.[37] The judges tend to be more powerful than is typical in Civil Law systems, they may engage in law making, and are usually drawn from the practicing bar.[38] The question is then whether the judiciary/ies of international law are similar in character to those of the Mixed Jurisdictions.

The international law courts tend to be specialised and diffuse, not centrally organised or controlled from above. Furthermore, the use of precedent and *stare decisis* is new and while prevalent in some of the significant courts, is still considered problematic.[39] However, the international judges themselves may increasingly resemble the Common Law judges more than the Civil Law judges – coming from practice, not being civil servants, and increasingly viewing themselves as significant if not equal participants in the growth and development of international law. For example, the international law courts, like Common Law courts, tend to take powers for themselves that they view as necessary, such as creating procedural or other rules, as opposed to the legislatures (or for international law – the state parties to a treaty regime) being the sole source for such rules. While still unusual in international law, this is an issue that is showing up with increasing frequency as these courts mature. For example, the WTO has itself dealt with the issue of accepting *amicus* briefs, asserting that it had the power to decide the issue and then exercising it, much to the consternation of many WTO members.[40] Similarly, the ECtHR, now a mature court, has started to expand its reach into areas that it originally argued were beyond its competence.[41]

Consequently, with respect to this specific judicial characteristic of Mixed Jurisdictions, at most it can be said that the international law judiciary is beginning to resemble and *may* soon be like those of the Mixed Jurisdictions, but it is perhaps not yet at that point. Though this may be more of a function of the slow development of these new international law institutions as they increasingly challenge traditional notions of state

37 Id.

38 Id. at 37-38.

39 See Bhala supra n 33; Bhala supra n 34; and Bhala, R (2000) 'The Precedent Setters: De Facto Stare Decisis in WTO Adjudication (Part Two Of A Trilogy)' (9) *J. Transnat'l L. & Pol'y* 1

40 See e.g., WTO AB decision to allow amicus briefs. Appellate Body Report, United States-Import Prohibitions of Certain Shrimp and Shrimp Products ('Shrimp-Turtle'), WT/DS58/AB/R, adopted 12 October 1998. See also Keller, J (2005) 'The Future of Amicus Participation at the WTO: Implications of the Sardines Decision and Suggestions for Further Developments' (33) *Int'l J. Legal Info.* 449.

41 See Mowbray, A (2005) 'The Creativity of the European Court of Human Rights' (5) *Hum. Rts. L. Rev.* 57.

sovereignty. Accordingly, examination of this characteristic suggests that international law is perhaps an emerging Mixed Jurisdiction.[42]

Similar Linguistic Issues

As a consequence of the conquest by one and then another imperial power over an indigenous people and over non-indigenous colonists, Mixed Jurisdictions typically have serious linguistic issues.[43] There may be multiple official or working languages including an indigenous language, a language associated with the Civil Law tradition (the original colonial power), and one associated with the Common Law - English (following conquest by the United States or Britain). So long as both the Civil Law and Common Law languages remain viable, with jurists having working knowledge of both, the dual character of the system can be maintained. Problems start to occur when the language associated with one of the traditions, usually the Civil Law, ceases to be well known among jurists, lawyers, and members of the government.[44] In that case the vitality of the Civil Law within the Mixed Jurisdiction suffers.[45]

International law shares similar linguistic issues. Historically, the primary languages of modern international law were Latin and French, though there were attempts by the English, and later the Americans to make English one of the languages of international law.[46] International law jurists would be conversant and proficient in these languages, allowing them access to primary and secondary legal sources, typically from sources within the Civil Law system. Today, increasingly the international language is English, with the consequence that there is greater resort to writings, legal opinions, and texts written in English.[47] That trend suggests that those sources will then more likely reflect the legal traditions that employ English as their primary language – and those systems typically

[42] See Glenn, HP (2003) 'Mixing It Up' (78) *Tul. L. Rev* 79 at 85-86 (discussing the idea that systems can transform from one tradition to another – mentioning U.S. state of Michigan as an example of a system that was once Civil Law and yet where today there is little trace of that heritage).

[43] Or because of the other unique circumstances of their creation (e.g. Israel's citizens originally comprising migrants from all around the world), Palmer supra n 4 at 41.

[44] See Loubser, M (2003) 'Linguistic Factors into the Mix: The South African Experience of Language and the Law' (78) *Tul. L. Rev*. 105 at 144-47.

[45] See e.g., Örücü supra n 12 at 102 (noting the potential of this problem in Scotland where 'there are no longer "civilian trained" lawyers, nor are foreign languages well known').

[46] See Shelton, D (1997) 'Reconcilable Differences? The Interpretation of Multilingual Treaties' (20) *Hastings Int'l & Comp. L. Rev*. 611, 613-615.

[47] See e.g., Romano, CPR (2003) 'The Americanization of International Litigation' (19) *Ohio St. J. on Disp. Resol*. 89 at 115-116

come from the Common Law tradition.[48] In contrast, a working knowledge of Civil Law languages tends to be confined within those specific countries themselves, with English as the universal second language across even those countries within the Civil Law tradition. Sadly, the fact that international law shares similar linguistic issues with Mixed Jurisdictions means that, like the Mixed Jurisdictions, these linguistic issues may contribute to the decline of the role of Civil Law in international law.

Approach to Precedent and Legal Sources

Unlike many modern Civil Law systems with aspects of Common Law, the Mixed Jurisdictions employ precedent, at a minimum as a *de facto* primary source of law, if not as a *de jure* primary source.[49] In light of the role precedent plays in marking the difference between the Civil Law and Common Law, it should not be surprising that the issue of precedent should be a defining characteristic of Mixed Jurisdictions. Indeed, the failure to employ, at a *de facto* level at a minimum, precedent and stare decisis as a primary source of law may end up ruling out many systems from classification as a Mixed Jurisdiction. The question is then whether international law satisfies this criterion.

Supposedly inferior to treaty law, according to the ICJ statute, an authoritative statement on the sources of international law, judicial decision are only meant to comprise a secondary source of law in international law. [50] And yet, in reality, they live somewhere between the Common Law's view that at times they may be considered primary law and the Civil Law's view that they are secondary law. This judicially created international law is usually in the form of the authoritative precedent, *stare decisis*. While not

[48] See Loubser supra n 44 at 107 (noting that the language structure may itself influence the development of the law and using German as an example of a language whose structure may have contributed to the German legal system's style).

[49] Palmer supra n 4 at 45-46.

[50] Article 38(1) of the Statute of the International Court of Justice provides that:

> The Court, whose function is to decide in accordance with international law such disputes as are submitted to it, shall apply:
>
> a. international conventions, whether general or particular, establishing rules expressly recognized by the contesting states;
> b. international custom, as evidence of a general practice accepted as law;
> c. the general principles of law recognized by civilized nations;
> d. subject to the provisions of Article 59, judicial decisions and the teachings of the most highly qualified publicists of the various nations, as subsidiary means for the determination of rules of law.

Statute of the International Court of Justice, Article 38, available at http://www.icj-cij.org/documents/index.php?p1=4&p2=2&p3=0#CHAPTER_II (website of the ICJ, last checked Jul. 3, 2007).

binding as a *de jure* matter, it is increasingly *de facto* binding.[51] For example, studies of the use of precedent in the most dynamic of the present-day international tribunals, the WTO Appellate Body, show its increasing use and importance.[52]

Thus, international law, like the Mixed Jurisdiction, employs an approach to precedent that is, as a practical matter, somewhere between the Common Law and the Civil Law, with a definite tilt towards the Common Law approach. Consequently, this specific Mixed Jurisdiction characteristic appears to be satisfied as far as international law is concerned.

Reception of the Common Law

This Mixed Jurisdiction characteristic refers to a pattern of impact of Common Law into specific fields of the private law of Mixed Jurisdictions.[53] Generally, the Common Law has impacted some fields more than others, with the most impact in the area of delict, and the least in property.[54] Of course, such an analysis for international law is difficult in light of the public nature of international law and the limitations on an exact correspondence between domestic and international legal fields.[55] But, if instead of focusing on specific fields, the focus is on the style and the patterns of the reception, it is possible to find these characteristics present to some extent within international law.

While not understood completely, some preliminary consideration of the style of reception of the Common Law into Mixed Jurisdictions suggests that the reception occurs when the Civil Law field is, relatively speaking, both general and vague.[56] Those criteria then open the door to Common Law intrusions, as in certain areas of delict, such as negligence.[57] In contrast, it may be that the Common Law fails to be received into those fields where the Civil Law and Common Law concepts are diametrically opposed,

[51] See Bhala supra n 33.

[52] See id. See also, Haazen, OA (1997) 'Book Review Precedent In The World Court. By Mohamed Shahabuddeen' (38) *Harv. Int'l L.J.* 587 at 587-588.

[53] Palmer supra n 4 at 53. The reception is usually Common Law into the Mixed Jurisdictions and on top of the Civil Law system, due to the nature of the origin of the Mixed Jurisdictions (usually, Common Law conquest of the Civil Law jurisdiction– though Israel provides an example of the opposite direction).

[54] Reid supra n 3 at 25; Palmer supra n 4 at 57; Fassberg, supra n 1 at 156 (describing similar reception during the English U.N. Mandate over pre-independence Israel).

[55] Indeed, Palmer notes that both Israel and Quebec cannot fit into this criteria because of some of their unique aspects. Palmer supra n 4 at 54.

[56] Palmer supra n 4 at 59

[57] Id. at 57.

such as in property.[58] Also reception fails where there are strong cultural connections to the law, as in family law.[59] Those cultural connections prove to be a hardy barrier to any foreign Common Law characteristics.

These notions may also apply to the pattern of Common Law intrusion into international law. For example, the greatest impact of the Common Law in international law may be in judicial behaviour – perhaps this is because the judicial institutions and the regulation of international judges are both new and vague. It is, after all, unclear just what should be the role of international law judges, and in any event it is questionable just how would one control them if they strayed off the permitted path. In contrast, those areas of international law that are specific and/or closed may be less receptive to Common law characteristics. An example may be the field of interpretation of treaties which, as noted earlier, might be the international functional equivalent of contract law within the private law. The detailed and clear Vienna Convention on Interpretation of Treaties may have been more impervious to the influence of the Common Law than other parts of international law. This is an area that needs further exploration, though as an initial matter, it might be fair to suggest that international law has suffered its greatest Common Law 'infection' in those areas that are general and vague – as has largely been the case in the Mixed Jurisdictions.

The role of culture in international law is less clear. While cultural relativism has been bandied about, it and culture otherwise is a problematic concept that has not found an easy reception within international law.[60] As such an equivalent concept within international law is not so easily identified. One such concept, raised but not examined here, is whether it might be the case that where international law has been created as a result of specific historical factors, it might be less amenable to the gradual Americanisation, with its Common Law approaches, that is perhaps present in so many other parts of international law. However, consideration of that issue is not pursued here. It is sufficient that international law, like the Mixed Jurisdictions, might be more common law-like in those parts that are more general and vague than in its parts that are more structured and specific.

Creativity

This criterion is less a definitional requirement and more of a description

58 Id.

59 Id. at 57-59

60 See, Wyman, JH (1997) 'Comment, Vengeance is Whose?: The Death Penalty and Cultural Relativism in International Law' (6) *J. Transnat'l L. & Pol'y* 543; Teson, FR (1985) 'International Human Rights and Cultural Relativism' (25) *Va. J. Int'l L.* 869.

of the creativity that accompanies the mixing of the two primary members of the Western Legal Traditions. Unique devices are created through the interaction of the two bodies of law.[61] International law, as already pointed out, also has no shortage of unique devices, some a consequence of the two traditions interacting. For example, it has been argued that the new rules of procedure for the new International Criminal Court may fairly be described as 'unique', and were the result of the blend of the two traditions resulting in a system that arguably does not belong to either.[62]

Reception of Anglo-American Procedure

Palmer points out that the 'juxtaposition of civil law in alien procedural surroundings is a phenomenon unique to [the Mixed Jurisdictions]'.[63] The alien procedure is of course the common law style of procedure.[64] Furthermore, channelling the substantive Civil Law through a Common Law procedural mechanism will have a noticeable impact on the substantive law.[65] Common Law procedure in this context includes, among other things, common law oral adversary proceedings with a correspondingly larger role for the attorneys than is traditionally found in the Civil Law procedure, Common Law style witness cross-examination, the finality of the first instance judgment and the limited role of appeals, the 'various writs', and the overarching presence of the 'jury' whether actually employed or not.[66] Of course, there are differences among the systems depending on the many different histories of the different systems. For example, the level and type of Common Law procedural penetration may depend on what was the stage of development of the legal system when the common law was introduced.[67] Goldstein argues that perhaps the 'primary explanation' for the application of Common Law procedure 'is the emotional, almost religious attachment of the adherents of the Common Law procedure to their

[61] Palmer supra n 4 at 61-63. An example is the Scottish form of a trust (it does not divide the equitable and legal ownership). Id. at 63.

[62] Kress, C (2003) 'The Procedural Law of the International Criminal Court in Outline: Anatomy of a Unique Compromise' (1) *J. Int'l Crim. Just.* 603 at 604-605

[63] Palmer supra 4 at 63, though Goldstein notes that Scotland is anomalous in this regard. Goldstein, S (2003) 'The Odd Couple: Common Law Procedure And Civilian Substantive Law' (78) *Tul. L. Rev.* 291 at 292.

[64] Though perhaps there is not as large a difference between the Civil and Common Law procedure as some claim, but rather for the most part it is simply a matter of 'degree.' Goldstein, supra 63 at 296.

[65] Palmer supra n 4 at 63 and 66,

[66] Id, and Goldstein supra n 63 at 297.

[67] Palmer supra n 4 at 63-65.

system.'[68] Might this same passion by common law trained international jurists result in a form of Common Law procedure being applied in the international system? As we shall see, indeed, it appears that international law is undergoing the same experience as that of the Mixed Jurisdictions.

But, international procedure, unlike domestic procedure, is hard to identify with any degree of uniformity due to the diffuse and independent nature of international adjudicatory bodies. Nonetheless, the method of formation of these many and different procedural systems can be considered together. They are typically created through two methods. As an initial matter, the state parties to a tribunal will usually decide on the procedure, either through a treaty, such as the WTO's Dispute Settlement Understanding (the 'DSU') or by mutual agreement before arbitration begins. The second method of procedure formation derives from the fact that despite the parties' attempt to create the procedure in anticipation of the litigation, it is usually not possible for all procedural issues to be resolved ahead of time. Accordingly, the court must itself then end up, as in the Common Law,[69] deciding on procedural issues itself as it is not easy to go back to the state parties to get them to agree on changes or additions to the previously agreed procedures, particularly where the procedures are memorialised in a multilateral treaty.

The former attempt, pre-agreement between the state parties on the procedural rules, will often result in a procedural system that is a mix of Common and Civil Law ideas - given the involvement of Common and Civil Law states in the development of the rules.[70] That in itself is an insertion, a reception, of Anglo-American procedures into a system historically more Civilian than Common law-like. The second method, judicial creation of the rules, also opens the system up to Anglo-American procedure, particularly where the arbitrators/judges or parties are trained in the common law procedure and hence might feel 'passionately' about the superiority of common law procedure over that of the Civil Law.[71] Indeed, the idea that the court can set up its own procedural rules is itself quite Common Law-like and typical for Mixed Jurisdictions.[72]

68 Goldstein supra n 63 at 293.

69 Palmer supra n 4 at 65

70 Costa, JE (1998) 'Double Jeopardy And Non Bis In Idem: Principles Of Fairness' (4) *U.C. Davis J. Int'l L. & Pol'y* 181 192 ('The Draft Statute for an International Criminal Court embodies both Common Law and Civil Law principles. The drafters incorporated elements of both legal systems and blended them together to fashion an international law satisfactory in both civil law and common law countries.')

71 Goldstein notes that this passion is even evident in the use by Common Law attorneys of the pejorative word 'inquisitorial' to describe Civil Law procedure. Goldstein supra n 63 at 293.

72 Palmer supra n 4 at 65

Furthermore, when we examine the procedural systems of international bodies, we see a strong Common Law influence – even though the jury is typically absent from the system. For example, the limited role of appeal at the WTO accords well with the Common Law idea of limited appeals. The WTO's Appellate Body, as a formal matter and as its primary method of practice, will typically only hear appeals of law, and not of the facts that were developed at the initial panel hearing.[73]

Of course, there are plenty of Civil Law aspects to the procedure employed in international law. There are even some procedural devices that are unique, as all legal systems have unique features. But it may be fair to say that the procedures found in international law are frequently of a Common Law style and hence, as in the Mixed Jurisdictions, the substantive law may be filtered and altered by this Common Law overlay. Nonetheless, despite Common Law aspects to the procedures frequently employed in the international law system, it can not be said that the procedure is entirely or even significantly Common Law-like due to the diffuse nature of that body of international procedural law. Once again, one of the integral characteristics of Mixed Jurisdictions is more suitable to domestic systems than to the international system. So, although international law may have tendencies that satisfy this Mixed Jurisdiction characteristic, over all perhaps, international law does not satisfy this characteristic. Of course, not all Mixed Jurisdictions satisfy all of the criteria. Indeed, it has been asserted that Israel and Scotland do not satisfy this procedural reception characteristic, as they never employed a civilian style of procedure that would then suffer a Common Law procedural incursion.[74] Accordingly, the quasi-failure of international law under this characteristic should not be fatal to this Article's attempt to find commonalities between international law and the Mixed Jurisdictions as a whole.

Commercial Law Has Become Common Law-Like

The final specific characteristic of Mixed Jurisdictions to be considered here is that Mixed Jurisdictions have usually adopted Common Law commercial law, eventually going so far as to totally replace their Civil Law-like commercial law.[75] Despite the fact that many of the Mixed Jurisdictions were the result of English or American conquest of formerly French, Dutch

[73] Dispute Settlement Understanding, Marrakesh Agreement Establishing the World Trade Organization, Annex 2, Appellate Review – Standing Appellate Body, art. 17.6, 33 I.L.M. 1125 (1994).

[74] Palmer supra n 4 at 64-65.

[75] Id at 66.

or Spanish colonies, this adoption of the Common Law-like commercial law was essentially carried out through voluntary assimilations.[76] In part the reasons for this voluntary adoption have had to do with the recognition that adoption of significant elements of the Anglo-American commercial law, the law of the 'dominant' economies of the world, would be in the financial self interest of the Mixed Jurisdiction.[77] Thus, over time the pre-existing Civil Law commercial law, often derived from the European Law Merchant, has been replaced.[78] The question is then whether we can discern a comparable move of international commercial law from a traditional Civil Law to a more Common Law form.

The possibility that this characteristic may be applicable to international law can be considered from two different perspectives – both somewhat artificial due to the disconnect that must necessarily exist between public international law and domestic legal fields, such as the private or commercial law. The first, and perhaps less contrived, is by the more directly comparable consideration of the existing international law that regulates individuals' transnational commercial interactions. The second method is through employment of analogy, as before in this Article, by substitution of states in the role of the private actors in commercial law and then by considering how the law impacting commercial relations between states has developed.

The international law governing individuals' transnational commercial actions has ancient roots, though the modern form is most closely associated with the law that grew out of the Law Merchant – Lex Mercatoria.[79] Historically, the law merchant was influenced more by the Civil Law, though it was to a great extent largely immune to the formal law – having been developed by merchants for merchants, largely outside the control of the public courts.[80] Gradually, however, the commercial law was brought into the public realm and at that point was influenced by the Civil Law tradition present in most of the commercial jurisdictions of the world.[81]

Centuries later, and with the tremendous growth and influence of the American and British economies, there is indeed evidence for a

76 Palmer examines this voluntary adoption in great detail for many of the Mixed Jurisdictions. Id. at 67-76.

77 Id. at 76.

78 Id. at 80.

79 Berman, HJ (1985) *Law and Revolution: The Formation of the Western Legal Tradition* Harvard Univ. Press at 333.

80 Id at 346-347. But see Kadens, E (2004) 'Order Within Law, Variety Within Custom: The Character of the Medieval Merchant Law' (5) *Chi. J. Int'l L.* 39 (critiquing Berman's depiction of the history of the Law Merchant and arguing that there was a greater and earlier role played by the state).

81 Berman supra n 79 at 348.

strengthening of the Common Law within international (or transnational) commercial law, particularly as a result of American dominance in the world economy in the twentieth century.[82] For example, the Hague-Visby Rules,[83] concerning bills of lading, are arguably Common Law in character, while the Hamburg Rules, an alternative set of rules for bills of lading, are arguably Civil Law in character, and so far the Hamburg Rules have encountered great difficulties in universal adoption.[84] This growing Common Law influence is no surprise; as with the Mixed Jurisdictions, this development probably reflects the strength of the Common Law economies and the need for other economies to harmonise with them in order to take advantage of the financial benefits of easier access to those markets. Thus, if this international commercial law is considered, then it is possible to discern this Mixed Jurisdiction trait, an emergence of a Common Law-like commercial law, within international law.

The problem with the preceding argument, however, is that it may be said to fall into the realm of 'private' international law, not public international law. True, there are treaties involved that set the tone for this private law, but this law does not typically involve the traditional actors of international law – the states. This issue can be circumvented as before by the employment of an analogy whereby the private actors in the domestic model are replaced with the states from the international law model, and then the consideration of international law that is the functional equivalent of the commercial law in the private context. The initial question is then what would be the functional equivalent to commercial law in this analogy – the law that regulates the economic relations between the states. The answer may be what we have come to know as 'international economic law'. That law consists of the laws found within the WTO and the other

[82] For discussion of the United States declining to enter into private law treaties because they were based on Civil Law ideas, see Nadelmann, KH (1954) 'Ignored State Interests: The Federal Government and International Efforts to Unify Rules of Private Law' (102) *U. Pa. L. Rev.* 323; see also, Golove, DM (2000) 'Treaty-Making and the Nation: The Historical Foundations of the Nationalist Conception Of The Treaty Power' (98) *Mich. L. Rev.* 1075, n 551 ('Private international law treaties provide a good example: the United States, like the British, long resisted joining because the conventions were based upon civil rather than common law premises.')

[83] Protocol To Amend the International Convention for the Unification of Certain Rules of Law Relating to Bills of Lading, Feb. 23, 1968, 1977 Gr. Brit. T.S. No. 83 (Cmnd. 6944) (entered into force June 23, 1977), reprinted in 6 Benedict on Admiralty doc. 1-2 (7th rev. ed. 2004); Protocol Amending the International Convention for the Unification of Certain Rules Relating to Bills of Lading, Dec. 21, 1979, 1984 Gr. Brit. T.S. No. 28 (Cmnd. 9197) (entered into force Feb. 14., 1984), reprinted in 6 Benedict on Admiralty, supra, doc. 1-2A.

[84] Tetley, W (2000) 'Uniformity of International Private Maritime Law–The Pros, Cons, and Alternatives to International Conventions–How to Adopt an International Convention' (24) *Tul. Mar. L.J.* 775 at 802.

Bretton Woods Institutions, the many Bilateral Investment Treaties, and so on. The question then is, 'Can these laws be said to be in any way more Common Law-like than Civil Law-like?' Or will the analogy simply not hold up?

One way to approach this question is to consider within the Mixed Jurisdiction model what characteristics of the commercial law are Common Law-like. As it turns out, in the Mixed Jurisdiction model it was not really a battle between substantive rules and understandings of the commercial law, but simply an effort to harmonise the Mixed Jurisdiction's commercial interests with American and British commercial interests. Applying that underlying rationale, the question then becomes whether we see anything similar in the development of international economic law – in other words whether there has been a move towards acceptance of Anglo-American rules and values about international economic relations. The consideration of that question is obviously beyond the scope of this Article. Yet, it is clear that the Bretton Woods and post-World War Two, and even post-Cold War era, are periods when there has been significant economic influence by the United States and Britain, as well as by Canada and Australia. London's place as the financial capital of the world, and Washington's grip on the Bretton Woods institutions as well as its overpowering economy cannot but have had significant influences on the development of international economic law. Furthermore, the WTO was moulded in significant respects by the common law countries.[85] Also, the accession agreements for new members are heavily impacted by America. For example, China's entry into the WTO took place only after it had acceded to American demands. Indeed, any new member of the WTO must secure the agreement of the United States (and the European Union) before it can truly take advantage of the benefits of WTO membership.[86] Thus, while this does not result in a specifically Common Law-like character to international economic law, it certainly imparts a peculiarly Anglo-American focus. In that respect, international law is similar to the Mixed Jurisdictions – in that both Mixed Jurisdictions and international law have generally adapted their economic law to Anglo-American rules and expectations.

[85] The role of Canada, the United States, the U.K., New Zealand, and Australia in the Uruguay Round leading to the birth of the WTO cannot be over stated.

[86] See, e.g., How to join the WTO: the accession process (WTO webpage) http://www.wto.org/english/thewto_e/whatis_e/tif_e/org3_e.htm (last visited August 10, 2007).

Application of the Mixed Jurisdiction Framework to a Subfield in International Law: International Trade Law

The above analysis focused on international law as a whole. Yet international law, unlike most domestic systems is not a unitary system. True, when viewed from above, the argument that international law resembles a Mixed Jurisdiction has some potency, for all parts of international law are governed by the fundamentals within international law – from the Vienna Convention on Treaties to the primacy of the UN Charter.[87]

But, perhaps the true test will be when the individual fields within international law are analyzed under the Mixed Jurisdiction framework. Just as consideration of the Common Law characteristics within the American system can be deduced from the federal law present in the United States, the real test of America's Common Law nature must be when the individual state legal systems are considered, for the U.S. system is significantly decentralised. So too, the Mixed Jurisdiction analysis of international law's subfields is a necessary part of the inquiry.

This short contribution cannot begin to fully consider the subfields of international law. That is best left for a larger work. This essay will, however, suggest that it is both possible and fruitful to do so and will very briefly consider one international law field within the mixed jurisdicition framework – international trade law. That subfield is particularly appropriate as at this time international trade law can be considered sufficiently developed and concrete for such an examination. Specifically, the main institution of international trade law, the World Trade organization, has after 15 years developed a large and sophisticated institution and body of jurisprudence.[88]

In truncated form – for this issue is otherwise presently being explored in greater detail by the author – following the Mixed Jurisdiction framework, the WTO and international trade law may be said to exhibits characteristics from both the Common and Civil Law. Those characteristics may also be considered to be building blocks of the field. Additionally, the dual character is indeed objectively apparent. The final characteristic of the

[87] See Charter of the United Nations, Article 103 ("In the event of a conflict between the obligations of the Members of the United Nations under the present Charter and their obligations under any other international agreement, their obligations under the present Charter shall prevail.")

[88] The WTO includes over 140 members, has extensive legal commitments in its agreements, and its dispute settlement system has handled over 400 cases in its short fifteen years. See the WTO website (www.wto.org).

classical Mixed Jurisdiction framework, that the public and private spheres of the system are respectively Common and Civil Law-like, is less clear.[89]

Concerning the first two defining characteristics of the classical Mixed Jurisdiction, a supporting example might be that the Common and Civil Law characteristics are visible in the WTO through the character of the judges in the WTO dispute settlement system – both as building blocks and as objectively identifiable characteristics. The WTO's initial dispute settlement panelists (akin to trial judges) may indeed share some similarities with the traditional Civil Law judges – who are themselves often civil servant in character.[90] Just as traditional Civil Law judges are promoted based on their performances, so too the civil servant-like panelists' future appointment as repeat panelists will likely depend on their performance – less akin to the independence of the Common Law judges, judges that often tend to remain in their initial appointment, with little promotion potential.[91] In contrast, and as an objective expression of the dual character of the system, the WTO appeals body judges might be thought of as being more akin to Common Law judges. Their appointment is for a term of years, ensuring their independence throughout their tenure. Additionally, their appointment may be considered to be somewhat political in that the more powerful members of the WTO exert influences on the ultimate selection of those judges. Also, they are themselves often former academics or significant members of their field at the end of a long and distinguished career – as is common in the Common Law judicial selection process.[92]

Other examples of dual Common and Civil Law components of the WTO include the absence of juries in the dispute settlement system, like the traditional Civil Law system, whereas appeals, as a de jure matter, are only of the law, not fact – like the Common Law systems.[93] Similarly, like public international law in general, the issue of precedent reflects both the Civil Law traditional view that cases do not as a de jure matter create law, but in reality, like the Common Law systems, they are very strong de facto souces of law. Another Civil Law characteristic present within international trade law is the significant role of scholars.[94] Just as in the Civil Law system, those scholars are often involved in the creation of the law itself as well as in its

[89] The seven or eight more specific defining characteristics of the classical Mixed Jurisdictions discussed earlier as applied to international trade law will be considered in a larger work presently under development by the author.

[90] See Glendon, supra n 2 at 167.

[91] See Glendon, supra n 2 at 167-168, 490-91, 499.

[92] See Glendon supra n 2 at 490-91.

[93] Article 17.6 of the DSU provides that an "appeal shall be limited to issues of law covered in the Panel report and legal interpretations developed by the Panel".

[94] See Glendon, supra n 2 at 179-181.

interpretation. But, a Common Law component is clearly visible through the very significant role played by Common Law origin scholars, such as John Jackson – the "father" of the field.[95]

As mentioned above, the final but thorny characteristic required for a system to be considered like one of the classical Mixed Jurisdictions, is that the Public Law should tend to be Common Law in style while the Private Law should tend to be Civil Law in style. But, this final characteristic is harder to show with respect to the WTO, just as it was with respect to international law in general. Yet, as shown above in the general international law discussion, through analogy and lateral thinking it may be possible to satisfy this final condition. While there is insufficient space in this essay to fully develop the idea here, one might argue that within international trade law the institutional aspects might be considered to be akin to the public law side, while the substantive law, the text of commitments, the obligations that exists between members, could be considered to be the functional equivalent of the private law. Applying this analogy one then needs to examine whether there are more Common Law characteristics within the institutional framework of international trade law and whether the substantive components reflect more of a Civil Law character. A cursory consideration suggests indeed that it may be that the institutional side, with its dispute settlement system, may be more Common Law like, even as the substantive commitments, in a code-like series of agreements, might be more Civil Law like. The analogy is not exact, and needs significantly greater development, but it, along with the earlier more applicable characteristics is at least sufficient to show the potential relevance of the Mixed Jurisdiction framework for subfields within international law.

CONCLUSIONS

After having briefly considered the nature and characteristics of international law alongside the specific and general traits of Mixed Jurisdictions, and when viewed in the totality, international law appears, at least in part, to share, in some significant respects, many of the characteristics of Mixed Jurisdictions. Of course, international law does not satisfy all of the criteria. After all, how could it? It is not a domestic legal system, and some of the criteria are particularly domestic law orientated. But then each of the different legal systems that comprise the Mixed Jurisdiction family also more or less satisfy most, but not all, of these criteria. In any event, perhaps

[95] See, e.g., the special issue in volume 20 of the *Michigan Journal of International Law* "A Tribute to John Jackson".

all these different criteria are not the sole measure of whether a system is a Mixed Jurisdiction. Some scholars have identified other specific criteria that are common to all or to a sufficient number of Mixed Jurisdictions.[96] Perhaps the most relevant for this Article is that of William Tetley, that Mixed Jurisdictions are those 'where debate over the subject takes place.'[97] Though that debate is not presently taking place in international law, hopefully this Article will set the stage for satisfaction of this characteristic – to general international law as well as to its subfields. Or, perhaps the notion of 'emerging' Mixed Jurisdictions is more appropriate for international law. In other words, there are some legal systems that are in the process of becoming Mixed Jurisdictions.[98]

Nonetheless, the congruence between the characteristics of international law and the Mixed Jurisdictions, as shown above, is sufficient to support productive comparative analysis. In particular, that analysis may be used to support international law 'borrowing' ideas from the Mixed Jurisdictions in order to help resolve emerging issues in international law. This is especially important in light of the fact that international legal institutions rely, often unconsciously, to a significant extent upon national legal systems for much of their present development - from substantive norms to procedural rules.

But what are the benefits for the Mixed Jurisdictions? Perhaps for the Mixed Jurisdictions, the real success of this exercise is to show the legal scholars of the world that Mixed Jurisdictions are potentially directly relevant to their own legal systems – be it a Common Law, Civil law, Islamic Law, or Socialist legal system, or some form of mixed system. The reason for this direct applicability is that international law is everyone's law. It is part of the domestic law, be it via domestically enacted legislation or directly applicable – whether applicable in a monist or dualist legal system. Even in 'isolationist' America, 'International law is part of [U.S.] law.'[99] And this is more and more the case with the constant growth of international law. This impact is now even applicable to individuals, as much of that new international law is directly applicable to them through human rights law. It is even applicable in the commercial world, through the direct effect of the regulation of economic actors as a result of the increasing prevalence of international economic law. In other words, because in every country international law is directly relevant, as such the study of Mixed Jurisdictions may be of vital importance for all countries of the world. If so, then the study and knowledge of those small and far-

96 See Reid supra n 3 at 21-25.

97 Tetley supra n 28 at 680.

98 Glenn supra n 42 at 79-80.

99 *The Paquette Habana*, 175 U.S. 677, 700 (1900).

flung Mixed Jurisdictions will take on a level not otherwise anticipated or predicted.[100]

Finally, if, through imagination it is possible to consider international law, a public law-based system that many consider sui generis, juxtaposed with these Mixed Jurisdictions, then through similar imagination, and courage, perhaps other systems can be laid alongside the Mixed Jurisdictions and perhaps with productive results for both. Indeed, the example presented in this Article suggests that there may be benefits in considering other seemingly disparate systems against each other and engaging in a comparative analysis. While many times the results may be frustrating or inconclusive, the fact that there may be successful and useful comparisons supports the idea that as comparativists, we need to be open minded to new avenues of research and comparison.

[100] That being said, some of the Mixed Jurisdictions are in fact often in the centre of world affairs, such as South Africa and Israel, or have issues that command the world's attention – such as the future of Quebec in Canada, or the on-going civil war in Sri Lanka, or even the calamitous events flowing from Hurricane Katrina in Louisiana. Furthermore, others of these Mixed Jurisdictions have played a role in the development of the modern world significantly beyond what their small sizes and populations would have suggested – such as Scotland 'where civilization was born' See, e.g., Herman, A (2001) *How the Scots Invented the Modern World: The True Story of How Western Europe's Poorest Nation Created Our World & Everything in It* Three Rivers Press.